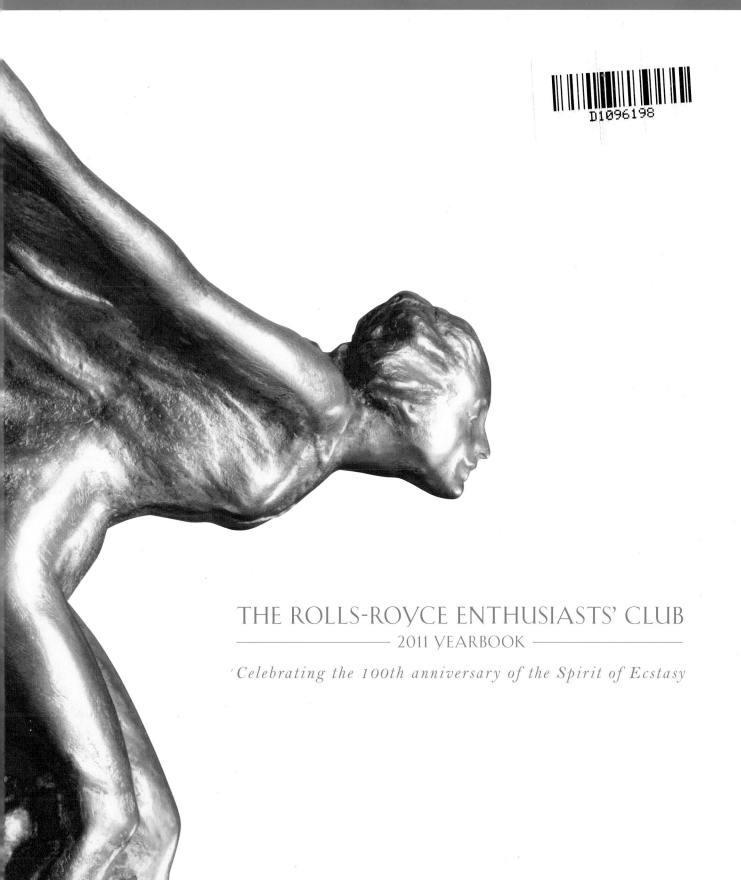

THE ROLLS-ROYCE ENTHUSIASTS' CLUB

— 2011 YEARBOOK —

Celebrating the 100th anniversary of the Spirit of Ecstasy

I'm these little silver fairy,
Your mascot of many a mile,
...... bringing you golden hours,
Guarding you safely the while.
2

Round the curves of the grey Rhone valley,
Through the scents of the Esterels,
In the evening light from the golf club,
Past the Mediterranean's spells.
2

I sooth you with tender daydreams
Of home or the girl that you love,
Or spurring you on to adventures,
Your skill and courage to prove.
2

I'm the little silver fairy,
Wed to the car of my choice,
Roaming the whole world over,
Enthroned on my grey Rolls Royce
2

April 1912.

INTRODUCTION

by Tony James, Chairman of the Rolls-Royce Enthusiasts' Club

The Rolls-Royce Enthusiasts' Club endeavours to:
Cherish the past
Appreciate the present
Preserve for the future
Rolls-Royce motor cars created since 1904 and
Bentley cars made since 1933

The heritage and history of Rolls-Royce and Bentley motor cars are enshrined at the heart of the Rolls-Royce Enthusiasts' Club. Combined with a forward-looking approach to the maintenance, restoration and use of these wonderful motor cars, the Club and its members contribute to the legendary reputation for reliability and survival rates of these two marques.

As a result of clever marketing by C S Rolls and the first Chief Executive of Rolls-Royce, Claude Johnson, the six cylinder 30 horsepower Rolls-Royce was advertised as the Best Car in the World in the *Autocar* magazine published on 25 November 1905. This accolade was inherited with merit by the 40/50hp model, subsequently known as the Silver Ghost, in deference to the original 40/50 named "The Silver Ghost" which ran continuously between Glasgow and London for a total of 14,371 miles without incident. »

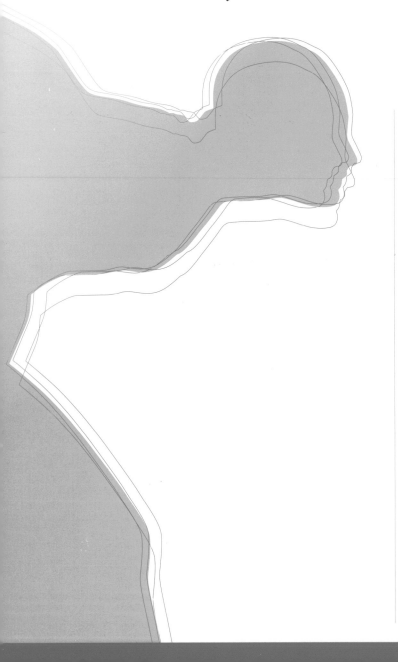

In Europe and the rest of the world, admiring observers acknowledge the high standards of finish and presentation of the cars owned by Club members

The marketing strategy was successful; wealthy men and women desired to own the best car in the world.

The year 2011 marks the anniversary of significant events in Rolls-Royce and Bentley lore. Bentley Motors was acquired in November 1931 by Rolls-Royce. For the next seventy two years, Bentleys were produced by Rolls-Royce.

From the beginning of 1911, all Rolls-Royce and later Bentley motor cars have, as an option available to the owner, been embellished by sculptured mascots created by the artist, Charles Sykes. The lady with rearward outstretched arms and diaphanous robes giving the appearance of wings titled "Spirit of Ecstasy" is without doubt Sykes' masterpiece. The flying 'B' which graces Derby Bentley radiators was also designed by Charles Sykes.

In the United Kingdom, rallies such as the Annual Concours and the celebration of the life of C S Rolls are graced with immaculate cars which, on display or in a parade, are greeted with appreciation and enthusiastic cheers or comment by crowds of observers who remark upon the elegance or impressive nature of these fine vehicles.

In Europe and the rest of the world, admiring observers acknowledge the high standards of finish and presentation of the cars owned by Club members. The international nature of the Club and its members is recognised in an article in this Year Book about Club rallies in Europe which includes narrative in several languages.

The factors which bind together all of these activities are the bonhomie and effort of members who combine in harmony and in care of our fine motor cars.

This Yearbook is the result of the skill and effort of the editorial team, volunteer authors and publishing personnel who have worked together with success.

FOREWORD

by Lt Col Eric Barrass OBE, President

> *The Club has developed hugely from its humble beginnings into the large prestigious international car club it is today*

The main medium of communication with members for the past fifty years has been the bi-monthly Bulletin and earlier this year it reached its milestone 300th edition. Here the Club's President recalls the early development of the Bulletin.

The Club has been in existence for over fifty-three years and during that time it has developed hugely from its humble beginnings into the large prestigious international car club it is today. Throughout the development of the Club, much effort has been put into providing information to members through the publication of many books, magazines and newsletters. This Yearbook, and the previous two, represent significant additional means of communicating with members and demonstrate the Club's desire to continually enhance the services it provides. However, the main medium of communication for the past fifty years has been the bi-monthly Bulletin. It began humbly as a locally produced single sheet of typed foolscap paper and has evolved into the full colour, professionally produced publication it is today. Earlier this year, the Bulletin reached its milestone 300th edition. It is interesting to recall the early development of the Bulletin and here are my recollections of its evolution during the first thirty years of the Club.

The Club was formed in 1957 and, after a slow start, the membership had reached 100 by the beginning of 1960. It was decided to introduce a publication for the increasing membership and so early in 1960 the Bulletin was established. It was a duplicated typed foolscap affair, but full of good stuff and it carried a note that "enquiries for spare parts, service sheets, and general information should be addressed to the Assistant Secretary, Nigel H Hughes". The first Bulletin offered a 1932 Phantom II for £150 and a 1925 Phantom I by Hooper for £130! The Editor accepted no responsibility for the accuracy, or truth of advertisements, though every care was taken to ensure both! »

In November 1962 the old duplicated circular Bulletin gave way to an offset litho production on nice shiny paper and the first list of members appeared as an appendix – and most impressive it looked. However, in November 1963 the Bulletin took a big step forward. The familiar foolscap format was replaced by an A5 magazine – a size and style which was to endure for the next forty-plus years.

The May 1965 issue of the Bulletin contained the first of the 'Secretary's Notes'. A paragraph of explanation may be worth repeating: "These [Secretary's] Notes are being introduced to act as a target for suggestions which will be published, either in digest or extract form, and if any particular problem or proposal emerges strongly from time to time, it will be pursued actively by the Committee on your behalf. It is after all, your Club, and you – the members – should steer it".

For the Bulletin issue of February 1966, a new format was adopted and a photograph appeared on the front cover. This showed Joe Fildes with his lovely open drive Silver Ghost limousine, taken at Bordeaux on the Club's first French Tour. In the summer of 1966, good 20/25s were being offered in the Bulletin at £200 to £400 (completely overhauled). Nigel Hughes was advising members to stock up with such items as gasket sets, pistons, valves, guides, etc, before prices started to rise!

The Bulletin for September 1967 was a bumper number with fifty pages. It contained an account of the second great Goodwood event. This great issue also saw the beginning of the Correspondence column, following a letter to the Secretary which ended; "It is a shame that such a fine Bulletin has no correspondence column, rather than dull stories by a fortunate minority who drive from one grape farm to the next." We only needed a hint! Tom Brahmer was an early correspondent, indeed he wrote an excellent article on the 1913 Alpine and the cars involved. He played a prominent part in the route reconnaissance and arrangements for the great event of 1973. Tom was also very much involved in the fast growing Swiss Section of the Club.

In 1967, Ralph Symmons, after a long and valuable innings, resigned as Club Chairman and became our first President. His Editorship of the Bulletin also ended and Derek Randall was appointed Editor, with his wife Carol as Art Editor (as befits a professional photographer). The Editorial Committee was completed by Nigel Hughes and Peter Baines, a very successful team which ran for five years.

Left to right: Cover of Bulletin Issue 100; Page 1 of Bulletin Issue 1; Cover of Bulletin Issue 200 **Previous page** Club President, Lieutenant Colonel Eric Barrass OBE

> *The May 1965 issue of the Bulletin contained the first of the 'Secretary's Notes'*

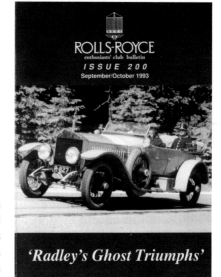

'Radley's Ghost Triumphs'

No. 1.   February 1960

ROLLS-ROYCE ENTHUSIASTS' CLUB
B U L L E T I N

EDITORIAL

The Club continues to grow, and its growth has brought about more work for our Secretary, Miss Harris. With this in mind, the Committee has decided that the responsibility for the club bulletin should be taken off her shoulders and has created the post of Assistant Secretary and Editor of the bulletin, which I hope adequately to fill.

We have decided that this bulletin should now be professionally duplicated, and that its scope should be enlarged. Whilst carrying announcements of meetings as before, we will try to give more details of the form of meetings, so that members will know what to expect when they turn up. We also hope to carry reports of club meetings and to include a 'Sales & Wants' column in which members will be able to place advertisements.

The Committee is always glad to receive any suggestions from members on the substance of the bulletin and the types of meeting they would like.

READ, MARK, LEARN AND INWARDLY DIGEST

Members should receive a copy of the club rules with this bulletin. A large number of members have failed to pay subscriptions for 1959. This is formal notice of the committee's decision to enforce the rules and strike them off the club list if the subscriptions are not paid within one month of receipt of this notice.

Subscriptions should be sent to Miss G.M. Harris, Paternoster Farm, Yarnton, Oxon.

THE SPIRIT OF ECSTASY

On December 1st, 1959, Mrs. Phillips (Jo Sykes) daughter of the late Charles Sykes, who designed the 'Spirit of Ecstasy', gave a talk to members of the club at 'The Chequers', Cassington. Unfortunately, it was the worst night of the year for weather, Oxford being blanketed by thick fog. Nevertheless, fourteen intrepid members turned up to hear Mrs. Phillips.

She started by saying that, about 1910, Rolls-Royce Ltd, suggested that a graceful mascot should be designed to replace the horrid little mascots that owners were fitting onto the radiator caps of their cars. Charles Sykes was inspired by the challenge of producing a mascot which belonged to the car as much as a carved wooden figure-head belonged to the ship of which it was a part. At the same time, the mascot should convey an impression of smoothness and speed, and the harnessing of mysterious power. His answer to this challenge was the 'Spirit of Ecstasy', which was born on February 6th, 1911.

Mrs. Phillips told us how, in 1920, and unknown to Charles Sykes, a photograph of the mascot had been entered for the World Competition of Radiator Mascots, in Paris, by Rolls-Royce, and had won first prize. She showed us the gold medal commemorating this, and the gold-plated mascot sent later for exhibition.

She then gave us details of how the mascots were made, of the various sizes which were produced, and of the production of the kneeling version on January 25th 1934. We were shown the bronze mascots, used for casting, and a pair of small silver-plated ones, 2⅝ inches high, one on a silver ash-tray, and the other supporting a goblet. The latter were made for presentation to exalted members of the firm and its associates.

The talk was followed by an extremely interesting question period, when more points came to light, and Mrs. Phillips denied the story that the figure of the Spirit was modelled from any particular person.

We recorded the meeting on tape, and an edited version has been sent to the Rolls-Royce Owners Club of America, together with a set of photographs of the original mascots.

Car prices by early 1968 had begun to rise sharply. It is noticeable that in the Bulletins' advertisements, and indeed in contemporary motoring magazines generally, prices were seldom quoted as they were rising fast. However, a 1931 20/25 Park Ward saloon was offered at £500 and a 1930 20/25 coupé by James Young was offered at £650. Amongst the 'hard stuff' was a 1921 Silver Ghost with an open two-seater replica body, and a Phantom II Continental by Mulliner – at just £4,000 each!

As we moved into 1972, we had broken the 2,000 membership barrier and had about £6,000 in the Club's kitty. In 1973 a new Editor was appointed – R J Gibbs ("Gibby" to us all), a professional newspaperman, highly disciplined and with vitriolic humour capable of slicing bread. There was no messing about when it came to deadlines. "Gibby" raised the Bulletin to a very high standard. Members' advertisements, still carried in the Club Bulletin at that time, included a 1932 PII Continental chassis with a hearse body at £2,750. The regular feature "Cars and Their Owners" had reached No 46.

Issue no 1 of the Advertising Supplement was produced in January 1975. This resulted from a strong feeling that the Club Bulletin might be swamped with commercial advertising if this were allowed, and so an insert was designed. The very first one was produced on our own second hand offset litho printing machine operated in a member's house, collated round the Secretary's dining room table by a bunch of volunteers and then hand stapled. The content was produced by Christopher Leefe who improved and developed it for many years. The first issue had sixteen pages.

Home production of further Advertising Supplements proved physically impossible on a do-it-yourself basis and the printing was transferred to Flo-Print of Tunbridge Wells. Only Members' adverts continued to be carried in the Bulletin.

From Bulletin 93 the printing of the Bulletin was transferred from the dubious ministrations of an eccentric Irishman in Oxford to our current printers, Acanthus Press of Wellington, Somerset. In the spring of 1976 the New Members list in the Bulletin carried thirty names. Bulletin editorial again emphasised the urgency of finding a permanent home.

The Club's permanent new home is, of course, The Hunt House in Paulerspury. The rest, as they say, is history. ▣

CONTENTS

1» RREC *The Rolls-Royce Enthusiasts' Club*

2 » STYLE

Fine Jewellery & Timepieces

3 » LIVE

Luxury Living, Interiors & Architecture

4 » ENJOY
Yachting, Leisure & Aviation

5» TRAVEL *Travel & Hotels*

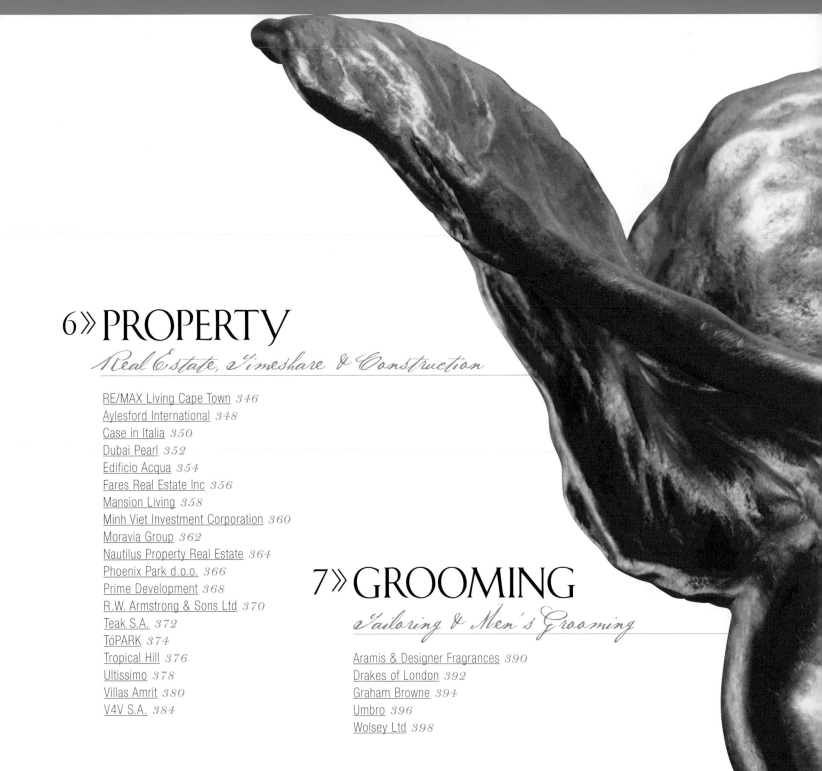

6» PROPERTY
Real Estate, Timeshare & Construction

7» GROOMING
Tailoring & Men's Grooming

8» INDULGE *Food, Drink & Hospitality*

9» CHAMPIONS

Best of British & Royal Warranty Holders

10» WEALTH

Investment Management & Philanthropy

RREC

1 » The Rolls-Royce Enthusiasts' Club

ONE HUNDRED YEARS OF THE SPIRIT OF
ECSTASY
by Ken Brittan

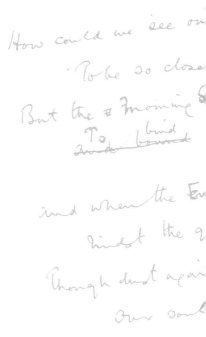

One hundred years ago in 1910 the Spirit of Ecstasy was proudly fixed to the radiator cap of a Rolls-Royce 40/50 motor car by Claude Johnson. Claude was the Managing Director of Rolls-Royce. In 1907 the 40/50 was declared to be 'The Best Car in the World'. In this article the author considers the key players in the formative period, when the sculptor Charles Sykes interacted with the motoring pioneers and the Spirit of Ecstasy was created. Changes in style, size and finish of the mascot have fascinated members of the RREC for many years. Here we discover the mascot's early evolution.

CHARLES SYKES - RESIDENT ARTIST AT *THE CAR*:

The Rolls-Royce 40/50 was initially developed by the design team at Manchester in 1904. In 1908 production was transferred to Derby. Frederick Henry Royce was the Chief Engineer and his designs ensured that the 40/50 Rolls-Royce would be the smoothest running and the most superlative driving machine that had ever been built. Charles Rolls was one of the most experienced drivers in the world and did much to promote the pre-eminent position of the Rolls-Royce Company.

Claude Johnson was a friend of John Scott Montagu, well known to him at the turn of the century in 1900. He visited John Montagu in Piccadilly, London where he was editor of the weekly magazine *The Car*. It was here that Claude Johnson first admired the art works of Charles Sykes, resident artist at *The Car*. He admired the bronzes created for Lord Montagu including the masterpiece 'Adam and Eve' which was exhibited at the Paris Salon in 1909.

Inside the offices of *The Car* in Piccadilly, John Scott Montagu MP often entertained his friends. He also encouraged Charles Sykes. John Montagu's day-to-day affairs were managed by his secretary, Miss Eleanor Thornton. Recent research has shown that Eleanor Thornton was the brains behind the business and when Sykes joined *The Car* in 1903 it was Miss Thornton who welcomed him with a cup of tea. Eleanor played a key part in motivating Sykes within the extraordinary framework which was developing at *The Car*. ≫

Left to right: The last piece of art work which was signed by Sykes just a few months before he died; Chromium plated mascot on cap for 20/25s, 1936

Sykes was commissioned by Johnson for the paintings which were reproduced in the Rolls-Royce 1910-11 sales catalogue

PAINTINGS FOR ROLLS-ROYCE SALES CATALOGUE: Whilst in the employment of John Montagu, Sykes was commissioned by Johnson for the paintings which were reproduced in the Rolls-Royce 1910-11 sales catalogue and also, significantly, for a figurehead to be placed on the radiator of the 40/50. He was fortunate because he travelled in the cars used by Rolls and Johnson. He also travelled extensively in the cars used by Lord Montagu of Beaulieu who frequently journeyed from London to Hampshire.

At that time, Sykes was living in London whilst his wife Jessica lived in Newcastle-on-Tyne with daughter Josephine. According to his letters, he was overloaded with work for *The Car*, John Scott Montagu and Claude Johnson. Charles and Jessica found time to take their daughter Josephine to Beaulieu Parish Church where she was christened by permission of Lord Montagu.

THE SPIRIT OF ECSTASY – A WORK OF ART: Charles Sykes was an accomplished sculptor. He attended the life modelling class at the Royal College of Art. He was trained in the use of clay, plaster and also the conversion of wax into cast bronze. He was an accomplished metal worker in repoussé, whereby the metal is raised with fine tools from a thin metal sheet. Charles was also familiar with chasing and finishing techniques. A self portrait of Charles Sykes, which was converted to a lost wax bronze, is shown in the accompanying photograph dated 1900. We see therefore that Charles was well equipped to produce for Claude Johnson the figurehead which he called 'The Spirit of Speed'. Soon it was to be renamed by Johnson the 'Spirit of Ecstasy' and assigned by Sykes to Rolls-Royce Ltd. It was agreed that it would be manufactured as a work of art. This meant that all of the production would receive special attention. Claude Johnson got what he wanted: the paintings for the Rolls-Royce catalogue and the figurehead for the 40/50 - the mascot for 'The Best Car in the World'.

There has been much conjecture concerning the role of Eleanor Thornton at *The Car* and as a model for the Spirit of Ecstasy. Charles knew Eleanor very well indeed. It was a special relationship, which ended prematurely when Eleanor died in December 1915. During his lifetime until 1950 Charles was not able to talk about Eleanor, although he may have told his daughter Josephine many years after 1910 as Josephine grew to be part of the business in her twenties. Later, Josephine was often asked about Eleanor and the Spirit of Ecstasy before she died in 1988.

Left to right: Type 3 mascot for early 20hps; Type 1 mascot for early Rolls-Royce 40/50s

Her reply "Eleanor was a lovely person. It is an interesting story and if it makes you happy, let the myth prevail". The reticence of Josephine was noticeable and well-founded.

Charles, the accomplished sculptor, did not need a model for the Spirit of Ecstasy but he needed his friend Eleanor. Charles knew exactly how to interpret the messages which he received from the motoring pioneers. He created the image which has maintained the iconic value of the Spirit of Ecstasy for a hundred years. For these reasons, we should remember Eleanor and Charles. Together they worked in the formative years. They gave us the Spirit of Ecstasy and they bequeathed to us the mystery, which still beckons.

MAKING THE SPIRIT OF ECSTASY:

In 1911, when Charles Sykes started to manufacture the mascot, it was hurriedly fitted to the existing radiator cap. This was a Royce design which had originated in 1904 and was not to be altered. This cap, which had a small hexagon head, was fitted to the first type of mascot and it became known as the hollow base mascot because the hexagon head of the radiator cap was covered by the hollow base. A good example of this earliest mascot is on display in the Club's headquarters. »

> *These mascots were impressed on the base with the full signature of Charles Sykes*

Charles Sykes made two types of smaller mascot for the 20hp known affectionately as the 'large cheese' and the 'small cheese'

This particular mascot was probably fitted retrospectively in 1911 to a 1909 40/50 motor car. A slightly later version of this mascot, Type 1, was produced without the hollow base. Many variations were made by Sykes following requests from coachbuilders. Those mascots were manufactured from 'yellow metals' such as brass, bronze and gun metal. Some were manufactured from an alloy of nickel and copper called nickel silver. Many were electroplated with nickel and some were given a heavy coating of pure silver. These were the first proper 'Silver Ladies'. These mascots were impressed on the base with the full signature of Charles Sykes which he inscribed into the wax before casting. The name Rolls-Royce and the date 6.2.11 were also inscribed and thereafter appeared on all subsequent standing Sprits of Ecstasy.

The Club's Concours Rally is an annual opportunity to see the variations of these first type hollow base mascots. You will see many variations but note that very few of these mascots came from the hand of Charles Sykes. There are very many acceptable looking replicas made since 1965. The majority of original mascots have over the years been damaged and many of them discarded.

LATER DERIVATIVES OF THE MASCOT:
A derivative of the hollow based mascot, Type 2, appeared towards the end of World War I. A new radiator cap had been designed by Rolls-Royce and resolved the mounting difficulties of the hollow based type. This was fitted to 40/50 Silver Ghosts between 1918 and 1925. This mascot was also fitted to the early New Phantoms in 1925, thus ensuring continuity of mascot production between Silver Ghost and Phantom I. Many Type 2 mascots were made in solid nickel silver and closely matched in colour the metal used to construct the radiator shell and sometimes the radiator cap.

In 1923 the Company announced the 20hp car which was manufactured between 1923 and 1929. The 20hp had a significantly smaller radiator but the cap was exactly the same 2" diameter screw thread as used on the 40/50. Charles Sykes made two types of smaller mascot for the 20hp known affectionately as the 'large cheese' and the 'small cheese'. They are distinctly different from each other. Type 3 is not very often seen whereas Type 4 is for the most part regarded as the 20hp mascot. Very many replicas have been made.

THE ORMOLU SPIRIT:
We now come to a very significant event in the mascot story. When World War I ended in 1918 Charles Sykes had found a new associate, Dennis Bradley. Dennis Bradley and Sykes had both been critics of the war. They lunched together in central London on 11 November 1918. During the war Sykes had been kept busy with commercial art, some of it for Bradley. He also made bronzes for Bradley and it was Bradley who was soon to view a magnificent new Spirit of Ecstasy finely chased by Sykes and unusually finished in Gold Ormolu.

This unique bronze was an exhibition piece which grew out of the first mascots made by Sykes. It was a celebration at the end of the Great War and the Spirit of Ecstasy in Ormolu lifted the spirits of Sykes and Bradley. It was never intended for use on a motor car. This Spirit of Ecstasy gained both the first prize and the gold medal awarded to Charles Sykes in 1920 at the Paris Salon. This special Spirit of Ecstasy was guarded by the Sykes family and by Josephine Sykes in particular. Josephine treasured it as the essence of her father's most well-known work. He was forty three years old in 1918. Claude Johnson now had 'The Best Mascot in Paris' to fit 'The Best Car in the World'.

Whereas the Ormolu Spirit was an exhibition piece of 1918, it was to be five years later before a new Rolls-Royce motor car, the 20hp, emerged from Derby in 1923. This is where the form and detail of the Ormolu Spirit were first incorporated. The very first of these small mascots for the 20hp car, that is the 'large cheese' mascot, bears a strong resemblance to the Ormolu Spirit. However, the fully detailed form of the Ormolu Spirit was never viable on the 20hp. It was subsequently modified and a smaller simplified version Type 4 became the accepted 20hp mascot until about 1928.

The Ormolu mascot of 1918 was to permanently influence the subsequent design of standing Spirit of Ecstasy mascots for small horsepower Rolls-Royce used until 1929. 1918 was a defining year for mascot design. »

Left to right: A self portrait of Charles Sykes converted to a lost wax bronze and dated 1900; Type 4 mascot for later 20hps; Type 2 mascot for later Rolls-Royce 40/50s

KNEELING LADY AND BENTLEY MASCOTS: The Rolls-Royce motor car was being continually developed and this development was nearly always reflected in the mascot. For example, 'Staybrite' radiators were introduced in 1929/30. This meant that radiator caps were made of stainless steel and often the mascots were chromium plated to match. The kneeling lady mascot was introduced in 1934 and was fitted by Rolls-Royce to late 20/25s, 25/30s, Wraiths, also to late Phantom IIs and to Phantom IIIs. These kneeling lady mascots manufactured by Sykes during 1934 were magnificent but those manufactured later by Le Jeune were quite different.

Charles Sykes also designed most of the Bentley mascots which appeared on the 3½ and 4¼ Bentleys and the Mark V Bentley in 1939. There was a public competition with a prize of £50 offered by Rolls-Royce. It was Charles who received the prize money.

When Sykes was a student before 1900, he was taught by Eduardo Lanteri. Lanteri was acknowledged as the best modelling teacher who taught Rodin and whose teaching methods are as effective today as they were in 1898. Hannah Sykes, mother of Charles, played a crucial part which led him to the Royal College of Art. Eleanor Thornton became 'Alice in Motorland' in the hands of Charles Sykes and we know that every Christmas at *The Car* Charles celebrated with Eleanor. During Christmas 1910 those celebrations, hosted by John Scott Montagu, reached their highest point of perfection, the Spirit of Ecstasy. ▣

(This script has been paraphrased from the researches of the Charles Sykes Heritage Group. This group seeks to access and understand the archive materials which support the story of Charles Robinson Sykes 1875-1950 and those associated with him. A comprehensive account is being prepared in a book called 'Towards the Dawn' a title chosen by one of our group members. We are more than grateful to the many participants who have already helped us to put together new commentaries which enlighten the Charles Sykes story.)

Above: Kneeling lady by Le Jeune, 1937

> *Eleanor Thornton became 'Alice in Motorland' in the hands of Charles Sykes*

80 YEARS OF THE
DERBY BENTLEY

by Douglas Reece and James Tucker

Eighty years ago, in 1931, Rolls-Royce acquired Bentley Motors and after a somewhat lengthy gestation period commenced the production of a Bentley motor car at their works in Derby. The Derby Bentley was launched in 1933.

TAKE OVER OF BENTLEY MOTORS: In 1930 W O Bentley introduced the magnificent 8 litre car which was capable of carrying luxurious coachwork at 100mph and in complete silence. In a shrinking market following the depression, this car began to make serious inroads into a traditional Rolls-Royce market. Jack Barclay found that it was increasingly difficult to sell a Phantom II Continental alongside a Bentley 8 Litre.

Money was always tight at Bentley Motors and the racing programme together with the cost of launching the 6½ litre necessitated the raising of further capital in 1925. Woolf Barnato, one of the 'Bentley Boys', injected considerable sums of money to keep car production going, but by 1931 the situation was becoming dire. The expense incurred in the launch of the 8 litre and 4 litre cars and a supercharged version of the 4½ litre required more capital if the Company was to stay afloat. The 4 litre was not a success, much to the relief of Rolls-Royce who feared competition with their 20/25 model, and the sales of the 8 litre were not sufficient to keep the Company afloat.

Various approaches were made including one to Rolls-Royce suggesting a merger, but all to no avail and on 11 July 1931 a receiver was appointed. In desperation W O Bentley approached Napiers who, following negotiations, agreed to buy the Company and to recommence car production which they had given up in 1924. An announcement appeared in the *Autocar* of 14 August 1931 headed "Bentley Napier Fusion".

Rolls-Royce felt sufficiently threatened by this potential Napier take over – their old aero engine and quality automobile manufacturing rivals - that they decided to take action. When the official receiver appeared in court to present the Napier offer to the presiding judge they made an anonymous bid for Bentley Motors through the Equitable Central Trust Ltd. This bid was successful and Rolls-Royce acquired Bentley Motors Ltd for about £125,000 on 13 November 1931. This included the services of W O Bentley himself. Once the legalities had been completed Rolls-Royce formed a new company 'Bentley Motors (1931) Ltd. »

Left to right: Derby Bentley (B22BN) H J Mulliner streamline dhc; Derby Bentley (B16FB) Park Ward saloon
Overleaf (top to bottom): Derby Bentley (B105AE) Vanden Plas tourer; Derby Bentley (B186EF) Gurney Nutting fhc

EARLY DEVELOPMENT OF THE DERBY BENTLEY:
The engineering department at Derby had no warning of the imminent takeover of Bentley Motors and had nothing to offer the sales department to market as a Bentley.

By the end of 1931 Sir Henry Royce and his team based at his home in West Wittering began to think about a new model, codenamed 'Bensport', and what they were initially contemplating bore little resemblance to the first Derby Bentley. Due to the economic depression, a smaller model of about 3 litres and different from current Rolls-Royce models was contemplated. Half of sales from the Cricklewood works had been the 3 litre and sales of larger cars had been declining. Royce was considering a supercharged engined car to reflect its sporting heritage. The Company started trying out other sports cars including an Alvis Speed 20 and Roy Fedden's blown straight 8 Alfa Romeo, but decided this was not the type of car they wanted to produce.

A SMALLER ENGINE PROJECT:
Due to the prevailing economic situation, Royce had had a smaller four seater owner-driver saloon designed at Derby, code name 'Peregrine', with a mono-block cast iron engine of 2364cc capacity, a possible successor to the 3.6 litre 20/25 model. The car was ready for road testing in June 1932 and was favourably commented upon. However, when taken to France it developed very high oil temperatures when driven flat out. The Babbit metal big end bearings suffered and began to break up. An oil cooler could have been a solution but would have to have been massive to cope. The small engine could not produce acceptable performance on the winding British roads without a rear axle ratio which gave a continuous 5000rpm in France. The solution of an overdrive was not available. The project was dropped, but as the basis of the 'Bensport' the chassis had distinct possibilities which Royce recognised.

Consideration was given to supercharging the Peregrine engine, but issues such as where to site the unit and finding a suitable source delayed development - the Rootes and Powerplus units not being considered suitable. They even considered developing their own supercharger, but the cost would have been prohibitive. A Peregrine so equipped had suffered from blown head gaskets and low speed detonation which threatened reliability. Time was going on and discussions continued; an overhead camshaft version of the Peregrine or adding two more cylinders of similar capacity to produce a straight eight engine were some of the ideas. Royce's failing health was beginning to affect his decision making. Meanwhile the Sales Department had no offering for the old Bentley customers and there was fear that competitors could move in and take the market.

A COMPROMISE IS REACHED:
During this impasse the engineering department at Derby were amusing themselves by considering alternatives to the non-existent supercharged engine and found that they could fit an existing 20/25 engine and gearbox into the Peregrine chassis with little modification. The resulting hybrid had lively performance and handled well with all the Rolls-Royce attributes of smoothness and silence.

In September 1932 Hives launched a carefully considered attack on the supercharged engine programme and pressed for the use of the J1 engine in the Peregrine chassis which he considered an ideal combination. The J1 engine was the same as the 20/25 but with a new six port crossflow head, a modified camshaft, a compression ratio of 6.4:1, (up from 4.6:1) and fitted with twin SU carburettors on a new induction pipe. Power output was 110bhp. This configuration had been road tested on a 20/25 and was the 3½ litre engine as we now know it. Royce eventually agreed to this combination, but was still hankering for a blown engine. ≫

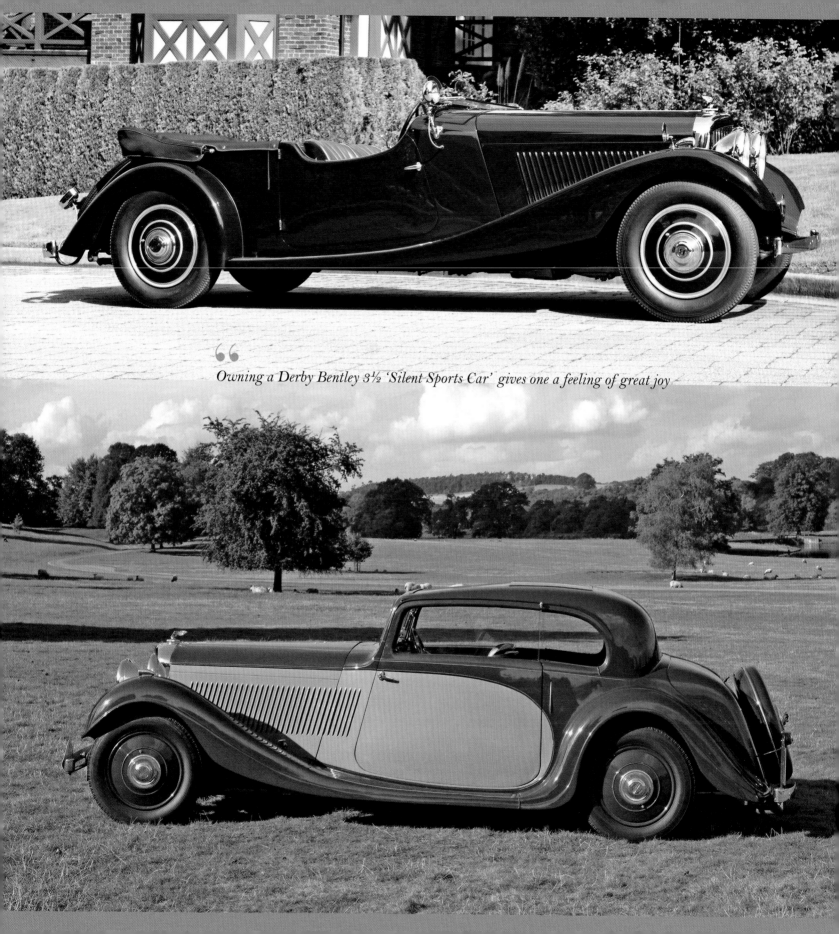

Owning a Derby Bentley 3½ 'Silent Sports Car' gives one a feeling of great joy

Woman's Love

Fashion forbids me speak to thee
Save by a glance or sigh
My aching heart must bear its load
Acting its daily lie
Were I a man I'd take by storm
Thy lips so proudly cold
I'd steal thy heart unstolen before
With Love so hotly told

> **Taking all things into consideration, I would rather own this Bentley car than any other car produced under that name**

THE FIRST DERBY BENTLEY:

By November 1932 Hives was pressing on with the J1 Bensport and had the first mock-up Bentley on the road by mid January 1933. He comments 'With J1 it is far better than any sports car that is being sold today.' The car, a four door Park Ward close coupled saloon, was taken to West Wittering reaching an indicated 95mph on the way, so Sir Henry did see it some three months before his untimely death on 22 April 1933 at the age of 70.

Hives decided to use the 20/25 gearbox and commented that Bensport would be economical to make as it was almost all 20/25 and Peregrine pieces. W O Bentley was not involved in the design process but helped with prototype testing. He took the car to Brooklands and reported most favourably commenting "Taking all things into consideration, I would rather own this Bentley car than any other car produced under that name". He was delighted with the performance of the car following an extensive Alpine excursion. Four experimental Bentleys were on the road by June 1933, two saloons, a drop head coupé and a tourer. There was concern that the new product was too quiet for a sports car but this was to be skilfully exploited by the Company. All work on the Peregrine project had stopped and production at Cricklewood ceased.

LAUNCH OF THE 3½ LITRE BENTLEY:

The new car was shown to the press in September 1933, the final release being at the October motor show. The fourth of the prototypes, an open tourer with a 3.9 axle, was used on press day. It was a very fast car and was reputed to have lapped Montlhery at 95mph. The car had an instant appeal and was marketed by the Sales Department as 'The Silent Sports Car'. Bentley was back at Olympia for the first time since 1930 and had three examples on their stand including a sports tourer by Vanden Plas priced at £1380. The chassis price was £1100, £50 more than a 20/25. Several examples were on display by the leading coachbuilders including a sedanca coupé from H J Mulliner, sports saloons from Arthur Mulliner and Hooper and a drophead coupé from Thrupp and Maberly.

The press reception was most favourable. In 1934 the Company published a booklet entitled *Some Opinions* which ran to four editions and contained articles about the new Bentley taken from motoring magazines and newspapers.

PRODUCTION VOLUME AND SURVIVAL:
The public's response to the new 3½ litre Bentley was encouraging and 540 cars were sold in 1934. Taken together with 890 examples of the 20/25, this more than offset the declining sales of the Phantom II. Total sales of the 3½ litre were 1177 by 1937, the new 4¼ litre model being introduced in 1936.

The survival rate of these cars is known to be 73% and this is likely to be a slightly conservative estimate - 75% is often quoted. Examples are still occasionally coming to light. A remarkable rate for a vehicle that was underrated for many years and a testament to the build quality and loyal following these wonderful cars enjoy.

FAMOUS OWNERS:
The new Bentley appealed to previous owners of Bentleys from the old factory. Famous names such as its previous chairman and a director of the restructured company, Woolf Barnato, and his wife, owned five between them. Britain's land speed breaker, George Eyston owned two and his great rival Malcolm Campbell had three. They were popular cars with British racing drivers such as Raymond Mays who had a series of four all painted black with distinctive chrome wheels and blue upholstery. A very successful racing driver, involved in the conception and campaigning of ERA racing cars, he used his Derby Bentleys for high speed travel on the continent and practice sessions on race circuits. His testimonials following extensive use of the cars were used by Rolls-Royce as promotional publicity material. Prince Birabongse (B Bira) used his 3½ litre for similar activities.

Captains of industry were good customers for the new car. Several pillars of the British aviation industry chose Derby Bentleys including Richard Fairey of Fairey Aviation, Sir George White and Roy Fedden of Bristol Aircraft Co. and R J Mitchell designer of the Supermarine Spitfire. Parts suppliers to the company owned them: Gordon Smith of Smiths Industries; C L Breedon of Wilmot & Breedon bumpers; F W Bluemel (steering wheels); Alexander Duckham of Duckhams oils and Bernard Hobbs of Lodge Sparking Plugs.

HRH The Duke of Kent had two Derby Bentleys delivered which were often used for official visits and both of which featured a division, a very unusual fitting for these sports saloons. He was a keen driver and was often photographed at the wheel. This confused doormen who, on the car drawing up, would open the nearside rear door only to find the Duke alighting from the offside front! »

Left: Derby Bentley engine (nearside)
Above (top to bottom): Derby Bentley (B64FB) Barker saloon; Derby Bentley (B136CR) Mann Egerton saloon; Derby Bentley (B203CW) H J Mulliner sedanca

> *The survival rate of these cars is known to be 73% and this is likely to be a slightly conservative estimate*

BESPOKE COACHWORK: The 1177 3½ litre cars manufactured at Derby as rolling chassis and engines were all dispatched to various coachbuilders for bespoke bodywork built to the specifications chosen by their purchasers. The lucky first owners chose from a wide number of styles - with four door light saloons being exceedingly popular but with a few tourers, coupés, and cabriolets adding to the sporting image. There were enormous variations in the detailing, both of coachwork and interior and exterior fittings. The top coachbuilders were Park Ward with 529; Thrupp and Maberly, 111; Vanden Plas, 77; H J Mulliner, 64; Hooper, 61; Barker, 44; Freestone & Webb and Gurney Nutting both 39 and James Young, 35. The other 178 were bodied by around 40 coach builders, some in the UK and some in Europe.

The larger coachbuilders offered a variety of styles of body with the user then deciding on what further fitments and accessories they wished. Park Ward initially offered a saloon body with the spare wheel mounted on the boot lid. However, with four seats, the inside of the boot was rather small and so an alternative design was offered with a more upright and rather larger rear end. Their drophead was very popular with an elegant line and considerable seating space for four people. Numerous variants were produced and also special bodies commissioned by Jack Barclay including a beautiful 2-door streamline coupé. Smaller coachbuilders such as Oxborrow & Fuller were commissioned by individuals to create cars to their desired specification. Offord & Sons bodied one of the most famous racing cars of the period when they built the Eddie Hall car for the Ulster TT races.

Inevitably with closed cars being the most popular and demands being for more comfortable seating, sound proofing and extras such as radios and cocktail cabinets and tables, the overall weight of the coachwork increased and this encouraged the move towards a larger more powerful engine - the 4¼ litre, and again Park Ward was the major supplier of bodies.

Inevitably, the chassis, steering column and scuttle set the base for the line of a Derby Bentley and so all the cars have a family likeness. However, the variations in style, finish, colour and detailing ensure each car offers a fresh perspective and a unique feel.

THE DERBY BENTLEY 3½ LITRE: Owning a Derby Bentley 3½ 'Silent Sports Car' gives one a feeling of great joy; - pride in the pedigree and history, delight in the coachwork and excitement at the anticipation of driving. The driving is easy with light and responsive steering, good handling, a lively engine and sure footed brakes. It is a car to enjoy regardless of weather, road conditions, or distance. In the 1930s several well known racing drivers used these cars, not just as every day transport but, as the cars were fast, smooth, and had superb road holding, as the means of

learning the various European race tracks they competed upon.

During the manufacturing life of these chassis - 1933 to 1936 - a number of modifications were introduced as lessons were learnt from their world-wide usage. Much of this revolved around improved dampers and stiffened mountings and supports, probably because of their high speed use on European roads less well surfaced than they are now. The Peregrine chassis that was adopted for use in these cars was relatively lightweight and flexible with no cruciform bracing and intended for a less powerful car. One of the early teething troubles experienced was that of the front of the car shaking with vibrating wings and headlamps on poor roads. This was cured by fitting Wilmot Breedon harmonic front bumpers and lowering the front cross member. A few instances of piston seizure were cured by the adoption of Aerolite components. Con rods were modified with a central drilling replacing an external oil pipe. Additional cylinder lubrication was added and first Dunlop road wheels and then Rudd Whitworth wheels were fitted.

MODERN REFINEMENTS:

In more modern times further refinements have been introduced, largely to bring the cars into line with current motoring conditions. Perhaps the most important is the addition of an externally mounted modern full flow oil filter. This allows the use of current multigrade detergent oils affording greater engine protection and less wear. Overdrives or high ratio rear axles add much to the pleasure as the higher gearing is ideal for fast cruising on motorways enabling one to keep up with modern traffic conditions and speeds without stressing the engine in any way. New aluminium heads can be fitted in place of worn out original cast iron examples, thus removing any concerns over fuel and offering greater economy. And finally, to top off the modern feel, a satellite navigation system can be added thus providing a totally over the top superior classic car with which to tour the world! ▣

(Acknowledgement: Pictures in this article are from the Fraser and Knapek Collection as shown in the book *Bentley Beauty* and with many thanks to Neill Fraser for allowing their use.)

Left to right: Derby Bentley (B93EJ) Vanden Plas tourer; Derby Bentley (B73FC) Park Ward dhc

HEADS IN THE
CLOUDS
by Malcolm Tucker

Left to right: Phantom V with Park Ward landaulette coachwork to design 1104 (this car was commissioned for HM Queen Elizabeth The Queen Mother); Sales catalogue illustration for the launch of the 1955 Silver Cloud

It's been nearly fifty years since the last steam engines ran the length and breadth of British railways, and yet, if you ask a child to draw a train the chances are that an approximation of a steam engine will be the result. If you ask the man in the street to draw a Rolls-Royce, then it's a sure bet that something akin to a Silver Cloud will be the result. Such is the strength of the image of that beautiful John Blatchley-designed body.

LAUNCH OF THE SILVER CLOUD: Launched in 1955, the initial design stages of the Silver Cloud go back at least to 1950. At this time the last Derby designed cars were being manufactured at Crewe: the Bentley Mk VI and the Rolls-Royce Silver Dawn and Silver Wraith models. These were a range of cars that would be able to benefit from a commonality of parts - the 'Rationalized Range'. The first of these to enter production in 1946 was, for political reasons, the Bentley Mk VI rather than the Rolls-Royce Silver Dawn. One of Harvey-Bailey's crucial design decisions was that the 'Rationalized Range' cars would have a separate chassis that would take coachbuilt bodywork as well as a standard steel body, making them the first Rolls-Royce produced cars to leave the factory as complete vehicles, in any number. Standard steel bodies were never designed for the longer wheelbase Silver Wraith, which was designated for bespoke coachwork only.

When the company began to address the problem of a replacement for the 'Rationalized Range', Dr Llewellyn Smith, head of the post-war car division, and his chief engineer, W A Robotham, realized that the financially successful 'Rationalized Range' concept must be continued.

This was a time when, despite the majority of cars being ordered with the factory-fitted standard steel bodies, there was still a strong demand for more specialized, bespoke bodies by such coachbuilders as Hooper, James Young, H J Mulliner and, of course, the Company owned Park Ward. This made a chassis-based car inevitable. The new Bentley experimental cars were designated 'Siam' and the Rolls-Royce versions 'Siam Dawn'.

DEVELOPMENT OF THE MODEL: In overall concept the Silver Cloud chassis followed that of its predecessor the Silver Dawn. The great improvement was that instead of a riveted channel section, a lighter and much stronger welded box-section was chosen; still with a massive centre cruciform, but now nearly fifty per cent more rigid. »

Running gear was transferred from the earlier cars, except the straight six cylinder engines were now bored out to 4.9 litres, as were the earlier Bentley R Type Continentals. Suspension and braking systems were redesigned and in all respects the myriad of changes to the mechanical components effected an improvement in virtually all respects over the preceding model. The continued concept of commonality of parts showed itself in the chassis being offered in standard and long-wheelbase forms at 10' 3" and 10' 7" and on the coachbuilt-only chassis of the Phantom V and VI with a wheelbase of 12' 1".

The manual gearboxes were relegated to special order only. The automatic General Motors four-speed unit first seen in the Silver Dawn and R Type Bentley was again chosen to be built under license by Rolls-Royce to their own standards. The *Autocar*'s contributor Ronald 'Steady' Barker wrote of this box "No one at Crewe is under the illusion that this transmission is completely smooth, but it has the overwhelming asset of transmitting full engine-braking in the overrun through any of the four gears. Where a compromise has to be biased towards smoothness or controllability (and thus safety), the latter wins."

Space for power-steering and air-conditioning was allocated to the chassis, although both of these offerings were initially extras. The new car was some three inches longer, with a wider track front and rear, which with the engine and gearbox moved slightly forward, allowed the passenger accommodation to be increased, as was the boot area.

CONSERVATIVE ELEGANCE AND LUXURY:
There can be no doubt that elegant and beautiful though the body is, it was more than a little reactionary. Led by the American influence, the mass-market was well into curvaceous designs with wing and waist-lines running steadily from front to rear, making use of the full width of the vehicles for the accommodation of occupants. Rolls-Royce had merged and flared elements of the Silver Cloud

Top to bottom: Silver Cloud III bodied by H J Mulliner Park Ward Ltd and commissioned by the Australian government for HM The Queen's tour of Australia in 1963. Two were built: CAL37 and CAL39 - both using the codename 'Tasmania'; Silver Cloud interior - more spacious and with plusher seating compared with the Silver Dawn **Right:** Straight-six-cylinder 4.9 litre engine of the Silver Cloud

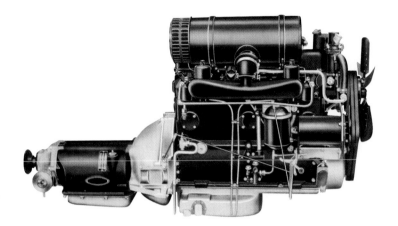

compared with their former designs, but the result can only be called conservative. In fairness, this was an accepted trend for the better quality British cars such as Jaguar's Mk VII, Mk VIII and MK IX, Daimler's offerings throughout the range and Armstrong Siddeley's Sapphire. That having been said, it can be argued that the Silver Cloud is one of the most attractive cars ever produced. All elements are in harmony, and the eye can sweep across its lines from any angle and not a glitch or hitch will cause an exclamation of disapproval by the viewer.

Inside, the luxury was increased over that of the Silver Dawn, with thicker seating and larger side bolsters for weary rear-seat passengers. The lit, mirrored companions became a little larger and the 'duchess' straps were retained. The fold-down rear compartment picnic tables became a shade more stylish and sheepskin over-rugs complemented both front and rear. A new dashboard layout greatly enhanced the view from the front seats, the instrument and control layout being up-to-date; a great contrast to the pre-war offering on the Silver Dawn. More light was let into the cabin by the adoption of stainless-steel window frames, their thin section allowing a much greater glazed area compared with the thick metal frames on the previous model.

DEVELOPMENT OF THE V8 ENGINE:
By 1959 the Silver Cloud, still accepted as gracious and imposing, was lagging behind in performance. By 1951 the development of a new V8 engine was underway, and just as the 'Swinging Sixties' were about to change Britain, the new engine was ready. As with all Rolls-Royce products, continuous improvements and changes were made, almost on a chassis-by-chassis basis. The new V8 engine weighed thirty pounds less than the old six-cylinder in-line engine and power was up to at least 200bhp and the swept volume was some 27.5% greater. All this

meant vastly improved acceleration in any range accompanied by no worse fuel consumption figures.

The only other significantly noticeable changes to the car were to the ventilation system that now sported face-level vents at the ends of the screen rail, atop the instrument facia. The Company considered these changes worthy of a new appellation. The V8 powered car became the Silver Cloud II.

SILVER CLOUD III – REDESIGNED BODYWORK:
For the 1963 model year, a totally re-styled front end showed a twin headlamp system, with the sidelights and indicator flashers mounted on the leading edges of the wings. Perhaps this was a gentle lead-in to the 1965 launched Silver Shadow, for which both items were carried over. The Silver Cloud III bonnet dropped gently towards a shortened radiator grille, which allowed slightly better forward vision for the driver. Under this new bonnet was the same V8 engine, but now enhanced to give a 15% increase in power. The drum brakes, perhaps the best in the world, were the last of their type to be fitted to a super-luxury car. The soon-to-be-announced Silver Shadow would at last feature disc brakes all around.

A change in seat design, obvious by the use of individual front seat cushions, allowed a gain in usable cabin space as they contained less padding, at no diminution in comfort. An increase in power steering assistance was coupled to a smaller steering wheel with a thinner rim.

BESPOKE COACHBUILDING:
The minority of chassis that were fitted with coachbuilt bodywork naturally included all the engineering changes from which the standard steel bodied cars benefited. Although there were no Rolls-Royce Continental cars in the mechanical sense, there were some Continental-style bodies fitted, some of which are now amongst the most valuable Silver Clouds. »

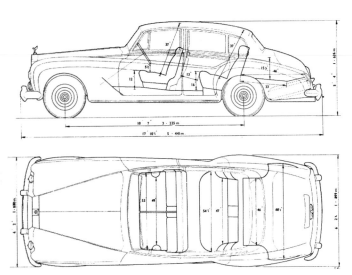

Top to bottom: Silver Cloud III shows its dual headlights, wing mounted indicator and side-lights, neat bumpers and lower bonnet line to the reduced-height radiator grille; Silver Cloud III dimensions - the tapering bonnet line compared with the Series I and II cars is easily seen

James Young made a four-door saloon version, design SCT 100, that is arguably more balanced and attractive than the standard steel body, and H J Mulliner adapted the standard body to form a two-door drophead coupé which looks particularly elegant.

SILVER CLOUD – STILL BRINGING A SMILE:
The Silver Cloud is a large car but they are a joy to drive. The six-cylinder engine was the last derivative of its type and as such had benefited from years of development, a fact which shows in its creamy smoothness and quietness. The V8 engine had some initial troubles, all of which have long since been sorted out. The sheer brilliance of this engine's post-war design can be best illustrated by the fact that Crewe-built cars today are still using the unit, albeit much refined in terms of hugely increased power output and vastly reduced pollution, all accompanied by a very high percentage reduction in fuel consumption.

All three models of the Silver Cloud and Bentley S series are more than capable of cruising at legal limits and keeping up with the cut and thrust of modern traffic. One small criticism is that, compared with the earlier Silver Dawn, a Silver Cloud is not as easy to steer precisely. Constant input at the wheel is needed to keep as close to the road's edge when passing in narrow lanes, and trying to hit the apex of a corner when motoring-on is more serendipity than skill. That having been said, the whole experience of driving a Silver Cloud is vested with the best of Rolls-Royce features, not least being the precision of all controls (steering excepted). Couple this with the complete absence of feeling the need to compete with other traffic, and a Silver Cloud journey is relaxing and smile-inducing. Comparisons are drawn with the latest products of lesser manufacturers but one has to remind oneself that these cars are at least forty five years old and derived from a design dating back sixty years. ▣

SILVER CLOUD

H J MULLINER DESIGN 7413

by Davide Bassoli

Above: Silver Cloud I (LSWA104) painted a lighter colour, parked in London in February 1970

After WWII, Rolls-Royce produced complete standard bodies on their chassis. However, coachbuilding companies could still provide bespoke bodywork for customers who preferred exclusivity. This is the story of a one-off drop head coupé body that was fitted to a 1955 Silver Cloud chassis.

BESPOKE COACHBUILDING: The success of the Silver Cloud and S Type standard steel saloon designed by John P Blatchley reduced the general request for special hand-crafted bodies. But for customers who still preferred individuality and exclusivity, the most important British coachbuilders could still offer a range of models, hand-built in small batches.

Of course, it was even rarer for customers to pay for one-off body designs due to the considerable costs involved in the design and manufacture. An American, Blevins Davis, was one of those wealthy "lucky few" who could afford to indulge in commissioning a one-off body. He ordered a Silver Cloud chassis with the intention of fitting a special coachbuilt drop head coupé body. Chassis LSWA104 was delivered at the end of 1955 to H J Mulliner whom Mr Davis had commissioned to tailor the bodywork.

OWNER SPECIFICATIONS: The American customer, who had residences both in London and the United States, ordered the chassis with left hand steering, having the intention to ship the car one day to his home in Missouri. »

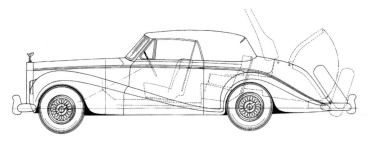

ROLLS-ROYCE SILVER CLOUD DROP-HEAD COUPÉ

MULLINER & CO. LTD.,
CHISWICK, LONDON W.4.

DRG. No. **7413**

Left to right: Exposed spare wheel on Silver Cloud I (LSWA104); H J Mulliner Drawing Number 7413 for Silver Cloud (LSWA104); Silver Cloud I (LSWA104) with P100 headlamps and Diana Ross

Mr Davis had definite ideas as to how he wanted his car to look, from the distinctive front to the swept tail with exposed spare wheel.

Another special feature requested for this car was a disappearing hood under a "U-shaped" cover, behind the rear seats. It is important to underline how this feature, common today for all the modern drophead coupés, was highly innovative in 1955.

H J MULLINER'S DESIGN:
The H J Mulliner Drawing Office produced drawing number 7413 which included all of Mr Davis' special requests. The shape was inspired by early post-war designs for drophead coupés, with front and rear wings still prominent. To replace some of the space lost in the boot due to the need to house the disappearing hood, the spare wheel was moved outside onto the boot lid, pivoting rearward to allow its opening.

H J Mulliner's premises were very busy during this period due to their production of cars with their "standard" Design Numbers 7409 and 7410 for drophead coupés and Design Number 7400 for the 'Fastback' Bentley Continental chassis. As a result, the one-off body for Mr Davis' chassis took a long time to complete and he did not take delivery of the car until May 1958!

Unfortunately, the Club does not have any photographs of the car delivered when new, but a copy of Drawing Number 7413 is preserved at The Hunt House. The H J Mulliner body card shows the car was painted in Blue with all the wings Black and the upholstery Dark Blue (VM8090). The car was specially equipped with an altimeter on the dashboard and a single lamp on the front bumper.

HEADLAMP MODIFICATIONS:
It is unknown if the car ever went to the United States with Mr Davis, although it was fitted with a "GB"

> *LSWA104 is now in the tender care of
> a private collection in the United States*

plate on the back when new. In a lot of photographs recently discovered, some show LSWA104 parked in London. They are dated August 1966 and clearly show the modification of the car to twin headlamps, introduced in October 1962 for the Silver Cloud III.

In another photograph, taken in February 1970, LSWA104 still has the twin headlamps but has been repainted in a lighter colour, probably Grey or Sand. It is not known if the car at that time was still owned by Mr Davis. Two photographs of LSWA104 are shown on page 211 of *Rolls-Royce – The Classic Elegance* written by Lawrence Dalton.

This Silver Cloud reappeared years later in the United States, with the twin combination of paint colours of Sand and Maroon, and two P100 headlamps that replaced the previous modification. A poor quality undated photograph, taken in the United States, shows LSWA104 with this new configuration. It comes from the journalist Rob De La Rive's personal archive and on the back of it is written "Liz Taylor". Perhaps LSWA104 was once owned by the famous actress. The car also appeared in a more recent photograph with American singer Diana Ross.

After three different headlamp treatments, LSWA104 is now in the tender care of a private collection in the United States. In 2003 the car was displayed in the Peterson Museum Exhibition "Rolls-Royce: a Century of Elegance". ▣

A GREAT SHADOW TO EMERGE IN THE SIXTIES

A HISTORY OF THE ROLLS-ROYCE SILVER SHADOW 1965-1976

by Tony Flood

After the initial launch in 1965, the main production did not begin in earnest until 1966 and during that year two 2-door versions of the Silver Shadow and T Series were introduced

The 'Swinging Sixties' were half way through their decade when the Rolls-Royce Silver Shadow and its very important sister the Bentley T series motor cars were launched. Introduced in the autumn of 1965 and at the height of Beatlemania they were the result of several years of development. The Company decided to rid itself of what was seen as a rather stuffy image as all previous models certainly gave that air about them and were in the main intended for the owner to be seen in the car driven by a chauffeur.

A TOTALLY DIFFERENT DESIGN: The new Silver Shadow was a totally different beast to its previous relatives as it had been designed without a chassis, had independent suspension, a triple braking system, a hydraulic levelling system that operated on both the front and rear of the car and had two separate transmissions, one four speed for right hand drive cars (RHD) and a three speed for left hand drive cars (LHD). The four speed transmission was entirely manufactured within the Crewe factory and was a development of the previous type that had been fitted to the previous range of cars namely the Silver Cloud series, whereas the three speed type was entirely produced by General Motors (GM) in the USA. It is interesting to note that the company had seriously investigated using GM produced transmissions for Silver Cloud cars built purely for the USA market but refrained from installing it in either a Rolls-Royce or Bentley until the introduction of the Silver Shadow/T Series.

It is also interesting to note that in the first ones built, air conditioning was not a standard fitting but merely a customer request item, although the majority of customers did request it to be initially fitted. Also the now long forgotten dynamo was fitted to the early cars as the car battery did not have to contend with the number of ancillaries that were fitted as standard in later years. The price of the Silver Shadow at launch was £6,557 and the T series was £6,496.

SCEPTICISM AND LEGISLATION: Once launched, it was not universally "loved" by everybody since, as usual, the "prophets of doom" were vocal, feeling Rolls-Royce had totally lost its way and the Silver Shadow and Bentley T would never sell as it no longer "looked like a Rolls-Royce" and now just looked like any other car. How wrong they were! It must be pointed out that unlike any previous Rolls-Royce or post Silver Shadow models from Crewe none had to contend with so much forced legislation that had to be incorporated during its years in production. »

Left: Rolls-Royce Silver Shadow II
Above: Silver Shadow 2 door saloon by H J Mulliner Park Ward

> *At the time, the Rolls-Royce Silver Shadow LWB
> division car was only the second car in the entire world
> that had two independent air conditioning systems*

Most of this legislation came from the USA but other countries to a lesser degree also imposed their legal demands. Adapting the car to meet legislation is a time consuming and costly process but not an option if the Company desired to satisfy all markets and is a true testament to the people who designed, developed, built and in no small way serviced the car. A great deal of the legislation made the car much safer for the occupants. This of course does not mean the Silver Shadow and T Series were not safe cars, they were, but were safer cars for having the benefit of many of the enforced changes incorporated. In parallel with these many legislative driven features, many other changes took place over the years to update the vehicles for the benefit of the driver, and it is timely to look at the continuous change that took place over the years in both the legislative and other important modifications. It would be impractical to cover all changes but the significant legislative and visual changes that took place will now be discussed.

FULL PRODUCTION AND ROYAL PATRONAGE: After the initial launch in 1965, the main production did not begin in earnest until 1966 and during that year two 2-door versions of the Silver Shadow and T Series were introduced. These were the short lived 2-door saloon produced by coachbuilder James Young (only thirty five Silver Shadows and fifteen T Series were built) and the much more attractive 2-door saloon produced by the Rolls-Royce wholly owned coachbuilder H J Mulliner Park Ward (MPW). The following year, 1967, the 2-door convertible was added to the range and this body style would remain in production for twenty eight years although then known as Corniche. Also during 1967, ten long wheelbase (LWB) cars were built. The difference between these LWB cars and the standard Silver Shadow is that the body was lengthened by four inches (100mm) in the rear occupant area to give more leg room. One of these initial ten cars was ordered by HRH Princess Margaret.

SAFETY LEGISLATION COMPLIANCE: 1968 was the year that brought the first amount of tremendous change to the car in line with USA legislation. Exhaust emissions from the engine had

Above: Silver Shadow 2 door convertible by H J Mulliner Park Ward **Right:** Bentley T Series 2 door saloon by James Young

to be controlled in order to keep pollution levels in the USA (notably carbon monoxide emissions) to required limits set by each state in general and California in particular which resulted in the fact that the engine had to be greatly modified to enable it to satisfy these requirements. It must be pointed out at this stage that every year thereafter the exhaust and also fuel emission regulations were reviewed and tightened and the Company had to prove to the Federal authorities that Rolls-Royce could satisfy them before they would grant permission to continue selling the product in the USA each year. Cars destined for Canada were also built to the same specification.

In parallel with the introduction of emission modifications to the engine, the interior of the saloon had to be greatly redesigned to improve occupant safety. This meant that all interior areas of the car that could likely cause an unnecessary injury had to be filled with a certain type of foam that, in an impact situation, would absorb a great deal of energy resulting in less chance of serious injury for the occupants. Also, the steering column was redesigned to collapse under collision conditions similarly reducing the risk of injury. The main non-legislative changes to the car in this year were that air conditioning and the three speed transmission became standard fitments. Very close on the heels of the USA legislation for emission controls, the Japanese authorities introduced similar controls but made them slightly more rigorous and had to be met in order to sell Rolls-Royce and Bentley cars in Japan - not a great market at the time for volume sales but one the company did not intend to lose.

TWO INDEPENDENT AIR CONDITIONING SYSTEMS:

Leaving legislative changes to one side for the moment, we can now look at what happened the following year, namely 1969. Firstly, following the initial ten LWB Silver Shadows which had been built in 1967, this model was formally launched in 1969, initially for the USA market and later introduced for all countries. »

It was made available with or without a centre division and in the majority of cases had a small back window and Everflex (fabric) covering to the roof. Those built with a centre division enjoyed two independent air conditioning systems whereby the front and rear occupants could operate independently of each other which meant that in practice with the division in the "closed" position the rear occupants could have cool air in their compartment while the driver could have warmer air or not require the system operating at all. At the time, the Rolls-Royce Silver Shadow LWB division car was only the second car in the entire world that had two independent air conditioning systems, the first being the Rolls-Royce Phantom VI, so it was in good company. The division car also had two separate radios so that the driver could listen to one programme and the passengers another without a conflict of interest, assuming the division was in the closed position. The price at launch for the Silver Shadow without a centre division was £9,950 and for those with a centre division the price was £10,603.

IN-CAR ENTERTAINMENT AND THE FIRST 'FLEET':

A controversial engineering decision was taken during 1969 which was the deletion of the hydraulic front levelling system, not unanimously supported in the Company boardroom. A great deal of resistance to this change came from the then engineering director John Hollings. However, he was overruled and it was deleted owing to the fact that its benefit was very limited and it was extremely expensive to manufacture. On the lighter side, towards the end of the year, the Silver Shadow was equipped with in-car entertainment of the stereo variety and electrical door locking, items that all modern day very basic cars have fitted as standard.

1970 was the year whereby the famous V8 engine capacity was increased from 6230cc to 6750cc and items such as cruise control were introduced, initially as a customer option, but it was soon to become a standard item. It is worth noting at this stage that during this year the first 'fleet' of cars were built. Eight were delivered to the famous Peninsula Hotel in Hong Kong for use as transport for guests to and from the airport. These cars featured in the 1974 James Bond film "The Man with the Golden Gun".

BANKRUPTCY OF ROLLS-ROYCE LTD:

1971 was a year never to be forgotten since, no sooner had it begun, the entire future of not only the Silver Shadow was at stake but that of the entire Rolls-Royce Motor Car Division. On 4 February 1971, Rolls-Royce Ltd was declared bankrupt owing to the escalating costs in the Aero Engine Division of producing the RB 211 engine destined to power the Lockheed TriStar airbus. The result was the car business was split off and in 1973 floated as an independent company. It is ironic that, following this debacle, demand for the Silver Shadow was stronger than ever and that was very important as legislation from thence onwards became even more stringent.

INTRODUCTION OF COMPLIANT SUSPENSION:

The following year (1972), after criticism from owners that the car ride was uncomfortable, a revised front suspension was introduced known as 'compliant' which had mountings with rubber inserted within the construction that attached the body to the sub-frame replacing the previous steel wire variety. This revised installation not only compensated for up and down movement of the suspension but also in the forward and rearward modes. In line with change, the front brake discs were modified with ventilation features to enhance cooling. This year saw the reinstatement of the reversing lights back into the light clusters on both rear wings from its former place on the boot lid that had been a feature from the early 1970s. »

> *The new Silver Shadow was a totally different beast to its previous relatives*

Owing to the unfortunate rise of terrorism in the world, particularly following the ill fated Munich Olympic Games, the Company was asked by the Government to build several cars for use by our Foreign Offices in such far flung places as Rio de Janeiro, Buenos Aires, Tokyo, New Delhi and several others including most European capitals. The cars had built-in protection in the doors, thicker glass to windscreen and door windows and improved security door locking and an onboard siren. A small number of private customers also had these features fitted to their cars, particularly if they were being exported to parts of the world that could be unstable!

SAFETY ENHANCEMENTS AND CATALYTIC EXHAUST SYSTEMS:

Significant changes took place the following year whereby the outward appearance changed for two markets in particular. Firstly, cars destined for Sweden from mid-1973 had to be equipped with a headlamp wash/wipe facility, the only country in the world at the time to make this mandatory, and for cars destined for the USA totally new energy absorbing front and rear bumpers were fitted. These bumpers had to withstand a 5mph frontal and a 2½mph rear impact without damaging the body or breaking the car lights. The body had to be greatly strengthened to ensure these loads could be absorbed and owing to this fact the front lower body vents had to be deleted and the body fixing slots eliminated. From mid-1973, following the introduction of energy absorbing bumpers, no further Bentley T Series cars were offered for sale in the USA owing to the fact that very few were previously sold in that market and to ensure the Bentley T complied with the Federal legislation concerning energy absorbing bumpers at the time would not have been cost effective.

The body changed again the next year when the front wheel arches were produced considerably larger to compensate for suspension and wheelbase revisions. During 1974, electronic ignition distributors were installed onto the engine and thereby consigned the old-fashioned contact breaker type to history. The much heralded but sadly short lived quadraphonic in-car sound system was introduced during the year's latter months, replacing the stereo sound system. Unfortunately, with the soon-to-be-available cassettes which many owners preferred, the quadraphonic system was soon deleted.

Above: Silver Shadow Standard Saloon

66

1975 was the year when the term "catalyst" became part of the factory vocabulary since all cars destined for the USA and Canada needed to be equipped with this unit

1975 was the year when the term "catalyst" became part of the factory vocabulary since all cars destined for the USA and Canada needed to be equipped with this unit now forming an important part of the exhaust system in order to reduce exhaust emissions. During this year, a major revision to the car's braking system took place whereby the former triple system was replaced by a dual system which dispensed with the master cylinder from the brake actuation box assembly.

A REMARKABLE SALES LANDMARK: We now come to the final year of Silver Shadow and T Series production, namely 1976. Other than the USA market, the vehicles destined for other parts of the world did not change significantly to be worthy of discussion. However, major revisions had to take place to the car body for the USA and Canada destined cars. This was on account of legislation that dictated that no fuel must leak from the car in the event of a "roll over" and at the same time the fuel tank must not rupture following a rear end impact. The outcome was that the entire luggage area of the car had to be redesigned to allow a totally new fuel tank to be installed behind the rear seat and, in conjunction with this, the fuel filler was now positioned in the rear body pillar adjacent to the rear door frame. Non-USA destined cars retained the fuel tanks in the boot floor. In this final year, a truly remarkable sales landmark was achieved since for the first time in Rolls-Royce history over 1,000 cars were sold to the USA. In fact the final total for the year was 1,200 cars sold to the USA and the number for the year worldwide was 3,261. This year witnessed a significant split between cars destined for the state of California and the remaining forty nine states in so much that a revised engine was installed with extra emission ancillaries for California only. During this year a second fleet of eight Silver Shadows were delivered to the Peninsula Hotel in Hong Kong.

THE END OF PRODUCTION: The final cars were completed in November of that year with the selling price of £19,662 for the standard saloon (Bentley selling prices were identical to those of the Silver Shadow since 1972) and £22,979 for the long wheelbase saloon without a division and £24,327 for those with a division. By this time its successor the Silver Shadow II and Bentley T2 were in full production and would prove to be equally successful replacements for the next three years until 1980 when the Silver Spirit, Silver Spur and Bentley Mulsanne took to the road. ▣

30 YEARS OLD

by Ian Rimmer

The SZ series of models, introduced in 1980, consisted initially of the Silver Spirit, Silver Spur and Bentley Mulsanne. Several derivative models followed. There can be no doubt that the SZ series of cars hold a very significant position in the evolution of the two marques, Rolls-Royce and Bentley.

GENESIS OF THE SZ MODELS:

The Rolls-Royce Silver Shadow and derivatives, known within the Company as 'SY', were replaced in 1980 after fifteen years of successful production. The initial replacements, under code 'SZ', were named Silver Spirit, Silver Spur and Bentley Mulsanne. However, work had started some ten years earlier on producing this next series of models. Initially, a restyled version of the Silver Shadow was considered but this gave way to more technical refinement in the form of the Silver Shadow II in 1977.

Five quarter-scale SZ models were progressively produced by Fritz Feller's styling department and differed mainly in the treatment of the exterior lamps, more especially the headlamps. The final style was a full-size model and carried large rectangular moulded headlamp units in contrast to the twin round lamps of the previous models. The overall shape of the body was much more angular and the area of glazing considerably increased.

The first two prototype cars were built to an intermediate style with four round headlamps but by the time they were built in 1975 they were considered obsolete and were relegated to testing systems rather than the whole car. The original concept was to use Dunlop Denovo run-flat tyres, eliminating the need for a spare wheel but this idea proved unsuccessful and so cars reverted to conventional wheels and tyres. »

Left to right: Silver Spirit Standard Saloon; First SZ quarter-scale model; Second SZ quarter-scale model

SIGNIFICANT NEW FEATURES: The most significant mechanical features of SZ were the rear suspension and hydraulic system. On Silver Shadow cars, under severe cornering, the rear suspension allowed the rear wheels to deflect out of line. To overcome this on SZ, a space frame joining the suspension and transmission crossmembers was adopted which ensured the rear wheels always ran true to the direction of travel. The rear suspension springs of the previous model were reduced in size but augmented by hydraulic struts. These struts had triple functions: as dampers; height control rams; and, as part of gas springs. Since improved lubricity was required the hydraulic fluid was changed to a mineral oil. This in turn allowed proprietary spheres to be used and these were obtained from Citroen.

The change of model required significant changes to the factory, especially the build and test departments. In preparation for the introduction of SZ one car was used for training, being built, stripped and rebuilt several times with different teams of workers. Eventually a new-model centre was set up to prepare the first batches of cars for sale and to learn of any repetitive faults.

Initially, there were just three models under the SZ banner – the Silver Spirit replacing the Silver Shadow II, the Bentley Mulsanne replacing the Bentley T2 and the long wheelbase Silver Spur replacing the Silver Wraith II. Interestingly, the name Silver Spur was a late change for what was originally planned as the Silver Wraith III. The long-wheelbase version of the Mulsanne was made available shortly afterwards. The three existing two-door models, the Corniche saloon, Corniche convertible and Camargue, retained their designations but all incorporated the new rear suspension and hydraulic systems which were actually fitted during 1979 to gain experience on limited volumes prior to the total switchover onto the four-door models. The new models were launched in the UK during late 1980 but were deferred until 1981 in North America. As an economy, due to low volumes during the late 1970s, Bentley T2 cars were fitted with Rolls-Royce logos on the rocker covers, instruments and pedal rubbers but with the introduction of the Mulsanne the correct Bentley logos were reinstated. On cars for the North American market the single large headlamp units were replaced by smaller twin rectangular lamps to comply with legislation. The engine and transmission were largely 'carry-overs' from the previous models.

Launch prices for the new cars displayed significant increases over their predecessors. The Silver Spirit and Mulsanne, at £49,629.02 in the UK market replaced the last Silver Shadow II and Bentley T2 priced at £41,959.67. The Silver Spur at £56,407.59 replaced the Silver Wraith II at £49,447.13. However, these prices rose steadily over the following years. Similar percentage price increases were applied to the two-door cars.

SUCCESS OF THE TURBOCHARGED ENGINE:
Initially, sales of the new cars were good, which is to be expected of any new models, but this soon started to shield the effects of a world recession and within a couple of years sales had fallen dramatically, leading to a downsizing of the Crewe workforce. There was, however, some respite on the horizon. The Company had been developing a turbocharged version of the current V8 engine, with plans to offer it in a Bentley version of the Camargue, but the low volumes of such a model would not recoup the large development costs so it was decided to offer it as an option in the Mulsanne and was introduced during 1982 as the Bentley Mulsanne Turbo. With a fifty percent increase in power a new level of performance was achieved and this started to be targeted at the younger clientele who were normally purchasing high performance sporting cars. With its matching performance and its enhanced comfort and refinement the Mulsanne Turbo rapidly gained a new customer base and was soon outselling the basic Mulsanne by a large margin. »

> The most significant mechanical features of SZ were the rear suspension and hydraulic system

For many years, sales of Bentleys had been very low; frequently less than five percent of total car output, but the Mulsanne Turbo triggered a revival in interest in the marque. In 1984 the Bentley Eight was introduced and was targeted as an entry model, based on the Mulsanne but with some cost saving features to create an affordable price level with a saving of more than £5,000. However, the most significant boost to the Bentley marque was in 1985 when the Mulsanne Turbo was replaced by the improved Turbo R. To the same exhilarating performance was added improved brakes and handling which enabled the true performance capabilities to be exploited. As an identifying feature the radiator shell was now painted in car colour as standard. A demonstration of the car's superb performance was seen when an example broke the one-hour endurance record covering 141 miles on a test track.

THE ONE HUNDRED THOUSAND ROLLS-ROYCE MILESTONE: A major milestone in the Company history was reached during 1985 when the 100,000th Rolls-Royce was produced. This was a Silver Spur and was given the title Centenary Spur. Twenty-five replicas were sold and a major celebration was held at the Crewe factory.

Demand for the Bentley Corniche during this period was still very small but in 1986 this picked up considerably following a change of name to Bentley Continental, reflecting the growing interest in the Bentley marque seen in the four-door range. The Rolls-Royce Corniche also enjoyed a boost in 1986 and was renamed Corniche II for the North American market and in 1988 for the rest of the world. Also in 1988 the Mulsanne was renamed the Mulsanne S. 1987 saw the end of the Rolls-Royce Camargue.

The revival of the Bentley marque during the 1980s continued and by the end of the decade sales of Bentleys were equal to the numbers of Rolls-Royce sales, something that had not been seen since the 1950s. While the Bentleys were enjoying most of the attention, the Rolls-Royce models were upgraded to the Silver Spirit II, Silver Spur II and Corniche III in 1990. Sales of all models reached their peak around this time but another World recession was about to happen. Within two years sales of cars had dropped to below half of the previous levels and the Company was now experiencing severe financial losses. The result of this was a large downsizing of the

Left to right: Extended Silver Spur by Jankel; Centenary Silver Spurs. **Previous page (top to bottom):** Silver Spur touring limousine; First representative SZ prototype car

workforce and the outsourcing of many components that had previously been made in-house. The machine shop was closed down. In spite of this setback the Company was able to launch an exciting new model, the Bentley Continental R, at the 1992 Geneva Motor Show. Now, Turbo R performance was available in a stylish fixed-head coupé and sales grew rapidly. Also in 1992 the Corniche III was upgraded to the Corniche IV.

A number of significant modifications were introduced during the life of SZ. Fuel injection and electronic engine management improved fuel consumption and increased power. Active suspension and ABS improved ride, handling and safety. Alterations to the air conditioning enhanced personal comfort. The three-speed gearbox was replaced by the new four-speed unit.

NEW MODEL NAMES AND THEIR DERIVATIVES:

By now the Company had realised that increased sales were generated not only by enhanced specifications but also by revised or new model names. This theme continued throughout the remaining life of the SZ range of cars. For 1993 the Bentley Mulsanne and Eight were discontinued but replaced by the new Bentley Brooklands which, like the Turbo R, also featured the painted radiator shell. 1994 saw the Silver Spirit II and Silver Spur II upgraded to series III designations. Further changes were made in 1996 but instead of the series IV suffix, the basic Silver Spirit and Silver Spur names were reused. Shortly afterwards the decision was taken to standardise on the long wheelbase body so Silver Spirit production came to an end. The replacement using the long wheelbase body was given the name Silver Dawn, a name last used in the 1950s. The final series of Silver Spurs were fitted with a low-pressure version of the turbo engine. Production of the Silver Dawn finally finished in 1998, to be replaced by the all-new Silver Seraph. »

However, the Silver Spur continued to the end of the decade, for the American market, since there was no long wheelbase successor and the Silver Seraph was introduced in North America later than elsewhere. The final series of the Brooklands was renamed Brooklands R and the Turbo R became Turbo RT.

Following the huge success of the Continental R, a convertible version was created by PininFarina and became known as the Bentley Azure. Two further adaptations followed – the muscular Continental T, shortened by four inches and with increased power output, and the Continental SC that featured the sedanca coupé style of coachwork with a removable hard top over the front seats. These two-door models continued beyond the end of the SZ four-door production run.

In addition to the various models mentioned above, there were other derivatives, based on these basic models, including limousines, special editions and Mulliner versions. With the proliferation of additional models during the 1990s, the number of distinct designations within the SZ banner totalled sixty one. The total number of cars built of the SZ family was over 38,000, of which 40% were Bentleys. However, the percentage of Bentleys had changed during the life of SZ from 5% at the start to 70% at the end.

COMPARISON OF THE SY AND SZ MODELS: So how did the SZ cars compare with those that went before and those that followed? The change from SY to SZ saw an improvement in handling, a much brighter feel internally with more space due to the curved door glasses. There was a slightly smaller boot space due to the fuel tank being relocated to behind the rear seat although there was a small storage well below the boot floor. The fuel filler was relocated from the right hand side to a higher position on the left. Internally, there were changes to the style of upholstery and woodwork but the unmistakable feeling of being in a Rolls-Royce or Bentley was retained and this was augmented by the retention of a number of those traditional detail items. Perhaps a more controversial comparison related to the exterior styling. SZ clearly displayed a more modern look, with its sharp edges and flatter topped

And me for thee he chose?

=

A little dust, some vapour green

In space lay hid somewh...

From them the Lord made flesh

And a human soul for...

=

Born wide apart, we knew

Had ever framed her f...

front end, compared with the more curvaceous look of SY cars. However, as is often quoted 'beauty is in the eye of the beholder' and this remains one of personal preference although there was some criticism of the shape at the time of launch. As time has progressed the shape has become more universally accepted, perhaps more so with the Bentley which has evolved during the life of the series to portray its sporty heritage.

The transition from the SZ cars to the new Silver Seraph and Bentley Arnage, known internally as 'P600', was much more radical with very little read-across. First impressions are that the new cars are much more compact and this is borne out when comparing dimensions. Interior space is notably smaller, especially in the rear compartment and, with a long wheelbase version not being immediately available, this was more pronounced. The exterior styling perhaps enjoyed more favour. Its more curvy shape took certain styling cues from the 1950s Silver Cloud. Again, like both SY and SZ, both Rolls-Royce and Bentley body shells were similar but with add-on features to distinguish the two apart. The most significant changes on 'P600' were the engines. The Silver Seraph utilised the 5.4 litre V12 BMW engine while the Arnage had the 4.4 litre V8 BMW, fitted with turbochargers by associate company Cosworth. Whilst these engines could match the power of the V8 in the SZ cars their low speed torque was noticeably less, resulting in a different driving experience. Although a long wheelbase version of Arnage became available later to combat criticism of reduced rear seating space, the Silver Seraph did not enjoy that benefit. The biggest boost to the Arnage came at the turn of the century when the Turbo R's 6750cc engine was adapted to fit in the Arnage.

Looking back over thirty years since the Silver Spirit, Silver Spur and Bentley Mulsanne emerged, there must be no doubt that these cars hold a very significant position in the evolution of the two marques, Rolls-Royce and Bentley. ▣

Clockwise from bottom left: Silver Spirit and Bentley Mulsanne facia; Silver Spirit and Bentley Mulsanne rear interior; Rolls-Royce Flying Spur

ROLLS-ROYCE AND BENTLEY
MOTOR CARS OF THE

MAHARAJAS

OF BARODA, INDIA

by John Fasal

The rulers of the State of Baroda, India were early pioneer motorists and in the early 20th Century took an increasing interest in the motor car products of Rolls-Royce. The Maharajas amassed a stunning collection of over thirty bespoke Rolls-Royce and Bentley cars befitting their great wealth and taste. This article describes the evolution of the Baroda dynasty and the Rolls-Royce motor cars enjoyed by H.H. The Maharaja Sir Sayajirao III of Baroda and his son and heir, Major General H.H. The Maharaja Sir Pratapsinhrao Gaekwar of Baroda.

Left to right: H.H. The Maharaja Sayajirao III aged 18 at the time of his investiture with full ruling powers in 1881. Seen wearing the 'Star of the South' diamond of 128 carats; 1914 40/50 hp 'Silver Ghost' (1AB) Hooper open-drive landaulette

THE ORIGINS OF THE RULERS OF THE STATE OF BARODA:

The origins of the Rulers of the great State of Baroda date from the 18th Century decline of the Mogul Empire and the rise of the British East India Company. With the military prowess of fellow adventurers like the Holkars of Indore and the Scindias of Gwalior, Damaji Gaekwad of Baroda rose to Deputy Commander in the ranks of the army of the Maratha Peshwa. It was his successor who drove out the Moghul forces from Gujarat and captured the town of Baroda in 1734 where the family finally established its capital in 1766.

The vicissitudes of their large domain, one of the most fertile agricultural regions in the country, continued with power struggles amongst the extended Gaekwad family amid much intrigue and maladministration. Sayajirao II died in 1847, to be succeeded by his eldest son Ganpatrao, who ruled until 1856; but as all of his three sons died before him, he was succeeded by his next surviving brother, Khanderao, who ruled for the next fourteen years. He was the epitomy of what a 19th Century Maharaja might conjure up in the imagination – a magnificent all-round sportsman, blessed with good looks, strength and courage, a generous host and lavish spender, a connoisseur of precious stones and, importantly, popular with his own people and the British. It was he who in 1867 purchased 'the Star of the South' a massive diamond of 128 carats that once formed part of the crown jewels of France and was larger than the Kohinoor diamond that found its way into the British Crown jewels. To his staggering jewel collection he added a necklace made up of 288 graduated pearls interspersed with 168 diamonds. »

The origins of the Rulers of the great State of Baroda date from the 18th Century decline of the Mogul Empire and the rise of the British East India Company

Left to right: The impressive façade of the Laxmi Vilas Palace built between 1878-1890 (Photo courtesy of Antonio Martinelli, Feb. 1991); H.H. The Maharaja of Baroda on the throne in the Durbar Hall of the Laxmi Vilas Palace, February 1939

Another commission was the making of the famous Pearl carpet of Baroda composed entirely of inwrought pearls, rubies, emeralds and diamonds sewed on deerskin and silk and said to have cost a crore (ten millions) of rupees.

OVERWHELMING HOSPITALITY: The French traveller and author Louis Rousselet describes his stay with the Maharaja Khanderao from the 11 June 1865 and the overwhelming hospitality of His Highness who would not let him leave until 2 December of that year. Witnessing a procession he writes ". . . . The nobles of the realm, the ministers, the governors of provinces, all mounted on twenty four elephants, whose immense coverings of gold-fringed velvet hung down to the ground." Finally he sees the Maharaja's elephant ". . . That on which the King sits is a gigantic animal. The howdah, of massive gold – a present from the Queen of England – sparkles with jewels. The Gaekwad is seated in it on embroidered cushions. He wears a red velvet tunic, over which is a profusion of magnificent jewels; his turban is adorned with an aigrette of diamonds, amongst which blazes the "Star of the South". On the footboards, on each side of the elephant, stand four men, clad in elegant attire. One of them carries the hookah presented to His Majesty by the Viceroy of India; the others wave fans composed of peacocks' feathers. Amongst them is the King's herald. The King's elephant is completely hidden under his ornaments, resembling a mountain of gold sparkling with diamonds." Khanderao died in November 1870 at the age of forty-two. His younger brother Malharrao acted as Regent of Baroda but his misrule came to the attention of the Viceroy. When Malharrao attempted to end the days of the British Resident, Colonel Robert Phayre, by spicing his regular glass of sherbet with a cocktail of arsenic and diamond dust, the Viceroy, through Sir Lewis Pelly, had Malharrao deposed in 1874 and exiled to Madras. His heirs were debarred from further succession. His elder brother Khanderao, who had shown great loyalty to the British Government during the 1857 Sepoy Mutiny in Lucknow, acceded to the request of his widow Maharani Jamnabai to select and adopt a member of the Gaekwad as future ruler. She wanted a young boy untarnished by the corrupt courtiers of recent times and a heart and mind that could be moulded to meet the exalted position that lay ahead.

FROM FARMER TO MAHARAJA!:
In the early part of 1875 Her Highness summoned three boys from the Kavlana Gaekwads, descendants from Prataprao, one of the brothers who separated after the Battle of Panipat in 1732 and settled in Kavlana to take up farming. Palace officials plucked the boys from relative obscurity to accompany them with a police escort and a senior British officer, the three hundred miles to the City of Baroda for the daunting interview. Questioned by the Maharani as to why they had been brought to the palace, the younger two gave unsatisfactory replies but the 12-year old Gopalrao confidently responded "to be Maharaja!" It is said that he also impressed the Maharani by emulating her table manners. Her choice was endorsed by Sir Richard Meade, the Agent to the Governor-General.

On the morning of 27 May 1875, with the appropriate Hindu ritual, the boy was handed over by his father and adopted by the Maharani Jamnabai as her son. After being placed on the gadi (throne) traditionally in the shape of a large brocade covered cushion, the installation ceremony took place in the Durbar Hall (hall of public audience) investing him as Maharaja with his new name Sayajirao III. A salute of one hundred and twenty two guns was fired by the Baroda artillery and a further twenty one guns by the British artillery. Like a fairy-tale the peasant boy was transformed into a Prince with unimaginable wealth and privilege. In 1875 the palace jewels were estimated to be worth £4,000,000. He was destined to rule the leading Hindu State of 8,164 sq. miles with an hereditary 21-gun salute, an honour accorded to only five major Princely States.

VISIT BY KING EDWARD VII:
Some able men were appointed by the Government to run the State such as Sir Tanjore Madhav Rao as the Dewan (Prime Minister) and F A H Elliot as tutor to the young Prince. His early studies were interrupted with the visit to India of the Prince of Wales, the future King Edward VII in November 1875. About forty Indian Princes and chiefs gathered in Bombay to greet their future King-Emperor and Baroda put on an impressive display sending down 1500 of his State troops together with ceremonial gold and silver cannons. »

His studies were broken again at the end of 1876 when he made his first Indian tour of nearly 3,500 miles, during which he attended the Delhi Durbar at which the Viceroy Lord Lytton informed him that Queen Victoria bestowed upon him the title 'Farzand-i-Khas-i-Daulatp-i-Inglishia' (Favoured son of the British Empire) and received the gold 'Empress of India' medal of 1877 and other gifts. On his return to Baroda he had begun his career as a traveller which was later to bring him criticism from the Government for spending too much time away from his State.

A VAST NEW PALACE: Not content with the old City Palace, the Moti Bagh Palace, the Nazar Bagh Palace, the Makarpura Palace and the Pratap Vilas Palace, the foundation stone of the vast Laxmi Vilas Palace was laid on 12 January 1880. This monumental residence designed in the Indo-Saracenic style by Major Charles Mant, an officer of the Royal Engineers, was set in 720 acres of parkland which contained several of the earlier summer palaces and ten miles of footpaths. The western façade stretched some 525 feet in length and the Durbar Hall was designed to accommodate a thousand courtiers. Major Mant died, aged forty, before the building was completed in 1890.

Sayajirao III was invested with full ruling powers in December 1881, a year after his marriage to Princess Laxmibai who took the name Chimnabai and bore him a daughter and a son Fatesinghrao. This Maharani died in May 1884. Within a year he married a Princess from Dewas State who took the name Chimnabai in remembrance of his first Maharani. She was a formidable character who encouraged the abolition of the purdah system.

AN AUDIENCE WITH QUEEN VICTORIA: His Highness was not enjoying good health and his doctor ordered him to Europe, a momentous decision in the eyes of pious Hindus to cross 'the black water'. Accompanied by Maharani Chimnabai, his personal physician and a suite of over fifty people including two cooks and large stocks of their own food with two cows to provide fresh milk, they sailed from Bombay on 31 May 1887. The two cows had died before they reached Aden! During his successful trip to Europe he visited Queen Victoria at Windsor Castle on 2 December and was invested with the insignia of the G.C.S.I., finally returning to Baroda in February 1888. He became

Left to right: 1937 Phantom III (3-CP-112) Windovers saloon trimmed in leopard skin for Prince Pratapsinhrao Gaekwad of Baroda; Major General H.H. The Maharaja Sir Pratapsinhrao Gaekwad of Baroda, G.C.I.E., LL.D. in 1941, festooned in diamonds and pearls

> *The King's elephant is completely hidden under his ornaments, resembling a mountain of gold sparkling with diamonds*

a well-known figure in Britain and was amusingly depicted in the *Vanity Fair* cartoon of January 1901 as 'The Gaekwar' holding his cane and wearing the famous necklace of flat-cut diamonds. Only the British spelt the name as 'Gaekwar'.

AN EARLY PIONEER MOTORIST:
His Highness was one of the early pioneer motorists. In the records of Messrs. Turner, Hoare & Co., engineers of Bombay, they exhibited Renault and Peugeot cars at the 1903 Delhi Durbar (the occasion to celebrate the Coronation of King Edward VII). Many native princes purchased cars from them including H.H. The Gaekwar of Baroda. Montague Grahame-White recounts in *The Car* of 25 February 1903 ". . . One instance of the number of carriages arriving by train at Delhi Station, which will give the reader some idea of the magnitude of the traffic, when the Maharaja of Baroda brought with him 117 carriages and three times the number of horses, two huge elephant carts, a Lifu steam wagonette, and two small motor cars. By no means is this a solitary example of the conveyances brought by each maharaja attending the Durbar."

A GROWING INTEREST IN ROLLS-ROYCE:
When the Motor Union of Western India proposed to hold reliability trials in 1904, His Highness offered a handsome silver trophy known as 'The Gaekwar's Cup'. This prize was for the car which underook the trials with the least number of voluntary stops over a distance of 880 miles between Delhi and Bombay from 26 December 1904 to 2 January 1905. It is interesting to note that S F Edge sent out to India a 20 hp Napier that was driven in these trials by Basil Johnson, the brother of Claude Johnson, the latter to play a major role in the formative years of the Rolls-Royce Company. Records are scanty as to other makes acquired by the Baroda State Garages and sent to India or retained in Europe but they included at least two French De Dietrich cars and a 1910 45-50 hp Mercedes landaulette by Brainsby & Sons. Thenceforth came a growing interest in Rolls-Royce with:

1911 Silver Ghost (chassis 1721) Barker "Whitmore" landaulette in dark blue with cloth upholstery with ivory interior handles. This is most likely the car rebodied as a tourer by the French Motor Car Co. of Bombay in 1916 for Prince Dhairyashilrao.

1914 Silver Ghost (1AB) Hooper open-drive landaulette in dark blue with grey silk brocaded upholstery. Nickel fittings. Reg: R-1959. »

Top to bottom: 1946 Bentley Mk VI (B30AK) H J Mulliner saloon bearing the flag showing the sword surmounted by the crown, the crest of Baroda; 1934 Phantom II (104SK) Kellner enclosed-drive landaulette on the Kellner stand at the Paris Salon, 1934. Supplied to Her Highness The Maharani of Baroda; 1946 Bentley Mk VI (B-42-AK) H J Mulliner drop head coupé handed over to the chauffeur to H.H. The Maharaja of Baroda on 8 August 1947 **Right:** The Baroda Coat-of-Arms depicted on a car badge

1914 Silver Ghost (60LB) Colonial L to E, H J Mulliner open-drive landaulette in maroon with fawn cloth upholstery. Nickel fittings. Reg: R-2349 (Formerly owned and restored by the author, now surviving in America).

1919 Silver Ghost (36LW) Rothschild open-drive landaulette. Nickel fittings.

1920 Silver Ghost (55CW) Barker tourer finished in French grey with dark green lines with dark green leather. For Prince Jaisinhrao.

1921 Silver Ghost (109LG) Hooper side-light cabriolet in dark blue.

1924 Silver Ghost (106EM) Barker enclosed limousine in dark blue with dark green silk cloth upholstery for Prince Dhairyashilrao.

1925 Silver Ghost (30EU) Barker Pullman limousine fitted with Dunlop steel artillery wheels. Nickel fittings. For H.H. The Maharaja.

1927 Phantom I (71RF) A Mulliner enclosed-drive landaulette.

1928 Phantom I (75EH) A Mulliner landaulette de ville.

1929 Phantom II (70WJ) Barker tourer finished in ivory and blue with blue leather upholstery. India Trials Car. Reg: X-6551 sold to Prince Pratapsinhrao. Recess for revolver in off side front door. Nacrolaque instrument board. 2 Alvis nickel plated Lucas wing lamps.

1929 Phantom II (101WJ) Kellner cabriolet de ville for H.H. The Maharani.

1930 Phantom II (101GY) A Mulliner landaulette exhibited at the October 1930 Motor Show and sold to Prince Pratapsinhrao.

1933 20/25 (GTZ27) Thrupp & Maberly landaulette sold new to Mrs M Herbertson Dawson, Kent. Sold second-hand to Prince Pratapsinharao.

1934 Phantom II (30SK) Windovers drop head coupé for Prince Pratapsinhrao.

1934 Phantom II (104SK) Kellner enclosed-drive landaulette with white finish to the instruments with black figures. Exhaust cut-out fitted. Lalique mascot mounted on the scuttle. Exhibited on the Kellner stand at the Paris Salon and supplied to Her Highness The Maharani.

1934 20/25 (GAE3) Kellner enclosed-drive limousine exhibited on the Kellner stand at the Paris Salon for the Prince of Baroda.

1934 20/25 (GAE45) Hooper sports saloon for H.H. The Maharani.

1935 20/25 (GBJ71) Thrupp & Maberly landaulette finished in grey and black with West of England cloth interior for H.H. The Maharaja.

1936 Phantom III (3-AX-201) Hooper enclosed limousine with sun roof finished in blue and black with red line and blue brocade

upholstery. Front seat black leather. Gold plated fittings. Bracket for flagstaff at base of kneeling lady mascot. Heraldry: Crown and sword emblazoned on waist rail. CD plate at rear.

1937 Phantom III (3-BU-106) Kellner enclosed drive limousine fitted with Marchal headlamps, ivory white equipment including steering wheel, change gear and brake lever handles; white dials with black figures; 6 Ace wheel discs with chrome plate ribs. For H.H. The Maharani.

1937 Phantom III (3-CP-112) Windovers saloon finished in 'Wilcolac' emerald green throughout. Trimming: Leopard skin, supplied by client; carpets front and rear in leopard skin; ivory finish to facia board, steering wheel and control knobs. Note: Heater, Rolls-Royce mascot, spare wheel covers, sunshine roof – not required. To the order of Prince Pratapsinhrao Gaekwar.

1938 Phantom III (3-DL-96) Park Ward tourer originally supplied to the Yuvaraja Saheb Mahendra Sinhji of Morvi. Second owner: The Prince of Baroda.

1938 Wraith (WXA37) Park Ward saloon used as a trials car. Reg: EYX 362 and featured in *The Autocar* 22 September 1939. Sold in January 1940 to H.H. The Maharani.

1938 Wraith (WRB20) Binder saloon for Princess Poniatowska, Paris. Sold second hand to H.H. The Maharaja of Baroda, c/o The Dorchester Hotel, London, June 1945 – February 1946.

1946 Bentley Mk VI (B8AK) Vanden Plas saloon in silver and blue grey for H.H. The Maharaja. Shipped to Bombay per S.S. 'Nirvana' on 25 January 1947.

1946 Bentley Mk VI (B30AK) H J Mulliner saloon in two shades of blue and grey. Perspex panel and sliding roof in rear. For H.H. The Maharani.

1946 Bentley Mk VI (B42AK) H J Mulliner drop head coupé in 'Belco' grey. Car handed over to H.H.'s chauffeur on 8 August 1947 for H.H.The Maharaja.

1946 Bentley Mk VI (B194AK) Bentley Motors saloon in pearl grey and sold via Dadajee Dhackjee & Co., Bombay, for H.H. The Maharaja of Baroda.

1948 Bentley Mk VI (B273BG) H J Mulliner drop head coupé in red and black for H.H. The Maharani.

1951 Silver Wraith (ALW2) H J Mulliner limousine with beige tapestry upholstery and gold fittings for H.H. The Dowager Maharani Chimnabai.

1956 Silver Wraith (LELW97) H J Mulliner touring limousine for H.H. The Maharani Sita Devi of Baroda and used in France.

1963 Phantom V (5-LVA-69) James Young touring limousine for H.H. The Maharani Sita Devi of Baroda and used in France.

FROM FEUDAL PAST TO MODERN TIMES:

H.H. The Maharaja Sir Sayajirao III, G.C.S.I., G.C.I.E., LL.D. (1863-1939) had brought his State from the feudal past into modern times. His achievements and improvements within his kingdom were considerable. Increasing the State owned railways from 59 to 642 miles, building irrigation plants, hospitals and schools; he was the first Ruler in India to make primary education free and compulsory among his subjects. He made vast financial contributions for the Great War effort, becoming a much loved and respected Ruler. He was succeeded by his son, Major General H.H. The Maharaja Sir Pratapsinhrao Gaekwar of Baroda, G.C.I.E., LL.D. (1908-1968). He was to witness the last days of the British Raj and see his own State merge with Bombay in 1949. With his demise ended a colourful life in the fast lane, of fabulous wealth, beautiful women, race horses and magnificent cars. The end of an era indeed! ▣

(Material extracted from one of the 67 chapters of the eagerly awaited definitive two-volume work "ROLLS-ROYCE & BENTLEYS IN PRINCELY INDIA" by John M Fasal to be published by the author in 2011.) © John M Fasal.

CONTINENTAL SECTIONS

A ROUND UP OF SOME RECENT ACTIVITIES

by Julian Spencer

The Club's continental sections represent a large percentage of Club membership and contribute significantly to the Club's global footprint. These sections arrange many high profile events each year. This article describes a few of the Club's continental sections' activities and is reproduced in English, French, German and Italian to underline the true international nature of this Club.

GERMANY SECTION: The Germany Section participated in three traditional fairs for classic motorcars during 2009. The first one was the Bremen Classic Motor Show 5 - 7 February where the Section had a stand together with the ASC (Allgemeiner Schnauferl Club, a club for all classic cars but mainly pre-war). Club members Dr Egon Schäfer and Dr Axel Zogbaum organized the stand and displayed a 1962 Bentley S2 standard saloon, a 1932 Phantom II boat tail tourer and a 1935 Bentley 3½ litre open tourer by Vanden Plas.

From 13 to 15 March, the Section had a stand at the Retro Classics in Stuttgart. Four interesting cars were on display: GPG73, which now sports a new body built as an exact replica of Charles Rolls' Balloon Car; 86XJ, a Phantom II tourer built for the Maharajah of Rewa for the purpose of hunting game; 79JH, a Springfield Silver Ghost Pall Mall tourer which won the first prize in Stuttgart for being the most impressive open tourer exhibited; and, 59LC, a fully restored Phantom I tourer once built for Don Carlos de Salamanca with a one-off body by Manessius of Brussels. The Section's stand was framed by two Goodwood Phantoms (one saloon, one drophead) which belonged to Auto-König of Munich.

Finally, later in 2009, the Germany Section members were at the Techno Classica in Essen where they used a part of the stand which belonged to Steenbuck Automobiles. Space was not as plentiful as in Stuttgart, but it was big enough to show Rolf Kuhnke's fine Bentley 3½ litre (B118CR) Kellner drophead coupé. »

Left: French Section in the Place des Lices in St Tropez; La sezione francese in Place des Lices a St Tropez; Section France, sur la Place des Lices de Saint-Tropez; French Section auf dem Place des Lices in St.

Tropez **Above right:** Switzerland Section at the 2009 BCCM Concours d'Elegance; La sezione svizzera al 2009 BCCM Concours d'Elegance; Section Suisse au Concours d'Élégance 2009 BCCM; Switzerland Section auf dem BCCM Concours d'Elegance 2009

Before
w
The

A
Fr

ITALY SECTION: In April 2009, the Italy Section had its first rally in the Piacenza hills where they visited four marvellous castles. The meeting point was in Pianello, not far from the Rocca d'Olgisio Castle. Many cars attended the event including a 1930 Phantom II, Silver Clouds, a Bentley S1 Continental, Silver Shadows, Corniches, a Silver Seraph, a Continental S and a Flying Spur that travelled from Monaco. Also it is interesting to mention that one of the first Silver Clouds built (SWA130) and a 1984 Bentley Continental owned in the past by Sir Elton John participated in the rally. After lunch the Section went to visit the feudal Agazzano Castle, now completely restored, where they were treated to a piano recital by Francesco Ghignone. The accommodation and Gala Dinner were inside the Rivalta Castle. The Section members were shown around the castle by Count Orazio Landi Zanardi. HRH Princess Margaret stayed at the castle several times on her visits to Italy. The rally ended on the Sunday with a visit to San Pietro in Cerro Castle.

In late April 2009, Italy Section members attended the Concorso d'Eleganza Villa d'Este. It was the chance for them to see beautiful concours Rolls-Royces and Bentleys restored to the highest standards. Rolls-Royce Motor Cars were present with the prototype 200EX, now in production as the Ghost model. Parked nearside, was a rare Rolls-Royce Silver Cloud III drophead coupé by H J Mulliner and the Pininfarina Rolls-Royce Hyperion, the two-seat one-off car, based on the Phantom dhc. The concours included three Phantom Is (one coachbuilt by Brewster), a beautiful Bentley 4¼ litre Carlton cabriolet and one of the two built Bentley R Type Continental Park Ward fixed head coupés.

SWITZERLAND SECTION: The 16th British Classic Car Meeting (BCCM) took place during 10 -12 July 2009 in St Moritz. The event is not devoted to one make but a large proportion of the cars that take part are Rolls-Royce and Bentley. The Switzerland Section members were there in force. The field of competitors this year was led by fifty seven Rolls-Royce and thirty six Bentleys of all ages. In addition, there were twenty two Aston Martins, a Lagonda, four Daimlers, fifty six Jaguars, seventeen Austin Healeys, and several other makes represented by one or two models.

Right: Germany Section at the Retro Classics in Stuttgart; La sezione tedesca al Retro Classics di Stoccarda; Section Allemagne du salon Retro Classics de Stuttgart; Germany Section auf der Retro Classics in Stuttgart

❝

*One of the first Silver Clouds built (SWA130)
and a 1984 Bentley Continental owned in the
past by Sir Elton John participated in the rally*

There are two main aspects to the BCCM which keep it at the top of the list of classic car events in Europe. First, there is total dedication to exclusiveness – the admittance of a car doesn't depend on its age, but on its rareness, appearance and condition. The second aspect for success is that the rally route is altered every year, so that an experienced competitor faces a new challenge while a newcomer is not disadvantaged. This year the route was set eastwards towards Italy and partly to Austria, climbing and descending countless mountain passes.

The 'Run', which is held just within one day, is a challenge for every car, no matter how young. The oldest Rolls-Royce to take part was a 1928 Phantom I Speedster owned by Silvio Zanolari from Chur, followed by a 1930 Phantom II tourer which was driven from England to Switzerland and back again by Robert Watson with supporting family and friends from Rolvenden! The most impressive engine was that of the 1938 Phantom III Mulliner sedanca de ville of Antonio Pasquale from Morcote. The largest car bodies were the 1967 Phantom V of Norbert Seeger from Vaduz and the 1968 Phantom VI of Martin Lechner from St Moritz. A very special car of the modern range was the 1985 Camargue Boano convertible driven by the owner Adrian von Lerber from Bern.

Sunday was devoted to the Concours d'Elegance. Honours this year in the Rolls-Royce category went to: Antonio Pasquale from Morcote in Switzerland with his 1938 Phantom III Mulliner sedanca de ville in the pre-war category; Norbert Seeger from Vaduz won the post-war category with his 1967 Phantom V; and, Gerhard Trümmel from Dübendorf won the 'Youngtimer' category with his 1976 Corniche. In the Bentley category, Jörg E. Meyerhans from Weinfelden won the post-war category with his 1957 S1 Hooper and Walter Steinemann from Mörschwil won the 'Youngtimer' category with his 1996 Azure. »

before the dawn of the...
When the Morning Star arose,
the Lord gave thee my mate to be,
and me for thee he chose.

=

A little dust, some vapour grey,
In space lay hid somewhere,
From them the Lord made flesh and blood,
And a human soul put there.

=

The BCCM 'Run' and Concours d'Elegance is a wonderful opportunity to savour the atmosphere of St Moritz and beyond. The event offers a unique combination of sheer luxury and pure enjoyment of driving in spectacular countryside.

For several years the Switzerland Section has held an annual car appraisal day known as the 'Greasy Fingers' Day. It is an excellently well organised car inspection day and in 2009 it was held at the Ministry of Transport (MOT) testing station in Schafisheim. The instructors from the UK were Steve Lovatt, Eric Healey and William Pullar who joined the experienced team in Switzerland of Markus Schatzmann, Roger Bachman, Renato Naef, Dominik Luescher, Eligio Camina, Eduard Rungg. Close scrutinies of members' cars were made by the experts and the Section members received valuable knowledge on the use, care and preservation of their cars.

FRANCE SECTION: A major event in the French Section's calendar for 2009 was a rally to Le Canadel, where Sir Henry Royce lived and worked from 1911 to 1931. In this region on the south coast of France, near St Tropez, Rolls-Royce Motors built three villas: one for Sir Henry Royce, another one for the engineers and mechanics, and the third one for use as a workshop. These properties were sold when Sir Henry Royce died in 1933.

The rally took place between 8 - 11 October 2009. The first evening was spent in the Hotel du Bailli du Suffren where the participants were welcomed by the French Section officers and enjoyed a splendid cocktail reception. Before dinner, the members visited the beautiful Jardins de la Méditerranée.

The next morning the cars set off in convoy to Château de la Mole, a beautiful privately owned 14th Century castle with its own airstrip. After coffee, they then journeyed to St Tropez for lunch and shopping. Saturday involved a visit to a large sophisticated vineyard, Château de Berne, where the participants were joined by members of the Italian Section. That evening, a Gala Dinner was held at which the guests of honour were Jacques and Catherine Gueirdet, who currently own Villa Jaune. Villa Jaune was originally occupied by Claude Johnson, frequently referred to as "the hyphen in Rolls-Royce".

On Sunday morning the group gathered at the Citadel which sits on the hill above Le Canadel where they were greeted by the Mayor of Rayol-de-Canadel. From there the members proceeded to Villa Jaune where they enjoyed drinks and a finger buffet. »

❝ *The oldest Rolls-Royce to take part was a 1928 Phantom I Speedster owned by Silvio Zanolari from Chur*

Club Chairman Tony James and his wife Mary participated in the event and decided to have a photo session with the Rolls-Royce Phantom in front of the entrance to Villa Mimosa, the winter home of Sir Henry Royce. They were greeted by a kindly gentleman who invited them in. He and his wife had acquired Villa Mimosa three years previously. While they were enjoying drinks on the terrace the owner disappeared then re-appeared carrying pre-1913 Rolls-Royce magazines and blueprints which he had found in a cupboard. They were annotated and signed by Sir Henry Royce! The Club Chairman stated "It was a great privilege to visit Sir Henry's home and it was the highlight of my year".

AUSTRIA SECTION: The Austrian Section held a highly successful Section Annual Rally last year based at the Seehotel Europa, situated on the shores of Worthersee. As well as Austrian members, there were Club members from the Netherlands, Belgium, Germany, Switzerland, Russia and the UK with a good turn out of around forty Club cars.

The first afternoon was spent relaxing on the hotel's lower lawns and terraces overlooking the lake. The conclusion of the day began with a champagne reception by the lake followed by dinner on the hotel terrace where members enjoyed superb views across the lake to the Slovenian mountains in the far distance.

After a leisurely breakfast the following morning, the cars set out in convoy for a ninety minute drive through the magnificent Carinthian countryside to St Oswald, taking minor roads, skirting picturesque lakes, and through alpine valleys. The high alpine meadows were at their best and were carpeted with a wide variety of colourful flowers. At St Oswald members took a cable car up to around 1900 metres where there was

Right (top): Germany Section on a drive to Hersbruck; La sezione tedesca in viaggio per Hersbruck; Section Allemagne, sur la route d'Hersbruck; Germany Section auf einer Fahrt nach Hersbruck **Right (bottom):** Germany Section at the Techno Classics in Essen; La sezione tedesca al Techno Classics di Essen; Section Allemagne au salon Techno Classica d'Essen; Germany Section auf der Techno Classics in Essen

> *Villa Jaune was originally occupied by Claude Johnson, frequently referred to as 'the hyphen in Rolls-Royce'*

a restaurant with panoramic views of the mountains. After lunch they returned to their cars and drove back to the hotel by a different route, again through spectacular scenery.

Friday's activities started relatively early with a two and a half hour drive through the mountains to the 'Heinrich Harrer Museum'. Harrer was an Austrian explorer who had connections with Tibet and became a personal friend of the Dalai Lama. The group then drove on to the castle of Pockstein. The castle had recently been acquired by a new owner and it was completely empty and semi derelict but was architecturally very interesting. It is intended that the castle will be completely renovated.

Saturday morning was a more leisurely start and the members drove to the town of Villach which, although a busy commercial area, has kept its centre in the old style and has been pedestrianised. Drinks and refreshment were kindly laid on by the Town Council. Following an introduction to the town's history through a loud speaker system, the members were welcomed by the Burgermeister. The inhabitants of Villach showed considerable interest in the cars and for around three quarters of an hour they became the central attraction.

From Villach the group drove on to the town of Ossiach on Ossiachersee where there is a well known monastery with a beautiful church adjacent to the lake. Although the monks are now long departed, the buildings remain well maintained and are open to the public. The church, still used for services, is a renowned venue for international music festivals. The members enjoyed a superb lunch, which included a selection of some of Austria's best wines, laid on in a large marquee on the lawns of the Stiftsschmiede restaurant, adjacent to the monastery. The restaurant building was formerly the monastery's Smithy. The evening commenced with a champagne reception on the hotel terrace overlooking the Lake, followed by a sumptuous gala dinner. ▣

SECTIONS CONTINENTALES

RÉCAPITULATIF DE QUELQUES SORTIES RÉCENTES

de Julian Spencer

Above: Switzerland Section - 1985 Camargue Boano convertible; Sezione svizzera - 1985 Camargue Boano decappottabile; Section Suisse - cabriolet Camargue Boano 1985; Switzerland Section – 1985 Camargue Boano Convertible

Les sections continentales du Club représentent un pourcentage important des adhésions au Club et contribuent largement à son empreinte mondiale. Chaque année, ces sections organisent des événements amplement médiatisés. Cet article reproduit en français, en anglais, en allemand et en italien pour souligner la véritable internationalité du Club, décrit un échantillon des activités de ses sections continentales.

SECTION ALLEMAGNE: La Section Allemagne a participé à trois rencontres traditionnelles de voitures anciennes en 2009. À commencer par le « Bremen Classic Motorshow » (Salon de la voiture ancienne de Brême) organisé du 5 au 7 février et au cours duquel la Section partageait un stand avec l'ASC (Allgemeiner Schnauferl Club), club dédié à toutes les catégories de voitures anciennes et principalement, aux voitures d'avant-guerre). Le Dr. Egon Schäfer et le Dr. Axel Zogbaum, tous deux membres du Club, s'étaient chargés de l'organisation du stand mis en valeur par une berline standard Bentley S2 1962, une Phantom II « boat-tail » 1932 et une Bentley 3½ litre cabriolet 1932 carrossée par Vanden Plas.

Du 13 au 15 mars, la Section était aussi présente au salon Retro Classics de Stuttgart. Les visiteurs ont pu y admirer quatre modèles pour le moins intéressants : GPG73, désormais dotée d'une nouvelle carrosserie, copie conforme de la « Balloon Car » de Charles Rolls ; 86XJ, Phantom II Tourer construite pour le Maharajah de Rewa pour la chasse au gibier ; 79JH, Springfield Silver Ghost Pall Mall Tourer, désignée comme étant le cabriolet le plus impressionnant exposé au salon et lauréate du premier prix à Stuttgart et 59LC, Phantom I Tourer entièrement restaurée, construite à l'origine pour Don Carlos de Salamanca et dotée d'une carrosserie inédite créée par Manessius de Bruxelles. À l'entrée du stand de la Section trônaient deux Goodwood Phantom (une berline et une Drophead) appartenant à Auto-König, Munich. »

Above: Switzerland Section - 1938 Phantom III Mulliner sedanca de ville; Sezione svizzera - 1938 Phantom III Mulliner sedanca de ville; Section Suisse - 1938 Phantom III Mulliner sedanca de ville; Switzerland Section – 1938 Phantom III Mulliner Sedanca de Ville **Right:** French Section – Rolls-Royce Phantom at the gateway to Villa Mimosa, once the home of Sir Henry Royce; Sezione francese – Rolls-Royce Phantom all'ingresso di Villa Mimosa, in passato residenza di Sir Henry Royce; Section France – Rolls-Royce Phantom aux portes de la villa Les Mimosas, ancienne demeure de Sir Henry Royce; French Section – Rolls-Royce Phantom am Eingang zur Villa Mimosa, einst der Wohnsitz von Sir Henry Royce

Et pour terminer l'année 2009, les membres de la Section Allemagne se sont rendus au salon Techno Classica d'Essen pour partager le stand de Steenbuck Automobiles. Bien que plus restreint qu'à Stuttgart, l'espace était suffisant pour faire admirer la belle Bentley 3½ litre Kellner Drophead Coupé de Rolf Kuhnke (B118CR).

SECTION ITALIE: En avril 2009, la Section Italie profitait de sa première sortie dans les collines de Plaisance pour visiter quatre châteaux. Les membres se sont retrouvés à Pianello, non loin de la forteresse de la Rocca d'Olgisio. Les voitures étaient nombreuses au rendez-vous, que n'ont pas manqué une Phantom II Silver Cloud 1930, une Bentley S1 Continental, des Silver Shadow, des Corniche, une Silver Seraph, une Continental S et une Flying Spur venue de Monaco pour l'occasion. Citons également au passage, la participation à la sortie d'une des premières Silver Cloud jamais construites (SWA130) et d'une Bentley Continental de 1984 ayant appartenu à Sir Elton John. Après le déjeuner, la Section est allée visiter le Château féodal d'Agazzano dans toute sa splendeur restaurée et écouter un récital pour piano donné par Francesco Ghignone. Elle a passé la nuit au Château de Rivalta, après le dîner de gala également organisé au château. Les membres de la Section ont visité le château en compagnie du Comte Orazio Landi Zanardi. Son Altesse royale la Princesse Margaret a fait plusieurs escales au château, à l'occasion de séjours en Italie. La sortie s'est terminée le dimanche, après une visite du château de San Pietro in Cerro.

Fin avril 2009, les membres de la Section Italie ont assisté au Concours d'Élégance Villa d'Este, à l'occasion duquel ils ont pu admirer de magnifiques Rolls-Royce et Bentley de concours, restaurées au plus haut niveau de qualité possible. Rolls-Royce Motor Cars était de la partie, avec son prototype 200EX désormais produit sous l'appellation Ghost. Une Rolls-Royce

> 66
>
> *Une des premières Silver Cloud jamais construites (SWA130) et une Bentley Continental 1984 ayant appartenu à Sir Elton John ont participé à cette sortie*

Silver Cloud III Drophead Coupé rare carrossée par H. J. Mulliner et une Pininfarina Rolls-Royce Hyperion, deux places inédite basée sur la Phantom DHC, stationnaient non loin de là. Le concours mettait notamment en lice trois Phantom Is (dont l'une carrossée par Brewster), un magnifique cabriolet Bentley 4¼ litre Carlton et un des deux coupés FHC Bentley Continental Type R Park Ward.

SECTION SUISSE:

La 16ème édition du British Classic Car Meeting (BCCM) s'est déroulée à St. Moritz, du 10 au 12 juillet 2009. Cet événement n'est pas dédié à une seule marque, mais les Rolls-Royce et Bentley occupent une place de choix parmi les voitures présentées. Les membres de la Section Suisse y étaient venus nombreux. La liste de concurrents de cette année était menée par 57 Rolls-Royce et 36 Bentley de toutes les époques. Deux Aston Martin, une Lagonda, quatre Daimler, 56 Jaguar, 17 Austin Healey et plusieurs autres marques représentées par un ou deux modèles étaient également présentes.

Deux aspects permettent surtout à cette manifestation de dominer le calendrier des rencontres européennes dédiées aux voitures anciennes. Premièrement, ses maîtres-mots sont « exclusivité totale » – la participation d'une voiture ne dépend pas de son âge, mais de sa rareté, de son apparence et de son état. Deuxième facteur de réussite, le tracé de la sortie change chaque année. C'est ainsi que les habitués font face à un nouveau défi à chaque participation et que les nouveaux venus luttent à armes égales avec eux. L'itinéraire de cette année pointait vers l'Est et plus précisément vers l'Italie en effleurant l'Autriche, gravissant et redescendant une multitude de cols de montagne. Le « Run », qui ne dure qu'une journée est une véritable épreuve toutes voitures confondues et quel qu'en soit l'âge. La plus ancienne Rolls-Royce participante était une Phantom I Speedster 1928 appartenant à Silvio Zanolari de Chur, suivie par une Phantom II Tourer 1930 engagée dans un aller-retour Angleterre-Suisse-Angleterre par Robert Watson avec le soutien de sa famille et de ses amis de Rolvenden (Kent) ! Le moteur le plus impressionnant appartenait à la Phantom III Mulliner sedanca de ville 1938 d'Antonio Pasquale, de Morcote. Les plus grandes carrosseries étaient celles de la Phantom V 1967 de Norbert Seeger, de Vaduz et de la Phantom VI 1968 de Martin Lechner, de St. Moritz. Notons parmi les voitures très spéciales de la gamme moderne le cabriolet Camargue Boano 1985 conduit par son propriétaire Adrian von Lerber, de Berne. »

La journée de dimanche a été consacrée au Concours d'Élégance. Cette année, les lauréats de la catégorie Rolls-Royce étaient : Antonio Pasquale de Morcote, en Suisse avec sa Phantom III Mulliner sedanca de ville 1938, catégorie avant-guerre.

Norbert Seeger de Vaduz a remporté la catégorie après-guerre avec sa Phantom V 1967 et Gerhard Trümmel de Dübendorf la catégorie « Young-timer » dans sa Corniche 1976. Pour les Bentley, Jörg E. Meyerhans de Weinfelden a remporté la catégorie après-guerre dans sa S1 Hooper 1957 et Walter Steinemann de Mörschwil la catégorie « Young-timer » sans son Azure 1996. Le « Run » BCCM et le Concours d'Élégance sont des occasions idéales pour profiter pleinement de l'ambiance de St. Moritz et de ses environs.Cet événement est une synthèse unique de luxe pur et de l'agrément naturel que présentent les routes d'une campagne spectaculaire.

La Section Suisse organise depuis plusieurs années une journée annuelle d'évaluation des voitures baptisée « Greasy Fingers' Day » (Journée de la mécanique). En 2009, cette journée d'inspection des voitures toujours particulièrement bien organisée s'est déroulée à la station de contrôle technique du Ministère des Transports de Schafisheim. Les trois instructeurs Steve Lovatt, Eric Healey et William Pullar du Royaume-Uni y avaient rejoint l'équipe suisse expérimentée composée de Markus Schatzmann, Roger Bachman, Renato Naef, Dominik Luescher, Eligio Camina, Eduard Rungg. Les experts ont minutieusement examiné les voitures des membres, qui ont pu en tirer des conseils précieux sur l'utilisation, l'entretien et la préservation de leurs véhicules.

SECTION FRANCE:
La sortie vers Le Canadel, là où vivait et travaillait Sir Henry Royce de 1911 à 1931, compte parmi les grands événements du calendrier de rencontres de la Section France. Rolls-Royce Motors a fait construire trois villas dans cette région du Sud de la France, près de Saint-Tropez : une pour Sir Henry Royce, une pour ses ingénieurs et mécaniciens. La troisième servait d'atelier. Ces propriétés ont été mises en vente en 1933, à la mort de Sir Henry Royce.

La sortie s'est déroulée du 8 au 11 octobre 2009. Les membres ont passé la première soirée à l'hôtel Le Bailli de Suffren, où ils ont été accueillis par les officiels de la Section France à l'occasion d'un splendide cocktail. Avant le dîner, les membres ont visité les magnifiques Jardins de la Méditerranée.

Le lendemain matin, le convoi de voitures s'est rendu au Château de la Mole, demeure privée du 14ème siècle dotée de sa propre piste d'atterrissage. Après le café, les participants ont mis le cap sur Saint-Tropez pour le déjeuner et faire les magasins.

Le samedi avait été réservé à une visite d'un grand vignoble sophistiqué, le Château de Berne, où les participants ont été rejoints par les membres de la Section Italie. Un Dîner de gala avait été organisé pour le soir en compagnie de Jacques et Catherine Gueirdet, invités d'honneur propriétaires actuels de la Villa Jaune. À l'origine, la Villa Jaune était habitée par Claude Johnson, fréquemment appelé le « trait d'union de la marque Rolls-Royce ».

Le dimanche matin, le groupe s'est rassemblé à la Citadelle perchée sur la colline dont le sommet domine Le Canadel, où il a été accueilli par le Maire de Rayol-Canadel-sur-Mer. Les membres se sont ensuite rendus à la Villa Jaune où les attendaient buffet et boissons. Tony James, Président du Club et son épouse Mary ont profité de l'événement pour se faire photographier avec la Rolls-Royce Phantom devant l'entrée de la villa Les Mimosas, demeure d'hiver de Sir Henry Royce au Canadel. Un gentleman bienveillant les y attendait, pour leur faire visiter. Lui et son épouse ont acheté Les Mimosas il y a trois ans. 》

La plus ancienne Rolls-Royce participante était une Phantom I Speedster 1958 appartenant à Silvio Zanolari, de Chur

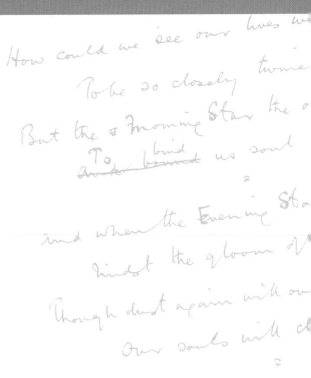

> *Explorateur autrichien, Harrer avait des relations au Tibet et comptait parmi les amis intimes du Dalaï Lama*

Above: French Section – the plaque at Villa Mimosa; Sezione francese – La targa a Villa Mimosa; Section France – plaque de la villa Les Mimosas; French Section – die Gedenktafel an der Villa Mimosa

Et pendant que les visiteurs se rafraîchissaient sur la terrasse, le propriétaire est allé chercher une pile de magazines et plans de Rolls-Royce datant d'avant 1913, trouvés dans une armoire de la villa. Ils portent les commentaires et la signature de Sir Henry Royce lui-même ! Réaction du Président du Club : « Visiter la maison de Sir Henry était un grand privilège, qui s'inscrit parmi mes grands moments de cette année ».

SECTION AUTRICHE: L'année dernière, la sortie annuelle de Section organisée avec brio par la Section Autriche était basée au Seehotel Europa, sur les bords du lac Wörthersee. En plus des membres autrichiens, la sortie a également attiré des membres du Club des Pays-Bas, de Belgique, d'Allemagne, de Suisse, de Russie et du Royaume-Uni, rassemblant en tout une quarantaine de voitures du Club.

Les participants ont consacré leur première après-midi à la détente sur les pelouses et terrasses inférieures de l'hôtel, avec vue sur le lac. Et pour finir cette belle journée, une réception au champagne avait été organisée sur la rive du lac, suivie d'un dîner sur la terrasse de l'hôtel où les membres ont pu profiter pleinement de vues magnifiques jusqu'aux montagnes slovènes voisines.

Après un petit déjeuné tranquille le lendemain matin, le convoi de voitures s'est mis en route pour une traversée de 90 minutes de la belle campagne carinthienne vers Saint Oswald, sur des petites routes, longeant des lacs pittoresques, à travers les vallées alpines. À cette époque, tapissées d'innombrables variétés de plantes et fleurs riches en couleurs, les prairies d'altitude donnent leur plus beau spectacle.

À Saint Oswald, les membres ont pris le téléphérique pour accéder à un restaurant situé à quelque 1 900 mètres d'altitude, où les vues panoramiques des montagnes sont véritablement imprenables. Après le déjeuner, les membres ont repris leur place au volant pour rentrer à l'hôtel en empruntant un itinéraire différent certes, mais toujours à travers un paysage spectaculaire.

Les activités du vendredi ont commencé relativement tôt, par une traversée de deux heures et demie des montages pour se rendre au Musée « Heinrich Harrer ». Explorateur autrichien, Harrer avait des relations au Tibet et comptait parmi les amis intimes du Dalaï Lama. Le groupe s'est ensuite dirigé vers le château de Pockstein. Bien que complètement vide et quasiment à l'abandon, ce château qui venait d'être racheté par un nouveau propriétaire n'en est pas moins très intéressant sur le plan architectural. L'intention du nouveau propriétaire est de le rénover à 100 %.

Départ plus relax pour les membres samedi matin avec, au bout du trajet, la visite de Villach, dont le centre-ville à forte vocation commerciale transformé en zone piétonne n'a rien perdu du charme de ses origines. Le Conseil municipal avait aimablement organisé une collation pour les visiteurs. Après avoir écouté l'enregistrement d'une introduction au passé de la ville, les membres ont rencontré le Bourgmestre qui les a chaleureusement accueillis. Les habitants de Villach ont manifesté un intérêt considérable pour les voitures qui, pendant trois quarts d'heure, ont retenu toute leur attention.

Puis de Villach, le groupe a mis le cap sur Ossiach, ville située sur le lac Ossiachersee célèbre pour son monastère et la magnifique église érigée tout près du lac. Les moines ont quitté la ville depuis longtemps, mais ces édifices sont parfaitement entretenus et ouverts au public. L'église, où l'on célèbre encore la messe, est un lieu bien connu du calendrier annuel des festivals de musique internationaux. Exquis, le déjeuné a notamment permis aux membres de découvrir une sélection des meilleurs vins autrichiens, sous un grand chapiteau érigé sur les pelouses du restaurant Stiftsschmiede, tout près du monastère. Mais le bâtiment n'a pas toujours servi de restaurant. Autrefois, il abritait la forge du monastère. La soirée a commencé par une réception au champagne sur la terrasse de l'hôtel avec vue sur le lac et s'est terminée par un somptueux dîner gala. ▣

CONTINENTAL SECTIONS

EINE ZUSAMMENFASSUNG KÜRZLICHER AKTIVITÄTEN

von Julian Spencer

Left: Germany Section members in northern Bavaria; I membri della sezione tedesca nella Baviera settentrionale; Les membres de la Section Allemagne en Bavière du Nord; Mitglieder der Germany Section in Nordbayern

Die Continental Sections des Clubs repräsentieren einen hohen Prozentsatz der Clubmitglieder und tragen erheblich zur weltweiten Präsenz des Clubs bei. Diese Sections organisieren jedes Jahr viele hochkarätige Veranstaltungen. Dieser Artikel beschreibt einige der Aktivitäten der Continental Sections des Clubs und wird zur Verdeutlichung der wahrhaft internationalen Natur dieses Clubs in englischer, französischer, deutscher und italienischer Sprache veröffentlicht.

GERMANY SECTION: Die Germany Section nahm 2009 an drei traditionellen Oldtimertreffen statt. Das erste war die Bremen Classic Motor Show vom 5. bis 7. Februar, auf der die Section zusammen mit dem ASC (Allgemeiner Schnauferl Club, ein Club für alle Arten von Oldtimern, jedoch hauptsächlich Vorkriegsautomobile) auf einem Stand vertreten war. Clubmitglieder Dr. Egon Schäfer und Dr. Axel Zogbaum organisierten den Stand und stellten einen 1962er Bentley S2 Standard Saloon, 1932er Phantom II Boat Tail Tourer und 1935er Bentley 3½ Liter Open Tourer von Vanden Plas aus.

Vom 13. bis 15. März hatte die Section einen Stand auf der Retro Classics in Stuttgart. Dort wurden vier interessante Fahrzeuge ausgestellt: GPG73, jetzt mit einer neuen Karosserie als exakter Nachbau des Ballon Car von Charles Rolls; 86XJ, ein Phantom II Tourer, der für den Maharadscha von Rewa als Jagdfahrzeug gebaut worden war; 79JH, ein Springfield Silver Ghost Pall Mall Tourer, der in Stuttgart den ersten Preis für den eindrucksvollsten offenen Tourer gewinnen konnte; und, 59LC, ein vollständig restaurierter Phantom I Tourer, der einst für Don Carlos de Salamanca gebaut wurde und eine einmalige Karosserie von Manessius aus Brüssel aufweist. Der Stand der Section wurde von zwei Goodwood Phantoms (einem Saloon und einem Drophead) flankiert, die Auto-König aus München gehörten.

Später im Jahr 2009 nahmen Mitglieder der Germany Section an der Techno Classica in Essen teil, auf der sie einen Teil des Stands von Steenbuck Automobiles nutzten. Der dort zur Verfügung stehende Raum war beengter als in Stuttgart, aber immer noch groß genug, um Rolf Kuhnkes außergewöhnliches Bentley 3½ Liter (B118CR) Kellner Drophead Coupé zu zeigen! »

"
*Einer der ersten gebauten Silver Clouds
(SWA130) und ein früher im Besitz von
Sir Elton John stehender 1984er Bentley
Continental nahmen an der Rallye teil*

ITALY SECTION: Im April 2009 führte die Italy Section ihre erste Rallye in den Hügeln von Piacenza durch, wo sie vier sehenswerte Burgen besuchte. Der Treffpunkt war in Pianello, nicht weit von der Burg Rocca d'Olgisio entfernt. Die Veranstaltung wurde von vielen Automobilen besucht, einschließlich einem 1930er Phantom II, Silver Clouds, einem Bentley S1 Continental, Silver Shadows, Corniches sowie einem Silver Seraph, Continental S und Flying Spur, die aus Monaco angereist waren. Weiterhin ist es interessant zu erwähnen, dass einer der ersten gebauten Silver Clouds (SWA130) und ein früher im Besitz von Sir Elton John stehender 1984er Bentley Continental an der Rallye teilnahmen. Nach dem Mittagessen besuchte die Section die feudale Burg Agazzano, die heute vollständig restauriert ist, wo ein Klavierkonzert von Francesco Ghignone auf dem Programm stand. Die Unterkunft war in der Burg Rivalta, in der auch das Galadinner stattfand. Die Mitglieder der Section erhielten eine Führung der Burg von Graf Orazio Landi Zanardi. Ihre Königliche Hoheit Prinzessin Margaret übernachtete bei ihren Besuchen in Italien mehrmals auf der Burg. Die Rallye endete am Sonntag mit einem Besuch von San Pietro in der Burg Cerro.

Ende April 2009 besuchten die Mitglieder der Italy Section den Concorso d'Eleganza Villa d'Este. Sie hatten die Möglichkeit, wunderbare Rolls-Royces und Bentleys zu sehen, die nach höchsten Standards restauriert waren. Rolls-Royce Motor Cars war mit dem Prototyp 200EX vertreten, der jetzt als Ghost-Modell in Produktion gegangen ist. Direkt daneben waren ein seltenes Rolls-Royce Silver Cloud III Drophead Coupé von H. J. Mulliner und der Pininfarina Rolls-Royce Hyperion, der einmalige Zweisitzer auf der Basis des Phantom DHC, abgestellt. Das Treffen umfasste drei Phantom I (mit einer Karosserie von Brewster), ein schönes Bentley 4¼ Liter Carlton Cabriolet und eines der beiden gebauten Bentley R Type Continental Park Ward Fixed Head Coupés.

SWITZERLAND SECTION: Das 16th British Classic Car Meeting (BCCM) fand vom 10. bis 12. Juli 2009 in St. Moritz statt. Die Veranstaltung ist keiner einzigen Marke vorbehalten, und ein großer

Teil der teilnehmenden Fahrzeuge sind Rolls-Royces und Bentleys. Die Mitglieder der Switzerland Section waren in hoher Zahl vertreten. Das Teilnehmerfeld wurde in diesem Jahr von siebenundfünfzig Rolls-Royces und sechsunddreißig Bentleys aller Altersstufen angeführt. Zusätzlich wurden zweiundzwanzig Aston Martins, ein Lagonda, vier Daimlers, sechsundfünfzig Jaguars, siebzehn Austin Healeys und mehrere andere Marken ausgestellt, die mit jeweils einem oder zwei Modellen vertreten waren.

Zwei Hauptaspekte gewährleisten, dass das BCCM ganz oben auf der Liste der Oldtimertreffen in Europa steht: Zuerst liegt der Schwerpunkt vollkommen auf der Verpflichtung zur Exklusivität, d. h. die Zulassung eines Automobils hängt nicht von seinem Alter, sondern seinem Seltenheitswert, Erscheinungsbild und Zustand ab. Der zweite Grund für den Erfolg des Treffens ist, dass die Rallyeroute jedes Jahr geändert wird, sodass sich erfahrene Wettbewerber immer einer neuen Herausforderung gegenüber sehen, während sich Neulinge nicht im Nachteil befinden. In diesem Jahr verlief die Route in östlicher Richtung nach Italien und teilweise nach Österreich, wobei zahllose Bergpässe zu erklimmen und entsprechende Talfahrten zu absolvieren waren.

Der innerhalb eines einzigen Tages abgehaltene „Run" ist eine echte Herausforderung für jedes Fahrzeug unabhängig von seinem Alter. Der älteste teilnehmende Rolls-Royce war ein 1928er Phantom I Speedster von Silvio Zanolari aus Chur, gefolgt von einem 1930er Phantom II Tourer, der von Robert Watson aus Rolvenden in England samt unterstützender Familie und Freunden in die Schweiz und wieder zurückgefahren wurde! Der beeindruckendste Motor war der des 1938er Phantom III Mulliner Sedanca de Ville von Antonio Pasquale aus Morcote. Die größten Karosserien hatten der 1967er Phantom V von Norbert Seeger aus Vaduz und der 1968er Phantom VI von Martin Lechner aus St. Moritz. Ein ganz besonderes Exemplar aus der modernen Baureihe war das 1985er Camargue Boano Convertible, das von seinem Eigentümer Adrian von Lerber aus Bern gefahren wurde. »

Left: Italy Section cars in front of Agazzano Castle; Le vetture della sezione italiana davanti al castello di Agazzano; Voitures de la section Italie devant le Château d'Agazzano; Automobile der Italy Section vor der Burg Agazzano

Der älteste teilnehmende Rolls-Royce war ein 1928er Phantom I Speedster von Silvio Zanolari aus Chur

Der Sonntag stand ganz im Zeichen des Concours d'Elegance. Der erste Preis in der Rolls-Royce-Kategorie ging an Antonio Pasquale aus Morcote in der Schweiz mit seinem 1938er Phantom III Mulliner Sedanca de Ville in der Vorkriegskategorie. Norbert Seeger aus Vaduz gewann die Nachkriegskategorie mit seinem 1967er Phantom V, und Gerhard Trümmel aus Dübendorf wurde Sieger in der „Youngtimer"-Kategorie mit seinem 1976er Corniche. In der Bentley-Kategorie gewann Jörg E. Meyerhans aus Weinfelden die Nachkriegskategorie mit seinem 1957er S1 Hooper, und Walter Steinemann aus Mörschwil belegte den ersten Platz in der „Youngtimer"-Kategorie mit seinem 1996er Azure. Der BCCM „Run" und Concours d'Elegance stellen wunderbare Gelegenheiten dar, die Atmosphäre von St. Moritz und seiner Umgebung zu genießen. Die Veranstaltung bietet eine einzigartige Kombination aus schierem Luxus und reinem Vergnügen des Fahrens in einer spektakulären Landschaft.

Die Switzerland Section hat seit mehreren Jahren einen jährlichen Automobiltag abgehalten, der als „Greasy Fingers Day" bekannt ist. Dabei handelt es sich um einen hervorragend organisierten Fahrzeuginspektionstag, der 2009 auf dem Gelände des Straßenverkehrsamts (TÜV) in Schafisheim stattfand. Die Ausbilder aus Großbritannien waren Steve Lovatt, Eric Healey und William Pullar, die mit dem erfahrenen schweizerischen Team aus Markus Schatzmann, Roger Bachman, Renato Naef, Dominik Luescher, Eligio Camina und Eduard Rungg zusammenarbeiteten. Die Experten nahmen die Fahrzeuge genauestens unter die Lupe, und die Mitglieder der Section erhielten wertvolle Informationen über Nutzung, Pflege und Erhaltung ihrer Automobile.

FRANCE SECTION: Ein bedeutendes Ereignis im Kalender der French Section im Jahr 2009 war eine Rallye nach Le Canadel, dem Ort, an dem Sir Henry Royce von 1911 bis 1931 lebte und arbeitete. In dieser Region an der französischen Südküste in der Nähe von St. Tropez baute Rolls-Royce Motors drei Villen: eine für Sir Henry Royce, eine weitere für die Ingenieure und Mechaniker und die dritte zur Verwendung als Werkstatt. Diese Immobilien wurden nach dem Tod von Sir Henry Royce im Jahr 1933 verkauft.

Die Rallye fand vom 8. bis 11. Oktober 2009 statt. Der erste Abend wurde im Hotel du Bailli du Suffren verbracht, wo die Teilnehmer von den Repräsentanten der French Section im Rahmen eines großartigen Cocktailempfangs willkommen geheißen wurden. Vor dem Dinner besuchten die Mitglieder die schönen Jardins de la Méditerranée. Am folgenden Morgen startete der Konvoi von Fahrzeugen zum Château de la Mole, einer wunderschönen, im Privatbesitz stehenden Burg aus dem 14. Jh. mit eigenem Landestreifen für Leichtflugzeuge. Nach einer Kaffeepause ging die Fahrt nach St. Tropez zum Mittagessen und Einkaufen. Am Samstag stand ein Besuch des großen Weinguts Château de Berne auf dem Programm, wo Mitglieder der Italian Section zu den Teilnehmern stießen. Am Abend fand ein Galadinner mit den Ehrengästen Jacques und Catherine Gueirdet, den gegenwärtigen Besitzern der Villa Jaune, statt. Die Villa Jaune wurde ursprünglich von Claude Johnson bewohnt, der häufig als der „Bindestrich in Rolls-Royce" bezeichnet wird.

Am Sonntagmorgen sammelte sich die Gruppe vor der Zitadelle auf dem Hügel über Le Canadel, wo sie vom Bürgermeister von Rayol-de-Canadel begrüßt wurde. Von hier fuhren die Mitglieder zur Villa Jaune, wo Ihnen Erfrischungen und ein Buffet mit Appetithappen angeboten wurde. Club Chairman Tony James und seine Frau Mary nahmen an der Veranstaltung teil, und man entschied sich zu einem Fototermin mit dem Rolls-Royce Phantom vor dem Eingang zur Villa Mimosa, dem Winterhaus von Sir Henry Royce. Die Gruppe wurde von einem freundlichen Herrn begrüßt, der die Mitglieder in sein Haus einlud. »

> *Die Villa Jaune wurde ursprünglich von*
> *Claude Johnson bewohnt, der häufig als der*
> *„Bindestrich in Rolls-Royce" bezeichnet wird*

Er und seine Frau hatten die Villa Mimosa drei Jahre zuvor gekauft. Während die Mitglieder einen Drink auf der Terrasse genossen, verschwand der Eigentümer, nur um kurze Zeit später mit Rolls-Royce-Magazinen und Entwurfsplänen aus der Zeit vor 1913 zu erscheinen, die er in einem Schrank gefunden hatte. Die Dokumente waren von Sir Henry Royce mit Anmerkungen versehen und unterschrieben! Der Club Chairman erklärte: „Es war eine besondere Ehre, Sir Henry's Haus zu besuchen, und für mich der Höhepunkt des Jahres!"

AUSTRIA SECTION: Die Austrian Section veranstaltete im letzten Jahr ihre äußerst erfolgreiche jährliche Section Rallye am Seehotel Europa am Ufer des Wörthersees. Abgesehen von österreichischen Mitgliedern waren Clubmitglieder aus den Niederlanden, aus Belgien, Deutschland, der Schweiz, Russland und Großbritannien mit guter Beteiligung von rund vierzig Clubfahrzeugen angereist.

Der erste Nachmittag war der Entspannung auf dem unteren Rasen und den Terrassen des Hotels mit Blick über den See vorbehalten. Der Tag endete mit einem Sektempfang am See, gefolgt vom Dinner auf der Hotelterrasse, von der die Mitglieder wunderbare Aussichten über den See auf die fernen slowenischen Berge genießen konnten.

Nach einem gemütlichen Frühstück am folgenden Morgen setzen sich die Automobile im Konvoi zu einer neunzigminütigen Fahrt durch die großartige Landschaft Kärntens nach St. Oswald in Bewegung. Die Strecke verlief über Nebenstraßen, an hübschen Seen vorbei und durch Alpentäler. Die alpinen Hochalmen mit einer Vielzahl bunter Wiesenblumen standen in voller Blüte. In St. Oswald fuhren die Mitglieder mit einer Seilbahn auf die luftige Höhe von 1900 Metern zum Mittagessen in einem Restaurant mit Panoramablick über die Berge. Anschließend kehrte die Gruppe zu Ihren Fahrzeugen zurück und schlug auf der Rückfahrt zum Hotel eine andere Route ein, die wiederum spektakuläre Aussichten auf die atemberaubende Landschaft bot.

Das Programm am Freitag begann recht früh mit einer zweieinhalbstündigen Fahrt durch die Berge zum „Heinrich Harrer Museum". Harrer war ein österreichischer Forscher, der Verbindungen nach Tibet hatte und zum persönlichen Freund des Dalai Lamas wurde. Danach fuhr die Gruppe zur Burg Pockstein weiter. Die Burg war vor Kurzem von einem neuen Eigentümer gekauft worden und stand im halb verfallenen Zustand vollkommen leer, erwies sich jedoch als architektonisch sehr interessantes Gebäude. Der neue Eigentümer beabsichtigt die komplette Renovierung der Burg.

Der Samstagmorgen begann gemütlicher, und die Mitglieder fuhren nach Villach, eine Stadt, die trotz starker Gewerbetätigkeit dennoch den alten Stil ihres Zentrums beibehalten und es zur Fußgängerzone gemacht hat. Dort bereitete der Stadtrat den Gruppenmitgliedern einen Empfang mit Getränken und Erfrischungen. Im Anschluss an eine Einführung in die Stadtgeschichte über eine Lautsprecheranlage wurde die Gruppe vom Bürgermeister willkommen geheißen. Die Bevölkerung von Villach zeigte starkes Interesse an den Automobilen, die für eine Dreiviertelstunde zur besonderen Attraktion wurden.

Von Villach fuhr die Gruppe nach Ossiach am Ossiacher See, einer Stadt mit einem bekannten Stift und wunderschöner Kirche am See. Obwohl die Mönche schon vor langer Zeit ausgezogen waren, sind die Gebäude gut erhalten und für Besucher geöffnet. Die weiterhin für Gottesdienste benutzte Kirche ist ein bekannter Veranstaltungsort für internationale Musikfeste. Die Mitglieder genossen ein ausgezeichnetes Mittagessen mit einer Auswahl der besten Weine Österreichs in einem großen Zelt auf dem Rasen des Restaurants Stiftsschmiede direkt neben dem Stift. Das Gebäude des heutigen Restaurants war früher die Schmiede des Stifts. Der Abend begann mit einem Sektempfang auf der Hotelterrasse mit Blick auf den See, gefolgt von einem ausgezeichneten Galadinner. 🔲

Left (top): Switzerland Section - Greasy Fingers' Day in Schafisheim, Switzerland; Sezione svizzera - Greasy Fingers' Day a Schafisheim, Svizzera; Section Suisse – journée des « Greasy Fingers » à Schafisheim, Suisse; Switzerland Section – „Greasy Fingers Day" in Schafisheim, Schweiz **Left (bottom):** Switzerland Section - Greasy Fingers' Day in Schafisheim, Switzerland; Sezione svizzera - Greasy Fingers' Day a Schafisheim, Svizzera; Section Suisse – journée des « Greasy Fingers » à Schafisheim, Suisse; Switzerland Section – „Greasy Fingers Day" in Schafisheim, Schweiz

SEZIONI CONTINENTALI

SINTESI DELLE RECENTI ATTIVITÀ

di Julian Spencer

Left: Italy Section - Bentley 4¼ (B44MR) Carlton dhc at Villa d'Este; Sezione italiana - Bentley 4¼ (B44MR) Carlton dhc a Villa d'Este; Section Italie - Bentley 4¼ (B44MR) Carlton DHC à la Villa d'Este; Italy Section – Bentley 4¼ (B44MR) Carlton DHC vor Villa d'Este

Le sezioni continentali del Club rappresentano percentualmente una grande parte dei membri del Club e contribuiscono in maniera significativa alle dimensioni complessive del Club. Ogni anno queste sezioni organizzano numerosi eventi di alto profilo. L'articolo descrive alcune delle attività delle sezioni continentali del Club ed è disponibile in inglese, francese, tedesco e italiano al fine sottolineare la natura internazionale del Club.

SEZIONE TEDESCA: Nel corso del 2009, la sezione tedesca ha partecipato a tre eventi tradizionali per vetture d'epoca. La prima manifestazione è stata il Bremen Classic Motor Show che si è tenuta dal 5 al 7 febbraio. La sezione tedesca ha condiviso lo stand con l'ASC (Allgemeiner Schnauferl Club, un club per vetture d'epoca anteguerra). I membri dr. Egon Schäfer e dr. Axel Zogbaum hanno organizzato lo stand esponendo una berlina Bentley S2 standard del 1962, una boat tail tourer Phantom II del 1932 e una open tourer Bentley 3½ litri del 1935 di Vanden Plas.

Dal 13 al 15 marzo, la sezione è stata presente con uno stand al Retro Classics di Stoccarda esponendo quattro interessanti vetture: una GPG73, che ora sfoggia una nuova carrozzeria che è una replica esatta della Balloon Car di Charles Rolls; 86XJ, una tourer Phantom II realizzata per il Maharajah di Rewa per le battute di caccia; 79JH, una tourer Springfield Silver Ghost Pall Mall che ha vinto il primo premio a Stoccarda come migliore open tourer in esposizione; e una 59LC, una tourer Phantom I completamente restaurata per Don Carlos de Salamanca con una carrozzeria personalizzata di Manessius di Bruxelles. Ai lati dello stand della sezione erano esposte due Phantom Goodwood (una berlina e una drophead) appartenenti a Auto-König di Monaco di Baviera.

A fine 2009 i membri della sezione tedesca erano presenti alla Techno Classica di Essen dove hanno utilizzato una parte dello stand di Steenbuck Automobiles. Lo spazio espositivo non era esteso come alla manifestazione di Stoccarda, ma era sufficiente a presentare la stupenda drophead coupé Bentley 3½ litri (B118CR) Kellner di Rolf Kuhnke. »

[handwritten manuscript, partially legible]

...ve by a glance or sigh

...hing heart must bear it' load

...cting it's daily lie

a man I'd take by storm

Thy lips so proudly cold

...al thy heart unstolen before

...ith love so hotly told

...thou not known a woman's heart

...s from the world concealed

...ve for one

To one alone

M. Beaubon

SEZIONE ITALIANA: Nel mese di aprile 2009, i membri della sezione italiana si sono riuniti per la prima volta sulle colline di Piacenza dove hanno avuto l'occasione di visitare quattro meravigliosi castelli. La sede del raduno era a Pianello non lontano dalla Rocca d'Olgisio. Numerose vetture hanno partecipato alla manifestazione, incluso una Phantom II del 1930, alcune Silver Cloud, una Bentley S1 Continental, alcune Silver Shadow e Corniche, una Silver Seraph, una Continental S e una Flying Spur arrivata da Monaco. È inoltre interessante menzionare la partecipazione al raduno di una delle prime Silver Cloud mai fabbricate (SWA130) e di una Bentley Continental del 1984 appartenuta in passato a Sir Elton John.

Dopo il pranzo, i membri della sezione si sono recati in visita al castello di Agazzano, ora completamente restaurato, dove era in programma un recital pianistico di Francesco Ghignone. I membri erano ospitati all'interno del Castello di Rivalta dove si è anche tenuta la cena di gala. I membri della sezione hanno visitato il castello con una guida d'eccezione, il conte Orazio Landi Zanardi. Il Castello di Rivalta ha ospitato più volte Sua Altezza Reale la principessa Margaret durante i suoi soggiorni in Italia. La manifestazione si è quindi conclusa la domenica con una vista al castello di San Pietro in Cerro.

Alla fine di aprile 2009, i membri della sezione italiana hanno partecipato al Concorso d'Eleganza Villa d'Este. È stata questa l'occasione per ammirare vetture Rolls-Royce e Bentley restaurate secondo i requisiti più stringenti. Rolls-Royce Motor Cars era presente con il prototipo 200EX, ora in produzione come modello Ghost. Era poi possibile ammirare una rara drophead coupé Rolls-Royce Silver Cloud III di H J Mulliner e una Pininfarina Rolls-Royce Hyperion, la biposto one-off, basata sulla Phantom dhc. Il concorso includeva tre Phantom Is (una coachbuilt di Brewster), una bellissima cabriolet Bentley 4¼ litri Carlton e una delle due fixed head coupé Bentley R Type Continental Park Ward.

SEZIONE SVIZZERA: La sedicesima edizione del British Classic Car Meeting (BCCM) si è svolta dal 10 al 12 luglio 2009 a St Moritz. La manifestazione non è dedicata a un solo marchio ma una larga parte delle vetture presenti erano Rolls-Royce e Bentley. La sezione svizzera era presente con una nutrita rappresentanza. Le vetture in concorso includevano cinquantasette Rolls-Royce e trentasei Bentley di tutte le età. In aggiunta, erano presenti ventidue Aston Martin, una Lagonda, quattro Daimler, cinquantasei Jaguar, diciassette Austin Healey e diversi altri marchi erano rappresentati da uno o due modelli. »

"
La Rolls-Royce più anziana era una Phantom I Speedster del 1928 di Silvio Zanolari da Chur

The Lord gave th

and me for

A little dust, so

In space

From them the

And a

Born wide a

Had eve

That we sho

The W

> "
> *Villa Jaune era originariamente residenza di Claude Johnson, conosciuto come 'il trattino di Rolls-Royce'*

Vi sono due aspetti principali che rendono il BCCM l'appuntamento di maggior richiamo per le vetture d'epoca in Europa. Innanzitutto la totale esclusività, l'ammissione di una vettura non dipende dall'anzianità ma piuttosto dalla rarità, dall'aspetto e dalle condizioni. Il secondo aspetto del successo di questa manifestazione consiste nel fatto che il percorso cambia ogni anno, in maniera tale che il concorrente esperto affronti una sfida sempre nuova mentre i concorrenti che partecipano per la prima volta non si trovano in svantaggio. Per l'edizione di quest'anno, il percorso puntava a est, verso l'Italia e parzialmente verso l'Austria e prevedeva l'ascesa e la discesa di innumerevoli passi di montagna.

La 'corsa', che si svolge in un'unica giornata, è una gara impegnativa per qualsiasi vettura, non importa quanto giovane. La Rolls-Royce più anziana a partecipare era una Phantom I Speedster del 1928 di proprietà di Silvio Zanolari di Chur, seguita da una tourer Phantom II del 1930 che aveva viaggiato dall'Inghilterra alla Svizzera e ritorno guidata da Robert Watson, sostenuto dalla sua famiglia e dagli amici di Rolvenden! Il motore più impressionante è stato quello della Phantom III Mulliner sedanca de ville del 1938 di Antonio Pasquale da Morcote. Le carrozzerie più grandi sono state quelle della Phantom V del 1967 di Norbert Seeger da Vaduz e della Phantom VI del 1968 di Martin Lechner da St Moritz. Una vettura davvero speciale della gamma moderna è stata la decappottabile Camargue Boano del 1965 guidata dal proprietario Adrian von Lerber da Berna.

La giornata di domenica è stata dedicata al Concours d'Elegance. Quest'anno i riconoscimenti nella categoria Rolls-Royce sono andati a: Antonio Pasquale da Morcote in Svizzera con la Phantom III Mulliner sedanca de ville per la categoria anteguerra; Norbert Seeger da Vaduz ha vinto nella categoria dopoguerra con la sua Phantom V del 1967 e Gerhard Trümmel da Dübendorf è

stato il vincitore nella categoria Youngtimer con una Corniche del 1976. Nella categoria Bentley, Jörg E. Meyerhans da Weinfelden ha vinto nella categoria dopoguerra con la sua S1 Hooper del 1957 mentre Walter Steinemann da Mörschwil ha vinto nella categoria Youngtimer con una Azure del 1996. La 'corsa' e il Concours d'Elegance del BCCM è una meravigliosa opportunità per assaporare l'atmosfera di St Moritz e dintorni. L'evento offre una combinazione unica di puro lusso e di puro godimento della guida in uno scenario naturalistico davvero spettacolare.

Per molti anni la sezione svizzera ha tenuto una giornata annuale di valutazione delle vetture conosciuta come 'Greasy Fingers' Day'. È una giornata di ispezione dei veicoli organizzata in maniera eccellente e nel 2009 e si è svolta presso la stazione di revisione del Ministero dei trasporti (MOT) di Schafisheim. Gli istruttori provenienti dal Regno Unito erano Steve Lovatt, Eric Healey e William Pullar che si sono uniti al team di esperti svizzero composto da Markus Schatzmann, Roger Bachman, Renato Naef, Dominik Luescher, Eligio Camina, Eduard Rungg. Un attento esame delle vetture dei membri è stato condotto dagli esperti e i membri della sezione hanno avuto modo di ricevere preziose conoscenze sull'utilizzo, la manutenzione e la conservazione delle proprie vetture.

SEZIONE FRANCESE: Il più importante evento nel calendario 2009 della sezione francese è stato il raduno a Le Canadel, dove Sir Henry Royce ha vissuto e lavorato dal 1911 al 1931. In questa regione della riviera francese, vicino St Tropez, Rolls-Royce Motors aveva costruito tre ville: una per Sir Henry Royce, un'altra per i tecnici e i meccanici e una terza da utilizzare come officina. Queste proprietà furono poi vendute dopo la scomparsa di Sir Henry Royce nel 1933.

La manifestazione si è svolta dall'8 all'11 ottobre 2009. I membri sono stati ricevuti in serata all'Hotel du Bailli du Suffren dai dirigenti della sezione francese con uno splendido cocktail di benvenuto. Prima della cena i membri hanno visitato i bellissimi Jardins de la Méditerranée. Il mattino successivo le vetture si sono trasferite in carovana verso Château de la Mole, un magnifico castello del 14° secolo dotato di pista di atterraggio privata. Dopo il caffè, gli equipaggi si sono spostati a St Tropez per il pranzo e lo shopping. La giornata di sabato prevedeva la visita a un vigneto, Château de Berne, dove i partecipanti sono stati raggiunti dai membri della sezione italiana. In serata, la cena di gala vedeva come ospiti d'onore Jacques e Catherine Gueirdet, gli attuali proprietari di Villa Jaune. Villa Jaune era originariamente la residenza di Claude Johnson, conosciuto come 'il trattino di Rolls-Royce'. »

Left: Austrian Section in Villach town centre; I membri della sezione austriaca nel centro di Villach; Section Autriche, dans le centre-ville de Villach; Austrian Section im Stadtzentrum von Villach

La domenica mattina il gruppo si è riunito alla Citadel, sulla collina che domina Le Canadel, dove hanno ricevuto il saluto del sindaco di Rayol-de-Canadel. Il gruppo ha quindi proseguito per Villa Jaune dove era previsti un buffet che proponeva specialità di finger food. Il presidente del Club Tony James e sua moglie Mary hanno partecipato all'evento e sono stati protagonisti di una sessione fotografica di fronte all'ingresso di Villa Mimosa, la residenza invernale di Sir Henry Royce. Tony James e sua moglie erano stati invitati a entrare nella villa da un distinto gentiluomo che aveva acquistato Villa Mimosa tre anni prima. Mentre si godevano un drink sulla terrazza il proprietario della villa si assentava, per poi ritornare con una serie di riviste e progetti Rolls-Royce precedenti al 1913 che aveva trovato in un armadio. I progetti erano annotati e firmati da Sir Henry Royce! Il presidente del Club ha dichiarato: 'È stato un grande privilegio visitare la dimora di Sir Henry e questo è stato sicuramente l'avvenimento più importante dell'anno'.

SEZIONE AUSTRIACA: L'anno scorso la sezione austriaca ha organizzato un raduno annuale di grande successo presso il Seehotel Europa, sulle sponde del Worthersee. Oltre ai membri austriaci, erano presenti membri da Paesi Bassi, Belgio, Germania, Svizzera, Russia e Regno Unito per un totale di circa quaranta vetture iscritte al Club.

Il primo pomeriggio è trascorso all'insegna del relax sui prati e le terrazze dell'hotel. La giornata si è conclusa con una coppa di champagne in riva al lago seguita dalla cena sulla terrazza dell'hotel da cui era possibile godersi lo spettacolare panorama del lago con lo sfondo delle Alpi slovene.

Il mattino seguente dopo una colazione gustata con comodo, gli equipaggi sono partiti in carovana per un tragitto di novanta minuti attraversando la magnifica campagna della Carinzia fino a raggiungere St Oswald, viaggiando su strade secondarie, costeggiando laghi pittoreschi e attraversando valli alpine. I prati alpini erano al massimo della fioritura, punteggiati da una grande varietà di fiori di tutti i colori. A St Oswald i membri hanno preso la funivia per raggiungere il ristorante a 1900 metri di altezza da cui si godeva uno spettacolare panorama delle montagne circostanti. Dopo avere pranzato i membri sono ritornati alle vetture per dirigersi verso l'hotel, questa volta seguendo un percorso diverso ma sempre assolutamente spettacolare.

"

Harrer era un esploratore austriaco che aveva viaggiato in Tibet diventando amico personale del Dalai Lama

To be so closely turned?
But the Morning Star the order
To bind us soul and
and when the Evening Star had
lindst the gloom of the Jua
Though dust again with our bod

Le attività della giornata di venerdì sono iniziate relativamente presto con un tragitto attraverso le montagne di due ore e mezzo con destinazione l'*Heinrich Harrer Museum*. Harrer era un esploratore austriaco che aveva viaggiato in Tibet diventando amico personale del Dalai Lama. Il gruppo si è quindi diretto al Castello di Pockstein. Il castello è stato di recente acquistato da un nuovo proprietario ed è al momento completamente vuoto e in stato di semiabbandono, ma i membri hanno avuto modo di apprezzarne il notevole interesse dal punto di vista architettonico. È infatti previsto il completo restauro del castello.

Il sabato mattina si è aperto all'insegna del relax e la carovana si è diretta verso Villach che, sebbene sia un città molto attiva commercialmente, ha conservato inalterato lo stile antico del centro storico che è stato completamente pedonalizzato. Il consiglio comunale ha gentilmente offerto drink e snack agli equipaggi. Dopo un'introduzione storica sulla città diffusa da un sistema di altoparlanti, i membri sono stati accolti dal Burgermeister, il sindaco della città. Gli abitanti di Villach hanno mostrato un notevole interesse nelle vetture d'epoca che per quarantacinque minuti sono diventate l'attrazione principale della città.

Da Villach la carovana si è quindi diretta verso la città di Ossiach, per visitare il monastero con annessa la bellissima chiesa adiacente al lago Ossiachersee. Sebbene i monaci abbiano lasciato il monastero da tempo, gli edifici sono in buono stato di conservazione e aperti al pubblico. La chiesa, ancora aperta al culto, ospita famosi festival musicali internazionali. I membri hanno quindi gustato un eccellente pranzo che includeva anche una degustazione dei migliori vini d'Austria, in un padiglione sui prati del ristorante Stiftsschmiede accanto al monastero. L'edificio che ospita il ristorante in passato era la fucina del convento. In serata, i membri sono stati accolti da con una coppa di champagne sulla terrazza dell'hotel affacciata sul lago, per poi continuare con una sontuosa cena di gala. ▣

Left: French Section at Villa Jaune; La sezione francese a Villa Jaune; Section France, à la Villa Jaune; French Section vor der Villa Jaune

IN COMMEMORATION OF

THE HON C S ROLLS

by Kelvin Price

How could we see on
To be so close
But the ~~#~~ Morning S
~~And bound~~ To bind u
and when the Eve
Midst the g
Though dust again
Our soul

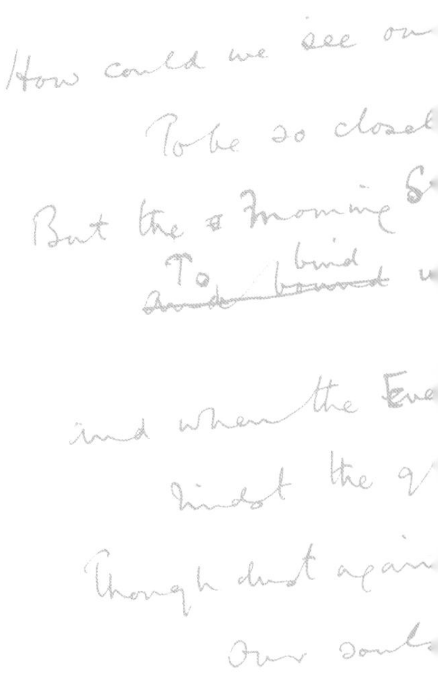

Much has been written over the past century about the Honourable Charles Stewart Rolls since his untimely death just weeks short of his 33rd birthday in a flying accident at Southbourne near Bournemouth on Tuesday 12 July 1910. This article explores the Club's events to commemorate the centenary of Rolls' early demise.

SETTING THE SCENE: Frederick Henry Royce (1863-1933) was the engineer, or 'mechanic', as he dubbed himself, but without the vision, enthusiasm and entrepreneurial skill contributed by Charles Rolls, it is conjecture whether what they established between them would have achieved such worldwide renown as it enjoys today.

Charles Rolls was born in London on 27 August 1877 into a very privileged and well-to-do family. He was the youngest of four children, having two brothers and one sister. The wealth came from his predecessors' prudent purchase of rural freeholds and leaseholds in Surrey on both sides of what today is called the Old Kent Road, long before London's urban expansion. By marriage, the family holding expanded to take in areas of Bermondsey, Camberwell, Newington and Southwark, as well as land just west of Monmouth on the Welsh Borders. Charles' grandfather decided to move the family seat to Monmouthshire and Charles' father, who later became the 1st Lord Llangattock in 1892, expanded the farmhouse cum shooting lodge to build a grand mansion in Victorian Gothic style called The Hendre, still standing today in a delightfully tranquil and unspoiled part of rural Monmouthshire.

Charles Rolls was fiercely competitive and adventurous in everything he did. He raced bicycles, he raced many types of motor cars, he entered his balloons in competitions, he took to powered flight in an airship and finally in an aeroplane, the best available at the time. He became friendly with American pioneer aviators Wilbur and Orville Wright. On 2 June 1910, Rolls became the first man to fly from England to France and back to England without stopping. He seemed to possess a passion to succeed in everything he did. In business, it was this competitive spirit that motivated him to want to build the best car in the world. »

Left: The Hendre, near Monmouth, the Rolls' family home

and blood,

ONE HUNDRED YEARS ON:
And so it was exactly 100 years later to the day, on 12 July 2010, that a full congregation of well over 100 people attended a service of thanksgiving for the life of Charles Rolls at St Cadoc's Church, Llangattock Vibon Avel, the small parish church of the estate where, along with relatives, he is buried. The church was beautifully decorated including a floral display incorporating 'RR', a model of one of his balloons and a life size image of the man himself. The Lord Bishop of Monmouth, the Right Reverend Dominic Walker, gave a very personal address and readings were made by Simon Harding-Rolls (descendant of the Rolls family) and Roger James of Rolls-Royce plc, Bristol. Afterwards, the congregation was invited to lay individual tributes on Rolls' grave in the churchyard.

Later, a service was held in the larger St Mary's Priory Church, Monmouth conducted by the Vicar of Monmouth, The Reverend David Mc Gladdery followed by a civic reception in the nearby Shirehall in Agincourt Square. High up on the front of the building on a plinth is a statuette of King Henry V who was born in the nearby castle.

At 1430hrs, Lord Raglan led a rededication of the Rolls statue standing prominently outside the Shirehall by unveiling a plaque presented by the RREC and Monmouth Town Council, to match one placed there in 1977 to commemorate the century of his birth. The famous statue itself depicts Rolls holding a model of his Wright bi-plane, finely sculptured by Sir Goscombe John which Lord Raglan's grandfather originally unveiled in 1911.

County and town dignitaries were in their finery and speeches concluded with that of the Mayor of Monmouth expressing her appreciation. The RREC then provided a parade of ten cars ranging in age from 1926 to 2003 which drove past a large and appreciative public audience in Agincourt Square, down the main street and through the arch of the bridge over the River Monnow to the Rolls family seat at The Hendre for refreshments. Unfortunately, poor weather in eastern England prevented the RAF Battle of Britain Memorial Flight from taking off from their home base in Lincolnshire for what was hoped to be an historic aerial display.

A TRIBUTE INDEED:
A fortnight later the Rolls-Royce Enthusiasts' Club held a weekend rally, based at the Hilton Hotel, Newport, to commemorate Rolls' achievements. Although billed as an international Club tribute, the committee of the Welsh Section of the Club planned and executed

Left to right: Many early Rolls-Royce cars carried mascots which reflected individual owners' tastes; Statue of Charles Rolls, Agincourt Square, Monmouth

the event. Cars attended from all over the UK and from abroad and ranged in age from 1909 to 2003. The friendly atmosphere of the Club was soon evident as friends met up again and new acquaintances were made.

Parked under the hotel portico was the magnificent 1922 Silver Ghost (43TG) Park Ward barrel sided tourer driven by George Simpson. It was commissioned by a Glasgow shipbuilder, Arthur C Connell, responsible for the construction of over 500 vessels including ocean liners. It was fitted with the coveted 'Alpine Eagle' high compression engine and especially ordered with all the brightwork in brass. Incredibly in eighty eight years it has covered less than 43,000 miles from new, primarily due to it being conserved both in the Sword Collection in Scotland and the Milligen Collection in Norfolk prior to its present ownership.

Another Silver Ghost was the 1920 car of Derek Allan (16LE). The chassis was built at Rolls-Royce's Derby Factory and shipped to the USA for Salamanca style coachwork to be fitted by Brewster of New York. The detail work is superb reflecting the extremely high quality of build by this American Company.

By far the oldest car was Tony and Vivien Dyas' 1909 Silver Ghost (1179) with open »

66

Lord Raglan led a rededication of the Rolls statue standing prominently outside the Shirehall by unveiling a plaque presented by the RREC and Monmouth Town Council

Roi de Belges style coachwork. Close examination of such early cars brings home just how much ahead of the field Rolls-Royce was at that time. Watch this perform on a hilly road in company with other cars of its era and one is convinced how swift and silent they really were compared with their contemporaries.

The Phantom I, the Silver Ghost's successor, was represented by two examples: the concours 1926 (110TC) open tourer of George and Sharon Miller, on which George has performed a tremendous amount of restoration work himself; and, the much travelled and lovely 1929 (23OR) Barker limousine de ville of Trevor Lewis.

As usual at Club events, the small horsepower cars were well represented notably by Jenny and Derek Johnson's 1926 20hp (GCK78) Hooper saloon and Graham and Mary Moore's 1928 Park Ward (GWL16) award winning car in which they cover a substantial mileage each year and during their ownership of some forty years has become part of the family.

Tod Marshman's 1932 20/25 (GKT23) Park Ward drophead coupé was a real gem in terms of both design and condition and, along with Chris Mott in his 1937 Bentley 4¼ litre (B47JY) Van den Plas drophead coupé, they were able to indulge in open air motoring. Almost every post-war model was represented including Karl Pathe from Germany in his 1949 Silver Wraith (WDC35) fitted with sedanca de ville coachwork by H J Mulliner.

There seemed to be every variation of Rolls-Royce Silver Shadow, Silver Spirit, Silver Seraph as well as Bentley Eight, Turbo, Brooklands and Arnage. Every one was beautifully turned out for the occasion, reflecting owners' model preference and pride of ownership of each example. After dinner Jim Myson gave an excellent slide presentation on Charles Rolls' achievements and his cars from images he had gathered from very many sources.

EXPLORING THE HERITAGE OF WALES:

Saturday morning took our party westwards to the outskirts of Wales' capital city Cardiff to the Museum of Welsh Life at St Fagans. This open air museum depicts, on a large scale, Wales' heritage and what life was like in Wales in centuries past. Over forty historic buildings have been brought to the site from the length and breadth of Wales and painstakingly re-erected and restored on this site donated over half a century ago by the Earl of Plymouth. Early buildings date from the medieval period while more recent additions are those from Wales' industrial past. An outstanding reconstruction is that of St Teilo's church, an unspoiled medieval place of worship, moved in recent years from alongside the M4 motorway near Llanelli, West Wales. During dismantling it was found that the painted wall murals, once common in medieval churches, had largely survived under layers of overpainting and thus could be faithfully reproduced during restoration.

On Saturday evening we were treated to a champagne reception while we listened to the melodious yet powerful voices of the Pontypridd Male Voice Choir. No such prestigious occasion in Wales should be without such a treat. The choir had a vast repertoire of traditional songs and ballads and some of our party even joined in. For the gala dinner the dining room had been especially prepared to reflect our event and a spectacular sight it was too. Above each of the twelve dining tables rose a dark blue air balloon bearing C S Rolls' name and in the basket beneath was a small teddy bear. A side table was adorned with a bust of Rolls with an illuminated balloon behind. It was a fitting backdrop in which to enjoy a splendid meal and enjoy the friendship and companionship that our Club engenders. After a toast to the achievements of Rolls and a few appreciative words from Club Chairman, Tony James, the Four Men in Harmony struck up ≫

Left: 1935 Rolls-Royce 20/25 (GLG 68) Windovers saloon with division. Owner, Robert Stanley
Above (top to bottom): 1936 Rolls-Royce 25/30 (GUL18) Hooper limousine owned by Kelvin and Rita Price; 1926 Rolls-Royce Phantom I (11OTC) Leyshon James tourer owned by James and Sharon Miller; 1928 Rolls-Royce Phantom I (71AL) Hooper landaulette owned by Nigel Taylor

We'll meet in Heaven or the grey between,
Where purged all sin will be,
And ask the Lord to make two souls,
One for Eternity.

with popular themes and had couples gyrating until the early hours.

THE ROLLS COMMEMORATIVE DAY:

Sunday, the big day, started with a run to Chepstow at the mouth of the River Wye past the famous horse racing course and on up the steep sided Lower Wye Valley, the scenery becoming richer by the mile. At this point the river itself becomes the boundary between Wales and England. The first significant village is Tintern, famous for its Cistercian Abbey which springs into view on the floor of the valley. Today its structure is open to the skies but the walls, doorways and soaring arches remain, a mixture of building works covering a 400 year period between 1131 and 1536. On 3 September 1536 Abbot Wyche surrendered Tintern Abbey to King Henry VIII's officials at the time of dissolution of the monasteries in Britain and ended a way of life which had lasted for 400 years. Tintern Abbey was only the second Cistercian foundation in Britain and the first in Wales. It remains the best preserved medieval abbey in Wales.

The route then followed the line of the river passing through a series of picturesque riverside villages on the way to Monmouth where the rendezvous point for our cars was the newly established show ground site just south of the historic town itself. It was an opportunity for occupants to take welcome refreshment. The number of Rolls-Royce and Bentley cars was swelled by those joining in for the day with the total now approaching 100. These included Simon Buck's 1952 Silver Wraith (WOF58) by Freestone and Webb, a number of pre-war small horsepower cars and even more post-war models. The lines of Anthony and Teddy Beach-Thomas' 1929 Phantom II (81XJ) Barker ≫

Above: 1964 Silver Cloud III (SFU619) James Young four door saloon
Opposite (top to bottom): 1936 Rolls-Royce 25/30 (GUL18) Hooper limousine owned by Kelvin and Rita Price at Tintern Abbey; A personal choice of mascot on 1935 Rolls-Royce 20/25 (GLG68)

" The number of Rolls-Royce and Bentley cars was swelled by those joining in for the day with the total now approaching 100

With a police escort, our procession drove into Monmouth past the Rolls Hall that was built by the Rolls family

sedanca de ville were quite outstanding, parked alongside Anthony and Gilly Armitage's 1928 Phantom I (65CL) polished aluminium tourer. An outstanding Phantom I was the Hooper landaulette (71AL) of Nigel Taylor resplendent in claret and black livery looking every bit as good as the day it was delivered to its first owner Lady Michaelis in 1928.

With a police escort, our procession drove into Monmouth past the Rolls Hall that was built by the Rolls family as a public assembly hall and is currently in use as the town's library. After a brief pause, we entered streets closed to other traffic but lined by the general public all of whom were keen to see our parade pass slowly into Agincourt Square past Charles Rolls' statue and on down the main street over the 13th Century stone bridge spanning the River Monnow. The crowds were out in great numbers, all cheering and waving enthusiastically. The Klaxon horn on the early cars was most popular with the public. The crowds thinned on the far side of the town as we headed out into open country towards Rockfield village and on to The Hendre, Rolls' family home.

THE HENDRE: The mansion itself has not been fully utilised since the 1970s when it was used as a residential school for children with special needs. Some years ago the grounds were adapted for use by the Rolls of Monmouth Golf Club. Members use the garage, built for Charles Rolls in 1905, as their club house. The golf club also uses the outbuildings as well as part of the mansion when special events are held such as ours. We parked as many early Club cars as possible in the quadrangle in front of the main entrance, a backdrop to many early photographs. We were greeted by a most welcome Pimms followed by an excellent high tea. Although the unused parts of the house were out of bounds to the curious, Andrew Helme, Curator of Monmouth Museum, »

Left (top to bottom): Detail of rear wheel of early Rolls-Royce Silver Ghost; 1909 Rolls-Royce Silver Ghost (1179) with Roi de Belges coachwork owned by Tony and Vivien Dyas
Above: 1979 Silver Shadow II (SRH36828) four door saloon

displayed photographs and artefacts appertaining to the mansion itself. The museum holds many Rolls related photographs and a number of exhibits including a recently acquired trophy awarded to the Rolls-Royce 4 cylinder Light 20hp (40523) in Florida in 1907 and long thought to have been lost.

Before our departure, a presentation was made by the RREC to Mrs Harding-Rolls who lives locally, her family having inherited the name from Patty, an aunt of Charles Rolls.

A leisurely run back to the hotel rounded off a memorable occasion which will be a vivid reminder to participants and spectators alike. Each car received an even more tangible reminder in the form of a china plate especially made to commemorate the occasion by the Monmouth China Company depicting scenes from Charles Rolls' activities with a suitable inscription around the perimeter.

THE LEGACY: Today when one takes a flight in a modern airliner, as one cruises some seven miles above the earth's surface in reasonable comfort, it is sobering to reflect just how far man has come in conquering the skies since Charles Rolls' days. Back on the ground an all too familiar symbol often catches the eye, on the engine cowling, of two interlocking Rs above which in bold capitals is the name Rolls. What better epitaph could any man have to his vision a century on? ▣

Above: Cars assemble in the quadrangle in front of the main entrance at The Hendre

THERE'S A NEW

GHOST

IN THE HOUSE

by Tom Stewart

Rolls-Royce has resuscitated an ancient and honourable name, or very nearly, with their newest model, the Ghost. As you might expect, it embodies a haunting mixture of tradition and technology

The Ghost name was born in 1907 when Rolls-Royce's MD, Claude Johnson, silver-plated the fittings of a 40/50hp model and painted the coachwork silver. Making an immediate impact, the car quickly became known as The Silver Ghost – a name that aptly reflected both its silent running and appearance.

Now scroll forward some 103 years to May 2010, when the company announced the Rolls-Royce Ghost Design iPhone app, which allows potential customers and enthusiasts to configure their own Ghost from a large variety of paint schemes, veneers, leathers and wheel designs, and, when complete, save their favourites in a virtual garage.

Mr Johnson would no doubt have struggled to comprehend the concept of an iPhone, or indeed any of its apps, but he'd surely have been hugely impressed and indeed proud to learn that the Ghost name would eventually return – which it did at the 2009 Frankfurt motorshow.

POWERFUL AND PURPOSEFUL: Little was seen of the new car, codenamed RR4, until the spring of 2008, when Rolls-Royce released the first official sketches. The styling was instantly recognisable as a Rolls-Royce, although less traditional than previous models. As Chief Designer Ian Cameron said at the time: "The RR4 has a more informal presence than the Phantom models with a greater emphasis on driving. In design terms this is expressed through its slightly smaller dimensions, yet with powerful, purposeful proportions. It is a true and uncompromising Rolls-Royce in every sense."

The Ghost is built around a steel monocoque body, which allows for a reduction in exterior dimensions while preserving interior space. Consequently, although the Ghost is some 400mm shorter than the Phantom saloon, its interior space is comparable.

Powered by a brand new, unique-to-the-model 6-litre twin-turbo V12, the direct-injection engine produces 563bhp – enough to propel the Ghost from 0-60 mph in just 4.7 seconds and on to an electronically-governed 155mph top speed. With 780Nm of torque available at just 1,500rpm, power is transmitted to the rear wheels via an 8-speed, shift-by-wire, automatic ZF gearbox.

According to the car's press material, the Ghost is 'more driver-focused than any Rolls-Royce before it', while 'delivery of power is both immediate and extremely smooth'. "Our challenge,"

Above: Details of the new Ghost, with its impressive, high-tech interior
Right: The distinctive lines of its highly illustrious ancestor, the Silver Ghost

blood,
e.

late

> 66
>
> *The most modern, dynamically*
> *interesting drive ever in a Rolls-Royce*

said Engineering Director Helmut Riedl, "was to preserve the prerequisite levels of comfort while delivering the most modern, dynamically interesting drive ever in a Rolls-Royce."

Having had the privilege of a short time at the wheel of a Ghost on a demanding test circuit I can testify to the above. At almost two tonnes unladen this car is no flyweight, but with double-wishbone front suspension and multi-link rear suspension working in conjunction with an intelligent air-suspension system and electronic variable damping, the response and accuracy of its steering, the seemingly relentless surge of strong acceleration, coupled of course with a suitably compliant ride, all mitigate the car's substantial mass and proportions.

And did I detect the subtle presence of a sporting engine/exhaust note? I think I did, although while being chauffeured briskly around the same route there was nothing to compromise the refinement, comfort and indeed opulence of the back seat experience. Within the Ghost's ample doors and high shoulder line, occupants feel serene, cosseted and safe. In the rear, the intimate ambience of the lounge seat is emphasised by its positioning behind the C-pillar, heightening the sense of privacy. Further enhancing the interior ambience is the 600-watt, 10-channel audio system that delivers up to 600 watts

of sound through no less than 16 speakers. The strong sense of well-being and security is further supported by a abundance of up-to-the-minute safety features. Beams in the front and rear doors combine with progressive rear crumple zones to absorb impacts, while the Ghost's Advanced Crash and Safety Management system takes measurements 2,000 times per second from sensors around the vehicle. Other electronic safety aids include Anti-Roll Stabilisation, Dynamic Brake Control and Dynamic Stability Control, all working together under dual Integrated Chassis Management systems.

ADEQUATELY SOLVENT: The first Ghost customers took delivery of their cars at the end of December 2009. Rolls-Royce won't be drawn on the relative production volumes of each model, but suffice to say that when production is fully 'ramped-up', more Ghosts will leave the Chichester factory than Phantoms, and with an on-the-road price of around £200,000 – some £75,000 less than the standard-wheelbase Phantom saloon – Ghost customers are also likely to be 'adequately solvent'.

The Ghost adds to the current Rolls-Royce line-up by providing a more involving driving experience in a slightly less formal guise.

Although not entirely pertinent, it is nonetheless tempting to make comparisons between today's Ghost and certain Rolls-Royce models of yesteryear. Is it perhaps the contemporary equivalent of an HJ Mulliner Silver Cloud 'Flying Spur' saloon of the late '50s/early '60s? Or, going back to pre-war times, could the Ghost be considered the 2010 incarnation of a sporty short-chassis Continental saloon of the early 1930s?

Or, travelling back in time even further, might it be akin to the Continental's forebear – the Silver Ghost? And thus we've come full circle… although I don't believe there was an iPhone app for any of the older models. ▣

A VINTAGE YEAR FOR

BENTLEY

by Tom Stewart

made flesh and ...
... soul put there.
... , we knew not Fate
... ed her plan
meet, an autumn eve,
... for the man.

Bentley has had a fine 2010, building on past glories to unveil exciting new models, expand globally and even move into the world of sustainability with its alternative fuel strategy

In the 91 years of Bentley Motors' illustrious existence, 2010 may not have been quite as sensational or turbulent as some, but the year nonetheless saw significant progress and proud achievement at Crewe, particularly with regard to new and exciting model developments.

The culmination of four years' work, Bentley's magnificent new Mulsanne made its world debut at the Pebble Beach Concours d'Elegance event in August 2009, with detailed specifications and the subsequent press launch of the car following in the Spring of 2010. With the long-serving Arnage having ceased production a year earlier – the last of the Final Series Arnages going to customers in the Autumn of '09 – the company was effectively without a flagship, four-door 'big Bentley' until deliveries of the new Mulsanne commenced in late September 2010.

As part of the company's ongoing investment in both new models and the Crewe factory itself, a new body assembly facility had been built specifically for the Mulsanne. However, no more than about 700-800 Mulsannes will be built per year, a figure representing around 10 per cent of Crewe's annual production volume.

No-one was too surprised when company Chairman and Chief Executive Dr Franz-Josef Paefgen declared the new Mulsanne to be "the best car Bentley ever made" but equally importantly, according to Bentley's Worldwide PR Director Mike Hawes, "public reaction to the Mulsanne has been phenomenal. By late Summer 2010 production was already covered right through to the end of 2011, so customers who placed an order in late 2010 will probably have to wait until early 2012 to take delivery – a healthy situation for any manufacturer."

GREENER AND CLEANER: FlexFuel technology forms one part of Bentley's three-part strategy to reduce its cars' impact on the environment. According to Hawes, "We believe that sustainable biofuels offer great potential to reduce the overall emissions of the transport sector." Consequently, at the Geneva show in early March, Bentley announced that FlexFuel, pioneered on the 2009 Continental Supersports Coupe, would now extend across the 2011 Continental range, including the new 630 horsepower Supersports Convertible. This, the most potent Bentley drop-top ever, would subsequently make its public driving debut at the Goodwood Festival of Speed in July. »

We believe that sustainable biofuels offer great potential to reduce the overall emissions of the transport sector

Just five days later at the 60th Pebble Beach Concours the company announced the debut of two limited-edition dropheads, the Continental GTC and GTC Speed 80-11 models. Designed exclusively for the North American market, just 80 of each will be built in 2011.

WEB SHOW: Arguably the most significant and certainly the most novel Bentley event of 2010 occurred in early September when the new 2011 Continental GT was first revealed online. This allowed viewers to experience the drama and excitement of a formal motor show unveiling before the Paris show in October. Following the car's press launch in November it's expected that the first 'new Continental' customer deliveries will take place at the end of the first quarter of 2011.

Launched in 2003, the previous Continental spearheaded Bentley's renaissance by offering an entirely new driving experience. Over 22,000 Continental GT models have been delivered to customers, while the strength of its engineering and design inspired the Flying Spur saloons, and, more recently, the GT Speed, the convertible GTC and the astonishing 204mph Supersports variants.

Prior to revealing the new Continental GT, Mike Hawes commented, "The Continental has become very symbolic of the company. It's loved by so many of our customers and it was very clear that in the new car we had to retain the essence of what made it an iconic car, but at the same time invigorate the styling, completely overhaul the interior and bring the car's infotainment up to date with the very latest technologies."

From late 2011 the Continental will, for the first time, be available with a choice of powertrains, as an all-new, high-output 4-litre V8 will join the existing W12 engine in the range. In addition to giving customers a frugal alternative, the new V8 will honour Bentley's environmental commitments by lowering CO_2 by 40 per cent, which in turn will help the company toward its commitment to reduce average fleet emissions by 15 per cent by 2012.

CHANGING TIMES: Bentley as a company has seen considerable change since the late 1990s. Back then sales were as few as 1,000 cars per year, but following VW's takeover and its investment both in the Crewe plant and new product between 1998 and 2002, sales increased massively from 2003 onward.

In 2007, for example, 10,014 cars were sold, mostly Continentals, with sales of the Arnage remaining level at around 600 to 800 cars per year. Not many by the standards of some, but, just as it will be for the new Mulsanne, such levels ensured the Arnage's exclusivity and individuality, while also being in-line with Crewe's production capacity for the bespoke car.

It's perhaps too early to officially declare 2010 a vintage year for Bentley Motors, but it was a very fine one and the company's future is certainly looking rosy.

With apologies to Pablo Picasso, 'Bentley doesn't grow older, it grows riper'. ▣

Above: The very rapid Supersports

STYLE

2 » *Fine Jewellery & Timepieces*

2» STYLE

DESIGN EXCELLENCE

JESPER VELLING BLENDS AESTHETIC COOL WITH ENGINEERING
EXCELLENCE IN HIS JEWELLERY CREATIONS

> *The process of commissioning a bespoke piece of jewellery is intensely personal. The result should be special and, of course, unique*

Those who appreciate the astonishing beauty that can be formed from a combination of engineering brilliance and aesthetic genius will appreciate the work of Jesper Velling.

An extraordinary mix of engineer, architect and jeweller, each piece from Jesper's collection is packed full of surprise and ingenuity. He enjoys playing with form and provoking surprise, astonishment and incredulity in equal measure.

Take, for example, his spiky choker, which he designed and constructed as part of a project, while studying at the Kent Institute of Art & Design, looking at reflective surfaces. Each spike is cast in silver and intricately hinged together to form a beautiful, bold, wearable sculpture.

'I love the whole process, from generating an idea, thinking in three dimensions and working with precious materials to overcoming challenges, and ultimately creating something that is truly unique and exquisite,' he says.

His diamond twist necklace demonstrates how much engineering prowess Jesper employs. The necklace is made from 25 links that are joined together to give the appearance of a continuous spiral. The spiral is made from four interlinked wires and each of the four sides is channel set with diamonds. The result is extraordinary – a necklace with a diamond weight of approximately 62 carats held in 126 grams of white gold that appears light, yet strong.

BEAUTY: Unsurprisingly, Jesper's collections have won many awards. The Goldsmiths' Craft & Design Council has bestowed upon him numerous accolades, including gold awards for craftmanship (diamond mounting, and setting) and a silver award for design, as well as being commended in the category of designer-finished pieces. Most prestigious of all, however, is the Goldsmiths' Special Council Award, which they bestowed on Jesper in 2007.

BESPOKE: Jesper is equally at home creating bespoke pieces for private clients. This might involve working on an entirely new creation, producing something to complement existing pieces or to overcome specific issues a client may have.

'My inspiration comes from the people I create jewellery for; matching the spirit and aspirations of a person is deeply satisfying,' Jesper says.

As with all his work, ingenuity lies at the heart of his bespoke creations. For one client with severe arthritis, Jesper's solution was to make a hinged replica of her engagement ring. For another, it was to turn a sentimental keepsake (a shell found on a beach on honeymoon) into a lasting, beautiful, wearable memory. The process of commissioning a bespoke piece of jewellery is intensely personal. The result should be special and, of course, unique. Jesper works hard to ensure every commission is suited to the style, personality and budget of the client.

'If there is an object, colour, shape, icon or memory that means something special to a client or someone they cherish, I can make that into something precious to carry with them,' he says.

Award-winning, stylish, with an extraordinary eye for form and an innate understanding of his precious materials and what they can achieve, Jesper Velling is a simply inimitable jeweller. ▣

CONTACT: www.jespervelling.com

A JEWELLERY
RENAISSANCE

AMRAPALI SHOWCASES THE
EXCLUSIVITY AND MAGNIFICENCE
OF HANDMADE JEWELLERY

In India, jewellery is treated with the utmost importance; it is considered an investment, a story, an heirloom. Virtually every family in the country has one or more pieces that are passed through generations. Embracing this ethos to create distinctive designs with a modern twist on the ancient and ethnic, Amrapali captures this heritage, quality and sincerity.

Amrapali is a family business started by Rajiv Arora in 1978 as a first-generation entrepreneur. His parents and grandparents were doctors or lawyers, and had wanted him to follow a similar 'secure' profession. But, Rajiv loved India's history and culture, and wanted to create something that represented this. Together with partner Rajesh Ajmera, they began a jewellery design and creation service that took the world by storm, today boasting 22 outlets globally.

> " With an Indian contemporary, ethnic-chic look, 90 per cent of Amrapali's jewellery is completely handmade

The company's grand and ornate necklaces, rings and bangles, encrusted with gold, silver, emeralds, rubies, sapphires, pearls and exquisite rose-cut diamonds regularly adorn the likes of Halle Berry, Megan Fox, Sandra Bullock and Freida Pinto on the red carpet. Amrapali is also the only Indian jewellery displayed on the Milan and New York fashion weeks' catwalks, and has featured in a Hollywood blockbuster, *Troy*, with the likes of Brad Pitt and Orlando Bloom wearing specially commissioned designs.

HERITAGE: Much of Amrapali's style expresses the influence of Kundan Jadau, a traditional method of gem setting and the oldest form in India. This process involves surrounding the base of precious stones with numerous 24-carat gold sheets to create a layered mount, and is believed to have originated in royal courts of Rajasthan and Gujarat.

To create its Indian contemporary, ethnic-chic look, 90 per cent of Amrapali's jewellery is completely handmade – no machine ever being able to achieve the intricacy, or care, that the human touch affords.

And while many jewellery companies only look at the front of a piece, Amrapali provides equal importance and attention to both sides, something known in India as *meenakari*. 'When you wear the jewellery,' says Tarang, the son of Rajiv and UK Director, 'the front is for the world to see, but the back is to enjoy and appreciate alone. This is very important in Indian jewellery; it's the completion of every piece. What you can't see needs to be as important as what you can.' To this end, all of Amrapali's designs have intricate enamelling on the unseen parts, and the company has even produced gold earrings that have the diamonds mounted in reverse. 'We are selling a piece of art,' adds Tarang, 'something that is more than just a piece of jewellery.'

The year 2010 saw Amrapali produce its most challenging piece to date: an elaborate gold necklace set with more than 95 carats of top-quality rose-cut diamonds, something Tarang describes as a 'statement piece'.

With Tarang's desire to make Amrapali 'the biggest, most popular Indian jewellery brand in the world,' and with its meteoric rise in popularity over recent years, it looks like the family business is set to become a household name synonymous with quality and luxury. ▣

CONTACT: www.amrapalijewels.com

BRINGING
IMAGINATION
TO LIFE

EVERY PIECE CREATED BY JACOBS JEWELLERY IS TRULY ONE OF A KIND

Imagination is what drives Barry Jacobs and his exceptional team of jewellery designers. Not just their own imagination but, more importantly, that of their clients. Making that imagination come to life is at the heart of Jacobs Jewellery Design. Every aspect of every piece of jewellery it creates is uniquely tailored to the imagination of the individual.

Discretion is what makes a piece by Jacobs Jewellery so desirable. It is not a household name, and its jewels do not appear on the must-have pages of glossy magazines. Jacobs Jewellery would not have it any other way. Everything the company does is bespoke for the client alone – making every piece one of a kind. As Barry Jacobs explains: 'Our job is to provide a service that is absolutely second to none, and which produces a piece that the client knows is unique because it has come from them.' It is this discretion that has won Jacobs Jewellery a fiercely loyal client-base, all of whom came to the company from word-of-mouth recommendation.

We provide a service that is absolutely second to none, and which produces a piece that the client knows is unique

Above all, it is the experience of using Jacobs Jewellery that clients recommend. Not only does it create exquisite, timeless pieces of lasting beauty, it also provides a unique experience – a journey – that is cherished as much as the work it produces.

UNIQUE: The small, family-run business's team of highly skilled craftsmen approach each task with a blank sheet of paper and 100 years of experience between them. Every piece commissioned from Jacobs Jewellery is crafted in the traditional manner using the finest raw materials: the metal that is teased into daring mounts with astonishing detail is always platinum or 18-carat white, yellow, or rose gold, and the precious stones are sourced from the world's most renowned gemstone markets in New York, Antwerp and Mumbai and are always conflict-free.

Once these raw materials have been sourced for the client, everything about the piece of jewellery is designed and created entirely in-house. Barry Jacobs himself will visit clients or welcome them to the workshop to discuss the piece they wish to create. In-house watercolour painters and artists will then prepare design mock-ups for clients to review, amend and approve. 'Only when every 'i' has been dotted and every 't' has been crossed, and the client is entirely comfortable that the design really reflects what they had in mind, will work begin,' explains Barry.

ACCOLADES: Because every element of a Jacobs Jewellery creation is completed in-house, coupled with the immense experience of its designers, the company has carved out a reputation in the industry for making complex pieces of great distinction and beauty.

In the last year this has been recognised at The UK Jewellery Awards, where Jacobs Jewellery was shortlisted for supplier of the year, alongside some of the biggest companies in the industry. Barry has also been asked by the board of directors of London Jewellery Week to be the ambassador for Hatton Garden in recognition of the work he has done there, not to mention the work he does to promote the diamond trade more widely and to encourage young people to join the industry. It is a great honour and well deserved, as Barry's passion for his craft is a rare thing in a very competitive industry. It can be summed up in his own words: 'I love this industry and the people in it, and I feel privileged to be part of it.' ▣

CONTACT: barryjacobs@jacobsjewellery.co.uk

BAYCO IS A RELATIVELY NEW NAME IN THE WORLD OF
PRECIOUS GEMSTONES, YET IT DRAWS ON THREE
GENERATIONS OF EXPERTISE TO REMAIN LARGELY
UNRIVALLED IN RARITY, ELEGANCE AND SOPHISTICATION

A QUEST FOR
PERFECTION

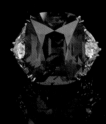 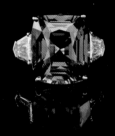

Marco Hadjibay, Managing Director of Bayco and grandson of fabled gem trader, Amir Hadjibay, says: 'For the splendour of our collection to be appreciated, it has to be seen. In the same way the world has come to know stones such as the Rockefeller Sapphire, there are sapphires that could have been named the Bayco Sapphire.' The awe-inspiring quality of Bayco's gemstones is equally present in the intricate work involved in producing each piece. Seamlessly fusing regional and temporal styles, Bayco's jewellery frequently incorporates aspects of classical, Mogul and modern-era design – a fusion of eastern and western aesthetics that bears accurate testimony to the company's origins in both worlds.

DREAMS: The story of Bayco is that of a family-run business spanning three generations over several continents, with the aim of providing the ultimate in luxury jewellery to a discerning elite. The story begins in 1945 when Amir, a 16-year-old Iranian entrepreneur in the textile trade between Iran and India, acquired his first gemstones. 'It was the mystique of the gemstones that first captured Amir's imagination,' explains Moris Hadjibay, the second of Amir's sons and father of Marco. 'For thousands of years, gemstones have been given as gifts to celebrate happy occasions, confer status or affirm bonds, and Amir was appreciative of how gemstones could take on social significance. For us, jewellery has always been about making somebody's dream come true.'

In the years following the Second World War, a thriving market for high-end jewellery and gemstones developed in Italy, and in 1957 Amir moved his family and business to Italy. By this stage, Amir had acquired considerable industry experience and a network of reliable contacts in jewel capitals across the world. He used this to his advantage, and quickly consolidated a reputation for delivering rare gemstones and jewellery of exceptional quality.

FUSION: Twenty-five years later, relocating the business had once again become a serious consideration. 'By the 1980s it was clear that if we wanted to remain at the centre of the gemstone market and develop a global brand, we needed a presence in New York,' recounts Giacomo Hadjibay, the youngest of Amir's three sons. 'So, in 1982, Moris and I established a second office in New York, eventually closing the office in Italy in 1995.' It was also in 1982 that the family business adopted the name Bayco. 'We needed a distinctive name for the business, so we created the name Bayco from the last three letters of "Hadjibay" and the first two letters of "company".'

As well as perfecting a trademark fusion of eastern and western aesthetics, Bayco has similarly perfected a balance of traditional and modern elements in aesthetic and business terms. 'Our company has changed a great deal over the years in trying to adapt to the changes that take place over time,' Marco explains. 'But we've always believed in keeping traditions as clean as possible. It's a very old trade, and a good reputation has always been a jeweller's lifeblood. So it's very much a quest for perfection: every step is under scrutiny – buying, designing, producing, selling… everything. We source only the finest stones, accept only the highest-quality workmanship and operate on only the most ethical of business principles. In our trade it's all about honour, and a handshake is worth more than a contract.' ▣

CONTACT: www.bayco.com

DESIGN
FOR DIAMONDS

A DIAMONDART DESIGN IS MORE THAN FINE JEWELLERY, IT IS FINE ART

Having grown up surrounded by artists and creatives, it had always been Assuntina Oliva's childhood dream to create beautiful, distinctive pieces of fine jewellery.

Today, with more than 20 years' experience under her belt, the Italian designer's creations have become recognised and loved for their composition, craftsmanship and true individualism.

Her company, Diamondart, was born through a realisation that many jewellery aficionados were not interested in 'the high-street look', but yearned for something as unique and distinctive as their own tastes. Only using platinum and gold upwards of 18ct, most of Assuntina's pieces are stone set using the highest-quality, ethically sourced, diamonds, rubies, emeralds and sapphires, while the choice of precious metals is a combination of what the client wants and what the design demands.

'We're all about luxury, beauty, elegance, sophistication and quality expressed through the design, the materials, and the workmanship lovingly applied to create each and every piece,' says Assuntina. 'We believe that jewellery is an extension of your personality; it says something about you, just in the same way that your clothes do, where you shop or what car you drive. Our task is building an understanding of clients' needs relating to the piece of jewellery we create for them. This way the result becomes an expression of the wearer – a piece that says "this is me".'

VISIONARY: Design challenges come in many forms to Assuntina. 'People often ask me what have been the most challenging commissions and my answer is all of them,' she says. 'The true task of any good designer is to match a client's expectations with the actuality of their unique piece of jewellery – from those gifting the piece to someone very special, to those who want a design to represent something unique.

'The gifting challenge is making sure that what I create is what the recipient wants, and because it is a gift and I don't have the wearer to discuss their likes and dislikes, I am totally reliant on the commissioner. My role in the initial stage is that of a detective, if you like. Clients bring me any favourite pieces of jewellery the recipient has (all very discreetly!) and any images of other jewellery that they may have commented on, both positively, and equally importantly, negatively. Once all this information is gathered I can then confidently start to put together designs that will be turned into a fabulous finished piece.

'The representational challenge is all about jewellery that looks like something specific, and this often takes the form of animals, in particular someone's pet. The challenge here is incorporating a high level of detail, balanced with the most important factor, wearability.'

SUPERIORITY: Diamondart uses the country's leading jewellery artisans, who incorporate the latest technology alongside traditional methods to create pieces that make a statement. And while the majority of commissions are through recommendations, client relationships are totally confidential. 'We enjoy being reserved and mysterious – it's another facet that differentiates us from ordinary jewellers. Our clients feel like they have joined a select few,' adds Assuntina.

Wearing a piece of exquisitely designed Diamondart is more than just fine jewellery – it is a piece of beauty and ingenuity; an heirloom that will speak of its owner for generations to come. ▣

CONTACT: www.diamondart.co.uk

CRAFTSMANSHIP, HISTORY AND CREATIVE DESIGN
ARE ALL SHOWCASED IN THESE STUNNING RANGES
OF BEAUTIFUL WATCHES

A s CYMA celebrates its 150th birthday in 2012 with the launch of Myriad, an incredible new range of products, it illustrates the company's reputation as an innovative specialist in developing and promoting luxury timepieces. As worldwide distributor of CYMA SA Switzerland products, E-Watch Suisse Sàrl offer the perfect blend of futuristic, technological prowess and unique creativity, combined with an unmatched knowledge of Swiss watchmaking traditions. The history behind this company reveals some stunning statistics, as CYMA has sold more than 40 million watches worldwide since it opened for business in 1862 and swiftly experienced a dazzling growth, becoming the biggest watchmaker of precision timepieces in Europe. In 1930 CYMA created The Captive, opening the way to the ladies' dream watch. Collette, the legendary French writer, described this beautiful timepiece in tones close to love. 'It is a captive in the most romantic sense of the word; we buy it, we sell it,' she said in her characteristic style, clearly captivated by its elegance and precision. 'Sensitive and easy, it gives in if you press it with

TIMELESS
TIMEPIECES

"

This visionary company produces the perfect blend of futuristic, technological prowess and unique creativity

master hands, reveals its face, divulging all its secrets, and every assent is one more charm in its favour.'

INDIVIDUALITY: While the company is clearly used to its products being worn by the rich and famous, this is not what drives the distinctive policy that has been an intrinsic part of the company ethos since the outset. A perfect combination of artistic, creative and innovative skills is the bedrock on which CYMA SA and E-Watch Suisse Sàrl have developed their reputation, with the unique Swiss watchmaking tradition enhancing an already enchanting product. The strangest value and main objective is always being as close as possible to the customers, recognising that every individual customer deserves the same respect and attention to detail.

The new collection, Myriad, is an excellent example of this concept, presenting a technological delight in a beautiful and elegant watch which doesn't need to be worn by someone famous to showcase all its properties, yet will undoubtedly appeal to many in the public eye. E-Watch wants

its customers to obtain an awesome, quality watch for a good price and wear it with pride, recognising the craftsmanship, history and creative design which all make up the stunning Myriad. A customer buying a CYMA or a Myriad product can be certain that the price paid for it reflects the valuable components and technology of the watch, and not the commissioning of a famous person.

TIMELESSNESS: The current CYMA collections and new Myriad collection will continue to draw customers who have a fervent admiration of beautiful timepieces, with quality and style which resonates back through the company history. Conversely, CYMA can be described as timeless, presenting classic designs and workmanship that have rendered some watches as family heirlooms, passed from one generation to the next in a way which reflects the strong links the company forges with so many of its customers.

The luxury of these watches lies not just in the appearance of the stunning creations, but in the knowledge of the watchmakers, the technological development, the quality of the components, the design of the timepieces and, of course, the value that each customer attributes to their own watch. What makes them truly luxurious is the choice in buying them, recognising a shared vision between company and customer, which celebrates the tradition, service, quality and exceptional care surrounding every watch at every step of manufacture before it leaves the workshops. As CYMA celebrates its 150th birthday, it also celebrates the integrity and quality that has made the company such a success.

CONTACT: www.myriad.ch; www.cyma.ch

JEWELLERY
WITH
PERSONALITY

The expression 'opposites attract' is certainly true of the design duo behind distinctive jewellery brand Francesca Sibylla Augusta. Zinzi Coetzee and Ursula Horton's individual tastes and styles merge to create a complementary, fresh and funky jewellery range that draws inspiration from diverse sources.

CONNECTION: Zinzi and Ursula first met while studying fashion at Central Saint Martin's College. 'We feel that it is the savvy, outlandish fashion perspective developed from our years studying that injects a cheeky, delicious indulgence into our jewellery,' explains Ursula. However, it wasn't until they took a trip to Tokyo together that they realised how a combination of their personal tastes could create fun and exciting jewellery designs, so they each undertook a Master's in Design Management at the London College of Fashion to transform their idea into a business reality.

With an aim to break the boundaries between disposable costume and traditional fine jewellery,

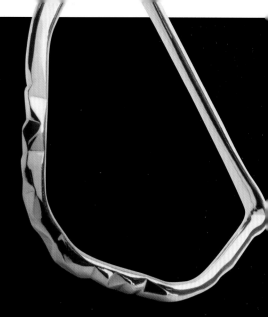

VIBRANT, ATTENTION-GRABBING DESIGNS
ENSURE FRANCESCA SIBYLLA AUGUSTA'S
JEWELLERY IS UNLIKE ANY OTHER

FSAugusta features three distinct collections: Fine, which uses 18-carat gold, diamonds and precious stones; Fashion Jewellery that is made with 18-carat gold plate, 925 silver and gemstones; and Silver Classics, which features silver pieces set with precious stones. All of these collections aim to combine traditional hand craftsmanship with modern styles and technology, while incorporating the brand's distinctive flair.

DAZZLING: Inspiration for the pieces comes from a myriad of eclectic sources, but Ursula explains that they have an underpinning design formula that can be categorised within four genres – art, fashion, innovation and classical jewellery – and this has seen the duo draw ideas from the work of Salvador Dali and Jeff Koons, style icons such as Lady Gaga, Grace Kelly and Marilyn Monroe, and the glitz and glamour of the Wynn Hotel, Las Vegas. 'The designing process is the most important, and I love the way that Zinzi and I can translate our ideas and inspirations into jewellery that is a wonderful mix of originality and luxury,' says Ursula. 'Our brand is constantly moving forward and our seasonal collections reflect the need for jewellery that is intelligent, witty and refreshing in the market, while building on a signature style that gives birth to timeless future jewellery classics.'

This enthusiasm and passion for jewellery, and the variety of inspiration, result in eye-catching, exclusive pieces, such as the popular Pig Ring, Dali Facet Bangle, Thorny Devil earrings and necklaces, Komodo Egg rings and the new signature FSA Bow. 'Our specific design structure for each season ensures we have a unique result when we produce our jewellery,' adds Zinzi. 'The key is to be aware and as open to new ideas as possible.'

ACKNOWLEDGMENT: Since its launch at the International Jewellery Show in September 2008, the company has grown at an astonishing rate with recognition from the fashion industry, professionals and customers alike; the jewellery has been featured in the pages of *Vanity Fair* and *Grazia*, as well as Vogue.com, and spotted adorning the likes of Rihanna, Fearne Cotton, Daisy Lowe and Ellie Goulding. In 2009, FSAugusta won the Coutts New Jewellers Award and Highly Commended Collections New Designer Award, sponsored by Stephen Webster who enthused: 'FSA has created an attention-seeking, fun collection – the one thing that everyone in the marketplace is looking for.'

The collections are currently sold in Kabiri designer jewellery stores in London and in Selfridges, as well as boutiques in Greenwich, Chelsea, Brighton, Sweden, Madrid and West Hollywood. And FSAugusta is set to expand even further, with a focus on evolving and marketing the brand internationally in Europe, the USA, Asia and Australia. 'The brand is totally self-sufficient and, in many ways, FSAugusta's strength lies in the motivation and working relationship that Zinzi and I have created,' explains Ursula. ▣

CONTACT: www.FSAugusta.co.uk

DISTINCTIVE
DECORATION

TAKING INSPIRATION FROM
BYGONE ERAS, KAJA GJEDEBO
BRINGS HER UNIQUE STYLE TO
A VARIETY OF ACCESSORIES

A ccessories are what give an outfit character, colour and individuality. Many people, therefore, aim to choose the most distinctive or unique adornments in order to truly reflect their personality, and Kaja Gjedebo Design fully understands how best to make an impact and complement any outfit with a pair of cufflinks or piece of jewellery.

Educated at Edinburgh College of Art, primarily in furniture design, Kaja was studying jewellery as a secondary subject but, after winning a Royal College of Art student award in the field, decided to focus on jewellery design after graduation.

VINTAGE: Drawing on her artistic background, Kaja's cufflink designs are creative and unique; handmade using original vintage materials. These include stamps she uses to embed into the cufflinks that date back to 1930s Russia, Germany and Eastern Europe, and some of her collection is

Cufflink designs are creative and unique; handmade using original vintage materials

almost 100 years old. Using resin in all her designs, Kaja creates a background for the cufflinks using images and text from sources as diverse as vintage postcards, posters and magazines. 'A neighbour was throwing out a lot of recipe books and brochures from the 1950s, which were perfect,' she explains. 'But I pick up images from everywhere – the Internet, shops and markets.' As an added distinctive flourish, Kaja creates miniature 3D dioramas within the cufflinks using small model figures and objects (largely from model train sets), which she says fit the vintage theme ideally: 'Because model railways were very popular as a hobby in the 1950s and 60s, all the figures are in period dress.' Customers are also encouraged to suggest their own ideas and Kaja has previously made cufflinks with images of cars, pets, boats and even, for one expectant customer, an ultra-sound scan.

ACHIEVE: Kaja's cufflink designs first became a hit when she began selling them from her jewellery stall at a fashionable outdoor market. Now, alongside receiving the accolade of Highly Commended at the International Jewellery London event in 2009, Kaja's designs are sold in a wide range of exclusive shops in Norway, Berlin, Hamburg, and London's prestigious Burlington Arcade and trendy Brick Lane, as well as to a number of private customers across the world. 'Now I really want to expand my range of female jewellery,' she says.

'Women tell me they love the cufflinks and have been asking me if I can recreate the style in rings, pendants and bracelets, which I really enjoy doing as I can indulge in details whilst producing larger designs.'

ORIGINAL: Having recently moved to a new home in Oslo, which has its own large studio attached and is surrounded by likeminded artists, Kaja hopes to be able to employ someone in the future to assist with her pieces. She is aware, however, that the personalised aspect of her company and the fact that she is responsible for every item, from design to production, is a positive aspect for her customers: 'As I do everything myself, my customers know that every design is different and that each image I use is unique. They are buying an original piece and there will be no one else with the same piece of jewellery or pair of cufflinks.'

With customers ranging from 18-year-old students to retired businessmen, it seems Kaja's designs are as unique and distinctive as the person wearing them. ▣

CONTACT: www.kgd.no
IMAGES: (L–R) Gentleman cufflinks © Chris Harrison; bracelet and bad guy cufflinks © Geir Dokken

SUBSTANCE AND
STYLE

*Every piece created is part of
a continuous and fascinating
experimental journey*

Intriguing, mysterious and exclusive, the jewellery conceived and created by Liana Pattihis is designed to make a contemporary statement. Using unique methods of fusing enamel on various types of silver and gold chains, her work mainly comprises brooches and necklaces that provide a fresh contrast to the more traditional styles seen in many high-street stores. A Liana Pattihis creation stands out from the crowd and is highly regarded and sought-after by collectors around the world.

Born in Cyprus, Liana has been living in London since 1980 and originally trained in interior design. However, needing a new challenge in her life, she undertook a four-year degree in jewellery at Middlesex University, gaining a First Class Honours. Today, Liana has her own jewellery workshop in north London.

'Every piece is part of a continuous and fascinating experimental journey which gives my work the freedom of constantly achieving something different and new,' says Liana. 'My aim is to try and stretch the boundaries of what can be achieved with glass powder as a medium, thus introducing a unique way of enamelling in the jewellery world as an alternative to what is already out there.'

APPEAL: Liana's work has been displayed at more than 30 jewellery exhibitions in the UK, Europe and United States, and in October 2009 was selected to present her work at the prestigious Goldsmiths' Fair where her vibrant offerings made a refreshing change to the more typical techniques seen on other stands.

'The unconventional process I follow in the making of my jewellery is a product of many months of experimenting with sifting and fusing enamels, which resulted in my pioneering a unique method of combining enamel on a movable chain base,' she says. 'Any new discovery in one piece is the starting point for the next. This enables my work to progress technically as well as aesthetically. Discovery is the goal.'

Even though Liana has endless sources of inspiration, looking into ancient Greek and Cypriot jewellery has had a tremendous influence on her work. Her style is distinctive and instantly recognisable, with an overwhelming appeal both nationally and internationally. She was first featured in The British Society of Enamellers' newsletter in 2007, and in the following months her work was spotted on Klimt02, a website featuring art jewellery from around the world, by a New York gallery owner who now shows her work in the United States.

'What makes my pieces luxurious,' says Liana, 'is the richness of the texture I can achieve with the enamels and the balanced relationship of the attention to detail of the design when making them, which doesn't detract from the desired free and organic result after firing.'

Future plans for Liana include solo exhibitions not only in the UK, but her birthplace, Cyprus, and a continued vision to create pieces that inspire others to embrace enamelling in a fresh and more contemporary manner. ▣

CONTACT: www.pattihis.com

131

REFLECTING
WHO YOU ARE

MATTHEW FOSTER'S BELIEF IN THE POWER
AND PERSONALITY OF JEWELLERY IS WHAT MAKES
EACH PIECE UNIQUE

With a true passion for the jewellery trade, its long and fascinating history, and a genuine excitement about the unpredictable mix of interesting people and colourful characters he has the opportunity to work with, Matthew Foster treats each item of jewellery as a treasure waiting to be discovered. 'To own a piece of period jewellery is not only to possess a beautiful jewel to be worn as an adornment, but also to make a statement about the individuality and taste of the person who wears it,' he enthuses. 'It is unique to them and a reflection of who they are.'

This belief in the power and personality of period jewellery is what has inspired Matthew throughout his career in fine jewels.

APPRENTICE:
Matthew began his apprenticeship in the jewellery trade working in the family business. Gaining invaluable experience, Matthew not only learnt about a wide variety of gemstones, but gleaned how to run a business, assist clients and make good contacts with trade buyers from around the world, as well as private clients and collectors.

ENTREPRENEUR:
In 1987 Matthew set up on his own, with a stand in the Bond Street Antiques Centre in Mayfair. At first specialising in fine Victorian jewellery, Matthew gradually leaned more towards concentrating on jewellery from the Art Deco period. This was a period of great style and glamour, with Art Deco permeating every aspect of daily life, from architecture and fashion to consumer products and film. Of course, jewellery was no exception, and the Art Deco movement had a profound effect on the designs of the period.

'The Art Deco style is probably one of the easiest artistic styles to recognise, with its modern, ultra clean lines, and trapezoidal shapes, stepped edges and arced corners,' explains Matthew. 'The designs often incorporate striking colour combinations of precious and semi-precious gemstones combined with innovative gem-cutting techniques to create strong and exciting geometric shapes.'

The Matthew Foster collection still includes an extensive range of Art Deco pieces, but now also extends into the Retro period of the 1940s and 1950s. This was a period of bold and colourful designs. Fun and whimsical, they were at the time an antidote to the austerity of the war years.

LOCATION:
In 2006, after almost 20 years of trading in the Bond Street Antiques Centre, Matthew Foster relocated to the current shop in the Burlington Arcade. A visit to this store is a pleasure in itself, a reminder of how life can be away from the hustle and bustle of city life.

'The Burlington Arcade is the longest covered shopping street in the capital and arguably the most beautiful,' says Matthew.

'It has long been associated with the sale of luxury items and prides itself on impeccable service, specialist knowledge and elegant surroundings.' Nowhere is this more pertinent than at Matthew Foster.

Whatever you are looking for, be it Victorian, Art Deco or rather more modern, the Matthew Foster collection encompasses a wide range of designs for all occasions. 'Each piece marries its own individual history with exquisite jewels, craftsmanship and timeless design,' Matthew concludes. ▣

CONTACT: www.matthew-foster.co.uk
IMAGES: (L–R) 1950s 18ct gold necklace by Cartier London; 1960s 18ct gold hoop-design earrings by Hermes, Paris; three diamond and gem-set rings from the Art Deco period

FLOWING
WITH INSPIRATION

To have a career you are passionate about is something that eludes many people. This isn't the case for Nina Koutibashvili, whose enthusiasm and creative talent allow her to invest in a career she really cares about and, additionally, to be her own boss.

As an experienced goldsmith, Nina wanted to find a career that allowed her passion for jewellery design, combined with her boundless ambition and inexhaustible energy, to push her to break new ground and offer customers something new and different that had not been designed before. After completing a BA in Jewellery Design at Central St Martins, Nina started her own business designing exquisite items of jewellery that are now worn by the rich, famous and fashion-conscious across the world.

ALLURING: Having always been fascinated by her first love of fashion, Nina says this greatly inspires her work: 'I have never been able to leave behind the fusion of fabric and fashion, and it is this beauty that I have brought to my jewellery design.' All of her pieces incorporate features that are borrowed from fabric – free-flowing movement, softness,

graceful tumbling – resulting in striking and original designs that are flexible and can be bent, shaped or manipulated by hand. 'Traditionally, there have been boundaries between jewellery and fabric,' she adds. 'My approach has been to break down that barrier so that fabric, metal and stones work and flow together in harmony, always complementing each other.

'Textures are lifelike; they are pieces of jewellery that people wear and can't help playing with.'

The designs are created in a range of materials, including gold, silver and platinum, precious stones and gems, all of which are ethically sourced in London; Nina ensures everything is fair trade. Her jewellery gives off a feeling of life – be it the intricacy or obvious love and attention to detail that has gone into each design – and the pieces don't boast about the wearer's personality, but add to it.

EXCEPTIONAL: With the huge amount of passion behind her designs, Nina's first collection won the Gold Award in the Fashion Jewellery category at the Goldsmiths' Craftmanship and Design awards. Many of the collections she has designed, particularly the first, hold specific significance. 'Most precious to me is my first "baby"; a gold necklace that helped me develop my trademark style,' Nina explains. 'I created this using a self-developed coiling technique based on uniquely tapered, handmade spiral forms.'

Nina's complex and striking designs have also seen her earn other prestigious awards, such as the Design Innovation Platinum Award, Coutts New Jeweller 2009 at the Coutts London Jewellery Week, and nominations as the Designer of the Year at the UK Jewellery Awards in 2008 and 2010. Her creations are sold in luxury retailers including Harrods, Selfridges and Harvey Nichols.

AMBITION: Possessing a great eye for detail and an ability to create beautiful, unique pieces, Nina says a late start to her career has allowed her the chance to really apply herself to what she wanted to do: 'I have been able to take my ideas and translate them into realities surpassing my wildest dreams.' ▣

CONTACT: www.ninakoutibashvili.com

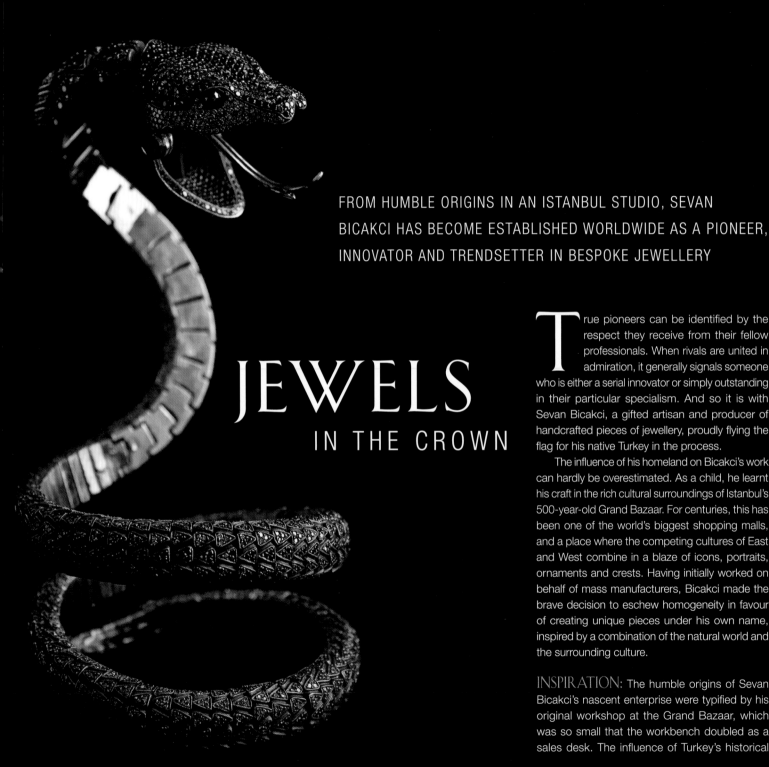

FROM HUMBLE ORIGINS IN AN ISTANBUL STUDIO, SEVAN BICAKCI HAS BECOME ESTABLISHED WORLDWIDE AS A PIONEER, INNOVATOR AND TRENDSETTER IN BESPOKE JEWELLERY

JEWELS
IN THE CROWN

True pioneers can be identified by the respect they receive from their fellow professionals. When rivals are united in admiration, it generally signals someone who is either a serial innovator or simply outstanding in their particular specialism. And so it is with Sevan Bicakci, a gifted artisan and producer of handcrafted pieces of jewellery, proudly flying the flag for his native Turkey in the process.

The influence of his homeland on Bicakci's work can hardly be overestimated. As a child, he learnt his craft in the rich cultural surroundings of Istanbul's 500-year-old Grand Bazaar. For centuries, this has been one of the world's biggest shopping malls, and a place where the competing cultures of East and West combine in a blaze of icons, portraits, ornaments and crests. Having initially worked on behalf of mass manufacturers, Bicakci made the brave decision to eschew homogeneity in favour of creating unique pieces under his own name, inspired by a combination of the natural world and the surrounding culture.

INSPIRATION: The humble origins of Sevan Bicakci's nascent enterprise were typified by his original workshop at the Grand Bazaar, which was so small that the workbench doubled as a sales desk. The influence of Turkey's historical

monuments was immediately evident, as he readily admits: 'My intention was to create jewellery which reflects my personal identity. Inevitably, the cultural heritage of Istanbul and Turkey has become a very important source of inspirations. It's the architecture, the lifestyle and legends from both the Byzantine and the Ottoman past as I have been spending almost every day of my life being surrounded by fantastic monuments. It's just these little things that inspire me, as they define my soul and my identity.'

Having spent almost a year perfecting 50 bespoke items, the inaugural collection of Sevan Bicakci's jewellery was unveiled in Turkey in 2002. The unique nature of these finished products initially worried jewellery retailers, concerned that they would be unable to re-order a popular design. However, their bespoke nature would ultimately become one of their greatest selling points, and today Bicakci's creations can be found across Europe, USA and the Middle East, commanding considerable sums in the world's leading auction houses.

HANDCRAFTING: Sevan Bicakci is now internationally renowned as an artist, with more than two decades of expertise in his highly specialised field. He is still based in a studio near the Grand Bazaar in Istanbul where he blends together gold, sterling silver, diamonds and uniquely cut gemstones. By collaborating with artists and artisans, from calligraphers to painters, each modern design is imbued with an inherent antiquity, and technology is still shunned in favour of handcrafting using simple tools. Bicakci describes the philosophy thus: 'Each wearer is a unique individual and should be wearing a unique piece, the one which is most meaningful to her or to him.'

Unsurprisingly, the international art world has been quick to celebrate this ingenuity and originality, with four Couture Design Awards and the Tanzanite Foundation award for Best Independent Designer collectively attesting to Sevan Bicakci's rare gift. As the artist himself points out: 'What I do with my heart seems to touch the hearts of some people, and others seem to be bored with mass production. There is no commercial thinking behind what I do and reaching out to the masses was never my consideration. I derive a much greater pleasure from observing people becoming collectors.' Considering the purity and exclusivity of every item he creates, it's easy to see why Sevan Bicakci's jewellery has become so sought-after and cherished by collectors and aficionados alike. ▣

CONTACT: www.sevanbicakci.com

EACH ITEM OF JEWELLERY
IN THE SHAMBALLA
JEWELS RANGE IS UNIQUE,
EXCLUSIVE AND PERSONAL

EASTERN
INSPIRATIONS

With a devoted following that includes world-renowned superstars Rihanna, Helena Christensen, Jay-Z, Michael Jordan, Beyoncé and Heidi Klum, Copenhagen-based jewellery company Shamballa Jewels creates outfit-enhancing designs that are simple yet cutting-edge, while symbolising a deeper meaning for the wearer.

SPIRITUAL: The jewellery is inspired by Indian and Tibetan mythology – Shamballa derives from the Himalayan mythical kingdom of the same name – as well as founder Mads Kornerup's passion for yoga and meditation. Each piece is distinctive to the individual wearer, and forming a personal connection is an integral philosophy. With the presence of the Star of Shamballa on every piece, Mads explains: 'It's there to remind us that we are all little shining stars that shine brighter when we smile. If a wearer looks at their piece of jewellery, hopefully it will make them smile and cause

> *There's good energy in everybody and my aim is that the designs will remind people of their inner power*

everyone around them to smile too. There's good energy in everybody and my aim is that the designs will remind people of their inner power.'

The company's signature piece, the Shamballa bracelet, is the item most customers are drawn to and fall in love with – Mads hears many stories about customers who simply refuse to take theirs off. Taking inspiration from Tibetan Mala beads, Mads originally designed the bracelet for himself and his brother, as well as his business partner, Mikkel. 'There wasn't anything similar available for men that carried the same meaning or symbolism,' says Mads.

MASCULINE:
Furthering this theme, designs are mainly aimed at men, and Mads creates pieces that he personally would choose to wear. However, the use of precious stones such as sapphires, rubies, emeralds and diamonds has seen more and more women attracted to the brand. 'They have become such a large part of our customer base that we have had to adjust our look a little bit,' says Mads, 'so it isn't as masculine as I would have maybe preferred! And, over the years, the women who work at the company have definitely influenced the designs.'

The bracelets are very versatile, complementing the laid-back, afternoon look of a T-shirt and jeans or adding to the character of an evening tuxedo. And they can be designed to incorporate individual touches, such as an engraving of the wearer's star sign or initials – Jay-Z chose for his fashion collection's Rocawear logo to be featured on his. Mads also sources distinctive

stones, whether they are 16-carat black diamonds, pink Argyle diamonds or earth beads – although around 90 per cent of men who buy the bracelets choose those with black diamonds, preferring their masculine and powerful style. 'I try to make each bracelet individual and special,' he adds. 'At a dinner party there could be 12 or 15 people wearing a Shamballa bracelet and not one of them would be the same; they would have different colour threads, various types of gold and a range of precious stones.'

DISTINCTION:
Having originally got into jewellery design purely by coincidence, Mads can now boast that, as well as a flagship store in Copenhagen, Shamballa Jewels' bracelets, pendants and rings are sold in luxury department stores and high-end jewellery shops across the world. In 2005, the company also received the Rising Star award at the prestigious JCK jewellery show in Las Vegas. 'The look of the pieces is very understated, but the stones and materials used are very high quality,' he says. 'In Basel, senior people from big jewellery companies, such as Bulgari and LVMH, were impressed with the style, stones and settings of the pieces. I think that was the biggest compliment we could ever get; that these other renowned jewellery designers praised us for our quality.' ▣

CONTACT: www.shamballajewels.com

ETERNAL
SHINE

EVERY ITEM OF JEWELLERY CREATED BY SINGHAL GEMS TELLS A
STORY OF DESIGN, CRAFTSMANSHIP AND ITS WEARER

"

Throughout the entire process, each gem is
checked for quality at least 100 times

Artist, poet and writer, Khalil Gibran once said: 'Trust in dreams, for in them is hidden the gate to eternity.' His words sum up the power of dreams and depth of emotion that lies behind Singhal Gems. The company was established with an aim to redefine excellence when it was set up in Jaipur in the 1990s, and has now become pre-eminent in the field of jewellery manufacturing, and the cutting and polishing of emeralds. The group delivers designs with unrivalled artisanship, and the belief that each precious gemstone is individual, with its own unique character and personality.

MARVEL: Royalty have long been known as connoisseurs of the finest emeralds and have been synonymous with Jaipur for many years. Seen as a unique and lustrous testimony of nature's bounty, emeralds are known for their antiquity and have been adored by different cultures throughout the centuries.

Singhal Gems is the leading cutter and polisher of this verdant precious stone in India. The company's artificers nurture every emerald with utmost regard to maintain consistency of shape and magnify the colour to its maximum effulgence. Every single stone procured at Singhal Gems undergoes a stringent process of selection, where each is scrutinised on its colour, cut, clarity and transparency, as only the highest-quality stones make the grade. This is followed by an equally meticulous procedure of manufacturing where the emerald's features are accentuated with the scientific techniques employed in cutting and polishing, and the accurate expertise of the traditional emerald artisans. Throughout the entire process, each stone is checked for quality at least 100 times. Singhal Gems holds a proud collection of the finest and rarest specimens of vitreous emeralds, each of which has its own resplendent beauty.

MAGIC: Another exciting facet of Singhal Gems is its mastery in making precision jewellery. The company's newest venture is Mirabelle, which specialises in elegant, handcrafted jewellery, from wedding bands, solitaire rings and bangles, to bracelets, pendants and necklaces. Each diamond and precious stone is exquisitely layered in metal to enhance its lustre and brilliance. The finest Italian craftsmanship and artistry ensure high quality and the finest surface finish on all bespoke pieces of jewellery. Each Mirabelle piece has consistent and unrivalled brilliance, with a perfectly cut and crafted diamond or stone nestled in an exceptional setting engineered at Singhal Gems. It would be no exaggeration to state that every item of Mirabelle jewellery is truly a work of art, widely appreciated and acknowledged as a prized possession. ▣

CONTACT: www.singhalgems.com; www.mirabellejewels.com

LIVE

3 » *Luxury Living, Interiors & Architecture*

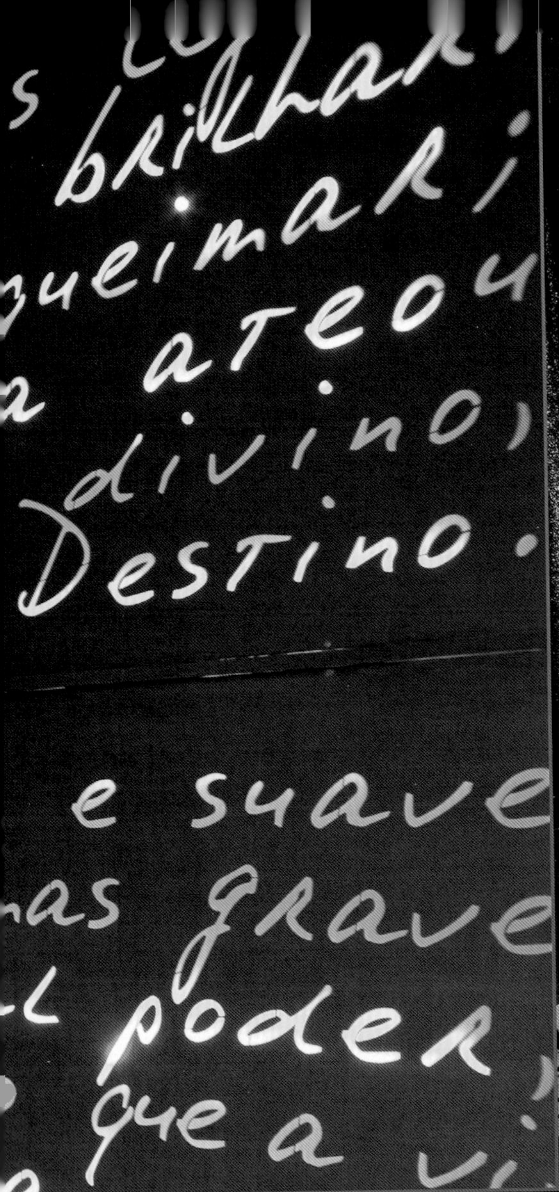

brilhan!
queimar!
a ateou
divino!
Destino.

e suave
mas grave
poder
que a vi

3» LIVE

CONTEMPORARY
CRUISING

TILLBERG DESIGN CREATES CRUISE SHIPS FOR THE 21ST CENTURY

Cruising makes up a large part of the tourism industry, providing a getaway for more than 18 million people worldwide. The amenities and facilities onboard a cruise ship, such as shops, restaurants, bars and suites, all contribute to the holiday experience. It is essential, therefore, that these are all designed and completed to a high standard, offering luxurious and comfortable surroundings.

With more than 40 years of experience in the industry, marine interior design company, Tillberg Design, is committed to bringing high quality to the cruise-ship industry. 'We see a steadily growing diversity, and many ship owners are moving away from strongly themed, over-decorated designs often associated with the cruise industry, towards more subtle, contemporary styles.' explains Partner and Senior Architect, Fredrik Johansson.

FOCUSED: Tillberg Design has created stylish interiors for an estimated 140 vessels including luxury yachts, high-speed catamarans, ferries and

Tillberg Design has created stylish interiors for an estimated 140 vessels

some of the world's largest and most prestigious cruise ships, such as *Queen Mary 2* and *Queen Elizabeth 2*. 'We work very much on our ships like we do with our land-based projects,' says Fredrik. 'We produce design documents to the builders – the shipyards – who then send them out to the sub-contractors who do the purchasing, building and installation.'

Tillberg's design teams are on hand to support the client – whether they know exactly what they want and give the company a clear brief, or leave it completely up to the designers. This is something that Fredrik believes sets the company apart: 'We try to strike that balance between being very professional, target focused and disciplined, but also to listen – we are known as the listening team.'

DIVERSE: The company can design everything from classic, timeless elegance to vibrant, cutting-edge interiors. Fredrik explains that working with a Norwegian or Asian cruise line is very different from designing for more traditional British or US

clients: 'We are blessed with some very open-minded and creative talents in our conceptual department. In fact, we have partly separate concept teams for each project, just to make sure the results are totally individual for each client.'

ADVANTAGE: Tillberg Design has also moved into land-based designing, with clients including hotels, restaurants and resorts, such as the recently completed interior design project for the Marriott hotel in Malmo, Sweden. This diversification is something that holds plus points for both types of clients and is an area Tillberg Design will continue to develop in the future, says Fredrik: 'Hotel owners appreciate the core skills and competencies we can bring from our work with cruise ships. We are very used to working with space-efficient planning, cost-effective designs and clever use of space, which is useful when planning hotels. And ship owners are always looking at what's happening onshore and want to bring the latest trends onboard.

'The cruise industry is partly a rather conservative one, and cruise ships are not historically known for having the best and most stylish designs onboard. We would like to change that. Imagine a cruise ship that is designed like a designer hotel. That is where we are heading; combining these two industries to the advantage of all parties involved.' ▣

CONTACT: www.tillbergdesign.com

A
FAMILY
FAVOURITE

THE ENDURING APPEAL OF AN AGA CONTINUES THROUGH THE GENERATIONS

To thousands of devotees across the world, the iconic AGA cooker is a way of life. It enjoys a loyal following, with many owners swapping stories about their beloved cooker. One such admirer went as far as to claim it was warmer, more reliable and considerably better looking than most men and that, if she had to choose between her husband and her AGA, she would waste no time in packing his bags! The range cooker also has a number of celebrity fans, including Elizabeth Hurley, Jamie Oliver and Rick Stein, who has said: 'The AGA is an iconic part of British life. I've cooked on an AGA since the day I was born, or at least my mother did. I'm very enthusiastic about it.'

INGENUITY: Dr Gustaf Dalén, who invented the AGA in 1922, is unlikely to have predicted the iconic status his creation would achieve. After gleaning how exhausted his wife was from cooking, the blind Nobel Prize-winning physicist wanted to develop a stove that was efficient and easy to use.

> **"**
>
> *With a dedicated fan base and the ability to last for generations, the AGA has secured its place in the family home for many years to come*

Working on the principles of heat storage and using cast iron because of its unique heat-retention properties, he combined a heat source, two large hotplates and two ovens to create the first AGA cooker.

Originally produced in Sweden, the AGA was first introduced to Britain in 1929 and quickly adopted by those living in large country houses, becoming a symbol of rural England and farmhouse kitchens. By the end of the Second World War, production had moved completely to the UK and, today, the cookers are still manufactured in Coalbrookdale, Shropshire, a United Nations world heritage site and birthplace of the Industrial Revolution.

VERSATILE: Almost nine decades after its creation, the AGA is as popular as ever. Its style and reputation mean that it is just as at home in a hip Hoxton loft as it is in a Hampstead townhouse or rambling country pile. There are many aspects that make the AGA special, but undoubtedly its core function of delivering delicious, well-cooked dishes, full of flavour and goodness, remains the most important.

While there have been many technological advances, the fundamental design has changed little over the years and, likewise, the cooker itself has incredible endurance, with many AGAs still in operation more than 50 years after their first use. In 2009, the company and *The Daily Telegraph* set up a competition to find the oldest AGA still in use; the winner, in a family home in Sussex, was installed in 1932. Often referred to as the 'heart of the home' because of the warmth it provides, the AGA creates a homely, sociable feel as the focal point of the kitchen.

PROGRESSIVE: The AGA can also boast environmental strengths and has been developed for today's busier lifestyle, with fuel options including oil, gas and electricity. Innovative technology means that the cooker can now also be fully programmable, so it can be ready when needed, or in slumber mode when not, giving greater control and versatility to the benefit of both the cook and the environment. The fact that each AGA is made from 75 per cent recycled materials and is 70 per cent recyclable itself only serves to emphasise its green credentials.

With a dedicated fan base and the ability to last for generations, the AGA has secured its place in the family home for many years to come. ▣

CONTACT: www.aga-web.co.uk

CLEVER AND
BEAUTIFUL

ALCHEMY DESIGN AWARD BRINGS BACK THE ESSENCE OF BESPOKE DESIGN, FROM THE HIGHLY CLASSICAL TO THE ULTRA-MODERN

The fabled alchemists of ancient Mesopotamia were said to be able to turn base metals into gold. While mysticism is not what Alchemy Design Award offers, the company's promise to provide rare and bespoke interior designs from the world's best designers does have the effect of making the seemingly impossible become a tangible reality.

The group has 20 years of experience acting as the connection between clients and their dream bathroom and home designs. Now, a new element has been added, which focuses on high-end, classical products, known as the Grand Tour Collection. Taking its name from the famous Grand Tour that travelled Europe in the 1800s, the pieces and designers included in this collection represent what Alchemy Design Award has always believed: that its clients deserve to have access to bespoke creations when they are furnishing or building their

dream homes. Ultimately, Alchemy Design Award removes the barriers between people and the designs of their dreams.

FREEDOM: The products that Alchemy makes available by way of the Grand Tour Collection are not everyday household items. The essence of the collection is a return to a period when people who knew what they wanted could have exactly what they desired.

'The Grand Tour,' says Managing Director Sean McGran, 'brings together, in one uniquely themed collection, some of the most prestigious Italian producers of classic bedroom and bathroom furniture, accessories, taps and showers. It takes the client on an inside journey across Italy, spotlighting the tradition and craftsmanship of some of its hidden treasures.'

Sean takes pride in this aspect of Alchemy's work. 'Most of the designers commissioned by ourselves work to the customer's specifications,' he says. 'In this way our clientèle can share an affinity both with the designer and the producer. There is something quite wonderful about that.'

ENVIABLE: One of the premier marques with which Sean and his team are currently working is Rubinetterie Stella, the original Italian tap company, formed in 1882. 'The lines we are now re-launching were some of the most sought-after designs of the 1920s,' says Sean. 'We're bringing back those very same classical fittings in precious-metal finishes such as silver and 24-carat gold and, in so doing, are applying those very same master-craftsman techniques.'

As any true connoisseur of design knows, the materials used are as important as the actual designs of the products themselves. 'For classic furniture designs our clients usually request beautiful finishes such as gold leaf, silver leaf, Venetian mirrored glass, fine wood veneers and pianoforte lacquers often incorporating genuine silk-print motifs, as in the case of Oasis Bagni,' Sean explains. 'For more contemporary designs, clients tend to favour sculptural, solid-surface materials which, in addition to sharing the visual and tactile qualities of natural stone, are seamless in nature and therefore ideal for creating a sleek, pure look and feel.'

'My view of luxury is that it's something that takes you to the place you need to be in your soul, your place of comfort,' says Sean. 'Rather than being surrounded by expensive possessions, real luxury is something that creates an overall sense of well-being; clever and beautiful design provides precisely that.' ▣

CONTACT: www.alchemyaward.com

ALLEGRA HICKS' STYLE IS ABOUT
CREATIVITY AND EXPRESSION

ECLECTIC
STYLE

> *With more than 400 fabrics created, Allegra has her own unique print vocabulary*

Allegra Hicks is a worldwide label found in boutiques in the most fashionable neighbourhoods. As a lifestyle brand, the collections encompass both women's luxury fashion and distinctive interior fabrics, and they are available in prestigious department stores such as Harrods and Harvey Nichols in London, and Saks Fifth Avenue in New York, as well as through popular fashion websites. The interior fabrics are primarily distributed in the USA, UK and Europe.

Originally well known for designing a successful, luxury home collection that included sumptuous rugs, beautiful fabrics and soft furnishings, Allegra felt it was a natural progression to expand into fashion design by personally designing the fabric prints for fashion collections. 'I studied design in Milan, specialising in textiles,' she says. 'With a passion for textiles, I began to design furnishings and rugs, and naturally evolved into a more product-related area – designing kaftans, throws and cushions.'

CREATIVE: As well as her home collection, Allegra designs two women's ready-to-wear collections per year and a cruise collection. Similar themes and colours are present throughout both the fashion and interiors collections. With more than 400 fabrics created, Allegra has her own unique print vocabulary that uses natural colours and subtle shades and is patterned with printed, embroidered or woven designs on materials including linen, silk, velvet and cotton, while her clothing range focuses on individual, bold, graphic prints.

'I think it is very important for a designer to develop their own "creative vocabulary",' she explains. 'It is their own form of expression, their design identity. When a customer purchases an item to wear or for their home they, in turn, are choosing to express themselves in a similar way.'

With her first, and signature, clothing design, Allegra was named the 'Queen of Kaftans' by *Vogue* and credited with reinventing the garment. She says she began designing kaftans when she was looking for one for a trip she was taking: 'No one else seemed to be producing high-end beachwear; there was a gap in the market and I really needed one!' Kaftans have now become much more than just a beach cover up, with women wearing them at home and as evening wear. 'Kaftans are so easy to wear and relaxed,' Allegra adds.

ECLECTIC: Allegra describes her typical customer as someone who is 'an elegant, naturally stylish, free-spirited woman who isn't a fashion victim and cares about quality'. The home furnishings reflect Allegra's relaxed yet sophisticated lifestyle and add a modern, yet organic, twist. 'I think the strength of my designs is that you can use the fabrics and prints in any type of home, whether it's contemporary or traditional,' she says. 'The best way to describe the prints is as eclectic – they are very distinctive.'

As part of the brand's design and development strategy, Allegra often collaborates with other designers to bring a fresh perspective to seasonal womenswear collections, and has plans to expand the brand in more ways than one: 'I would love to carry on these collaborations and design with, and for, other companies,' she says. 'Of course, I also want to focus on Allegra Hicks by opening new standalone stores and also expanding my interiors collection.' ▣

CONTACT: www.allegrahicks.com

EXCEPTIONAL HOMES FOR EXCEPTIONAL
PEOPLE

ARQUI+ DESIGNS SOME OF PORTUGAL'S FINEST LUXURY VILLAS

Each project is an innovation, not a repetition of previous designs – it is something that hasn't been seen before in the area

Every year, thousands of people visit the Algarve in Portugal to enjoy its Mediterranean climate, stunning scenery and golden beaches. These aspects have also been a drawing factor for the increasing number of expatriates who live in the country, or those owning a holiday home in the area.

EXPERTISE: Having studied and trained in architecture in South Africa, respected architect Vasco Vieira spent his first ten years in the Algarve at Vale do Lobo, one of the leading luxury resorts in Europe, as Chief Architect and Construction Director. 'This previous experience at Vale do Lobo really taught me about the market in the Algarve,' explains Vasco. Recognising the demand for luxury properties in this picturesque location, Vasco established ARQUI+ seven years ago to work on projects ranging from individual villas and holiday homes, to large commercial and leisure facilities such as hotels, restaurants, spas and shopping centres.

DISTINCTIVE: The villas that Vasco and his team design are luxury properties at the top end of the market, occupied by discerning clientele who desire their own exclusive residence in which to get away from it all. Each villa is designed to meet the client's individual requirements. 'Clients will give us a brief and we work with their input,' he explains. 'It is fundamental that each villa reflects the owner's personality. Therefore, although it has my own architectural style, it also contains the essentials they have specified.'

ARQUI+ has been instrumental in the introduction of a more contemporary architectural language in the Algarve, yet the designs maintain the essence of the region. 'Each project is an innovation,' says Vasco, 'not a repetition of previous designs – each design is something that is new in the area.' The designs are inspired by the location, utilising local materials, optimising use of light and incorporating the surrounding views. Vasco explains it as 'connectivity between indoor and outdoor', and many incorporate features such as wooden deck areas, expanses of glass, large external living spaces and infinity pools.

The designs also focus increasingly on sustainable features, such as solar panels, geothermal energy, and natural cooling and heating, with many ARQUI+ developments having been selected as some of the most environmentally friendly properties, including a ranking in *A Place in the Sun*'s Top 10 International Eco-Resorts 2009 survey.

EMERGING: ARQUI+ has also gained recognition in the property industry with a number of awards for villa designs. Additionally, Vasco has been selected as one of the top ten international architects by *Homes Overseas* magazine.

As each project is completed, Vasco and his team strive to constantly improve on their designs and continue to innovate in terms of their architectural style, the villa facilities and eco-friendly solutions. ARQUI+ is expanding and is now responsible for the creation of luxury villas in resorts located outside Portugal which include Brazil, Cape Verde, Angola and Morocco, as well as projects in Holland and Germany.

'The work we do is always at the top end of the market' adds Vasco. 'Increasingly people are spending more time in their own luxury holiday homes with facilities comparable with small boutique hotels, making these villas a great stay for all four seasons.' ▣

CONTACT: www.arquimais.com

FREEING THE SOUL

EVERY INTERIORS PROJECT CARRIED OUT BY
TALENTED DESIGNERS ATELIER NINI ANDRADE SILVA
DISPLAYS STYLE, CREATIVITY AND PASSION

Atelier Nini Andrade Silva is a Portugal-based architecture and interior design firm led by Chief Designer, Nini Andrade Silva, who has established herself and her firm as a brand of international reference. With a high level of quality and service, the company has a well earned reputation for excellence in the international world of architecture and interior design and is a several-times award winner.

The firm's work includes design, furniture design and interior architecture consultancy with an emphasis on the hospitality sector. Directed by the designer herself, the team's work is carried out by assistants, architects, interior designers and graphic designers throughout Lisbon and Funchal, and they are currently engaged in several projects worldwide, working with hotels, private residences, restaurants and offices.

VISIONARY: Recent projects have included the The Aquapura Douro Valley Hotel, which was selected by *Harrods Magazine* as one of the best 100 hotels of the world and was also recently included in *Tatler Travel Guide* 2009, which makes a selection of the top 101 hotels of the world. The five-star hotel is in Portugal's wine region, which is reflected in its design, combining eco-friendly philosophies with contemporary styles. The hotel uses earthy colours and natural materials to evoke tranquillity and calm. Each room glows with soft, natural light and is finished with bronze-lacquered furniture, four-poster beds and steel lamps. The hotel is a wonderful demonstration of Nini's work and unremitting search for the perfect conjugation between the human needs and the soul of the spaces she conceives and creates. 'I like to make an impact, a statement,' she explains. 'I take my inspiration from nature and add the unique and unusual.'

The Fontana Park Hotel, which has been considered by the judges of the European Hotel Design Awards as the Best Interior Design for Bedrooms and Bathrooms 2008, is also a member of the Design Hotels, which are both visionary and unique.

DEFINING: Nini's work is a living illustration of her work and continues to define her talent, as is illustrated by The Vine, a luxurious hotel in her birthplace, Madeira Island. It was nominated in the award category of Interior Design from the European Hotel Design Awards 2009 and also achieved the Best Design in Europe, as well as being selected as a candidate in the shortlist of the World Architecture Festival 2009.

The Theater Hotel, located in the historical downtown area of Oporto, is the latest architectural and interior design project of Atelier. As the name suggests, the Theater Hotel was developed around a concept directly related to its previous function, the legendary Teatro Baquet, which was the cultural hub of the city for more than 100 years.

'The interior architecture and design project integrates all its history and respect for the space's soul,' explains Nini, 'and what has come to life is an elegant and subtle environment.' The hotel is already a serious candidate for the European Hotel Design Awards 2010, the World Architecture Festival 2010 and the European Property Awards 2010, and it is set to bring Nini further acclaim.

ENDLESS: Nini's creativity seems endless and the demand for pieces created especially by her has resulted in the development of design collections of unique pieces for international brands, as well as the production of the firm's own interior and exterior furniture collection – Garota do Calhau – which ensures that it can supply all the design needs of its projects. In addition to this, Nini has been actively engaged in developing a private painting collection also called Garota do Calhau, which means 'girl of the pebbles' and is the name used to describe the free children walking on the pebbled beaches of Madeira Island. ▣

CONTACT: www.niniandradesilva.com

ESCAPE
TO THE COUNTRY

A SPECTACULAR LOCATION AND ATTENTIVE
SERVICE HAS MADE CHÂTEAU DE VAULT DE LUGNY
A FAVOURITE WITH DISCERNING GUESTS

The region of Burgundy, France, is the perfect destination for an idyllic getaway. Its lush countryside boasts unspoilt villages, historic abbeys, famous vineyards, charming châteaux and winding canals. The laid-back pace of life and the welcoming locals make it an attractive place to explore.

KINGS: The Château de Vault de Lugny is a luxuriously restored 16th-century castle located in the heart of this region. Surrounded by 100 acres of land, encompassing a park, forest and moat, the four-star hotel offers its guests an extraordinary experience. 'Here, nothing is standard,' explains General Manager, Pascal Bourzeix. 'Guests will sleep in a real château and can even stay in a room that was created especially for the kings of France.'

This room, the Le Roy suite, was reserved for French kings to stay in when they travelled through the region. Located at the end of a long corridor, the suite has unrivalled views of the surrounding countryside, an open, sculpted marble fireplace, sumptuous gothic chairs, a vast bathroom with a bathtub for two, antique tiling and beautiful peacock frescoes – it's easy to see why it was deemed fit for a king. The hotel features just 15 other rooms and suites, all individually decorated and luxuriously furnished. 'We only have a small number of guests at any one time, giving an atmosphere

The spa offers a range of body well-being and sculpting therapies such as the Maracaibo chocolate massage, which uses rich Swiss chocolate

of exclusivity and privacy,' says Pascal. 'Although only a happy few can enjoy a stay at Château de Vault de Lugny, our service and facilities are of the highest quality.'

ATTENTIVE: The hotel prides itself on providing *service sur mesure* (a bespoke service) and an atmosphere that feels like home. Staff strive to meet each guest's wishes and are on hand to arrange a plethora of activities, from medieval evenings, bowls games, croquet tournaments, hot-air balloon trips, horse riding and private concerts. Inside the château, located in the ancient vaulted cellars, guests can enjoy the indoor pool and Jacuzzi, while they are also encouraged to enjoy the surrounding park where animals roam freely and trout fishing takes place in the private, 800-metre stretch of Le Cousin. Mountain biking, hiking and jogging trails with detailed itineraries are also provided.

INDULGE: At the nearby Le Prieuré des Sources spa the hotel's guests can take advantage of an exclusive package that includes treatments and a limousine service. Located in an 18th-century priory, the spa offers a range of body well-being and sculpting therapies such as the Maracaibo chocolate massage, which uses rich Swiss chocolate created especially by Nicolas Noz for Le Prieuré des Sources, and leaves skin silky soft. As this treatment is

edible, guests can taste the delicious chocolate before it is rubbed onto their skin and can also take a bar home. All of the treatments at the spa use only natural ingredients, including earth, herbs, vegetables and flowers.

Château de Vault de Lugny's restaurant is situated in its former kitchens, in luxurious surroundings where dining is relaxed. Alternatively, glorious weather permits guests to eat outside in the beautiful gardens. The cuisine is inspired by Burgundy's rich countryside and seasonal produce is locally sourced or grown in the château's vegetable gardens and greenhouse. As Château de Vault de Lugny is in the heart of one of France's main wine-producing areas, its wine list is exceptional. 'We have our own cellar, which has the best bottles from around the world,' says Pascal. 'Many are matured for at least ten years before they are poured for our guests.'

RECOGNITION: Château de Vault de Lugny has been named on numerous occasions in Andrew Harper's Hideaway Report, made Condé Nast Traveller's Gold List in 2005, and is highly recommended by both Condé Nast Johansens and Michelin. As Pascal adds: 'Guests shouldn't come here expecting an ordinary hotel: a stay at Château de Vault de Lugny is a wonderful experience.' ▣

CONTACT: www.lugny.fr

ISLAND LIFE

CLIENTS' DREAMS AND CORFU CONSTRUCTION'S EXPERIENCE MAKE THE PERFECT MATCH

Houses are built in the charming, traditional style and blend in beautifully with the surrounding countryside

Flaunting a green and bucolic landscape in the glistening Ionian Sea, Corfu's sub-tropical climate and gentle pace of life creates an idyllic retreat for those fortunate enough to grace its shores. It is covered in olive trees, planted more than 400 years ago by the Venetians.

Offering a combination of cosmopolitan and time-honoured Greece, while many famous people from all over the world, such as Royal families, politicians and actors from Hollywood, are happy to escape to the island for a few weeks' holiday every year, those who realise its potential call upon the services of Corfu Construction to bring their housing dreams to life, be it a charming holiday cottage or grand luxury villa.

TRUSTED: Buying a property abroad can be a daunting prospect. However, using a professional company like Corfu Construction, which specialises in villas, takes the worry out of what could potentially be a complex and risky project. As experts on Greek property law, the company ensures that land is legally fit for building, ready for construction to start immediately and clear of any debts or boundary issues. This can save the buyer many months of bureaucracy, and sometimes heartache, offering total security and peace of mind in the purchase process. 'Buyers need to be in safe hands; to know that their interests are protected,' says Corfu Construction's owner, Theodoros Karametos, Civil Engineer.

Through providing the finest quality homes at realistic prices in a minimal amount of time, Corfu Construction has gained an enviable reputation across the world, winning the trust of both clients and investors.

BEFITTING: While offering its clients a turnkey service, Corfu Construction operates on a small scale, never building obtrusive or unsightly developments and leaving every olive tree untouched. 'We want to preserve the island's special feeling and try to become part of the landscape, not change it,' says Theodoros. 'Houses are built in the charming, traditional style and blend in beautifully with the surrounding countryside.'

From a small development in the tranquil centre of the island to the prized north-east coast, plots are in the best locations on the island, unmatched for sea views, accessibility, golf, marinas and excellent shopping. They provide total seclusion within reach of all amenities. And, as Corfu Construction is a developer not an estate agent, clients pay no commission. Furthermore, because of its reliability in the Greek market, Corfu Construction provides customers with the possibility of obtaining a loan from a Greek bank.

Properties are erected using only the finest materials, often custom-made for durability and style; and no matter how big the villa is, construction will take no longer than 12 months. As well as guaranteeing fittings for two years, Theodoros, as a qualified civil engineer, is responsible under Greek law for the structural integrity of his houses for his lifetime. When purchasing through Corfu Construction, clients can rest assured that they will be co-operated with, advised and consulted every step of the way. For 2010, Corfu Construction has introduced a new investment opportunity for its customers, allowing them to use their villas for rental purposes and maximise their income.

CARING: Corfu Construction continues to take a personal interest in clients after they've been handed the keys to their property. For a further two years it offers free general house maintenance and 'keeps an eye on it' while the owner is away.

Glowing customer testimonials include Louise Hynd from London: 'From designing the house with Mr Karametos and his specialised staff to getting it just perfect, watching it take shape and growing each day, the real miracle was that it only took seven months, which on a large house of 400 square metres must be a world record!' Edward Lyn, a chemist from Wales, adds: 'I looked into various properties in the Mediterranean and Dubai. House buying is a very stressful endeavour. I found that Corfu Construction answered all questions fully, and has gone above and beyond the call of duty for us on many occasions.'

Corfu's property prices are steadily rising due to strict building regulations which protect the island from overdevelopment, presenting an ideal time to invest in this idyllic small island. ▣

CONTACT: www.corfuconstruction.com

IMAGINATIVE, INSPIRING,
ILLUMINATING

MULTI-AWARD-WINNING DAVID BROWN LIGHTING IS CONSTANTLY REDEFINING PEOPLE'S UNDERSTANDING OF WHAT IS ATTAINABLE

L ighting is the extra dimension in architecture, the element that brings a building and its interior to life, and design-led consultancy David Brown Lighting promises an off-the-scale wow factor every time.

Whether it's a buzzing sales office, a luxury hotel garden, a grand hallway or a sophisticated drawing room, each project has its own distinctive requirements, overlaid by the client's unique design preferences.

The Edinburgh-based company boasts prestigious private-sector clients including Harvey Nichols and BSkyB, but it reserves its most creative designs for more intimate domestic projects.

To be expected, client confidentiality is an important part of the service. But David Brown has worked closely with top designers, including Celeste Dell'Anna, Julian Hunter Architects and Capital Interiors, to deliver some truly breathtaking lighting solutions.

DEXTERITY: Since setting up the company in 1988, the Managing Director, David Brown, has built an impressive team of interior and exterior, commercial and domestic experts. Just as important are the project management personnel who ensure that jobs run smoothly.

'Our ethos is quite simple: it's in the detail,' says David. 'It is essential to understand what the objectives are and what makes clients excited. One of our real assets is our understanding of light and space. Due to our design

training we can visualise how light works. We also know how to apply light and how to integrate it into an environment.

'We are generally involved at an early stage of the planning process as this enables us to contribute to the architectural details and cable management – the groundwork that makes a great design possible. Lighting shouldn't be an afterthought superimposed on a set of existing plans. The more integrated it is, the better it becomes.'

RADIANT: A private viewing of the company's lighting showcase at Leith Walk, Edinburgh, is the best way to experience the incredible effects that can be achieved. Featuring some of the world's finest lighting, this design treasure trove is crammed with stylish lamps, glittering chandeliers and sophisticated multi-level systems.

The David Brown team can offer expert advice on its beautiful interior products and ideas, selecting the ideal fixtures and fittings, and developing a tailored scheme to perfectly meet individual requirements.

There are also examples of how external lighting can be used to enhance landscapes, furniture, architecture and security. With a carefully designed scheme, outside lights can turn a darkened courtyard into a mystical clearing, a building façade into an artefact, and the night sky into a beautiful moving picture.

Always addressing both functional and aesthetic aspects, the company is constantly scouring the markets for inspired new technologies. A typical project will cover the development of a design concept, technical scheduling and product specification, design of bespoke lighting, and advice on efficient energy management.

David Brown also runs seminars for industry professionals — architects, designers, electricians and contractors — covering topics such as designing, specifying, fitting, controlling and operating lighting for both residential and commercial properties.

The language of light can dramatically alter any environment. It can realise a vision and influence visitors. With design integrity and an unwavering commitment to excellence, David Brown Lighting provides a world-class service.

CONTACT: www.davidbrownlighting.com

THE
ARTISANS
OF FINE SKILLS

THIS PIONEERING BRITISH BRAND IS
LEADING THE WORLD IN THE REVIVAL OF HIGH
CRAFTS, WHILE PRODUCING BESPOKE TABLEWARE
TO THE MOST METICULOUS STANDARDS

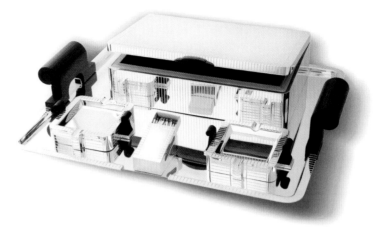

The word 'artisan' has largely disappeared from common parlance, yet it represents a very important and historic range of skills. Artisans are skilled workers with specialist talents for producing handmade items, and their lineage stretches back over many thousands of years. In the increasingly automated 21st century, such delicate arts are increasingly overlooked, but one British brand has dedicated itself to preserving them and introducing their beauty to a wider audience.

ILLUSTRIOUS: David Redman London is an illustrious and admired producer of completely bespoke tableware, from ceramic plates and champagne flutes to cigar boxes. Far more than accessories or accoutrements, these are handcrafted to the client's precise specifications, often inspired by family heirlooms or engraved with heraldic crests to integrate them with their owners' homes and belongings. As David Redman himself admits, his company was created as a reaction to the increasing homogeneity of modern design and manufacture: 'I felt luxury had become very "corporatised" in terms of the scale of corporate clients. Having spent a great deal of time with one particular brand, I felt the decision making by committee anaesthetised the design focus I was trying to achieve creatively. I was sure the receptive client would want some more cutting-edge solutions than these large businesses were offering.'

Having found a ready market for made-to-order tableware, the David Redman London brand has come to represent the very finest elements of British craft and design, as David explains: 'Our philosophy is to embrace a community of artists in their field of applied arts and offer specialised, bespoke solutions to discerning patrons. One important characteristic is our attention to unique British craft skills and important and relevant designs for the clients themselves, who may be from many parts of the world. We are not a one-size-fits-all business.'

METICULOUS: As a qualified design historian, David Redman employs some of the world's finest artisans for painstakingly meticulous tasks like raised paste work. This little-known art form involves painting reliefs onto fine bone china using liquid ceramic, and the intensive training required to undertake this process ensures it is a very specialised skill. The same is true of the goldsmithery David Redman utilises, ranging from solid gold castings through to fabulously delicate carvings. One piece of tableware can take weeks to produce, but the end products are items to treasure – instant family heirlooms whose purity and exclusivity makes them almost impossible to value, not to mention opulent enough for state dinners and banquets.

In David's pursuit of total perfection, he is understandably drawn to other like-minded brands, and recognises an affinity with Bentley and the new Mulsanne: 'The two posters in Bentley's West End showroom are headed "Craft" and "Design". This is Bentley's brand message to the public, and with our company philosophy and having visited Crewe, I feel a great empathy towards the brand – it is very clear that craft is fundamental to their quality, design-led business.'

Revitalising the high crafts of silversmithery and glass engraving is one welcome consequence of David Redman's eponymous brand, but this company also illustrates how British craftsmanship often leads the world. As David concludes: 'We are a community of genuine talent with a British focus... supporting a receptive and emerging customer base who truly appreciate the finer details in the application of genuine art.' ▣

CONTACT: www.davidredman.com

DESIGNER
LIFESTYLE

AESTHETIC DESIGN THAT DEFINES A WAY OF LIVING

Eva Solo epitomises state-of-the-art, designer homeware. 'The brand is one of a kind in adding distinctive, individual designs to functional appliances for outgoing, design-orientated people with an individual lifestyle reflected in the things that they own,' describes Marketing Manager Jette Lykke Siggaard.

Eva Solo rethinks traditional, complicated models, stripping them down to one simple, ingenious device that does the same thing, but better. These luxury modern appliances come in unique shapes and figures made from untraditional materials, transforming Eva Solo into one of the most sought-after homeware collections available.

INTELLIGENT: The company's versatile portfolio has won more than 150 awards in the 12 years since its inception. Born out of a Danish design company with almost 100 years of experience, Eva Solo's 2010 accolades include the International Forum Product Design Award and two Gold Design Awards by JIDPO.

'Our best products are thought up when the designers are in need of a special utensil at home and think "there must be a better way of doing this",' says Jette. 'If they can't find what they need, they develop it themselves.'

Inventions by Danish design duo Henrik Holbaek and Claus Jenson include a self-watering plant pot, an ice cube cooler, whisky glasses that create beautiful ripples in the drink, and an all-in-one cheese slicer and rind knife. 'The designs are often so basic that you wonder why they haven't been thought of before,' adds Jette.

SUPERIOR: The collection blends beautifully with modern and traditional homes, complementing all interiors. 'The products go well as part of a personal mix of possessions, in among things you've inherited, things you treasure, novelties and luxury items,' Jette explains. 'I live in a modern, contemporary apartment during the week and a traditional summer cottage on the weekends, and Eva Solo products look very attractive in both.'

Reinventing convention with superior designs that are made with highest-quality materials for unrivalled functionality and durability in elegant, contemporary forms, Eva Solo pieces are truly ingenious, such as the CaféSolo. Coffee beans and boiling water brew in the heat-resistant glass flask, and the coffee is automatically filtered by the drip-free filter funnel as it pours through the smart tip-up lid. Eva Solo's teamaker has a similar straining system, but tea leaves can be placed in a filter-holder, and a plunger stops the brewing process. Available in various sizes, with trendy, geothermal zip-up covers in sand, black and dark brown, these products have won 20 awards between them. The first cup of the day has never been so appealing.

Latest creations include an iced-tea maker and an easy-to-clean outdoor gas grill made exclusively from stainless steel. 'Design should always prompt a discussion,' Jette muses. 'People care about these inventions: they are provocative and spark a response.' ▣

CONTACT: www.evasolo.com

SLEEPING IN
LUXURY

THE MOST INNOVATIVE DESIGNS TEAMED WITH THE MOST DURABLE MATERIALS ENSURE
HÄSTENS' BED COLLECTIONS ARE BOTH QUALITY AND STYLISH

Sleeping is one of the most important functions the human body performs, yet very few of us regularly enjoy a good night's sleep, which can affect well-being and cause impatience, lethargy and irritability among other problems. With sleep accounting for an estimated one-third of a person's life, Brent Cooper, a sleep expert at luxury bed-makers Hästens, is dedicated to ensuring his customers can enjoy uninterrupted sleep in a bed that correctly supports them, making their waking hours calmer and more productive. 'Many people will spend more money on a personal trainer or car than on a bed, even though they would use it more often and for longer,' Brent explains. 'When people come into Hästens we want to change their mindsets to get them thinking properly about beds and achieving regular, restorative sleep.'

Hästens is a family-owned bed manufacturer based in Sweden, which has been making beds since 1852. Its products are sold in almost 200 outlets around the world, including department stores, specialist bed retailers and individually owned dealers who sell only the Hästens brand. Brent and his family hold responsibility for the three showrooms in the UK that are dedicated to selling Hästens' products – the UK flagship on the Kings Road, Crawford Street in London's West End and the Walton Bed Studio in Walton-on-Thames, Surrey. The three showrooms offer unparalleled service and expertise in both the products and sleep well-being, with the Kings Road store often ranking high within Hästens' listings for its best shop in the world.

EXPERTISE: Brent has many years of experience in the bed industry, having worked for more than 30 years with products by well-known brands such as And So To Bed and Vi Spring. While running his own shop, the London Waterbed Company in the Crawford Street location, Brent was approached by a representative from Hästens who wanted him to sell the brand in the UK. 'I travelled to the factory determined not be impressed,' he explains. 'But when I got there I was amazed by how quiet it is because the majority of the work is done by hand – there are hardly any machines.' After being left to spend almost 20 minutes laying on the Hästens' 2000T bed, Brent was sold on the brand: 'I was under the spell; I'd been in the bed industry for so long, working with different brands and designing beds so I knew how they should feel, but I'd never experienced anything like the 2000T – it had the most amazing support system.'

BESPOKE: Each Hästens bed is designed and handcrafted for strength and stability, and the models are available in a range of tensions – soft, medium, firm and extra firm – all individually tailored for the customers' needs; the bed can also be dual tension so that it is comfortable for both people sleeping in it. The exclusive beds are made using 100 per cent natural materials, including slow-grown pine, horsehair, flax, pure new wool and hand-tempered steel springs, and are available in bespoke sizes and colours, displaying the recognisable Hästens check print. »

I'd never experienced anything like the 2000T – it had the most amazing support system

The use of these materials ensures that the bed can adapt to any body shape to aid comfort and durability. 'There's no other luxury bed-maker like Hästens,' adds Brent. 'The detail that is put into the beds is unrivalled and quality is never compromised. If Hästens puts its name and blue check on it, then that bed is going to be the best it can possibly be.'

The most exclusive bed that Hästens creates is the Vividus; only 50 are made to order each year and expert craftsmen can spend between 140 and 160 hours meticulously constructing it, taking into account a client's weight, build, age and taste. The Vividus has received endorsement from celebrities and royalty, and – as with all Hästens beds – is accompanied by a 25-year guarantee. In fact, the company is so confident about the quality of its products that in 2007 a survey was carried out to find the oldest Hästens bed in daily use. 'Across Europe there were plenty of people who were using beds that were more than 50 years old,' says Brent. 'But there was one guy whose bed was made in 1908; the company offered to replace it with a new one for him but he refused because he still slept in it comfortably every night!'

ADVICE: Complementing Hästens' high-standard products is the advice given in the stores themselves by Brent and his family, who all have many years of experience in the bed industry. Hästens also trains its dealers from around the world in how to sell and communicate well to customers, and about various sleep disorders, in conjunction with the University of Stockholm, chiropractors and osteopaths. Brent offers customers a personal service, in which he puts this in-depth knowledge to use, involving a sleep analysis and lifestyle consultation to identify the correct support system needed. 'We want people to move away from just patting a bed to spending time laying on it, getting comfortable and laying how one should sleep – on their back, arms by their side and legs slightly apart,' he explains. 'When they experience a bed that is more in tune to what their body needs they are amazed by the support and relaxation.'

EXCELLENCE: Because beds and associated sleep matters are all that Hästens deals in, it has to excel in these areas – which it does through its products and support services. 'To help us achieve this we have quality people who are loyal, well trained, motivated, dedicated and who all make positive contributions towards our customers' satisfaction,' says Brent. 'We want every customer to leave our store with an indelible memory of their visit and, when they take delivery of their bed, their reaction to be: "I'm absolutely delighted that I invested in a Hästens bed." We never forget that all our customers must receive a lifetime experience that exceeds the value of their investment.'

CONTACT: www.hastenswestend.com

SILVER LINING

JENNY EDGE'S CHILDHOOD CURIOSITY LED TO A
NEW WAY OF LIFE AS A DESIGNER SILVERSMITH

As a child Jenny Edge, the granddaughter of Harry Hawker – an early aviator and an acquaintance of Henry Royce – was interested in the silver objects in her home; she was fascinated by their curves and the shiny, polished metal. This interest developed over time and led to Jenny pursuing silversmithing as a hobby; a pastime which has evolved to become her main business.

PASSION:
'My first career was as a medical researcher,' she explains, 'and I used to take some evening classes in silversmithing. Once I had my two daughters, I decided to look into it more seriously and train to become a qualified silversmith.' Jenny studied for City & Guilds qualifications in silversmithing and enamelling at John Cass College in London. Interested in an advanced technique called anticlastic raising, she was fortunate enough to attend the last course run by Heikki Seppa, a renowned silversmith who had introduced this technique to the modern industry, and who greatly inspired Jenny with his teaching and philosophy.

'Anticlastic raising has been used for a very long time, but it doesn't create a very practical shape, which is why traditional silversmiths use it just for things such as handles or spouts, and focus more on synclastic raising to create a curved, containing, bowl-like shape,' says Jenny. 'Anticlastic raising causes the curves to run in opposite directions, making "saddle-like" shapes that are very distinctive and quite unexpected.'

FLOWING:
The use of anticlastic raising is apparent in all of Jenny's work, and she often combines it with synclastic raising so that her designs can be used practically. Her collection includes grand candelabras, detailed bowls, swirling sculptures and delicate earrings. The items all incorporate flowing curves in their design and Jenny will often gild or enamel the inside of the curve with bright colours to create a strong contrast with the silver. 'I like to combine the bright colours of enamel with the flowing forms produced by anticlastic raising to make my work distinctive,' she says. 'Even when I make a practical item, such as a candlestick, it still has a flowing, sculptural form.' Anticlastic raising, welding and enamelling are all highly laborious techniques which are rarely seen in combination.

EXPLORE:
Jenny's work has developed and expanded over the past 20 years. She holds responsibility for her whole business from initial designs right through to sales, and says: 'I am very much a "one-man band". I exhibit work at Asprey and other galleries, but take part in various exhibitions as I like to sell directly to the customer.'

Her collection has also received awards for design, silversmithing and enamelling from the Goldsmiths' Craft and Design Council, and Jenny brought her passion for anticlastic raising to a new audience when she became a short-course tutor in the technique at both Birmingham School of Jewellery and West Dean College.

'I want to explore the technique of anticlastic raising further,' she says. 'I am always looking to produce more designs and shapes, especially in larger pieces. The joy for me is coming up with new shapes and new sculptural forms.' ▣

CONTACT: www.jennyedge.co.uk

> "
> *Taking his main inspiration
> from the building itself and its
> surroundings, Doug Atherley
> takes the light, space and
> atmosphere into account*

HELMUT NEWTON

INTERIOR
EXPERTISE

KINARI DESIGN'S WORK BRINGS CREATIVITY TO BUSINESS

Making a career change from international banking to join the world of interior design is a brave move, but one that Doug Atherley embraced after a banking career spanning more than 20 years.

PASSION: Doug's interest in design first began as a hobby when he bought a house in London in the early 1990s. Having initially hired architects, he took a 'hands on' approach to the refurbishment of the house – attending site meetings, designing layouts, and choosing all the materials and furniture. 'I have always been interested in the design and style of many things,' he explains, 'from cars to clothes, architecture and household objects. It was probably when I got bored with finance that I decided it should become more than just a hobby.'

After training at the New York School of Interior Design and the Inchbald Design School in London, Doug established Kinari Design in 2002. The international design consultancy specialises in the interior architecture, design and decoration of residential and commercial properties, as well as a growing presence in the property development field.

After a long career in the City, Doug has a good network of contacts and often finds himself working for acquaintances and customers from the financial, legal and corporate sectors, with his work gaining recognition through word-of-mouth recommendations. Key to his success is listening to clients to incorporate their ideas, from structural features, colours and furniture through to ornaments, artwork and door handles. 'I work with the clients every step of the way and they have huge input into the designs,' says Doug. 'Many are already very design literate and mainly need someone who can put all their ideas together and make them flow.

'Being able to build up a relationship with clients is a huge plus, and I share their enthusiasm and desire to have a beautiful property at the end of all the work.'

Taking his main inspiration from the building itself and its surroundings, Doug takes the light, space and atmosphere into account, and also draws inspiration from his extensive travels in Asia. Many clients also want their own exclusively designed features such as wine cellars, private cinemas and swimming pools.

SKILLED: Doug's background is a major selling point of Kinari Design, with his business experience assuring clients that their home is in capable hands. 'I ran a global sales operation dealing with clients around the world, who all had different agendas and requirements,' he explains. 'It's great experience to have because if you are running a project for a client they want regular updates and, on more complicated projects, I could be dealing with up to 15 other professionals such as sub-contractors, plumbers and architects. I can ensure that the whole project runs smoothly.'

SKILLED: Having recently returned as a freelance consultant to the British Institute of Interior Design (BIID), following a previous stint as a board director, Doug is working with the organisation to explore how the industry can grow and tie into business generally. He adds: 'Over the last few years interior design has changed dramatically with a more international, professional feel and the attitude to design has completely changed; there's a lot more publicity with books and magazines widely available.

'I think if someone is going to spend £5–10 million on a home, then they are more than likely going to hire a designer.' ▣

CONTACT: www.kinaridesign.com

DREAM
DESIGNER

ENJOY THE ULTIMATE IN INTERIOR DESIGN WITH
THE CREATIVE INSTINCTS OF THIS TALENTED AND
PASSIONATE DESIGNER

Over the last 20 years Pippa Toledo has established an enviable reputation as one of the leading interior designers in Malta and her company, Pippa Toledo Design Ltd, has become synonymous with style and quality. Such is her expertise that both commercial and domestic clients rate her in equal measure, which is due not just to the high standards of her work but as a reflection of her unfailing ability to take a client's dream and turn it into reality. While two decades of experience mean customers can have complete confidence in her design process, she sees her first talent as the ability to listen to the ideas behind a project before taking it forward. 'My aim as an interior designer is rooted in a philosophy I've followed from the outset,' she says. 'It's very important to me that I identify and showcase the client's individuality, because it is their personality and their taste I am reflecting through my work.'

DETAILED: Having so much experience in both commercial and domestic work ensures that Pippa is always at the forefront of the latest styles and developments. Clients are confident that she can apply the same expertise, time and attention to detail to every job, irrespective of size. Much of her work is bound up in the simple principle of respect, with the recognition that to every client their project is the most important. Pippa is able to put herself in their

66

Pippa considers the intrinsic elements of her approach to be style, originality, glamour and cheerful settings, which seem to work beautifully for all her clients

shoes and harness that emotion throughout the design process which constantly reflects and reiterates the client's involvement, enhanced and guided by her experience in both new developments and renovations. 'Attention to detail is equally important in every project,' explains Pippa. 'That's what makes a job not just a success but a joy – for both the customer and myself. The length of time I've been in business and the experience I have clearly make a difference, as I have developed the ability to recognise and move with particular trends and to remain contemporary at all times, with style and glamour being constant watchwords.'

METICULOUS: All projects begin with a design proposal, which is essentially a written brief that helps design the client's dream. Pippa begins work on this after a meticulous study of the space, producing various design presentations and eventually final computer-generated perspective drawings accompanied by a detailed costing document. She can supply drawings as well as service existing drawings for all contractors' needs and reflects her design according to each client's personality and preferences. Every project begins with a blank page and there are no preconceived ideas apart from the constant goal of aiming to surpass all original hopes for the project. Expert in the art and science of successful renovation, Pippa Toledo Design

can help transform space to meet needs and do so beautifully and with minimal upheaval.

SKILLED: Pippa considers the intrinsic elements of her approach to be style, originality, glamour and cheerful settings, which seem to work beautifully for all her clients, who have varying tastes and demands. Numerous high-profile commercial projects, which include offices, restaurants and cafes, and an equally wide variety of domestic ones testify to this, with every assignment adding to her list of satisfied customers. Her expertise and awareness of what works in a wide variety of settings and situations – whether colourful or minimalist, traditional or flamboyant – takes a very special talent, but this is a skill at which Pippa clearly excels. ▣

CONTACT: www.pippatoledo.com

PLAN FOR THE
FUTURE

AS IT CELEBRATES ITS TWENTIETH ANNIVERSARY, PLAN ASSOCIATED ARCHITECTS
CONSISTENTLY PUSHES FORWARD THE BOUNDARIES OF ARCHITECTURE AND PLANNING

With expertise in fields as diverse as architecture, town planning and interior design, Plan Associated Architects has developed an admirable portfolio of talents since its inception. The firm was founded by three young friends in 1991, including Portuguese architect and town planner Armando Dos Reis, whose role was to devise a long-term master plan for the country's Algarve region.

The inaugural project for Armando involved work on a luxurious residential and tourist development in the Algarve, named Quinta do Lago, where he was the supervisory architect and town planner. Over time, the company expanded its workforce and word-of-mouth recommendations began to draw in more business from elsewhere. Each new commission was viewed as a showcase for the company's design skills and quality-based ethos, and by the new millennium an eight-strong team was working on projects as diverse as town planning and interior design. By 2006, expansion necessitated a move to new premises, and the location chosen was a refurbished office on the cusp of Quinta do Lago itself. Adopting the moniker of Plan Associated Architects in 2008, the company

With expertise in fields as diverse as architecture, town planning and interior design, Plan Associated Architects has developed an admirable portfolio of talents

had truly come of age as a globally renowned organisation, celebrated as a leading exponent in its various specialisms. Today, it has a team of 16.

MULTI-DISCIPLINED: Currently celebrating its 20th anniversary, Plan Associated Architects draws on a wealth of multi-disciplined experience for each new project it undertakes. Every drawing and plan is completely bespoke, tailored to a client's precise requirements and reflecting the constantly changing priorities within society as a whole. Staff proudly admit that when asked to name their best project, the answer will simply be 'the next one', in recognition of an unswerving focus on constant improvement. As well as its core areas of expertise, Plan Associated Architects also offer a variety of other services, from feasibility studies through to cost control. The result is a one-stop shop from inception to completion, which not only simplifies things from the customer's perspective, but also results in better communication through the various stages and processes.

Praise for this pioneering approach has come from various quarters. An award-winning urban development in the Chinese province of Hainan earned Plan Associated Architects international

recognition, as did the similarly successful Tavira Bay waterside development in the Algarve. Here, two compact islands of properties are surrounded by cool blue water and connected to the main development by bridges; there is berthing for seven-metre boats underneath the curved bank of mainland properties, all of which are elevated above the water on stilts. With a water-levelling dam and nautical club (complete with bar and restaurant) also onsite, Tavira Bay received universal approval from the relevant environmental institutions, in recognition of its ingenious and pioneering design.

DIVERSE: Today, Plan Associated Architects is working on projects ranging from a home for the elderly through to a five-star beachfront hotel in the Portuguese town of Lagos. Involving 20,000 square metres of construction, this 220-room resort features huge swathes of open space punctuated by dramatic infusions of colour. The linear design brings to mind Dutch canal-side homes, and extensive use of balconies draws copious natural daylight into each room and suite.

With active projects around the world, from Brazil to Angola, clients of Plan Associated Architects are typically inspired by the company's ambitions and expectations. Each new project is expected to feature the very best elements of design, quality and exclusivity, intertwining modern technology and environmental awareness, in terms of both construction methods and synergy with the surrounding area. Simplicity is often overlooked in the pursuit of success, but many Plan Associated Architects projects achieve and surpass their stated aims without resorting to unnecessary embellishment. ◻

CONTACT: www.planassociados.pt

179

FIT FOR THE
KING

ROMANTIC ALLURE WITH IMPECCABLE SERVICE MAKES ROYAL MANSOUR MARRAKECH A TRUE ADVENTURE

The vision of a king is realised with the Royal Mansour Marrakech – a proud display of Moroccan national heritage. This hotel is a private project of King Mohammed VI, who wanted to create a place that would reflect the best of his country. The majestic buildings have a light and airy charisma, and the interior is handcrafted by local artisans.

Marrakech, one of few original Moorish cities, is a vibrant market town and the main square bustles with acrobats, musicians, snake charmers, whirling dervishes and dancers, as well as street vendors of all sorts. The Royal Mansour Marrakech is a medina within a medina, a community of 53 riads (traditional houses with interior gardens), built on 3.5 hectares and completely surrounded by its own 16-foot wall, one side consisting of the ancient city wall.

SERENDIPITY: Though the Royal Mansour Marrakech is literally only a stone's throw from the busy centre of Marrakech, it is an oasis of calm, beauty and comfort. Fountains and water displays contribute soothing sounds of water, interrupted only by birdsong and the occasional calling of the faithful to prayers from distant minarets.

At ground level the interior garden is the centre of the house, leading to a number of reception rooms with private quarters on the first floor. Above that you'll find a rooftop terrace with a swimming pool and an Arabic tent with plush Bedouin cushions, ideal for romantic evenings as well as the high noon sun. The interior is finished with local craft techniques: silk walls, decorated wood and hand-laid mosaics.

This hotel is a private project of King Mohammed VI, who wanted to create a place that would reflect the best of his country

Despite the ornamental and classical exterior, discreet modern conveniences are all there. Each room has a touch panel controlling lighting, temperature and sound, and there is high-speed Wi-Fi wherever you go. Some of the technological wonders guests will never notice until needed, such as rain sensors which automatically extend roofs over all two-, three- and four-bedroom riads and main building in the unlikely event of precipitation.

Attention to detail defines the Royal Mansour and the locally sourced fresh and dried fruit, handmade chocolates and other courtesy items are of outstanding quality. Upon arrival every guest is greeted with their own engraved and gilded stationery.

OPULENCE: Guests are offered great choice at The Royal Mansour Marrakech. The hotel has two gastronomic restaurants for fine dining, La Grande Table Marocaine and La Grand Table Française, run by Michelin three-star chef Yannick Alléno, along with La Table, a delightful loggia and al fresco restaurant.

The Royal Mansour Marrakech also houses various bars, including the main bar, a piano bar and Le Bar a Cigare, offering an impressive selection of vintage Armagnac complemented by one of the largest exquisite cigar collections in the world. The library is beautifully designed with wooden panelling, comfortable furniture and a vast collection of books and maps. It also holds an astronomical telescope, and the beautiful wooden ceiling is designed to display the greatest work of art at a push of a button – the starlit sky.

The Spa is on three floors and contains fitness facilities, two hammams, various massages and beauty treatments as well as a large swimming pool in an orangery-style glazed pavilion.

HOSPITALITY: The standard of hospitality is evident as soon as one touches Moroccan ground. Guests are met at the airport and hotel staff take care of immigration issues and luggage while the guest is offered refreshments, thus avoiding crowds and queues before a chauffeur drives them to the hotel. The 500 multilingual, respectful and friendly staff display a rare understanding of the finer points of service as an art form. A labyrinth of underground tunnels ensures separate staff access, allowing quick and effective service with the utmost privacy and discretion. The Royal Mansour Marrakech was not merely built by a king; it is also fit for a king. ▣

CONTACT: www.royalmansour.com

> *It is the understanding that furniture is a living, usable piece of design as well as a work of art that makes Sarah Davenport special*

FASHIONABLE
FURNITURE

The usual words that are evoked when thinking of bespoke furniture are 'classy', 'elegant' and 'understated'. Indeed, all these superlatives apply to the pieces created by Sarah Davenport. However, such is the individual approach taken by the firm that even the most articulate witness to a finished piece would be forgiven for simply saying one word: 'Wow'.

The company transforms the everyday into items of extraordinary beauty or quirky functionality that turns their original *raison d'être* on its head. A games room of the most beautiful polished black wood may look elegant, minimalist and design conscious, but tuck in a discreet top drawer, lined and ready to house billiard cues, all neatly nestled in individual housings, and it becomes inspirational, at once both simple and daring, obvious and audacious.

And anyone left in doubt about the skills of Sarah Davenport should ask to see the highly original piano – a piece of furniture art that rocks, rolls and has a concert set of ivories.

CONCEPTUAL: It is the understanding that furniture is a living, usable piece of design, as well as a work of art, that makes Sarah Davenport special. The firm takes inspiration from couture, music and the natural world, merging this with snippets of ideas from cultures around the globe to fashion its designs.

It specialises in making clients' environments fulfilling and inspiring through furniture by creating space for them to work, live and play with passion and enjoyment. It embraces a myriad of looks – from futuristic to reminiscent – and time is spent researching the worldwide rainbow of techniques, innovations, styles, materials and functions to provide complete freedom and choice.

INNOVATIVE: Sarah Davenport is renowned for innovation, the use of new materials and the seamless way that the designs marry invention and tradition. The focus is on mixing ideas to create new looks that are modern and unique – its projects are full of special bits and pieces created just the once. The company has also developed a keen ability to work with designers and manufacturers to create a methodology to turn innovation of design into a practical reality.

The materials demanded by cutting-edge design are also constantly changing. So, while Sarah Davenport is adept at fashioning walnut, birch, oak and maple, it is also equally comfortable working with arenastone, parapan, zebrano, granite, quartz, glass, perspex and leather.

In fashion, there is a difference between couture and haute couture: one is exclusive, the other is exclusively yours, packed with high drama and classicism. The result is a modern piece of wearable art. Similarly, with furniture, there is a difference between a bespoke approach and Sarah Davenport. For an intoxicating mix of drama, movement, beauty and ingenuity, there is no other choice. ▣

CONTACT: www.davenportinteriors.co.uk

CREATIVE
FREEDOM

DESCRIBED AS 'THE OUTSIDER IN INTERNATIONAL
DESIGN', CARLO RAMPAZZI'S WORK DEFIES CONVENTION,
TRANSCENDS FASHION AND RADIATES JOY THROUGH
ITS USE OF LIGHT AND COLOUR

> *Carlo likes to surprise clients with 'the unexpected', trying to realise their dreams by creating something they always wanted*

Born and raised on the Swiss shore of Lake Maggiore, interior designer and architect Carlo Rampazzi expressed, from an early age, a great aptitude for drawing and use of colour, which over time he applied to furnishings and design. Described as 'the outsider in international design', Carlo produces unconventional creations – going beyond the trends of fashion – that gain acclaim from critics and access to exhibitions and cultural events.

FREEDOM: It was 1985 when Carlo, alongside Anna Del Gatto, presented his furniture collection 'La Nuova Tradizione' at Abitare il Tempo in Verona. He had designed it to counter the minimalism that held sway at the time, in such an unconventional way, that it was a turning point towards new design. Hailed as a 'golden age' by *Vogue*, his style re-valued decoration, craftsmanship and the meaning of the unique piece.

Carlo, who established the architectural gallery Selvaggio in Ascona, Switzerland, began to emerge on the international scene with a professional profile of more unusual and original work. With highly skilled decorator Sergio Villa, he created the brand CR&SV, which encompassed furniture lines, objects and fabrics, displayed in their gallery NOI, located in Paris's antique and design district – Carré d'Or.

Carlo designs according to the principle of eclecticism; he creates immersed in a kaleidoscope of experiences, including traditional and modern art, contemporary culture and antiques, with a great emphasis on experimentation with materials.

DISTINCTIVE: Carlo's versatility has no boundaries, and his designs draw inspiration from the surrounding environment. Responding to the needs of his clients, Carlo's work is an ideal match for those who wish to have a project dedicated to their style of living; clients feel as if they are protagonists in their own work of art. Often these encounters turn into long term friendship and special clients are invited to festive happenings at the gallery in Switzerland and Paris.

With his philosophy, Carlo has redesigned private residences, luxury hotels, spas, yachts, cruising boats and boutiques. An important aspect of his creations is represented by his uninhibited and incredible use of colours. Through his chromatic choice, it is as though he has exalted some of life's most positive values – courage, freedom, harmony and serenity. He likes to surprise clients with 'the unexpected', trying to realise their dreams by creating something they always wanted to do or have, but did not dare or know how to implement. All of this is seasoned with a touch of lightness and self-mockery, such as the warm-up fruit bowl covered with mink for a mountain chalet or a mirror in the midst of fluorescent butterflies.

RENOWN: Carlo's sense of class and style determines his choices for clothing, his travels and hotel, his belongings and his books. Even his cars are special, and so only an unimaginable light-lime-green-coloured Bentley could satisfy him, as well as a lobster-coloured Porsche cabriolet for summer holidays!

Carlo's success is evident throughout the world; his works are published in the best international magazines, he is invited to the most important avant-garde design events. Some of his creations are sold at renowned international auctions and are always highly sought. ▣

CONTACT: www.selvaggio.ch; www.crandsv.com
IMAGES: © Reto Guntli/Zapaimages

SHOWER
POWER

For years, the bathroom was kept behind closed doors away from the prying eyes of visitors, with cleanliness and function taking priority. However, in the 1970s, a company in Warwickshire began to think along more innovative lines, and today that company has become a flag-bearer when it comes to the transformation of the British bathroom. With an expansive product portfolio and a solution for any bathroom or en-suite, Showerlux has firmly established itself as a market leader in everything from stylish enclosures and overbath screens to luxurious walk-ins and wetrooms.

There are many elements required to create a perfect environment for showering, and perhaps the most important of these is an appreciation of how the available space can best be utilised. For this reason, Showerlux has created a made-to-measure service, allowing a shower enclosure and its finishings to be handcrafted, thus maximising all available space and making use of unconventional areas. Sloping ceilings, dwarf walls, unusually sized

A bespoke bathroom is the ultimate luxury and can convert a simple space into a personal sanctuary

door apertures and many other challenges can be dealt with effortlessly, producing something truly unique in the process.

A bespoke bathroom is the ultimate luxury and can convert a simple space into a personal sanctuary. Providing a professional service Showerlux is on hand to oversee the transformation from the initial site survey and design stages right through to the installation. Minimalist or traditional, Showerlux can deliver the vision.

FLEXIBILITY: The made-to-measure range draws heavily on Showerlux's Designa Nexus products, which themselves offer a huge variety of configurations by combining different components together. This product range effortlessly blends engineering excellence with the finest-quality materials, including frameless 2-metre-high, 10-millimetre-thick tempered safety-glass panels. Walk-in showering areas are a popular option among Designa Nexus customers, with gorgeously tactile chrome brackets making a stunning statement out of something functional. In addition, hairline aluminium joins create an impression of floating glass, and a dedicated range of low-level trays further enhances the overall look, be that a contemporary statement or a minimalist solution.

QUALITY: As with all the finest products, finishing touches can make all the difference. Tactile materials and a sense of weight behind each handle and lever create an imperceptible but all-enveloping aura of quality, and

Showerlux has developed a range of accessories to satisfy its discerning client base. Engineered from brass and polished chrome, the SLX shower valves can be specified in a variety of styles, thermostatically regulating the water temperature to within one degree centigrade even when other taps or toilets are deployed throughout the house. A variety of showerheads include deluge and hand-held units, and Showerlux's outstanding Glass Shield delivers a final invisible flourish to each and every cubicle bearing the company's name. This protective coating comprises microscopic particles that prevent any build-up from forming. Water simply runs off, limescale has nothing to bind onto, and the glass retains its factory-fresh appearance for years, with minimal cleaning required.

As you would expect from such a prestigious brand, quality and peace of mind are central to the Showerlux experience. The company itself is certified to ISO 9001:2008, while the toughened safety glass used in every shower meets BSEN 12150 standards, and even the frames are constructed out of a BSI-approved high-grade aluminium alloy. With such a rigorous focus on quality, it's unsurprising that every Showerlux enclosure receives a ten-year guarantee, and comprehensive after-sales service provides further reassurance that the newly created centrepiece of your bathroom or en-suite will look just as good for many years to come. ▣

CONTACT: www.showerlux.co.uk

SOMETIMES UNJUSTLY OVERLOOKED, THE BATHROOM CAN BE A PLACE OF SUBLIME RELAXATION AND REJUVENATION

A QUIET SPACE

I n a fast-paced world in which professional, financial and family demands seem to mount unchecked, relaxation is at a new premium. And anyone familiar with the VitrA brand will understand how its bathrooms rejuvenate body and mind through a soothing, beautiful and escapist experience.

Inspired by the Turkish hammam rituals of human cleanliness, and drawing on millennia of Anatolian ceramic art, VitrA specialises in bathrooms that transport users to another world. 'VitrA considers the bathroom experience as a whole and aims to create preferred living spaces through colour, texture and ritual,' explains Berna Erbilek, Marketing Director at VitrA's holding company, the Eczacıbaşı Building Products Group. 'Ultimately the idea is to provide a calming and versatile environment for the individual, which might be used for personal care, reading or simply relaxing.'

INTERNATIONAL: While the VitrA brand emerged in 1966, the roots of the Eczacıbaşı Building Products Group lie in a small ceramics workshop established

in Istanbul in 1942 by Dr Nejat F. Eczacıbaşı. 'In the midst of the Second World War, international trade ground to a halt and an eight-man workshop was opened with the aim of producing earthenware products, ranging from tea cups to electrical sockets, to alleviate goods shortages in import-starved Turkey,' explains Berna. 'In the years following the war, trade picked up and the company began to grow. Sanitaryware was now its area of specialisation and production increased steadily. The company opened a production plant in 1958, and in 1977 it opened its first factory in Bozuyuk, then the world's largest factory for the end-to-end production of sanitaryware under a single roof. In 1991 a second factory was opened in Bozuyuk, this time for the production of ceramic tiles.'

Today VitrA stands as an award-winning brand and a preferred partner for prestigious projects across the world. As part of the Eczacıbaşı Building Products Group, the VitrA brand benefits from extensive infrastructural support, including 16 production sites across Turkey, Germany and France, with a 17th site under development in Russia. As such, the company is superbly geared for delivering bathrooms to customers around the world.

Reflecting on VitrA's customers, Berna explains: 'We're an increasingly international operation and our customers fall into two groups. The first group comprises sector professionals such as architects, interior designers and building contractors. The second group comprises private individuals and end users. And although these groups differ from one another in many respects, there is common ground: in each case VitrA appeals to the discerning customer who desires something different. It's a brand for the customer wanting a unique experience.'

INTEGRAL: The next decade promises exciting developments for VitrA. Building on an international reputation for delivering bathrooms of outstanding quality and matchless serenity, the company looks set to take a position among the top three European companies producing bathroom and tile ceramic products.

As a working method, VitrA fuses age-old traditions with innovative design and cutting-edge technology, and places great importance on consultation and attentive customer care. As Berna explains: 'At VitrA we listen to our customers, and we've established an organisational structure to meet their needs. We're flexible on design and production, but don't compromise on quality. In fact, we've made quality a lifestyle. In everything we do – every product and every service – we aim for the highest level of quality, and the customer is always our focal point.' And with this philosophy it is little wonder why VitrA is today playing an integral role in the bathroom's quiet revival. ▣

CONTACT: www.vitra.co.uk

PARADISE FOUND... WHERE ART, EXCLUSIVITY AND UNIQUENESS MERGE TO CREATE AN EXPERIENCE OF A LIFETIME

A PRIVATE
ISLAND
RESIDENCE

Nestled among granite boulders on the private island of Félicité in the Seychelles are the 16 sumptuous private villas that make up Zil Pasyon. Félicité is a 268-hectare undeveloped island covered with vanilla plants, coconut palms and takamaka trees, where the lush forests, secluded beaches and secret coves await their first settlers at Zil Pasyon – meaning 'Island of Passion' in the local Creole language.

These highly select villas vary in size from 612 square metres to over 1,400 square metres, each carefully placed among the magnificent granite formations and natural crevasses by multi-award-winning British architect, Richard Hywel Evans. 'Each individual residence and its positioning is unique, while the spectacular architecture will appeal to those who appreciate sublime beauty, absolute privacy, individuality and natural art, and who value owning a completely unique luxury residence,' affirms Developer Partner, Francis Savy.

> **"**
>
> *Our philosophy is to create the most awe-inspiring lifestyle for the most discerning clients, promising the ultimate in privacy and living space, with natural beauty and services to match*

EARTHY: Natural basalt surfaces meet large expanses of glass, allowing uninterrupted views of the glittering ocean from their 100-metre high perches. 'The organic chaos of the natural granite is the base, and the stonework emerges as an extrusion of the land,' says Richard. 'There is a sense of being embedded in nature, within the glimmering, Jurassic rock-faces.' Breathtaking panoramas from every room extend over curve-edged infinity pools averaging 20-metres wide, and bold contemporary interiors incorporate customised Bulthaup kitchens.

ENVIRONMENT: The entire development boasts a footprint of less than 3 per cent of the entire island. Zil Pasyon, one of the lowest-density developments in the world, has been lauded by the Seychelles Ministry of Environment as the benchmark for responsible development in sensitive environments. Rehabilitating Félicité to its indigenous state, Zil Pasyon is 'authentically transforming this already beautiful island back to the ecological jewel it once was,' explains ecologist Steve Hill. 'Among all the luxuries on offer from the island management and sophisticated infrastructure, the opportunity to live in such a magically evolving, 100-per-cent-authentic natural environment must be counted among the most significant privileges on earth.'

IRRESISTIBLE: With the aspiration to create truly memorable experiences, Managing Director Jenni Beggs comments: 'Our philosophy is to create the most awe-inspiring lifestyle for the most discerning clients, promising the ultimate in privacy and living space, with natural beauty and services to match. Island life offers everything from fishing, snorkelling and diving to swimming with turtles, nature trails and the world's finest luxury spa treatments. Residents can explore in their own electric GEM cars, or be whisked away to neighbouring La Digue Island to visit the cultural museum and enjoy the authentic Creole lifestyle, or visit nearby Praslin Island to play on the 18-hole championship golf course. This can be done in a few minutes by private helicopter or 15 minutes in a Sunseeker motor yacht.'

VIVID: As well as total privacy and seclusion, owners can also enjoy a vibrant, enticing social scene. Fine dining offers international cuisine and authentic Creole flavours, cooked with the finest organic ingredients freshly grown on the island. Together with local entertainment, bars and restaurants, decadent underground parties can be held in 'The Rock Cave', featuring the original Rolling Stones *Beggars Banquet* artwork as a centre-piece, and a wide selection of vintage wines stored in the granite rock.

It is little wonder that Zil Pasyon won Best Development in the Seychelles and Best Architectural Design at the 2008 CNBC Asia Pacific Property Awards. As Jenni says: 'Seeing is believing! Once you have visited and experienced the project first hand, you will be unable to resist.'

CONTACT: www.zilpasyon.com

ENJOY

4»ENJOY

FLYING
IN COMFORT

AERISTO TAILORS EXCLUSIVE INTERIOR LEATHERS FOR LUXURY AIRCRAFT

Supplying premium quality aviation leathers, Aeristo understands that its clients want more than the current status quo. The company is based at Dallas/Fort Worth International Airport in Texas, but all of its leathers are custom-made in Europe, and for more than 20 years it has built up a loyal and solid customer base that spans the Americas, Europe, the Middle East and Asia.

Aeristo researches, develops and distributes interior leathers and associated seating comfort products. As part of its ethos to provide clients with the best-quality products and service, the company employs a dedicated customer-oriented team of professionals and only partners with reputable, state-of-the-art and environmentally sound manufacturing organisations.

FIRST-CLASS: The company has a wealth of experience in the leather industry; founder and President Christian Schmidt grew up in the family leather business, which became one of the leading tanneries in Europe. Gaining the knowledge and skills needed to work with leather, Christian decided to venture into the aviation industry, which he had found to be a niche market for speciality leathers, and is now celebrating two decades in mastering the art of fine-tuning luxury leathers for bespoke aircraft interiors.

Establishing itself in early 1991, Aeristo introduced its first custom aircraft leather, developed and manufactured with Stuttgart's renowned C.F. Roser Tannery, which was for many years the exclusive supplier of leather to Mercedes-Benz.

> Celebrating two decades
> in mastering the art
> of fine-tuning luxury
> leathers for bespoke
> aircraft interiors

Connolly Brothers, leather tanners & curriers from England, chose Aeristo as its exclusive partner in the aviation industry. Together they developed Aerolux, a trendsetting technical luxury leather for the bespoke jet interior. Another joint success story was Raytheon's Jaguar Special Edition King Air.

CHOICE: Aeristo can provide clients with a variety of options. It stocks some 15,000 hides – probably the largest inventory of certified aviation leathers in the world – in more than 160 different colours. Its premium leathers include Aeronappa, Volaero, Aerolino and Belvedair, and it can boast prestigious clients such as Bombardier/Flexjet, Embraer, Gulfstream, Lufthansa Technik, Pilatus Aircraft and Virgin America Airlines among its 450 business relations.

With a highly qualified and professional team, every hide is inspected in detail as it arrives from manufacturing partners: diagrams and logbooks are kept per production lot for traceability purposes; each lot is tested for compliance with Federal Aviation Administration (FAA) requirements by independent laboratories for ease of mind; and abrasion tests are performed in house to guarantee best field performance of the leathers. Aeristo is dedicated to providing the highest-quality leather for the aviation industry.

ADVANCING: To enhance both passengers and pilots' comfort while airborne, Aeristo focuses on using ultra-lightweight and technologically advanced materials to provide an appropriate solution. Its most recent products have used technologies and materials established in the motor car industry that have been adapted to suit aviation requirements: VentiMesh is a passive seat ventilation and comfort material with fire-blocking capabilities; Fybairheat consists of lightweight heating foil systems used for seating, flooring and panels; and the Aerovitt seating system prevents fatigue on long journeys and promotes blood circulation. Air pads below the surface of the seat massage the upper thigh, hip and buttock area, relieve back and spinal muscles, and replenish fluids in the vertebral discs ensuring each journey is relaxing and in comfort.

In 2009, Aeristo expanded its operations with a new 50,000 square foot facility and a focus on continuing to provide value and extra services to clients. In tune with the aviation industry's goal of making aircraft greener, more efficient and lightweight, the company has invested in high-precision machinery that will reduce the weight and thickness of its leathers.

Aeristo measures its success not only by volume of sales, but by the successful relationships it holds with customers and partners, which it sees as a direct reflection of the quality of its products and the service it strives to provide. Christian explains: 'Aeristo is all about substance, performance, product development, quality control and customer satisfaction, proven by the fact that we thrive on referrals in what is actually a rather small but highly demanding industry.' ▣

CONTACT: www.aeristo.com
IMAGES: (L–R) Gulfstream G650 with Aeristo Belvedair Leather; Rotinda, Aeristo's Nubuck Leather Collection; Pilatus PC-12 featuring Aeronappa Leather by Aeristo

HIGH
FLYERS

"

Air Partner's legendary reputation for personal service has earned it the patronage and praise of the world's leading figures

OVER THE LAST 50 YEARS, THIS UNIQUE COMPANY HAS PROVIDED EVERY TYPE OF AIRCRAFT FOR EVERY CONCEIVABLE REASON, IN EVERY CORNER OF THE WORLD

Since its formation in 1961, Air Partner has established a unique niche in the air travel sector by providing every type of aircraft for every reason, in every corner of the world. With unparalleled levels of customer service, allied to absolute discretion and continual innovation, Air Partner has effectively become the airline of choice for royalty, business leaders and high net worth individuals.

PERSONALISED: Based at London Gatwick but operating 24/7, year-round, out of 20 offices worldwide, Air Partner's constant focus is on providing unsurpassed, private travel solutions, often overcoming enormous logistical challenges to co-ordinate and deliver perfectly tailored services, every time. The company's inherent belief that a client relationship is for life is reflected by the presence of a dedicated account manager for each customer, who brings together all elements of a trip, from before take-off to after landing, including helicopter or limousine transfers to hotel accommodation.

Air Partner's legendary reputation for personal service has earned it the patronage and praise of the world's leading figures. As the Supplier of Aircraft Charter to Her Majesty Queen Elizabeth II, the company holds the only Royal Warrant in the aviation industry, serving as a globally recognised mark of excellence.

Numerous other distinguished individuals have relied on Air Partner for decades, from heads of state to captains of industry. One of the company's most frequent flyers describes Air Partner as being able to 'deliver the impossible as a matter of routine'.

Air Partner is a world-leading, highly experienced air charter company with a specialist Private Jets division to cater for individuals through to groups of up to 20, and a Commercial Jets division that uses airliners to move larger groups. It even has its own in-house IATA travel agency and its relentless focus on excellence has seen it pass every audit ever carried out – by regulators, security services, aviation authorities and presidential protection teams alike.

Flying by private jet is flexible and convenient. First there is the utter pleasure of arriving at your local departure airport 15 minutes prior to take-off before being whisked effortlessly to a luxurious aircraft for a flight that takes you as close to your final destination as possible. Then, having the freedom to fly home from a different airport, even another country, adds flexibility to an itinerary and gives you more treasured quality time.

Air Partner prides itself on freeing its clients from the tyranny of crowded airport hubs and endless queues with pre-selected levels of luxury and refinement.

OPTIONS: Two private jet-flying options are available – bespoke ad-hoc charter, with no commitment beyond the flights themselves, and the competitively priced Air Partner JetCard. JetCard offers six categories of jet with fully-inclusive and transparent prices for 25 hours' flight time, discounts on qualifying return trips and the freedom to cancel at any time. A carbon-neutral JetCard can be purchased for a 2 per cent premium over standard JetCard rates.

With Air Partner, flying private means exactly that. Every detail of a journey – tailored schedules, routings and passenger information – remains confidential, providing complete privacy and security. It's an attractive, simple, stress-free flight option with the prospect of flight cancellations, delays and check-in queues firmly off the radar.

To date, Air Partner has organised more than half a million flights. VIP passengers have included prime ministers and presidents; celebrities and sports personalities; military personnel, troops and disaster zone evacuees; entrepreneurs and wealthy individuals. While similar companies may talk about success, Air Partner delivers it – to more than one million passengers every year. It builds relationships for life. ▣

CONTACT: www.airpartner.com

SUPER
YACHTS

AS THE SUPERYACHT INDUSTRY CONTINUES TO BOOM, THIS INTERNATIONAL CONSULTING COMPANY HAS THE EXPERIENCE AND EXPERTISE TO MEET EVERY SPECIALIST NEED

Argyra Consulting is an international consulting company providing unique business and management services to the maritime and luxury yachting industries, whether that is for a new-build yacht, a refit or an upgrade. With the required experience and expertise for all scenarios, Argyra is making life infinitely easier for customers by dealing with every aspect of their projects, facilitating what they are aiming for with minimum upheaval and ensuring that their specifications are fully met.

EXCITING: 'The super yacht industry is an exciting and growing industry, and a new sector for many businesses to target,' explains Managing Director, Scott Hay. 'The majority of our customers already have a boat and enough experience to give them a real sense of where they go next; our aim is to take that dream and turn it into reality. Some clients will be really involved and want to be a major part of the process, while others look for inspiration from us or have the bulk of their input at the planning stage. We're happy to help at any level, and confident that we can take our customers' concepts and produce exactly what they are looking for.'

TAILORED: Every project begins in the same way, with a detailed initial planning meeting to highlight exactly what the customer is aiming for and to allow Argyra, thereafter, to develop a very tailored project management service, delineating all requirements and the owner's needs for the duration of the project. This includes writing specifications to go to boatyards for tender, reviewing specifications forwarded by a yard prior to contract signing, overseeing full-build projects, or consulting and advising on specific areas of the yacht from upgrading an ageing communications system to giving an engine room an overhaul. Argyra oversees projects as the owner's representative for the duration of the build or refit, working closely with the yard and setting up an office on site for the duration of the project. A tailored project-management service ensures everything is completed in a timely and cost effective manner, as Argyra has the practical know-how and the business acumen to ensure the owner's best interests.

ASPIRATIONAL: 'We are a team of internationally experienced industry specialists, each bringing a different edge to the company,' says Scott. 'The result is a balanced mixture of practical maritime experience combined with the latest technology and information, to offer a truly cost-effective and valuable service.'

Argyra's collective marine industry experience of over 15 years, specifically to the superyacht industry for more than ten, results in an unrivalled, refined and dedicated expertise in two main service areas: business services to companies wishing to enter the yachting world, tailoring their profile to target this exciting industry; and consultancy services for owners wishing to build a new yacht, refit an existing one, or upgrade certain elements of one they currently own. Argyra works closely either with its own naval architects, or an owner's specific designer, to capture the dream desired.

'Valuable experience on board, at sea and in a business environment has given us unique insight into all situations,' says Scott. 'No dream is too great and we aim to provide solutions to all requests, no matter how big – or how bizarre – they may seem. We take care of every aspect, so the owner can sit back, relax and watch his dream materialise in front of his eyes.' ▣

CONTACT: www.argyra-consulting.com

AN OCEAN APART

CITADEL YACHTS SETS THE STANDARDS FOR AMERICAN-BUILT
STEEL EXPEDITION VESSELS

The Pacific Northwest Trawler is known for its distinctive commercial design, featuring an aggressive high bow, wide beam and forward-raking pilothouse. With stability and strength, it is capable of tackling the worst sea conditions on the planet in a commanding and reliable fashion – a heritage that is the keystone of Citadel Yachts.

The company's founder and CEO, Greg Ward, launched Citadel Yachts in 2004 with an aim of producing robust steel vessels that could transport their owners and crew safely on trans-oceanic voyages in maximum comfort. With that goal in mind, he gathered a highly experienced team to design a line of high-endurance, long-range vessels, and the company hasn't looked back.

Building luxury, world-class expedition yachts from 82 to 122 feet in length and crammed with creature comforts, each and every vessel created by Citadel is custom-tailored to each client's exacting criteria.

The beam of a Citadel yacht is, on average, 15 per cent wider than that of its competitors' models of similar – or longer – length

OCEAN-GOING: Greg started out in the commercial shipbuilding and fishing industries, and is firmly convinced that steel is the best material for safety and durability, resulting in less roll than either fibreglass or aluminium, and leading to a far smoother ride. 'We believe no other material is stronger or safer; and since all the major navies, commercial ships and offshore commercial fishing vessels in the world are using steel, we must be on the right path,' he enthuses. 'Steel offers high impact and abrasion resistance, structural fire protection, higher fuel and water capacities, and is easily repaired practically everywhere in the world. Secondly, building with steel allows us to be much more creative with our interior and exterior design. The strength of steel greatly reduces the need for load-bearing interior walls, which enables our clients to apply their own distinct layout and style. Each of our yachts is custom-built and handcrafted down to the smallest detail.'

Manufactured with the greatest attention to quality and detail, using the finest materials available, Citadel Yachts takes great care to choose the finest exotic woods which are finished with eight clear coats of lacquer, each application hand-sanded prior to the next. High-grade stainless steel is used extensively and polished to a mirror finish; and exterior painted surfaces take thousands of man-hours to prepare before final high-gloss coatings.

The beam of a Citadel yacht is, on average, 15 per cent wider than that of its competitors' models of similar – or longer – length, which provides substantially more interior square footage and increased stability. The end result is an expedition yacht with lower fuel, moorage and overall maintenance costs, that provides the same interior volume of a yacht 20 feet longer, but with fewer crew requirements and a more intimate experience.

Citadel's latest vessel, the 92-foot *Miss Lisa*, was described in *Megayacht News* as the finest expedition yacht ever built in the USA. Boasting a styled interior, the cabinetry is made from solid anigre, and the floors are polished marble in the en-suites and solid teak in all main living areas. *Miss Lisa* allows for long-range cruising in comfort through anything the elements can throw at it.

VISION: At Citadel Yachts, innovative design and construction techniques are constantly being studied and implemented for increased production efficiencies and reduced environmental impact. Some of these innovations include new propulsion methods, more efficient hull designs, reduced emissions and state-of-the-art waste-treatment systems.

'We are in this business because of our enthusiasm for adventure, boats and the sea,' says Greg. 'And we enjoy sharing our experience with clients in meeting their specific requirements to build a world-class yacht.' ▣

CONTACT: www.citadelyachts.com
IMAGES: © Neil Rabinowitz

SWIFT AND
EFFICIENT

THIS RAPIDLY EXPANDING AIRLINE IS SWIFTLY BECOMING THE CARRIER OF CHOICE FOR DISCERNING BUSINESS AND LEISURE TRAVELLERS

> *Providing convenient, hassle-free travel combined with award-winning service on high-frequency routes in the UK, Ireland and Europe, CityJet's extensive network offers a multitude of choices for business and leisure travellers*

Providing convenient, hassle-free travel combined with award-winning service on high-frequency routes in the UK, Ireland and Europe, CityJet's extensive network offers a multitude of choices for business and leisure travellers, with a host of convenient timings.

The largest carrier operating at London City Airport, CityJet currently offers a choice of nearly 600 flights a week from this conveniently located airport to 15 destinations in the UK, Ireland and mainland Europe. 'Offering a swift and efficient service to a wide range of destinations is our main priority,' says Catherine Stuyck, Corporate Communication Manager with CityJet. 'The reasons to fly CityJet are endless, including fast boarding and disembarkation, London City Airport's accessible location in the heart of the City, being able to check in online and earn Flying Blue miles.' As she points out, it's the customers who truly highlight the benefits of using CityJet, with the award-winning airline boasting more than 97 per cent of happy customers.

INCLUSIVE: CityJet's inflight service also has business travellers in mind, guaranteeing a quiet, comfortable inflight environment ideal for working or relaxing. CityJet has two fare families, CityValue and CityPlus, both of which feature complimentary drinks and snacks, plus luxury leather seats with ample legroom. CityPlus is CityJet's premium economy-class experience and is a totally flexible experience with no hidden charges, designed for business travellers who demand a high degree of flexibility and the highest standards. CityValue is a standard economy-class fare and is the most affordable approach to business travel, ensuring the modern business traveller gets from A to B with a minimum of fuss. Flying with CityJet means an end to uncivilised travel, with all seats assigned, all drinks and snacks included and all fares inclusive, with the welcome guarantee of no hidden fees, no credit card fees and no bag fees.

CENTRAL: At London City, the closest airport to Central London, passengers can take advantage of the no-queues policy and check in just 15 minutes prior to departure – the shortest of any UK airport – or just 20 minutes with hold baggage. Once on board, complimentary beverages and light meals are offered. London City Airport's location in the east of the capital allows easy access to all that the area has to offer. It is just three miles from Canary Wharf and connected to the London Underground via the Docklands Light Railway, providing desirable links to the City. And with a host of features tailored for business travellers, it is the UK's leading business airport.

London's premier international conference centre, Excel, which hosts numerous events from exhibitions, conferences and meetings to product launches, banquets, award ceremonies and sporting events, is within easy reach; and close proximity to the host boroughs for the London 2012 Olympic and Paralympic Games will prove invaluable for CityJet's customers in future.

Those flying in to London for pleasure rather than business will be delighted to find that The O2 is near to the airport, catering for their entertainment needs with restaurants, music, sporting and theatrical events, exhibitions and a state-of-the-art cinema. Alternatively, a journey into the West End and the heart of London's theatreland to sample award-winning shows and world-class shopping takes just 30 minutes.

With a great location, hassle-free flying and a host of destinations, it's no surprise that for many people CityJet is first choice. ▣

CONTACT: www.CityJet.com

A MEDITERRANEAN
GATEWAY

WITH ITS STUNNING AND CONVENIENT LOCATION, CLUB DE MAR-MALLORCA
IS THE MARINA OF CHOICE FOR THE DISCERNING YACHT OWNER

Visitors can rest assured they can relax and be taken care of in the ideal blend of land and sea that is Club de Mar-Mallorca

Highly spoken of in national and international leisure yachting circles, Club de Mar-Mallorca is the first and foremost sport yacht harbour on the south coast of the Balearic Islands. Its perfect location puts the cosmopolitan city of Palma on the doorstep, while the island's beautiful *cala*, or bays, renowned for their crystal clear waters, exquisite beaches and astounding natural beauty, are only a short trip away.

Offering a full range of exclusive services, ample space, and facilities for every size and type of seafaring vessel, the world-class marina of Club de Mar-Mallorca has provided a sheltered home at Palma's port since 1972. With berths ranging in size from 8 to 150 metres, and a waiting dock for those up to 350 metres in length, it is unique among nautical clubs and sport harbours in the Mediterranean.

Proud to be a marina of choice when it comes to the most important yachts of the world, its quays have accommodated, among others, the Royal Yacht *Britannia*, the *Nabila* and *La Belle Simone*. Currently, it is base port to *Lady Moura*, *Creole*, *Limitless* and *Al Mirqab*, all well known in the world of superyachts.

INCLUSIVE: Club de Mar-Mallorca is more than just a place to harbour a yacht. A hotel, bars and restaurants, swimming pool, discotheque, conference room, kids' club and a social clubhouse are all at the disposal of members and their guests; every facility is provided without a visitor needing to leave the marina. The club also has reciprocal agreements with similar establishments in Spain and abroad, permitting members to make use of their resources.

With a philosophy of discretion, security and exclusivity, the marina's main objective is to bring the highest quality of services in a privileged surrounding, using a team of professionals aimed at solving all requirements. Excellence is backed by awards such as the Blue Flag, highlighting cleanliness and care of environmental issues.

SPORTING: Since Club de Mar-Mallorca's inauguration nearly 40 years ago it has been, and still is, host and organiser of many prestigious regattas: the International Mediterranean Championship (Copa del Rey); dinghy races at the Princesa Sofía International Trophy, and the World Championship IMS in 2001. There are also regattas for classic and vintage yachts and cruisers; and following the club's sporting tradition, a sailing school for children was created in 2008 to address members' and the general public's needs.

As for the future, the main objective of Club de Mar-Mallorca is to continue with the modernisation of its premises, applying improvements and innovations to help the nautical, sporting and social activities to be carried out in the best quality conditions. Another priority for the club's board of directors, who understand the sensitive needs of the environment, is to stress among members and port users the importance of preserving natural resources, and applying an environmental management policy to guarantee quality and respect towards the marina's surroundings.

Whether choosing to stay onboard or reserve a room ashore, visitors can rest assured they can relax and be taken care of in the ideal blend of land and sea that is Club de Mar-Mallorca. ▣

CONTACT: www.clubdemar-mallorca.com

PRECISION

COMLUX AVIATION GROUP OFFERS ITS GLOBAL VIPS A COMPLETE SERVICE WITH
PROFESSIONALISM AND THE UTMOST DISCRETION

C omlux Aviation Group is one of the leaders in VIP charter services, operating worldwide with the highest standards of safety and quality. The experience and expertise it has gained since it was established in Zurich in 2003 has resulted in a quality of service which is simply superb, and a reputation that goes from strength to strength with every expansion and development. It operates with the highest standard requirements present in the aviation industry and its objective is to meet clients' expectations by always offering the best quality and the most cost-effective solutions for their aviation needs, while making confidentiality a major priority.

COMPREHENSIVE: Beyond charter operations, Comlux offers a comprehensive set of services to VIP customers who wish to have their own aircraft managed personally and professionally; and this includes exclusive aircraft management, sales and acquisitions, cabin design and completion, as well as maintenance and engineering services. Irrespective of whether a client is chartering an aircraft or having one built to specifications, the company has positioned itself in a very special market and goes far beyond just meeting the needs of clients by anticipating and pre-empting possible requirements. That can take many forms, whether working with architects, designers and developers, buying, selling or operating aircraft, or providing a complete crew

The experience and expertise it has gained since it was established in Zurich in 2003 has resulted in a quality of service which is simply superb

who speak the appropriate language and know the relevant culture of the client in the greatest detail. The quality of the service is such that once a client has experienced it they return time and again, and Comlux's excellent reputation has undoubtedly been developed on the ethos of perfection, from their welcome to briefing and timing.

DEVELOPING: Recent expansion has seen a Bombardier Global XRS joining the fleet, with a Challenger 605, another Global XRS, Airbus A318 Elite and A320 Prestige following suit, with all these brand-new aircraft being available for charter along with a 767-200ER BBJ aircraft. 'The development of our fleet is always a strategic decision, and for each and every new aircraft joining the fleet, market demand and customer satisfaction are our main objectives,' says Richard Gaona, President of the Comlux Group. 'With the arrival of the 767BBJ we will better serve our head-of-state and royal

customers. Together with our six Airbuses, we will confirm our position as the largest operator of VIP charter wide-body aircraft and we can offer aircraft management solutions to any customer.'

EXCELLENCE: The company takes huge pride in the quality of its service, working on the premise that once it has acquired a client it will never lose them, which it sees as a reflection of its Swiss origins. Everything recognised as the spirit of Switzerland is epitomised in the culture of Comlux, which is always prepared to put in the effort required to ensure excellence in every detail. As the company moves into Russia, the Middle East, Asia and China, it does so extremely confident in its service at every level, knowing that it is the luxury aircraft of choice for personalities, royalty, politicians and celebrities.

This was illustrated by Formula One World Champion Michael Schumacher selecting the company to provide his VIP flights during the Formula One Season 2010. 'I have been flying with Comlux for many years now,' says Michael. 'Travelling like this allows me to get fully rested before a Grand Prix so I always arrive well-prepared. I am excited to fly on its brand-new Bombardier Global Express XRS, which is currently one of the fastest jets in the world.' ▣

CONTACT: www.comluxaviation.com

DESIGNED AND
REFINED
AT SEA

FLEMING YACHTS ARE BUILT TO RELISH ADVENTURE

Fleming Yachts enjoy an unparalleled reputation for quality and craftsmanship. Producing three key models – the Fleming 55, Fleming 65 and Fleming 75 – the yacht developer works hard to ensure it maintains high performance standards and carries out regular sea trials to understand where new technology can work best to help it evolve.

A Fleming 55 model from 2010 may look broadly similar to a Fleming 55 from the late 1980s and may even handle in a similar way. But skippers of these yachts know only too well that technology can pack a punch where it most counts when the basic formula of success is kept constant.

FAMILY: A family-run business, founded by Tony Fleming, these days Tony's nephew, Adi Shard, his daughter, Nicky Fleming, and Duncan Cowie run the business. It remains small and tight-knit,

which means it can accommodate new ideas and adapt quickly, but also retain excellent control over day-to-day operations.

With a high level of customer-focussed attention and service that others cannot match for the price or the quality of the ocean-going ride, Fleming Yachts works out of the same single shipyard in Taiwan that Tony selected for his business 25 years ago. The Tung Hwa facility located near Kaohsiung in Taiwan was chosen because of the professionalism of the boat-building crew and the top-notch facilities.

CRUISING: 'Our original objective was, very simply, to build the best coastal and offshore cruising yacht using the experience acquired over many years of building and operating boats,' explains Tony, 'I took a fresh and objective look at every system and every piece of equipment, and selected only those which would be the best and the most practical

for a boat intended for serious blue-water cruising. The same philosophy still holds true today.'

These days Tony no longer runs day-to-day operations at Fleming Yachts. Instead he spends six months of the year cruising the world's oceans in his own personal Fleming 65. He uses this time to test out new ideas and technologies, the best of which are then adapted and incorporated within Fleming's production models.

This extensive, real-life ongoing research and development is a key reason why Flemings have become 'the ultimate cruising yacht': the best-designed and best-built in their class.

Little wonder that with more than 200 boats built to date, the Fleming 55 has become one of the most successful yacht models of all time. The 65 and 75 show every sign of replicating that success. ▣

CONTACT: www.flemingyachts.com

A DESIGN FOR
LIFE

Renowned for its meticulous attention to detail, and an unswerving commitment to perfection, Gore Design Completions produces symphonies of luxury for VIPs, heads of state and captains of industry alike. The phrase 'anything short of perfection isn't a solution at all' aptly describes the ethos of this world-leading turnkey centre for aircraft interiors.

Gore Design Completions is a rare example of a company where the staff and founders share the same vision and passion for what they do. Established in 1988 as a design firm, the company is spearheaded by the hugely experienced pairing of Jerry Gore and Kathy Gore-Walters, who serve as CEO and President respectively. As two of aviation's most respected designers, Jerry and Kathy oversee a team of experts in their respective fields, whose collective pursuit of perfection is imbued into every project bearing the company's name.

EXPERTISE: Gore Design Completions is based in a huge facility in the Texan city of San Antonio. The beating heart of its headquarters is a hangar large enough to accommodate five jets simultaneously, and patrolled around the clock by armed guards. This awe-inspiring space is home to a team of 500 people, including many of the world's finest artisans and craftsmen, who work together as a harmonious unit to maximise accuracy and expedite each completion, renovation or repair. As a turnkey completion centre, this is where

This company refuses to countenance anything less than the best, right down to the calibre of the fabrics used

WITH AN UNIMPEACHABLE PEDIGREE AND ILLUSTRIOUS WORLDWIDE REPUTATION, ONE COMPANY HAS TAKEN THE ART OF BESPOKE AEROPLANE INTERIORS TO NEW HEIGHTS

the initial designs are crafted and also where the final touches of luxury are applied, from hand-sewn upholstery to hand-carved woodwork. In the on-site manufacturing shop, each employee has an average of 15–20 years of experience in his or her particular niche.

From the moment a client approaches Gore Design Completions, a dedicated project manager will be appointed to take their vision from inception to completion, delighting the client at every step. This company refuses to countenance anything less than the best, right down to the calibre of the fabrics used, with a team of specialists responsible for creating opulent interiors out of the finest materials available and maximising space efficiency. Clients can be as involved in the design process as they wish to be; while many are happy to trust the expertise of a company with an unimpeachable pedigree, the more hands-on customers can request a private office on-site, from which they can supervise proceedings.

PERFECTION: A central tenet of the Gore Design Completions philosophy is that the journey is just as important as the destination. Each client has a different vision for how air travel can best be enjoyed, and the end result will be a standalone work of art, transforming every flight into an act of indulgence and pleasure. From the blank canvas of a functioning aeroplane, a bespoke interior will be crafted to delight even the most discerning eyes and exceed the most demanding expectations.

With expertise in fitting out both narrow and wide-bodied aircraft, Gore Design Completions has worked on Boeing and Airbus planes, with the rare distinction of being approved by both brands. It almost goes without saying that full industry accreditation and certification has been held for many years, while the team of 65 engineers responsible for each aeroplane's structural, internal and electrical designs are among the most skilled people in their fields. By giving the finest staff the best resources, a perfect marriage between ergonomic functionality and aesthetic excellence can be achieved in every project, right down to the choice of china crockery. At Gore Design Completions, results are limited only by imagination. ▣

CONTACT: www.goredesign.com

LETTING DREAMS TAKE
FLIGHT

LOMBARD PROVIDES THE FINANCING TO MAKE ITS
CUSTOMERS' DREAMS A REALITY

> *Lombard has used its long-term experience of financing assets to create a range of specialist funding solutions*

Many iconic British businesses owe their success and longevity to more than a dedication to delivering the highest quality of service and the very best in product standards. Often, the key to consolidating true potential lies in forming a partnership strengthened by a common purpose and shared brand values.

EXPERTISE : One hundred and fifty years ago, the first incarnation of Lombard was formed when The North Central Wagon Company, a railway wagon leasing firm, started up in Rotherham, South Yorkshire. The next century and a half would trace the development of Lombard through a number of strategic business partnerships into becoming what is now one of the UK's leading asset finance providers.

Developing a business over such an extensive period of time helps to shape its delivery and offering to customers, and Lombard has used its long-term experience of financing assets to create a range of specialist funding solutions to meet the needs of its most discerning clientele. In conjunction with high-profile private banking partners such as Coutts and Adams, Lombard has financed through its dedicated wealth division a variety of significant assets including superyachts, private jets and, of course, some of the finest vehicles in the world.

This experience of funding specialist assets has established Lombard's reputation in the aviation sector, where qualities of stability and strength are very important. Lombard Aviation works closely with a number of high-net-worth clients, as well as corporate customers, who are looking to fund a dream of owning their own private aircraft but don't want to be tied to one specific asset for a lengthy period of time. These clients demand the flexibility and control to acquire and interchange their aviation assets according to their business and personal needs, and Lombard can provide funding solutions that allow them to enjoy this freedom.

GUIDANCE: Aircraft acquisition can be a lengthy process, taking anything up to 18 months before delivery, so it is crucial that funding suppliers listen very closely to customer requirements and are prepared to guide them. Typically, clients will make initial contact with Lombard to discuss their specific plans, and the company will visit them and talk through individual needs. Establishing a bond of trust from the very beginning, each client is taken through every step of the process with a dedicated relationship manager – from advice on how best to retain or improve the aircraft's value over the ownership period to drawing up a purchase contract. Following a credit check, they will take the deal through to completion, working alongside any external third parties, such as lawyers, to ensure the transaction is as smooth as possible. Once financing is secure, all customers need do is wait for delivery of their aircraft.

There are a number of funding mechanisms available to aviation clients which take away much of the risk of ownership and depreciation, but the most common form adopted is the aircraft mortgage. This can be structured with a balloon repayment towards the end of the term, which can either be refinanced or the aircraft exchanged.

The beauty of an asset finance solution is that it allows customers to enjoy the aircraft they desire to own, for as long as they want, without paying more than they need or have to. Building a good relationship with the asset finance provider will help to ensure they consistently achieve the best deals they can, enjoying the full range of experiences that the aviation world has to offer. As Lombard's clients will testify: it's definitely worth the wait. ▣

CONTACT: www.lombard.co.uk/assets/aviation

WITH AN UNSWERVING FOCUS ON CREATING THE VERY BEST, THIS RESPECTED AND ADMIRED COMPANY HAS PRODUCED SOME OF THE FINEST BESPOKE INTERIORS EVER TO REACH THE SKIES

MAKING
TIME
FLY

In 1681, a German entrepreneur by the name of Johann Dietrich Rincklake opened a joinery workshop in his home town of Münster. There was no indication at the time that this modest enterprise would eventually inspire a global corporation, but 330 years on, Johann's direct descendants – the Rincklake van Endert family – have become one of Germany's most famous dynasties.

Among the many achievements of the family's descendants are the myriad business interests of the metrica® INTERIOR group, which today trades on three continents, employing 300 people across a spectrum of related industries. From hotel design to landscaping and technology solutions, this international organisation has become an established name in numerous market sectors, drawing on its rich history of craftsmanship and a traditional philosophy to set new standards across the board.

AVIATION: One of the three main divisions of metrica® INTERIOR – the others being yachts and residential property – concerns the creation or refurbishment of aeroplane and helicopter interiors, under the standalone metrica® aviation INTERIOR brand. Created in response to customer demand and with ambitious plans for future expansion, this now represents one part of the company's tripartite approach to lifestyle solutions, alongside the sea and land divisions. By employing the right people at the right place and the

> **In the years since its inception, metrica® aviation INTERIOR has produced a portfolio of truly outstanding completions**

right time, metrica® aviation INTERIOR has become synonymous with quality materials and handcrafted furnishings, creating bespoke solutions for aircraft of numerous disparate sizes and styles. Everything from complete refits to small repairs can be undertaken and, in especially urgent cases, the latter can be tackled within 24 hours.

In the years since its inception, metrica® aviation INTERIOR has produced a portfolio of truly outstanding completions. According to company founder Rudolf Rincklake van Endert, the metrica group shares its expertise freely between divisions, to the benefit of every brand: 'A particularly sensitive project was *Fortuna 2,* built for the royal house of Spain and probably still the fastest yacht in the world with a top speed of over 60 knots. Our experience in the construction of interiors for VIP aircraft helped us a lot in this case.' This cross-pollination of ideas and inspiration has helped metrica® aviation INTERIOR to produce tailor-made airline interiors for royalty, ministers and VIPs all around the world, helping them to realise their dreams of enjoying air travel to the absolute fullest.

PRECISION: It almost goes without saying that metrica® aviation INTERIOR attaches the highest standards to each and every project it tackles. Anything less would simply be unacceptable to the company's customer base, who typically view mistakes as unsatisfactory and anything less than the best as an unwelcome compromise.

The aviation division has become expert at delivering turnkey solutions customised to the specific needs of each customer, from airborne workstations to havens of relaxation. This process typically begins with design consultations where technical requirements are confirmed. It extends into the engineering itself, before concluding with the production and installation of each bespoke interior, incorporating luxurious fittings and typically Germanic levels of precision. Flexibility and lightness are key factors in the choice of recommended materials, in recognition of the need to save weight and space wherever possible, although customers can always opt for heavier materials to meet their own tastes and preferences.

Having already won awards for its market-leading solutions in the yachting industry, metrica® aviation INTERIOR continues to focus on balancing skilled craftsmanship and state-of-the-art design, allied to rigorous quality control. This global brand thoroughly deserves its place at the cutting edge of aviation, and will continue to successfully solve the very specific challenges of airline interiors for many years to come. ▣

CONTACT: www.metrica-aviation.de

The meticulously designed 'one touch' control experience is an essential part of the systems offered by Mobius Design Group

THE PERSONAL
TOUCH

MOBIUS DESIGN GROUP OFFERS A BESPOKE AND SIMPLE SOLUTION TO YACHT OWNERS' ONBOARD ENTERTAINMENT NEEDS

How liberating would it be to control everything in our homes – lighting, TVs, sound systems – all at the touch of a button? Making life easier and more convenient, it would also be an added bonus if there was someone knowledgeable on hand to help if any problems occurred. For yacht owners, there is a company that makes this dream a reality.

Mobius Design Group specialises in the installation of audio-visual, lighting and security systems onboard yachts, taking care of every aspect from planning and design to installation and service.

EXPERTISE: Founders Bob Horn and Vicki Shand-Horn each have more than 20 years' experience in the audio-visual industry, throughout Europe and the US, and it shows. 'We had both worked for companies, such as large banking groups and corporations, installing systems in boardrooms and similar environments,' explains Vicki.

The pair's experience also included live product launches and stage productions including *Chess* and *The Phantom of the Opera*, bringing a sense of theatre to their work. 'But our real passion was to install good audio-visual, entertainment and computer networks on yachts,' continues Vicki. 'We found that we really connected with clients who shared the same sense of adventure and an appreciation of innovation.'

The meticulously designed 'one touch' control experience is an essential part of the systems offered by Mobius Design Group, and has evolved from the company's use of Crestron products to provide customers with an integrated solution that is, Vicki adds, 'connected to everything so that the whole system can be controlled from one point.'

Bob himself is a Gold Level Certified Master Crestron Programmer – a rare honour, which is by invitation only and requires a lot of hard work. He also has a B.Sc. in computer science, adding technical expertise and knowledge to the mix.

'We wanted to bring all our experience together to offer a unique company that cares about the products and services it provides,' says Vicki, 'giving complete customer support and building long-term relationships.'

PERSONAL: Customers are the focus of Mobius Design Group's services. 'We listen to their ideas during the design process, tailoring the system to their specific needs, such as budget and the design of the yacht,' explains Vicki. 'We are always in contact with the customers, and the interior designer and crew, throughout the process.'

The yachts' crews are given full training in the operation of the system, and the company has remote access to each vessel's computer so that, with high-speed satellite connection, Bob and Vicki can dial in, wherever it is located, and give assistance. It is this aftercare service that Vicki says is a real strength of the company: 'There aren't too many companies who will answer the phone at midnight or at the weekend to dial into a boat and programme a system. We focus on offering our clients a personal and dedicated service because a connection and relationship with them are the main things that drive our business; we have loyal customers who recommend our services and, very often, become our friends.' ▣

CONTACT: www.mobiusdesigngroup.com

> *We view ourselves as a precision-class airport – designed, staffed, and operated specifically to accommodate the discerning private jet traveller*

AN AIR
OF CONVENIENCE

Discerning travellers have known for some time of the benefits in using Morristown Municipal Airport in New Jersey. And as word spreads of the convenience of this business airport, it is developing widespread appeal for a very good reason. While the traditional airports often associated with flying in and out of New York are well known, so too are the accompanying congestion, delays and undeniable stress of navigating travel in such a hectic environment. Just 27 stoplight-free miles from Manhattan and 18 miles from Newark International Airport, it is hardly surprising that as Morristown Municipal Airport makes its presence known to a wider audience, the positive practicalities in using this airport become very clear.

SUCCESSFUL: While practised international travellers are well aware of what makes their journey a success, from minimal delays to easy access to the finest amenities, they tend also to have had dispiriting experiences with the delays and pitfalls which can render a trip a nightmare. Morristown Municipal Airport is considerably less congested than its competitors and has significantly fewer delays, as well as being one of the most obvious metropolitan New York City options with all the infrastructure required to facilitate swift transfer and access to the finest amenities while being close to the New Jersey enclave.

THE CONVENIENCE OF THIS BUSINESS AIRPORT IS NEATLY SUMMED UP
BY SAYING THAT IT IS JUST 27 STOPLIGHT-FREE MILES FROM MANHATTAN
AND 18 FROM NEWARK INTERNATIONAL AIRPORT

New Jersey, being an urban state, is something the airport utilises to its best advantage, with four- and five-star hotels close at hand and a particularly attractive situation adding to its appeal, offering a suburban atmosphere but with all the expected urban amenities. 'We are often complimented on our park-like setting,' explains Maria Renner, AAE, Senior Director of Operations, 'and there is no doubt of the appeal of that to international travellers used only to experiencing airports situated in unmistakably dreary industrial areas.'

ACCOMMODATING: A number of major businesses have chosen to situate their corporate headquarters in the appealing and attractive surroundings of the Morris County area largely because of the availability of Morristown Municipal Airport, which provides a prime location with all the aviation amenities required to maintain a flight department within close proximity of company headquarters and one of the financial capitals of the world, New York City.

'Offering the accoutrements of a larger air-carrier airport without the associated overcrowding and inevitable landing and take-off delays, Morristown Municipal Airport makes the transition from air travel to ground destination seamless,' says Robert L Bogan, AAE, Deputy Executive Director. 'We view ourselves as a precision-class airport – designed,

staffed, and operated specifically to accommodate the discerning private jet traveller.'

DEVELOPING: Morristown Municipal Airport has a long and fascinating history, with construction finally commencing in 1941, more than ten years after the first plans for an airport in the area were discussed. On 11 November 1943, the completed airport was opened for public inspection and for the remainder of the Second World War it played an important role as a test site and training facility for Bell Laboratories. In August 1945, as the end of the war was nearing, the airport became a public-use facility and began to grow in conjunction with the community as the influx of companies and commercial development increased.

Over the years development has continued apace, with the continued introduction of facility improvements and relevant amenities ensuring that the airport has always kept abreast of technology, and in turn ensuring that its customers can depend on it being at the forefront of aviation development. The result is an airport with a reputation for swift and quality service, which has become an open secret amongst international travellers and continues to attract new customers interested in enjoying its benefits. ▣

CONTACT: www.mmuair.com

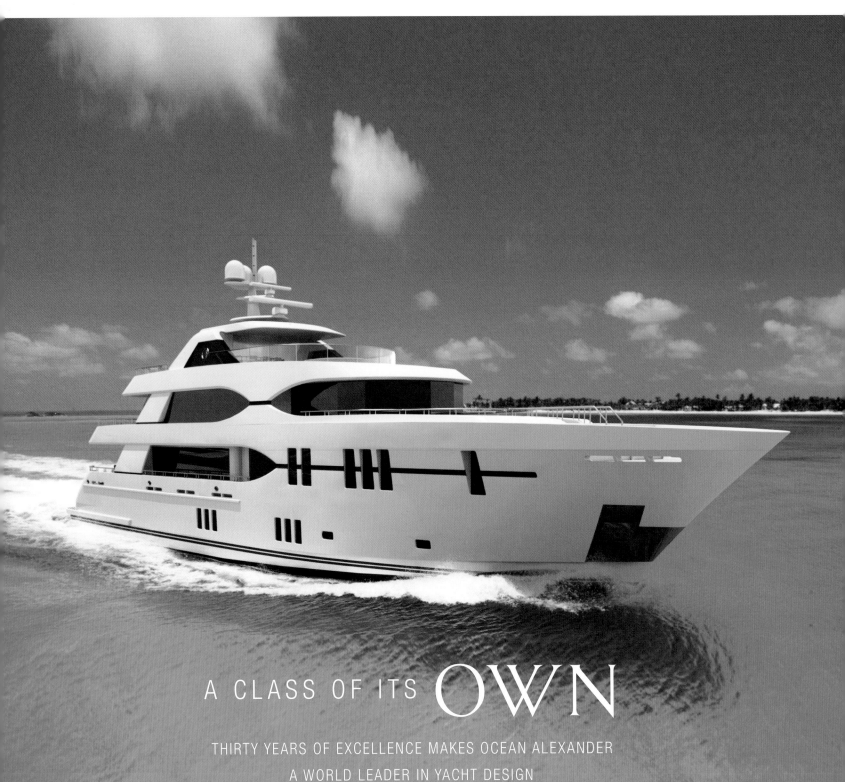

A CLASS OF ITS OWN

THIRTY YEARS OF EXCELLENCE MAKES OCEAN ALEXANDER
A WORLD LEADER IN YACHT DESIGN

> *The alliance with premier luxury yacht designer, Evan K. Marshall, resulted in the opulent styling and functionality of the new OA 120 Megayacht*

It is an indulgence to be on an Ocean Alexander yacht; when you step aboard you are instantly transported into a lifestyle of luxury, adventure and, above all, beauty. This is because Ocean Alexander understands that a motor yacht is not a necessity, but a luxury to be cherished and admired.

Each vessel is a labour of love, crafted using meticulous techniques, rare materials and applying processes that would normally be found only on custom designs. The result is an enviable series of luxury yachts that are eminently liveable, and at the same time among the most technically accomplished in the industry.

JOURNEY: The Ocean Alexander journey began 30 years ago under the leadership of Alex Chueh. Alex began with a dream to build the finest yachts in the world and formed partnerships with American design teams to make the dream a reality.

Their continued vision has seen Ocean Alexander develop from a respected family boat-building business into a world power in luxury yacht manufacturing, with vessels up to 155 feet, and new sales outlets opening across four continents.

PARTNERSHIPS: Today, Alex's son, John Chueh, continues the company's history of building excellence and commitment to innovative, independent engineering and architecture. This has led to new alliances with some of the world's finest nautical technicians, such as premier luxury yacht designer, Evan K. Marshall, who has won international acclaim for his innovative and advanced design concepts, which resulted in the opulent styling and functionality of the new OA 120 Megayacht. Ocean Alexander is also working with the well-known naval architect Gregory C Marshall and the luxury interior designer Destry Darr.

MEGAYACHTS: Thanks to John's energetic leadership and these new alliances, Ocean Alexander is now entering the most exciting period of its history and manufacturing some of the most enticing yachts of all time.

The most desirable of these are undoubtedly the new range of super yachts: 120 Megayacht (36.9 metres), 135 Megayacht (41 metres), and 155 Megayacht (47.2 metres), currently being engineered and constructed at the renowned American shipyard, Christensen Yachts, in Vancouver.

Ocean Alexander's highest-held principle is to constantly strive for perfection and their new Megayacht lines are testament to this philosophy. The custom-designed interiors have every luxury available, from exquisite custom-crafted furnishings, lavish upholstery and exotic wood fittings, to the latest in HD electronics and satellite technology. Hallmark Ocean Alexander exclusives include creative design concepts that maximise interior volume and utilise all space to optimise storage capabilities to accommodate the lengthiest of voyages. A unique pilothouse design in the Megayacht series will allow the owners and guests to enjoy the same magnificent view as the captain without hindering navigation from the helm.

Externally, the obsession with perfection continues. From thoughtfully designed outdoor entertainment spaces, to the hydrodynamic superiority of the hull tunnels, Ocean Alexander's commitment to safety and fine engineering is clear.

While guests are enjoying the decks and luxurious cabins, down below there is an impressive expanse of premier nautical equipment from the most well-known names in the industry. Meticulously placed systems exist for plumbing, hydraulic and electrical services, making it easy for the engineer and crew to access the yacht's primary systems.

It is this attention to detail, together with a breadth of vision, which has earned Ocean Alexander its worldwide reputation for exceptional quality and performance. ▣

CONTACT: www.oceanalexander.com
IMAGE: (L) Luxurious interior design by Evan K. Marshall

THE **BEST**
SEATS IN THE SKY

OFFERING A FULL PORTFOLIO OF PERSONALISED AIR TRAVEL SERVICES, TWO AFFILIATED COMPANIES AIM TO MAKE EVERY FLIGHT A DELIGHT

R egular air travel is often an essential component of modern life, and in the wrong hands, it can become a time-consuming and frustrating distraction. However, handled correctly, air travel can be a soothing and seamless method of transportation, and two affiliated companies have been cultivating an enviable reputation for delivering bespoke travel solutions around the world.

BRANDS: Although they are standalone brands, Oryx Jet and Rizon Jet are affiliated companies who work alongside each other to deliver unsurpassed business aviation solutions. The companies' respective slogans – 'Delivering you the skies' and 'The fine art of flying' – collectively highlight a focus on providing premium air travel for both private individuals and corporate clients. As world-class providers of charter aircraft, both brands combine dependable luxury with absolute professionalism, whisking people around the world in a fleet of luxury jets including Hawker 900XPs and Challenger 605s.

The differences between the two brands are subtle but significant. Rizon Jet is based in Doha, within the State of Qatar, and it flies to any destination within the Middle East, Europe, Africa and Asia. By contrast, Oryx Jet is proudly British, headquartered in Hitchin and specialising in European and Middle Eastern destinations. For the UK market, Oryx Jet is responsible for air travel, while Rizon Jet handles all the ground-based services, drawing on its considerable expertise in this area. However, both companies share

> **66**
>
> *Limousine or helicopter transfers from home or office whisk passengers to a dedicated VIP terminal, and then into a similarly exclusive lounge*

an over-arching aim of delivering value-driven solutions for time-pressed travellers.

OPERATIONS: The UK operations of Oryx Jet and Rizon Jet are based at Biggin Hill airport, just outside London. A brand new purpose-built terminal offers a complete portfolio of aviation services, all of which are replicated in the equally contemporary Doha facility in Qatar, creating exclusive gateways in and out of two different continents.

Epitomising the benefits of private air travel, the luxurious 70,000-square foot VIP terminal at Biggin Hill will be completed shortly, drawing stylistic inspiration from both Europe and the Middle East. Designed and operated by Rizon Jet, this airy two-storey environment combines open seating areas and private lounges with meeting facilities stocked with modern communication technology, all augmented by secretarial support for business travellers.

CUSTOMISABLE: When you travel with Oryx Jet or Rizon Jet, the journey doesn't begin on the boarding steps. Each trip is fully customisable, with limousine or helicopter transfers from home or office whisking passengers to a dedicated VIP terminal, and then into a similarly exclusive lounge. Queuing and waiting is eliminated in favour of a discreet, courteous service that is entirely tailored to the needs of each traveller and their itinerary.

An array of superbly maintained aircraft are available around the clock, tailored to individual requirements, right down to serving your favourite meals and snacks. The most challenging or lengthy journey can be transformed into a pleasurable and relaxing occasion, transporting travellers to their destination reinvigorated and ready for whatever awaits them. Even legal necessities like customs and immigration paperwork can be handled on their behalf.

In recognition of the fact that there is far more to air travel than the journeys themselves, Oryx Jet additionally offers a comprehensive portfolio of aircraft management for both private and corporate customers. From in-flight catering and staffing through to accounting documentation and aircraft registration, clients can be freed from the tyranny of regulatory red tape or maintenance responsibilities. Rizon Jet can assist with aircraft purchasing, sales, financing or consulting, and its maintenance expertise is hugely admired within the industry, with a talented team of engineers and technicians employed in both Qatar and the UK. ▣

CONTACT: www.oryxjet.com; www.rizonjet.com

"
Pensum Director Peter Gibbs was instrumental in making the Cayman Islands the world's number-one flag jurisdiction for large yachts

FLYING THE FLAG

PENSUM LTD PROVIDES A SAFE HARBOUR
FOR YACHTING ENTHUSIASTS

From its bases in those Caribbean paradises, the Cayman Islands and the British Virgin Islands, Pensum provides maritime consultancy to individuals, businesses and governments around the world. In fact, Pensum Director Peter Gibbs was instrumental in making the Cayman Islands the world's number-one flag jurisdiction for superyachts. Running Cayman's Maritime Administration from 1997 to 2004, by the end of his tenure 25 per cent of the world fleet of yachts over 40 metres/130 feet in length were Cayman-registered.

By comparison, chic cruising capital the British Virgin Islands (BVI) is a relative newcomer to this league, but it already boasts a large registry of 'smaller' yachts up to 30 metres /100 feet in length – still a fair size by any reckoning.

SOLUTIONS: Located outside any onshore taxing regime, Pensum's insurance division has had great success in arranging competitive cover for its high-net-worth clients' yachts, ships, aircraft, cars, real estate and personal property.

Pensum also offers a wide range of management and administrative services. 'We are in the business of "taking care of luxury", something I know that Rolls-Royce enthusiasts appreciate,' says Peter. 'Consistently, over several decades,

we have been diligent in finding suitable solutions to meet yacht owners' needs.'

With access to underwriters across the globe, Pensum can insure any asset anywhere in the world. For example, where a yacht is kept in North America, US coverage can be beneficial, particularly when US crew members are employed. Through an associate company, Pensum can assist with insurance in any US State. 'Where assets are registered offshore through a company, insurance arranged from there can help to establish the substance, mind and management of its registered office,' explains Peter. 'Indeed, servicing our existing corporate clients was what prompted us to enter the insurance field. Naturally, we are happy to quote at no cost for any yacht (or other asset), not just those for which we act.'

CHOICE: 'In terms of registration, the most frequently asked question is: "What is the purpose of a flag and why are certain flag states chosen over others?" The answer is not straightforward.

'First of all, no flag can be all things to all owners. Flags vary from country to country in what they are able to offer, just as clients vary from person to person in what they need. Patently, the objective is to find and adopt the nationality of a flag that best enables the owner to go where he wants and do what he wants in the most efficient and safe manner.'

Pensum's maritime consultancy covers a multitude of issues, with piracy prevention being one of the hottest topics. In another arena, very large yachts certified under international conventions as commercial cargo or passenger ships can be required to berth in commercial docks in countries such as the USA, rather than at a desired marina. Peter says his company has found a way to configure such vessels in a way that avoids such ignominy.

He continues: 'Company management involves not only the formation and operation of companies, but also any structuring necessary to address particular problems or objectives. Sometimes a multi-jurisdictional approach is the best way to solve the ever-increasing complexity in today's world. For example, for certain vessels registered under a flag subject to EU VAT and National Insurance, such as the Isle of Man, it is often best to employ and pay crew from a jurisdiction outside the EU that itself does not impose tax or other levies.'

So, when you next stroll along the dockside and admire the yachts, pause to examine their flags. You will be able to look knowingly and understand why international clients talk to Pensum when deciding which flag to fly and where to insure. ▣

Contact: www.PensumOffshore.com

EXCEEDING
EXPECTATIONS

AIRCRAFT BUILDER PILATUS IS LEADING THE WORLD IN TURBOPROP VERSATILITY AND CRAFTSMANSHIP

With a well-earned reputation for craftsmanship, the Swiss have long ruled the world in quality and precision. And when it comes to expert engineering, is there anywhere more important to have it than in a plane? Established in 1939 and based near Lucerne at the foot of the mountain that lent the company its name, the aircraft builder Pilatus has long been synonymous with excellence and superiority.

From its early P-2 model, which saw service with the Swiss Air Force between 1949 and 1982, to the company's current best-selling PC-12 NG, countless government and business organisations, as well as flight schools and private customers, have chosen Pilatus to meet their aviation requirements.

SPECIALIST: At the Pilatus factory, it is easy to see why the company is highly regarded: trained craftspeople are involved with every aspect of the assembly process. Working with state-of-the-art tools and machinery on a shop floor more akin to an operating theatre than a factory, each of the Pilatus engineers takes personal pride in their part. It is perhaps little wonder that many employees remain with the company from their apprenticeship until retirement.

> 66
>
> *Constructed using the latest techniques and technologies, its airframe is aerodynamically advanced, lighter, stronger and less prone to corrosion and fatigue*

VERSATILITY: Since its first certification in 1994, more than 1,000 PC-12 models have been sold, collectively clocking up an impressive 2.6 million flying hours. Offering the ability to whisk nine passengers 2,000 miles in absolute luxury and at great speed, the aircraft is versatile in every way. Constructed using the latest techniques and technologies, its airframe is lighter, stronger and less prone to corrosion and fatigue than less advanced aircraft.

Another invaluable feature is that its seats are not fixed, and can be moved about to suit requirements. Boasting a stylish and contemporary BMW Dreamworks-designed interior, trimmed in wood and cream leather, every plane is completely bespoke; and Pilatus is entirely flexible with the exterior painting and the cabin layout – no configuration or design is beyond the capabilities of this Swiss aircraft manufacturer.

It's the adaptability of the PC-12 that owners find irresistible, and the ease at which it can be integrated into both business and personal life. But possibly more impressive is that the PC-12's reliance on a single turbine engine does not mean compromise in terms of performance or specification. With its pressurised

cabin, impressive climb rate and high operating altitude, another benefit of the PC-12 is its ability to operate in challenging situations. The landing gear is robust enough to cope with rough terrain, and thanks to a short take-off distance, it offers the reliability needed for reaching areas that are often inaccessible to other aircraft.

In these times of austerity and fluctuating oil prices, aviation fuel costs can represent a significant financial burden; therefore the fuel savings offered by the PC-12 make it a tempting proposition for anybody in the market for a new aircraft. Combine this with the lower maintenance costs of a single-engined aircraft, as well as the obvious environmental advantages of using less fuel, and the PC-12 makes even more sense.

According to Fred Muggli of Pilatus, 'it's the quality and flexibility' that motivates customers not only to choose Pilatus aircraft, but to keep choosing them. The skies are never the limit when flying in a PC-12.

CONTACT: www.pilatus-aircraft.com

TECHNOLOGY IN THE
SKY

Whether a transcontinental flight or a short leap to another city, time spent in flight can feel like an interruption to a fast-paced lifestyle. However, the latest cabin electronics and information management solutions ensure that travellers can make the most of their time in the sky.

'We ask our customers what they want to accomplish during flight and present them with a solution that allows that,' says Tommy Dodson, Vice President and General Manager of Cabin Systems for Rockwell Collins. 'And because of our extensive experience as a systems integrator, we have the unique ability to provide passengers with the same systems they use in their offices and homes – ultimately creating a seamless transition for them while in flight.'

CONNECTED: In the cabin, connectivity has become an ever-more important feature as passengers and crew demand real-time access to information. Rockwell Collins has answered this call through innovative cabin solutions such as its Venue™ high-definition (HD) cabin management system, making each aircraft an extension of today's digital lifestyle and enabling productivity to continue in the air. The cabin management system allows passengers to plug in their laptops and view presentations or other applications directly on HD displays. Passengers also can print documents, use email and complete

In the cabin, connectivity has become an ever-more important feature as passengers and crew demand real-time access to information

ROCKWELL COLLINS UNDERSTANDS THAT CONNECTIVITY, PRODUCTIVITY AND ENTERTAINMENT ARE VITAL TO FREQUENT BUSINESS FLYERS

essential business communications as if in a regular office. Venue's media centre was developed for use with the latest consumer electronics technologies – from MP3s to gaming systems and Blu-ray discs – all featuring high resolution and compatibility with new high-definition standards such as HDMI.

When it comes to connectivity, Rockwell Collins provides comprehensive communications systems for both pilots and passengers. 'The quality and capability of communications equipment and systems available to business jet passengers continues to improve,' says Steve Timm, Vice President and General Manager of Information Management for Rockwell Collins. 'As technology continues to expand, we believe passengers can look forward to a quality of service that nears what you would expect on the ground via mobile phone or Voice-over-IP (VoIP) services.'

The company's Inmarsat satellite communication solution provides safety service communications for the cockpit and allows simultaneous operation by a passenger with the same equipment. Rockwell Collins eXchange™ is a real-time, two-way connectivity system. 'With eXchange in your jet's cabin, travel time is no longer an issue,' says Steve. 'You now have virtually instant access to the same information you have in your office. E-mail, FoIP, the Internet, VoIP telephony, and corporate Virtual Private Networks are all just a click away.'

SEAMLESS: Understanding that an executive's time is precious both in the air and on the ground, Air Routing, a Rockwell Collins company, goes beyond the cabin to enable a fast-paced lifestyle after the aircraft lands. While Air Routing's services focus on flight departments, the company is designed with the passenger in mind. Regional Trip Support, Air Routing's latest solution, combines the company's tools and experience in international flight planning to offer a new service, which provides pilots with access to a web interface with all the information they need to complete a flight. Air Routing's services extend to all aspects of a trip – including weather, over-flight permits, visas and passports, hotel arrangements, ground transportation and catering – to facilitate smooth, efficient travel anywhere in the world.

'Rockwell Collins recognises the value of a seamless experience from the time you leave home until you reach your final destination, and understands the vital role connectivity and information management play in making this happen,' says Steve. 'Coming soon is a day when the aircraft is synchronised in real time with the flight department and a passenger's world on the ground, to make business aviation travel truly transparent.' ▣

CONTACT: www.rockwellcollins.com

THE
SMOOTHEST
FINISH

> *The paint system is built up in many layers and the surface preparation for each application has to be perfect*

ROLLING STOCK GROUP COMBINES CRAFTSMANSHIP AND EXPERTISE TO PROVIDE ONE OF THE HIGHEST-QUALITY YACHTING SERVICES IN THE TRADE

Rolling Stock Group is made up of five divisions: Rolling Stock (chandlery), RSB Rigging Solutions (rigging), RS Shore Support (shore support agents), RS ProClean (interior carpet and upholstery cleaning) and RS Finishing & Refinishing (yacht painting), one of the world's largest superyacht finishing companies. Together they offer a complete yachting service supplemented by a wealth of experience in each area of yachting maintenance. This, combined with the most superior products, methods and technologies available, puts the Rolling Stock Group at the helm of the industry.

Beginning as a simple chandlery van cruising the docks of Palma de Mallorca, selling chandlery to boats directly in the marinas, Rolling Stock rapidly expanded into a comprehensive service, providing everything from supplies and maintenance to painting and rigging. The company now boasts more than 20 years of practice and has worked on some of the world's most prestigious yachts, including the 119-metre Yacht A, designed by Philippe Starck for a Russian billionaire.

CRAFT: Managing Director of RS Finishing & Refinishing, Rupert Savage, describes the craft and care dedicated to every yacht finished by the company: 'We spend an average of 20 hours of labour on every square metre of surface for a typical full system application. The paint system is built up in many layers and the surface preparation for each application has to be perfect. It's an extremely labour-intensive process that requires a high level of skill – there are no shortcuts. Every yacht that's created is different, because it's custom built. In the final stages we must pay scrupulous attention to detail – finding and fixing every scratch and pinhole, for the most flawless finish achievable.'

Operating from premises boasting state-of-the-art infrastructure and environmentally and safety conscious equipment, RS Finishing & Refinishing was the first yacht-painting service to be awarded Bureau Veritas certificates for environmental protection (ISO 14001), and quality control and management (ISO 9001).

UNIQUE: As the superyacht industry burgeons, yachting enthusiasts become increasingly discerning, with more customers wanting a design and style that is unique and that makes a statement. 'Our clients want a superior finish that says something about them, and we are increasingly raising the bar to cater to different tastes,' says Rupert. 'We paint an eclectic range of colour schemes, and are using more and more metallic and pearlescent paints, which require even greater finesse to apply.'

BESPOKE: Tailor-made designs are accompanied by tailor-made services, including superyacht rigging, bespoke marine supplies that customers can order from anywhere in the world and have delivered straight to their boat. 'Through our RS Shore Support service in Palma, clients need only to call and we can source anything for them – from silver spoons to private jets – like a concierge,' Rupert explains.

RS Finishing & Refinishing also has a fully mobile team that is able to respond quickly to clients requiring refits and new builds in locations including England, Germany, Italy, France, USA, Thailand, New Zealand and Australia.

Adding flair and distinction to a complete yachting service, the Rolling Stock Group provides comprehensive, high-quality services, putting luxury yachts in the safest of hands. ▣

CONTACT: www.rollingstock.es

JEWEL
IN THE CROWN

LINKING JORDAN WITH THE REST OF THE WORLD, ROYAL JORDANIAN AIRLINES IS THE ULTIMATE AMBASSADOR, SHOWCASING THIS VIBRANT NATION TO ITS BEST ADVANTAGE

Since 1963, Royal Jordanian Airlines has provided a superb service to discerning customers; and the last few years have seen exciting developments both in renewing its fleet and expanding its route network. Under the invaluable guidance and directives of His Majesty King Abdullah II, Royal Jordanian is following a very specific vision driven by a culture of excellence and attention to detail which puts customer satisfaction above all else.

PRESTIGIOUS: 'This company aims to become the airline of choice connecting Jordan and the Levant with the rest of the world,' says Hussein Dabbas, President and CEO of Royal Jordanian. 'We now cover and fly out to every available international airport in the region to connect them with each other and the rest of the world.' In 2007 the oneworld alliance furthered this ambition by inviting Royal Jordanian to join its elite membership, which includes American Airlines, British Airways, Iberia, Cathay Pacific and Japan Airlines among others and gives access to fly to more than 700 cities. Royal Jordanian is the first Arab and Middle Eastern air carrier to join the three global airline alliances of oneworld, Sky Team and Star Alliance.

LUXURIOUS: While route expansion is clearly important, attention to passenger comfort and convenience is perfectly illustrated by its Crown Class service. This first-class service for business-class fares epitomises the superb service offered by Royal Jordanian, with the result that for many travellers there really is no other airline of choice. The warm Jordanian hospitality onboard, as well as on the ground, plays a major part in that response, further enhanced by a host of luxurious details: elegant reclining leather seats with extra leg room on all aircraft types, and flatbed seats in the Crown Class on the A340 and A330 aircraft; first-class à la carte dining with vintage French wines and champagne; private in-seat video; and separate check-in desk. Extra baggage allowance,

double-points credit for frequent flyers and access to Royal Jordanian and oneworld's Business and First Class Lounges are further enhancements to an already excellent service, while extra seat pitch on all aircraft types distinguishes Royal Jordanian from all other European carriers operating to Jordan, and applies to the company's economy class as well.

INNOVATIVE: Royal Jordanian, the world-class award-winning airline, currently operates a fleet of 29 modern aircraft. The inauguration of four new routes within the last two years brought the airline's network to 59 destinations worldwide with plans for further expansion by introducing an average of two new routes per year. A range of IT systems makes it easier for passengers to complete all travel procedures electronically, including online check-in, thus ensuring that state-of-the-art technology keeps this forward-thinking airline flying high. Royal Jordanian has also concluded its short- and medium-range fleet modernisation programme by introducing 19 modern aircraft in the last five years, while planning for the arrival of the first of the 11 Boeing Dreamliner aircraft to join its fleet as of 2013. 'We aim to obtain the best airplanes in the market to service our regional flights, medium-haul and long-haul network,' says Hussein. 'And for the future we are looking forward to continuing to enrich and enhance our network.'

Royal Jordanian prides itself on superb customer service and sees itself as being the welcoming face of Jordan for many visitors, famed for its hospitality, outstanding comfort and efficiency. For nearly 50 years now it has achieved that aim, while embracing change and transforming challenges into opportunities, promising a future as innovative and exciting as its past. ▣

CONTACT: www.rj.com

SPECIAL PROJECTS AND SERVICES' CLIENTS KNOW
THEY CAN EXPECT AN INTEGRATED, PROFESSIONAL
AND DISCREET SECURITY PACKAGE

PROFESSIONAL
PROTECTION

Many high-net-worth individuals and large organisations have specific and demanding needs when it comes to ensuring the security of themselves, their companies, and even their families. With potential threats surrounding travel, homes, schools, businesses and assets, many people are searching for security providers who can tailor their services to meet all these needs.

EXPERIENCE: Established in 1991, Special Projects and Services (SPS) is a security, risk-management and consultancy firm that provides specialist, integrated services. Since its inception, SPS has provided services in more than 70 countries across the globe for clients including diplomats, royalty, senior professionals and multinational businesses. The company's highly skilled personnel come from backgrounds such as government, Her Majesty's Armed Forces, police and security services, and are handpicked

❝

Ninety- to ninety-five per cent of SPS's new work is derived from referrals by previous and existing clients

because of their personal integrity, loyalty and outstanding reputations.

SPS has expanded over the years to incorporate services in five core areas – consultancy, maritime security, physical security, training and support services – offering project management and consultancy, crisis management, travel management and logistics, close protection, and security audits and assessments in a range of low- to high-risk environments. One of the company's main areas of focus is the provision of services to high-net-worth clients, which encompasses superyachts, properties, and the security and welfare of them and their families. SPS currently has a number of personnel that are working on both land-based and maritime projects.

SERVICE: As part of SPS's goal to deliver a bespoke and consistent approach to security, clients are allocated their own dedicated senior project manager who works with them to devise the most appropriate integrated security package. The project manager provides regular updates to the client and is on hand 24 hours day, and there is also a back-up manager so they always have two personalised points of contact. The in-depth knowledge that a senior project manager provides, alongside continuity and a proactive service, allows trust to develop between all parties.

Services are developed to meet clients' specific needs and alleviate threat while also fitting their lifestyle and budget. SPS looks at the project in the long term, which can mean improving security measures that are already in place or dealing with complex pre-existing situations. Security provision can be rapidly scaled up or down, and the company will often transfer the knowledge and expertise of a case to trusted client staff or a small local security operation as a cheaper and more efficient alternative to 'parachuting in' a totally new and alien system.

REPUTATION: With a healthy customer base that includes the oil and gas, and banking sectors, the company is not complacent. The bulk of SPS's new work is typically acquired through referrals from new and existing clients, who are impressed by the company's discretion, flexibility and expertise. ▣

CONTACT: www.specialprojectsandservices.com

EARNING THEIR
SPURS

TOTTENHAM HOTSPUR IS ONE OF THE PROUDEST NAMES IN WORLD FOOTBALL, AND THE CLUB'S GLORIOUS HISTORY IS MATCHED BY ITS BRIGHT FUTURE

There is a unique cachet surrounding the name Tottenham Hotspur in domestic and international football. It is the stuff of dreams, of romance, of style, a true passion and loyalty that remains lifelong.

SUCCESS: Established in 1882, Spurs became the only non-League club to lift the FA Cup, in 1901, and to date the club has won the League Championship twice and the FA Cup a thrilling eight times.

In 1961, it did the cherished 'double', becoming the first side in modern times to lift both the FA Cup and League Championship title in the same season.

True, others have since done the same. But, now 50 years on, the Spurs achievement is still rated as the finest of all time – because it was achieved with such style.

The nucleus of that same side went on to lift the European Cup Winners' Cup and so became the first British club to win a major European competition. Those wonderful floodlit European encounters at White Hart Lane, when Spurs swept aside the cream of the continent, have since become known as the 'Glory Nights' – and this season sees their return.

In 1973 Spurs became the first club to win the Football League Cup twice; by 1974 it had become the first English club to have played in three major European finals, having lifted the UEFA Cup in 1972 – a feat that would be repeated in 1984.

After a seven-year hiatus the 'Lilywhites' obtained further domestic glory, winning the FA Cup in 1991. The following year the club was invited to play in the Premier League, in which it has remained since its inception.

Spurs' more recent successes have come in the League Cup with wins in both 1999 and a 2008 extra-time victory against west London rivals Chelsea.

EXPECTATION: Along with its illustrious past, Tottenham Hotspur has a future bursting with ambition. The club has now joined Europe's elite and is competing in the UEFA Champions League with a team of enviable talent famed for its attacking, fluid footballing style. Off the pitch, Tottenham Hotspur has attracted a series of new commercial partnerships, including a Barclays Premier League shirt sponsorship deal with Autonomy and a new shirt sponsorship for all domestic and European cup competitions with Investec, both listed on the FTSE 100. This, combined with the support of a large, passionate global fanbase, a season ticket waiting list of 32,000 and growing demand for the club's award-winning hospitality suggest the hallmarks of prosperity.

Work is already well under way on the development of an impressive training centre on a 67-acre site in Enfield to help the club attract, train and retain top-quality players along with nurturing and developing emerging talent.

Plans are already well in hand to build a stunning new state-of-the-art 56,250-capacity stadium that will be the envy of world football with plans incorporating many benefits for the local community that will help regenerate the Tottenham area. This will provide a new base for the Tottenham Hotspur Foundation, a registered charity established by the club that aims to positively impact the lives of young people in north London and the surrounding area. The club is currently seeking a stadium naming-rights partner to be part of this exciting, world-class development.

These are indeed exciting times for the north London club as it makes significant strides to achieve its long-term vision and reward the support of its growing throng of millions of passionate and loyal fans worldwide. ▣

CONTACT: www.tottenhamhotspur.com

TRAVEL

5 » *Travel & Hotels*

TRAVEL

17, 46

15, 16, 23, 24, 31

13

44

21

22

20

28

43

38

8

35

9

35

40

19

45

35

40

18

41

40

39

42

14, 27

1, 33

7

29

25

40

5

40

30, 32, 36

4, 19, 26, 35, 37

4, 40

2, 6, 10

PERFECTLY
PROVENÇAL

The sun-drenched good life of Provence has long captivated artists such as Vincent van Gogh, Roman legionnaires, travellers and even popes. And in the heart of this region, famous for its landscape, food and unique French-Mediterranean blend of cultures, is Auberge de Noves. North of the Alpilles, on the border between Bouches du Rhône and Vaucluse, sits this Manor located in 20 acres of countryside. The location of the Auberge is exceptional in its proximity to Avignon, the chic port of Marseille, the villages perched on the heights of the Lubéron and the famous market of Cavaillon – all within easy driving distance.

HISTORICAL: The building that houses the guest rooms at Auberge de Noves dates to the 18th century. It was previously used as a hunting lodge, and originally as a chapel. As Chef Robert Lalleman describes it: 'The atmosphere is like living alongside the past, among the landscape.' Two-hundred-year-old trees dot the property's 15-hectare park and shade the tennis court and swimming pool.

CUISINE: Robert's career as a cook began when he was 14 years old. Before the age of 24 he had worked in a new restaurant each year – from

Its 45,000-bottle wine cellar has been described as one of the most important in France

NESTLED IN THE HEART OF PROVENCE, AUBERGE DE NOVES GIVES GUESTS AND DINERS AN EXPERIENCE RICH IN LOCAL FLAVOUR

Le Manoir aux Quat'Saisons with the famous Monsieur Blanc, to restaurants in Germany and the Seychelles – and he attributes his culinary aptitude to this varied experience, although his family history may have played its part as well.

'I spent ten years, from 1990 to 2000, as a chef with my father at Auberge de Noves and I returned three years ago as head chef,' he explains. The essence of the cuisine at Auberge de Noves is its seasonality. 'I use the best produce that you can find on the market, and it is always local – my cooking usès the best of the region,' says Robert. 'We change the menu regularly, when new products are available, according to season. Cooking from Provence is very tasty; we use local olive oil and herbs.'

Auberge de Noves takes pride in its 45,000-bottle wine cellar, which has been described as one of the most important in France.

'My grandfather started buying wine very early, in 1954. His wife loved Bordeaux, so he bought a lot of Bordeaux, and my mother loved burgundy, so my father bought a lot of that. I am buying local wine.'

STAY: Every room and suite at the Auberge is decorated differently, with its own unique aesthetic. The hotel considers itself to be completely in tune with the personal needs of its guests and is described by Robert as somewhere between a large luxury hotel and a family establishment.

'We have a lot of guests returning each year and in the summer we have long-stay guests, sometimes for up to one month,' says Robert. 'They book one year in advance.'

Part of the attraction to Auberge de Noves, alongside the restaurant and chateau, is the opportunity to explore, from its perfectly central location, the surrounding area – whether it be in the direction of the sea, the river Rhône, shopping for antiques in Isle de Sorgue or Saint Rémy de Provence. The Auberge is located just ten minutes from Avignon airport and 15 minutes from Avignon TGV station.

And after a summer's day exploring the countryside, guests are invited to enjoy the outdoor dining atmosphere on the restaurant's terrace, which is replaced by an indoor lounge in the winter months.

'You can feel things here,' says Robert. 'There is a sense of history. We really are in the heart of Provence.' ▣

CONTACT: www.aubergedenoves.com
IMAGE: (L) Manuel Gomes da Costa

ASIAN
ESCAPE

A five-star sanctuary for rest, renewal and rejuvenation, The Banjaran Hotsprings Retreat nestles into 17 acres of tropical jungle, limestone cliffs, waterfalls and hot springs at the heart of historic Tambun in Malaysia. Twenty-five luxury villas measuring up to 2,800 square-feet are set in secluded grounds or along the banks of a sweeping canal. This natural beauty, coupled with the finest service South-East Asia has to offer, makes The Banjaran a haven in which body and mind can find comfort and refreshment.

FREEDOM: The Banjaran offers absolute privacy in a luscious setting. As Resort Manager Anita Khoo says: 'It is hidden away from the frenetic pace of civilisation, with an environment created to give each guest complete peace, a return to nature and time for self-reflection. We focus on health-enhancement and balance. The Banjaran's environment and philosophy promote relaxation, fitness, healthy eating and overall renewal, encouraging

a healthier lifestyle change for all who visit.' All-inclusive rates at the retreat encompass luxurious villas, attentive yet discreet butler service, meals, classes, use of facilities and selected treatments.

INDIVIDUAL: 'The location is completely unique,' Anita asserts. 'Integrated within the retreat are geothermal hot springs, a restorative thermal-steam cave which helps soothe, relax and detoxify, a meditation cave, an ice bath and an outdoor shower with cold, fresh spring water direct from the rainforest.' The Banjaran is environmentally aware and built on eco-friendly practices, with conservation high on its list of priorities. Within three months of its launch, the retreat was awarded the Malaysia Landscape Architecture Award for 2009 by the Institute of Landscape Architects Malaysia. 'The design encourages co-existence with the natural environment for an authentic, immersive experience,' Anita continues. 'It is a haven where nature nurtures.'

MALAYSIA'S FIRST LUXURY NATURAL WELLNESS RETREAT, THE BANJARAN OFFERS A LIBERATING EXPERIENCE FOR BODY, MIND AND SOUL

HARMONY: The Banjaran Spa and Wellness Centre is embodied by an extensive menu of treatments and therapies, with programmes tailored to the needs of each guest. Holistic Asian philosophies are embraced in rich health and beauty experiences, from Malay healing, traditional Chinese Medicine and Ayurvedic treatments to contemporary spa options using pure and natural ingredients.

Personal paths to wellness are found in wellness programmes ranging from 3 to 21 nights that include consultations, treatments, cuisine and exercise therapy. 'Our holistic exercise programme features disciplines such as Yoga, Qi Gong, Tai Chi, Water-cising and Meditation, all practised in completely natural surroundings,' says Anita. The Banjaran has been ranked fourth in *AsiaSpa*'s Top 10 Spiritual Retreats, which highlights some of Asia's most attentive retreats and spas committed to sharing the art of holistic healing, a potent way to achieve true health and well-being. 'We have our own line of aromatherapy skin and body-care products and amenities in the spa, made to international standards using natural and traditional recipes,' Anita adds. The Banjaran's Signature

Massage and The Luxurious Facial and Body Treatment have been awarded the Best Eastern Fusion Massage and the Most Luxe Organic Treatment by *Harper's Bazaar* (Malaysia) Spa Awards 2010.

PURE: The Banjaran's only restaurant, The Pomelo, also offers light, healthy and tasty spa cuisine cooked with fresh, wholesome, organic ingredients. The restaurant features a range of international organic wines to complement delicious appetizers, entrées and desserts designed to be well-balanced and easily digested. Guests can enjoy this fine cuisine within the peaceful surroundings of the restaurant, or at the gazebos charmingly housed above the hot springs.

'The Banjaran lifestyle creates the opportunity for escape, reflection and health transformation, guided by trusted professionals,' Anita concludes. The Banjaran is Malaysia's best-kept secret. ▣

CONTACT: www.thebanjaran.com

AN EXCEPTIONAL
RUSSIAN
HOTEL

FROM MOLECULAR HAUTE CUISINE
TO METICULOUS INTERIOR DESIGN,
THIS REMARKABLE HOTEL AND SPA
OFFERS A HAVEN FOR TRAVELLERS
TO MOSCOW

Every minute detail of the hotel's design has been honed by one of today's most sought-after designers, Antonio Citterio

In recent times, Russia has become one of the most influential and innovative countries in the world. During this period, Moscow has established itself as the country's cultural, business and scientific capital, attracting visitors from all over the globe in search of new beginnings and impressions. Located just eight kilometres from the capital, Barvikha is where big business meets politics, culture meets science, Russia meets the world and ancient tradition merges into bold innovation. It is here that Barvikha Hotel & Spa can be found, forming a cornerstone of Barvikha Luxury Village – an exclusive shopping area where the most important fashion and jewellery brands are represented, including Gucci, Prada, Chloé and Bvlgari.

ESCAPISM: Barvikha Hotel & Spa is a place of comfort, relaxation and tranquillity, with staff dedicated to making wishes come true. As soon as guests arrive at the airport, the hotel's own Bentley transfers them to the hotel. Should they wish to continue their experience with this magnificent car, they can take it for a test drive and purchase the preferred model in the Bentley showroom in Barvikha Luxury Village. Ferrari, Maserati and Lamborghini showrooms are also nearby, ready to be tested. Every guest has a personal butler at his or her disposal, and everything is designed to make each stay a unique experience, creating many pleasant memories. Every minute detail of the hotel's design has been honed by one of today's most sought-after designers, Antonio Citterio. Elegant simplicity is the trademark style of this new property, since Citterio favours natural wood and stone, as well as being inspired by the element of fire; a big fireplace welcomes guests at the reception area. The designer is also meticulous about small details and nothing has been left to chance, from doorknobs or lights to sofas or in-built closets. Materials such as beech wall panelling, Canadian cedar, natural stone and marble recur throughout the hotel's interior.

In total, Barvikha Hotel & Spa has 65 rooms, of which 58 are luxury suites (including a dozen with a steam bath and massage room), alongside the Presidential Suite. Antonio Citterio has designed the interior of each room exclusively for this hotel, with large terraces offering complete privacy, and some apartments even benefit from a real fireplace. Barvikha Hotel & Spa is one of the few resorts in the world using Frette bedding, towels and bathrobes.

ACCOMMODATING: Guests can make use of three conference rooms with a capacity of up to 20 people each, as well as a banqueting hall that can accommodate 100 guests at once. These spaces are perfect for meetings or business negotiations, as well as formal lunches, dinners, standing receptions or parties. Another cherished facility is the Spa Dominique Chenot, drawing on the work of Dr Henri Chenot – one of the world's most influential doctors and the founder of Biontology. His methods combine modern European medical knowledge and diagnostics with the ancient traditions of Chinese medicine, and each client receives a personalised healthcare programme. The spa itself covers more than 2,000 square metres, including various cabins, two facial care areas, a manicure and pedicure parlour, a hair care room and a spa cuisine restaurant. It also features a 21 metre by 5 metre indoor pool, Jacuzzi, steam baths, hot and cold pools, saunas and a tropical shower.

In terms of gastronomy, Barvikha Hotel & Spa welcomes its guests to the Anatoly Komm restaurant, serving a completely new interpretation of classic Russian cuisine. As the pioneer of molecular haute cuisine in Russia, Komm has become the most renowned chef in Moscow. The hotel's bar stocks a grand collection of wines from all over the world alongside vintage liquors, and the famous cocktail list is highly valued among Moscow's jetsetters. Barvikha Luxury Village also has two other restaurants: the exquisite European menu of A.V.E.N.U.E., and OPIUM, which is famous for serving some of the best Asian fusion cuisine in Moscow. ▣

CONTACT: www.barvikhahotel.com

AN UNFORGETTABLE
EXPERIENCE

Beachcomber Hotels are known for their outstanding levels of service, gourmet dining, elegant accommodation and fantastic facilities for sports, leisure and pampering.

Royal Palm is known as the flagship property in Beachcomber Hotels' portfolio of properties in Mauritius. This is the hotel where the great escape can occur to seek refuge from the hurly-burly of 21st-century life. The hotel truly epitomises luxury and exquisite natural beauty, and nurtures this so that the hotel remains the most prestigious address in the Indian Ocean.

The hotel effortlessly combines international standards of luxury with traditional Mauritian hospitality. Built on a prime site in fashionable Grand Baie, on a sheltered beach in the north-west of Mauritius, the hotel's signature haute cuisine and impeccable service creates the perfect setting for an unforgettable experience.

IMPECCABLE:
As an exclusive boutique-style all-suite hotel, with a ratio of three staff to every guest, the service is consistent, discreet and intuitive.

The La Goélette restaurant has an international reputation for outstanding gastronomy, and the stunning Le Bar Plage is the ideal place to enjoy a chilled glass of wine with a fresh seafood lunch.

Royal Palm also prides itself on the Spa by Clarins, described as 'simply magnificent'. It provides Thai massage, beauty treatments, body wraps, a sauna, relaxation area, a yoga pavilion and an algotherapy area.

SPORTS:
Sports are a special feature of the Beachcomber experience, and the water-based activities available make the most of the beach-side location. Guests are invited to partake in water-skiing, windsurfing, kayaking, sailing, snorkelling, and cruising in a glass-bottomed boat.

Land-based sports are also on offer at the hotel's superb Sports Studio, offering the latest equipment including Kinesis, Power Plates, Pilates, personal trainers, three tennis courts with coaches, and even a squash court.

With its customers' needs as central to the hotel's ethos, the concierge-service provides a Mini Club for children aged 3 to 12 and a babysitting service. Rolls-Royce Phantom, BMW X5 and helicopter transfers are also available.

TROPICAL:
Beachcomber's Trou aux Biches hotel opened in November 2010 on the north-west coast of Mauritius after an 18-month, £60 million facelift. This amazing hotel is situated on one of the best beaches – two kilometres of white sand and crystal-clear waters setting the stage for blazing sunsets.

This village-style hotel features suites set in lush gardens. Offering the perfect combination of tropical elegance and modern luxury, private villas are dotted throughout the tropical park, some even boasting a private butler service and personal pools.

Each villa is designed around a spacious open-air living area, with a free-form infinity-edge swimming pool and a large sun-drenched deck. »

*Private villas are dotted
throughout the tropical park,
some with a private butler
service and personal pools*

An outdoor barbecue allows guests to enjoy dining under the stars, and outdoor showers and deep-soak bath-tubs continue the al fresco theme.

Beachcomber Hotels has gone to great lengths to protect this site's unique flora and fauna, something that is clear when strolling through the abundant gardens, which have been carefully preserved throughout the resort's renovation.

Six restaurants offer a variety of international cuisines and each is designed to complement the warm climate and to focus on specialities sourced from around the globe that are prepared by world-class chefs.

From the authentic Thai and Indian restaurants to refined European gourmet cuisine, beach barbecues and local delicacies, Trou aux Biches offers the highest-quality dining in Mauritius. The Oasis Bar specialises in fruity tropical cocktails and delicious homemade snacks, while Caravelle Bar, set on the beach, is a stylish spot to enjoy aperitifs and a glass of champagne.

The Spa by Clarins is also offered to guests at Trou aux Biches. Echoing the tropical feel of the resort, the renovated spa comprises a string of individual thatched pavilions, quietly tucked away amidst palm trees and exotic plants, centered around a tranquil pool. Each spa pavilion blends outdoor space with the inside and guests can choose to enjoy their treatments either in the cool comfort of the air-conditioned interiors, or commune with nature outdoors under the shade of the thatched roofs. Classically luxurious in nature, treatments at the spa include massage, balneotherapy, algotherapy, shiatsu, a sauna, and hair and beauty treatments.

SEYCHELLES: Sainte Anne Resort & Spa, Seychelles, is Beachcomber's private island paradise. The hotel is on the island of Sainte Anne, just ten minutes from the main island of Mahé. This tropical hideaway sits in a marine park, offering spectacular diving. The hotel suites are elegant and all ocean-facing, many with private pools, a garden and an open terrace and/or a gazebo, and all with access to the same exquisite pampering of the Spa by Clarins.

The hotel's five restaurants include the 'must-experience' Le Robinson, which blends perfectly into the tropical gardens, while L'Abondance overlooks the pool and is edged with reflecting ponds, designed to evoke 'an island within the island'.

Adjacent to L'Abondance is L'Océane, a beach restaurant offering delights such as grilled fish, fresh seafood and Creole cuisine. Further enhancing the dining experience is Le Mont Fleuri restaurant, situated on stilts high above the beach, and the Le Sans-Souci bar, which provides guests with tantilising cocktails and home-mixed rum while overlooking the swimming pool and lagoon.

Private and romantic, indulgent and pampering, or luxurious and family-oriented retreats are all made possible with Beachcomber, the ultimate in ever-memorable and exquisite hotel experiences. ▣

CONTACT: www.beachcomber-hotels.com
IMAGE: (Overleaf) The pool at Royal Palm;
(Above) pool villas at Trou aux Biches

AMAZING
GRACE

INSPIRED BY CAPE TOWN'S RICH HISTORY AND STUNNING SCENERY, THIS AWARD-WINNING
HOTEL DELIVERS AN UNFORGETTABLE EXPERIENCE TO GUESTS FROM AROUND THE WORLD

Even by the exalted standards of South Africa, Cape Town is an extraordinarily alluring city. Developed by Dutch traders in the mid-17th century, it stands on the south-west tip of Africa, and today is one of the most visited destinations anywhere on the continent. That owes much to the city's unique blend of stunning scenery, world-renowned retail facilities and ever-popular tourist attractions.

Situated on a private quay, Cape Grace faces out over a harbour, a yachting marina and the Victoria & Alfred Waterfront, with the outline of Table Mountain forming a suitably dramatic backdrop. The hotel is especially stunning at night, when its brightly illuminated frontage reflects in the water. Nor is it merely in appearance that Cape Grace embodies the allure of Cape Town. The décor throughout this celebrated hotel has been studiously chosen to reflect the surrounding city's illustrious past, with priceless antique pieces, locally hand-painted fabrics and hand-forged metal fittings combined to remarkable effect. Each of the 120 guest rooms and

suites has been individually decorated and recently refurbished by a leading local interior designer to the very finest 21st century standards. Every suite incorporates views of the yacht marina or harbour through French windows, with fresh flowers and designer toiletries added by staff prior to check-in. It's possible to keep in touch with the wider world through satellite channels on high-definition flat-screen televisions, listen to music through iPod docks, while penthouses provide XBox 360 games consoles for the entertainment of guests.

AWARD-WINNING: A series of prestigious industry awards over the last decade serves as a glowing testament to the exceptional levels of customer service offered by Cape Grace's dedicated and experienced staff. Countless customer commendations further underline the hotel's consistently warm and welcoming environment, expressed by one guest as 'extraordinary and on the edge of perfection', with an impressive portfolio of services and facilities on offer.

Nothing illustrates this better than the *Spirit of the Cape* – a privately owned yacht available exclusively for use by guests of Cape Grace Hotel. This 56-foot vessel is moored beside the hotel and can be booked for bespoke excursions of varying lengths, with canapés and picnics prepared by the hotel's chefs before departure. It's the ultimate way to admire Cape Town's exquisite coastal surroundings – sipping champagne while watching another glorious sunset.

Back on terra firma, Cape Grace offers a wide selection of resources and indulgences, such as The Spa. Situated on the hotel's top floor and boasting spectacular views, it offers a portfolio of treatments inspired by African tradition and cultures, to pamper the body and relax the mind. By contrast, the 15-metre swimming pool is the perfect place to burn off energy, with the shops, restaurants, crafts and entertainments of the Victoria & Alfred Waterfront just a short walk away.

Despite the myriad of local attractions, many people will choose to relax and dine at Cape Grace, particularly considering the delights of the hotel's Signal restaurant, named after its views over the eponymous hill. In many ways the restaurant provides a microcosm of the hotel's character, with hand-painted silk curtains and hand-crafted chandeliers providing the surroundings for traditional foods inspired by Cape Town's multinational history, all blended together with international flair. After a fine meal at Signal, the Bascule whisky, wine & cocktail bar provides the perfect environment for post-prandial drinks, with the largest collection of whisky in the southern hemisphere, augmented by facilities for private collectors to rent storage space for their personal whisky or wine collections. It's even possible to enjoy soups and sweets in the Cape Grace Library, courtesy of the recently introduced Soup and Sugar Buffets – just one more reason why Cape Grace is a hotel unlike any other. ▣

CONTACT: www.capegrace.com

PERFECTION

SETTING NEW STANDARDS FOR
SERVICE, CAPELLA HOTELS AND
RESORTS OFFER PERSONAL CARE
IN SOME OF THE WORLD'S MOST
DESIRABLE BOUTIQUE HOTELS

Over recent years, Capella Hotels and Resorts has been quietly cultivating a reputation as a provider of top-tier accommodation in some of the world's most exclusive settings. Constantly aiming to set new standards in the hospitality industry, each Capella resort combines superb architecture and interior design with refined and discreet service, majoring on meticulous attention to detail. An ambitious programme of new hotels is set to augment an established presence extending from Colorado and Mexico through to Austria and Germany, and the grandeur of these resorts is epitomised by Capella Singapore – one of the world's finest destinations for the discerning traveller.

Situated on the island of Sentosa, ten minutes away from Singapore's financial and retail districts, this remarkable sanctuary was designed by Foster + Partners of London. Originally constructed in the 1880s by the British military, a pair of reclaimed colonial structures has been joined together in a sweeping figure-of-eight building whose stunning architecture pays homage to Singapore's rich British heritage. Indeed, many guests will arrive at Capella Singapore in the resort's own chauffeur-driven Rolls-Royce Phantom, as it glides towards the masterfully restored 19th-century frontage of the Tanah Merah buildings. Personal assistants then introduce each guest to a resort whose insistence on the finest components is reflected in the use of Japanese interior designers, San Franciscan artists and Swedish wellness specialists.

*Many guests will arrive at
Capella Singapore in the
resort's own chauffeur-driven
Rolls-Royce Phantom*

NATURE: Extending to 12,000 square feet internally, the unique Auriga spa typifies the attention to detail that has been lavished upon Capella Singapore. Exclusive treatments and 100 per cent organic products are available within nine suites, with herbal steam rooms and vitality pools centred on a relaxation lounge where the beverages served vary according to the current lunar cycle. This maintains Auriga's focus on matching signature treatments to each phase of the moon's monthly cycle, helping the mind and body to achieve greater equilibrium with nature.

ATMOSPHERE: Other elements of Capella Singapore maintain the meticulous standards set by Auriga. Named after an Asian spice, the Cassia restaurant serves Chinese fine dining within a dramatically presented space whose detailing is typified by the bronze butterfly-inspired lamps that illuminate it. With the option of private or al fresco dining, Cassia is rivalled by the cosy and intimate Knolls restaurant and bar lounge, which remains open around the clock. There are furnishings to admire and architectural flourishes to astonish in every communal area of Capella Singapore – nowhere more so than in the resort's ballroom, where a unique sculpture of 10,000 clear-glass tubes 'floats' beneath a domed glass skylight. Three cascading outdoor pools create a similarly spectacular feature within 30 acres of lush rainforest, incorporating more than 40,000 ferns, 125,000 shrubs and 5,000 trees from 60 different species.

TREAT: As might be expected, the accommodation on offer is surely the grandest anywhere in Singapore. Stylish flourishes include marble bathrooms, natural wood cabinets, touch-sensitive lighting and Bose stereo systems, while many accommodations offer captivating views over the South China Sea. A broad selection of 112 guest rooms, suites, villas and manors are available, with the 436-square-metre Colonial manors boasting private plunge pools and outdoor showers, alongside formal dining rooms and studies.

For those guests who can't bear to leave this pampering and cosseting environment, Capella Singapore has even introduced the option of extended stays, allowing people to live here for as long as they wish while still enjoying full access to the resort's numerous facilities. Long-stay guests have, in addition, exclusive access to a clubhouse with a pool and tennis court among its many facilities, while nearby Palawan beach's eateries, restaurants and bars are also close at hand. ▣

CONTACT: www.capellasingapore.com

INTO AFRICA

THIS FAMILY-OWNED SAFARI CAMP HAS BEEN MESMERISING VISITORS FOR OVER TWO DECADES,
COMBINING THE BEST ELEMENTS OF AFRICA IN ONE UNFORGETTABLE LOCATION

Within the majestic surroundings of the Lower Zambezi National Park (LZNP) and nestling under a grove of mahogany trees, Chiawa Camp is the original safari camp in this corner of Zambia. Founded in 1989, it was designed to introduce tourists and visitors to Africa, while simultaneously protecting and conserving this incredible wilderness for future generations to enjoy. At its inception, the camp's founder and owner Grant Cumings saw 'the opportunity to not only embark on a labour of love, but to be the first safari operators in what has since become one of Africa's most special wildlife reserves.'

As well as flying the flag for responsible tourism, Chiawa Camp aims to deliver the finest safari experience anywhere on this magnificent continent, with a team of 36 talented professionals allowing guests to get up close and personal with Africa's bounteous array of wildlife. As the maximum number of guests at the camp is 16, there are an impressive two members of staff per guest. Combining efficient personal service with a friendly and unpretentious atmosphere is a fine art, yet the long-serving team at Chiawa Camp manage it effortlessly, sending each

The animals are never far away from Chiawa's main accommodation areas, much like the 400 species of bird that live in the Lower Zambezi

visitor away with a lifetime of memories and extraordinary tales to tell about the LZNP. Through a combination of bush walks, game drives and river safaris, expert guides lead their guests through the numerous breathtaking features of this sprawling national park. With canoeing and fishing other popular options among visitors, no two days are ever the same.

EXPLORE: Chiawa Camp allows its guests to experience moments of true majesty – enjoying tea and cakes while bull elephants stroll past, for instance, or playing chess as monkeys chase each other through the branches of nearby trees. Guests are able to track lions and leopards on foot or in 4x4s, paddle past hippos or take part in catch-and-release fly fishing. A combination of motorboats, canoes and Land Cruisers are available to explore both the park and the Zambezi river, although the animals are never far away from Chiawa's main accommodation areas, much like the 400 species of bird that live in the Lower Zambezi.

Chiawa Camp has been constructed from natural materials to blend in harmoniously with its surroundings, typified by a thatched lounge area beside an alfresco dining veranda. Indeed, Chiawa has become synonymous with excellent cuisine: a fusion of African and European food is prepared with fresh local ingredients and often served in the bush or on a boat. Four-course dinners can be enjoyed under the stars, illuminated by camp-fire.

When the day is done and the indigenous inhabitants of the LZNP are settling down for the night, guests can retire to their safari tents on wooden decking. Each tent features super-kingsize beds with cool Egyptian cotton linens and en-suite bathrooms offering his-and-hers sinks alongside a choice of indoor and outdoor showers. Many tents have split-level timber decks overlooking the Zambezi River, while the furniture is locally made and pleasingly comfortable. A newly refurbished honeymoon tent provides the last word in luxury, with its huge bed proudly situated in the centre of this opulent environment.

ACCOLADES: In the last couple of years, Chiawa Camp's unique and innovative approach has seen it receive considerable acclaim. Its staff were declared the 'Best Guiding Team in Africa' at the 2008 Good Safari Guide Awards, and the camp itself was a finalist at the same awards ceremony, in the 'Best Safari Camp in Southern Africa' category – an achievement repeated in 2009. Chiawa Camp has also been declared one of the ten best safari camps in Africa by none other than *Conde Nast Traveller*, as well as being a shortlisted finalist for two years running in the 'Africa's Leading Safari Lodge' category of the World Travel Awards. ▣

CONTACT: www.chiawa.com

DISCOVER
AFRICA'S
HIDDEN SIDE

FORTY MILES FROM MARRAKECH YET A MILLION MILES AWAY IN SPIRIT, THIS EXTRAORDINARY MOUNTAIN RETREAT COMBINES THE FINEST ASPECTS OF AFRICA IN ONE RESORT

Nestling at the foot of North Africa's highest mountain, a cluster of traditionally designed buildings rise above wooded surroundings to create a visual and spiritual landmark. Standing in the snow-capped shadow of Jbel Toubkal in Morocco, this is Kasbah Du Toubkal – a spectacular mountain retreat that combines Berber hospitality and British innovation within the best resort of its kind in the country.

Kasbah Du Toubkal is the brainchild of brothers Mike and Chris McHugo, collectively the driving force behind Discover Ltd. Founded over 30 years ago, this Surrey centre of international travel has carved out an admirable niche, and Kasbah Du Toubkal encapsulates all the best elements of Discover's corporate ethos. The resort's origins lie in a chance meeting in 1978 between Mike McHugo and Hajj Maurice, and in 1989 this enduring friendship led to the purchase of a derelict building that would ultimately become Kasbah Du Toubkal.

Despite being just 60 kilometres from the city of Marrakech, this is Africa at its most peaceful and authentic – it is remote, yet with easy access on foot from the nearby village of Imlil, with mules carrying luggage for the short journey. Ensconced within this soothing haven is an eco-lodge and Berber hospitality centre, comprising a blend of informal salons with galleried sleeping areas, alongside more conventional guest suites. The undisputed highlight of the 14 different accommodation options is the self-contained garden apartment, where a glazed wall overlooks a waterfall with the Atlas Mountains forming a suitably majestic backdrop. Couples, families and groups can be housed with equal ease at Kasbah Du Toubkal, yet this is far from a conventional hotel – rather, it offers visitors the chance to experience Berber hospitality in an authentic environment, under the management of Hajj Maurice. As company chairman and co-founder Chris McHugo points out: 'Hospitality is a cultural obligation among the Berbers, so by guaranteeing to our Berber brothers that their larder will always be refilled, they can be generous without the concern that they may have to go without tomorrow.'

SYMBIOTIC:
Local involvement extends beyond mere hospitality at Kasbah Du Toubkal. The indigenous population helped to build the resort in 1995 using traditional construction techniques and local materials, and every room within the complex is imbued with North African furnishings and accoutrements. A close symbiotic relationship has developed between the neighbouring community and the resort, typified by the latter's support of local schools and ambulance services.

Understandably, given its location and ethos, Kasbah Du Toubkal has been warmly acclaimed by the world's press and hospitality experts. According to the *Cadogan Guides*: 'it is worth flying out to Morocco for just one night in this remarkable hotel, a role model for how tourism can help, not hinder.' Meanwhile, *Condé Nast Traveller* celebrated 'the best rooftop views in North Africa...this is the country's first and foremost mountain retreat'. Kasbah Du Toubkal was a proud entrant in *The Sunday Times*' most recent round-up of the world's 100 best hotels, and even Prince Charles has acknowledged this resort's good practice and standard-bearing levels of community involvement.

COMFORT:
Delightfully, this focus on sustainability and community integration hasn't reduced the levels of comfort on offer to guests at Kasbah Du Toubkal, where hand-woven carpets and carved walnut furniture are combined to stunning effect with modern technology and home comforts. Furthermore, Discover can call upon its enviable knowledge of Morocco to deliver everything from guided mountain ascents to educational tours of the surrounding region. Kasbah Du Toubkal's rich variety of visitors creates an ever-changing ambience, and the heart-warming Berber hospitality is one of the principal reasons that so many people return here again and again. As Chris points out: 'The visitors' book is full of wistful comments as guests prepare to leave Kasbah Du Toubkal – it is an experience rather than a destination.' □

CONTACT: www.kasbahdutoubkal.com/rrec

WHERE
DREAMS
COME TRUE

WITH A FULLY STAFFED YACHT AVAILABLE FOR
PRIVATE CHARTER ANYWHERE ON THE RED
SEA, DIVERS DREAM TOURS CAN DELIVER THE
ULTIMATE HOLIDAY FOR DIVING ENTHUSIASTS

Imagine beginning your day on a chartered yacht in the middle of the glorious Red Sea, diving into clear waters, with nobody else around and nothing to disturb your latest voyage of discovery. These dreams can be brought to life, courtesy of Divers Dream Tours, which allows people to charter a yacht for their own private use, before spending their days among coral reefs and ancient wrecks, swimming with dolphins and turtles in the ocean separating East Africa from the Arabian peninsula.

PASSIONATE: Divers Dream Tours is the brainchild of Belgian entrepreneur Maria Maraite. Inspired during an Egyptian holiday by the warmth of both the climate and the hospitality, Maria became a passionate fan of the country, and it was an obvious decision to make Egypt the base of operations for a pioneering holiday experience. Having chosen a suitable ship, Maria began fashioning what would become Divers Dream Tours – a fully crewed diving safari, creating the ambience of a luxurious hotel on the ocean waves.

Rebuilt in 2010, the Divers Dream Tours yacht is named *Aml Hayaty*, meaning 'Hope of my Life'. The 38-metre craft, which can accommodate up to 22 people within 11 en-suite equipped cabins and a beautifully finished dining salon, offers all the conveniences of modern technology. Stunning sunsets and seascapes can be admired from three different decks, and guests can spend anywhere between three and ten days being pampered in these rarefied surroundings by 11 skilled and experienced crew members.

PERFECTION: The team onboard *Aml Hayaty* aims to ensure that guests enjoy every moment of their live-aboard experience. This philosophy of perfection extends from delicious food served in a friendly atmosphere through to the presence of a dedicated diving expert, who can draw the most out of each dive for beginners and experts alike. Guests can complete four dives daily, the last taking the plunge at night if permitted in the area, with a pair of 40HP Zodiac motorboats on standby around the clock. Nitrox is available to certified divers, and certification can even be acquired during a holiday.

With the corporate slogan 'no problems, only solutions', each Divers Dream Tours experience is unique to its guests. Offering a choice of itineraries or the option to create a completely bespoke holiday, the boat can travel anywhere on the Red Sea. This is a marvellous venue for anyone with a love of nature, thanks to its coral reefs and more than 1,100 species of fish – a tenth of which are unique to these crystal-clear waters. Indeed, such is the experience of a diving holiday aboard the *Aml Hayaty* that guests are effusive in their praise, as well as being understandably keen to return. As Maria Maraite herself says: 'I invite all of you to follow your dream, because paradise is nearby, on the Red Sea.' ▣

CONTACT: www.diversdreamtours.com

WITH ALL THE HALLMARKS OF A FORMER BRITISH COLONY, PENANG'S CENTREPIECE IS THE BEAUTIFULLY APPOINTED EASTERN & ORIENTAL (E&O) HOTEL

EASTERN
PROMISES

In the late 19th century, wealthy European tourists began to visit far-flung destinations in Asia for the first time. They were able to take advantage of a burgeoning transport infrastructure, with the Suez Canal opening in 1869 to accommodate the new phenomenon of steamships. Britain had already colonised the Malayan island of Penang in 1786 and, a century later, a growing influx of visitors led to the creation of two colonial hotels here. Known as the Eastern and Oriental respectively, these establishments soon became combined into a single venue, described at the time as 'the premier hotel east of the Suez'. They attracted some of the era's most famous sons and daughters, such as Mary Pickford, Noël Coward and Rudyard Kipling, and some of these guests were subsequently honoured by having suites named after them.

DISTINCTIVE: Today, the E&O has become one of the world's legendary hotels, with its name serving as a byword for opulence. Those 125 years of heritage have left a deep impression on the hotel's character, with unmistakable colonial inspiration

> 66

*An illustrious pedigree and unmistakable sense of history are
now complemented by the best elements of modern hospitality*

visible in the architecture of this four-storey whitewashed building; even its address on the corner of Penang Road on Farquhar Street is in homage of colonial Governor Sir Robert Townsend Farquhar. The E&O lies within the historic charms of the Georgetown UNESCO heritage site, surrounded by shopping and entertainment amenities. From the hotel, looking across the bay of Gurney Drive, lies the master planned seafront development of Seri Tanjung Pinang where the E&O Group has extended its expertise in luxury hospitality to luxury lifestyle property, offering grand seafront villas and resort condominiums with sweeping views, fronting E&O's new retail marina enclave of Straits Quay.

An illustrious pedigree and sense of history are now complemented by the best elements of modern hospitality, with a complete refurbishment in 2001 transforming the E&O into a contemporary haven for visitors. The swimming pool is perhaps the ultimate encapsulation of this philosophy, with beautifully manicured surroundings flanked by lush tropical greenery, with uninterrupted sea views.

SUMPTUOUS: Further illustration of the E&O's calibre is underlined by the 100 hugely spacious and magnificently furnished suites. With eight different suite types on offer, each is equipped with a plethora of modern amenities, augmented by 24-hour butler service, attending to the specific needs of individual guests. Even the smallest deluxe suites feature adjoining living areas and spectacular sea views, while the Writers Suites are named after famous former guests, containing separate dining lounges, with twin sinks alongside claw-foot baths in each luxurious bathroom.

However, the ultimate in opulence can be found in the E&O's flagship suite, named after the hotel itself and undoubtedly one of South-East Asia's finest settings. It stands on the top floor of the building, with three bedrooms joined by a private study, a lounge and a walk-in dressing room with 'his and hers' en-suites. On top of this, there is a separate formal lounge leading to a private dining room capable of seating 22 people, a supported bar and butler's kitchenette, as well as dedicated male and female restrooms.

CHOICE: Colonial heritage has been retained in the E&O's communal areas as well, with the hotel's 400-seat Grand Ballroom still retaining the royal boxes that would once have been occupied by visiting heads of state. As in days gone by, diners are catered for in the fine-dining 1885 Restaurant, which mixes a traditional appearance with contemporary fusion cuisine, all blended together perfectly with fine wines, and is known for its famous afternoon tea. The colonial coffee shop Sarkies Corner (named after the E&O's founders) competes against the freshly prepared gastronomic delights of The Bakery, while the dark wood-panelled Farquhar's Bar is a quintessentially British affair, serving classic pub food alongside an excellent range of beers. ▣

CONTACT: www.e-o-hotel.com; www.seritanjungpinang.com
IMAGES: (L–R) The swimming pool at the 125-year old E&O Hotel; Martinique E&O Property's Villa-By-The-Sea at Seri Tanjung Pinang; E&O Hotel's Deluxe Seafront Suite

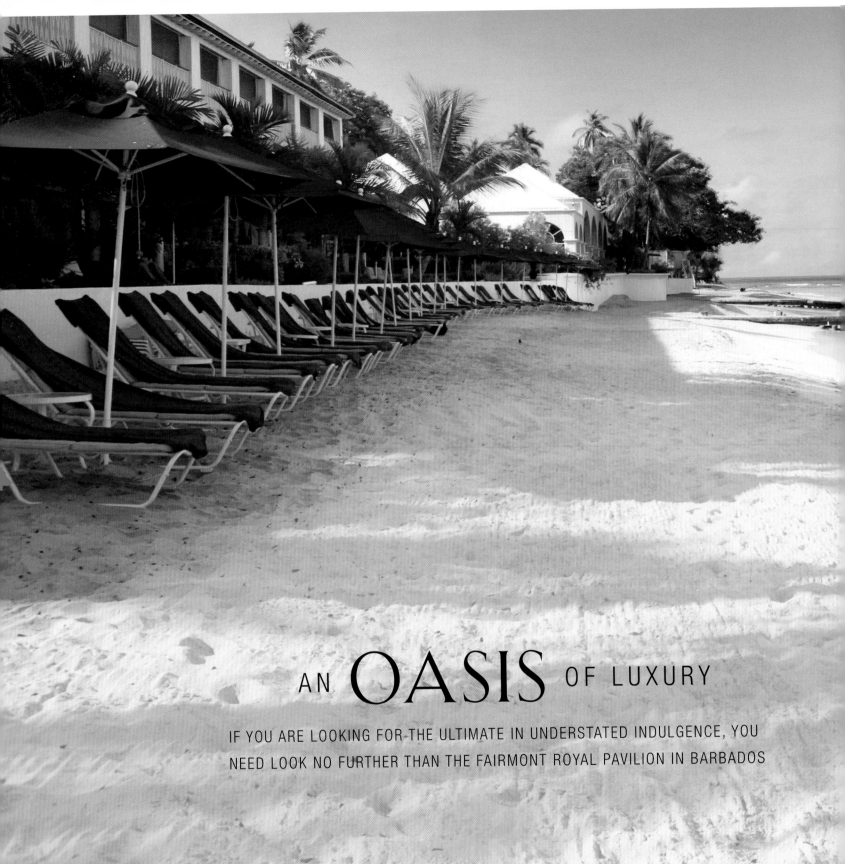

AN OASIS OF LUXURY

IF YOU ARE LOOKING FOR THE ULTIMATE IN UNDERSTATED INDULGENCE, YOU
NEED LOOK NO FURTHER THAN THE FAIRMONT ROYAL PAVILION IN BARBADOS

Perched on the eastern edge of the Caribbean Sea, The Fairmont Royal Pavilion is a truly magical oasis of luxury and has been sought out by discerning and sophisticated travellers for decades. Presiding over 11-acres of beautifully landscaped gardens with an unrivalled beach presence, this iconic, five-star award-winning resort is so at one with the Caribbean that it feels as if the ocean is just a hand's reach from any one of its 72 deluxe bedrooms.

HISTORY:
The Fairmont Royal Pavilion started life as The Miramar, the first hotel to be built on the world-famous west coast of Barbados. It was founded in the 1940s adjacent to the winter estate of the Cunard shipping legend Sir Edward Cunard.

In the 1980s The Miramar was redeveloped by the renowned British hotelier Mike Pemberton, and in October 1999, following the acquisition by the world-famous Fairmont Hotels and Resorts, the property was renamed The Fairmont Royal Pavilion, opening a new chapter of luxury, glamour and distinction.

EFFORTLESS:
Today, The Fairmont Royal Pavilion is a landmark in Barbados. The resort effortlessly intertwines the elegance of a traditional plantation home with the natural beauty of its surroundings. Its rich history has contributed to the island's legendary hospitality and to this day continues to embody the welcoming nature of the Barbadian people.

It is one of the most romantic settings in the Caribbean, and during the high season The Fairmont Royal Pavillion specialises in turning a holiday into the vacation of a lifetime. From each of its deluxe waterfront apartments guests can relax and watch breathtaking panoramic sunsets, while enjoying the modern luxuries of cable television and high-speed Internet. After wandering around the beautiful landscaped grounds, take time out to indulge in one of a variety of tailored in-room spa treatments, or make use of the innovative Beach Butler service offering a selection of cooling refreshments.

During the high season, the resort is primarily couple-oriented. However, children of all ages are invited to join their parents throughout the summer months, when the resort transforms itself into a family friendly environment between April 1 and October 31. There is plenty of fun for all the family, should you choose to bring the little ones along. The Kids & Teens Adventure Club will keep youngsters entertained all day long with complimentary activities for the under-4s, and watersports and movie nights galore for older children and teenagers.

SUSTAINABILITY:
The Fairmont Royal Pavilion is continually working towards becoming more sustainable. Wherever possible, its Michelin-star-experience chefs purchase local, organic, Fairtrade and sustainable foods – 75 per cent of vegetables purchased are from local suppliers; all chicken is hormone free and raised locally; there is an on-site herb garden; fruit trees are planted on the property and used in restaurant dishes; and sustainable seafood is served in all outlets.

The Fairmont Royal Pavillion also works closely with various agencies to protect the resort's marine environment, including regular reef checks of the island's endangered coral. It is also working with the Barbados Turtle Project to make sure that the turtles on the beach in front of the hotel are nesting and hatching in good conditions.

Whatever the purpose of your visit to The Fairmont Royal Pavilion, be it business or pleasure, a romantic getaway or a week of family fun, you can be sure of pure luxury and memories that will last a lifetime. This year The Fairmont Royal Pavilion is offering the Rolls-Royce Enthusiasts' Club an exclusive members' offer for a romantic or a family getaway. The special offer for couples includes private dining for two on the beach as well as chocolate-dipped strawberries and champagne on arrival. This offer is valid until 31st October 2011, excluding December 17th 2010 – February 28th 2011 and all public bank holidays and half-term weeks. Family members can enjoy a range of offers including 50 per cent off a second room as well as free meals for 0–5 year olds and daily complimentary activities for children of all ages. This offer is valid from 1st April 2011–31st October 2011. To make a reservation, please contact +1 800 441 1414 and quote RREC Special Offer. ▣

CONTACT: www.fairmont.com/royalpavilion

ISLAND
RETREAT

WITH THE OPPORTUNITY TO DO AS LITTLE, OR BE AS ACTIVE, AS THEY WISH, GUESTS
ARE SPOILT FOR CHOICE AT THE FISHER ISLAND HOTEL AND RESORT

Who wouldn't want to spend their holiday relaxing on a private island full of coconut palms and mangroves, surrounded by the Atlantic Ocean, taking in the sights of the nearby iconic Miami skyline? Located a mere seven minutes from the coast of Miami, and only accessible by auto-ferry or yacht, Fisher Island is a private residential community named after Miami Beach founder and developer, Carl Fisher. In the 1920s Fisher, then owner of the island, desired a yacht belonging to William Kissam Vanderbilt II, a millionaire sportsman and regular visitor to Miami. When Fisher proposed to Vanderbilt that he would trade 'my island for your boat', the offer was quickly accepted and Vanderbilt began laying the foundations for the exclusive retreat the island has become today.

WELCOMING: The focal point of Vanderbilt's plans for the island was a grand Mediterranean-style mansion surrounded by lush landscaping, spacious guest homes, tennis courts and swimming pools. The striking building provided Vanderbilt and his wife, Rosamund, with the perfect setting to entertain countless luminaries and distinguished guests. 'The historic Vanderbilt mansion still remains the centrepiece of Fisher Island Hotel and Resort,' explains Chief Executive Officer, Larry Brown, 'A newly completed $US60 million restoration project, Renaissance of Fisher Island, has seen the resort and its facilities returned to their former splendour and the recently upgraded surrounding guest rooms include new interiors, finishes and furnishings, private Jacuzzis, Wi-Fi high-speed Internet access and lots more.'

As a member of the Leading Small Hotels of the World, the sprawling 45-room boutique hotel's accommodation includes garden and ocean view suites, villas and cottages and one- two- and three-bedroom residences. Guests have all their needs catered for with a turndown service, complimentary toiletries, meals to suit any dietary requirements or special requests and, Mr Brown adds, 'the concierge is always available to answer any questions, concerns or requests that may arise during a guest's stay – from arranging a private yacht charter, to placing special orders for gear or apparel from the resort's pro golf and tennis shops.'

FREEDOM: Fisher Island boasts a private beach, complemented by a brand-new beach club offering guests full use of pool facilities, lounge areas and cabanas. Yacht owners are able to moor their vessels at either one of the resort's deep-water, surge-proof marinas, where 118 slips can accommodate yachts that are up to 250-feet in length.

With an emphasis on relaxation and rejuvenation, guests can pamper themselves at the Spa Internazionale, which features a state-of-the-art fitness suite overlooking the Vanderbilt marina and full-service Salon di Bellezza. Dedicated to promoting good health, beauty and wellness, the spa offers a full range of treatments carried out by professional and highly skilled staff, relaxation rooms, a Roman waterfall, lap pool, saunas and steam rooms. The 80-minute Organic Aromatherapy Massage uses Aromandina organic essential-oil blends ranging from 'Romance' to 'Relax', and even 'Exulto Fiesta', to provide an uplifting treat after a long night or day. »

> *Fisher Island boasts a brand-new beach club offering guests full use of pool facilities, lounge areas and cabanas*

Guests who wish to be more active can take advantage of the fitness centre's high-tech equipment or range of classes, from swimming and spinning to yoga. The island's nine-hole, 35-par golf course, The Links at Fisher Island, has recently been updated and now has new grass, laser-levelled tees, and rebuilt cart paths and bunkers. After a round or two, golfers can relax in the exclusive clubhouse with a refreshing drink or satisfy their appetites with a meal at its signature restaurant, The Grill. The resort also offers a refurbished tennis centre, which, alongside the golf course, has hosted visiting pros using the facilities for practice. The new centre includes a restored racquet club and 18 grass, Har-Tru clay and hard tennis courts with a sophisticated watering system, and modern surroundings including a courtyard fountain and improved lighting for night games.

CHOICE: After a long day relaxing or utilising the island's services, seven dining selections are available, ranging from the beach-side Sunset bar to The Beach Club, which offers Floridian cuisine in an al fresco setting, to the Garwood Lounge, an intimate piano bar located in the 1920s-era Vanderbilt mansion. Other gourmet choices include Italian, Mediterranean and à la carte menus offered in a range of settings, such as the mansion courtyard.

Fisher Island's close proximity to the bustling South Beach scene also allows guests to leave the resort, if they wish, to experience the world-class shopping of Lincoln Road or the gourmet dining and thriving nightlife along Ocean Drive, and enjoy Miami's renowned Art Deco architecture.

The resort's positioning, atmosphere and unrivalled range of facilities means that it attracts discerning customers from across the USA, Europe and South America who are looking for a one-of-a-kind, exclusive getaway. This ranges from couples of all ages and families, to those who want its picturesque and tropical setting to provide a romantic background for their wedding, which can take place in the Vanderbilt mansion itself or in the courtyard under Fisher Island's famous and distinctive Banyan Tree. The resort's wealth of business facilities, including free wireless Internet, hospitality suites, meeting rooms and dedicated event staff, also draws a number of corporate guests to the island.

ENHANCING: With brand-new and improved amenities due to the recent renovation, Mr Brown says that Fisher Island Hotel and Resort will continue with plans for development: 'Phase two of the restoration will focus on a thoughtful restoration of the Vanderbilt mansion, a complete renovation of 22,000 sq ft Spa Internazionale and the creation of a new town-centre experience.'

With a range of services always striving to cater to everybody's needs, and the best facilities, guests will have to tear themselves away from this island. ▣

CONTACT: www.fisherislandclub.com

AN ATMOSPHERE OF
ELEGANCE

With velvet-green valleys and commanding gritstone fells bisecting remarkable sweeps of heather-strewn moorland, the spectacular Ribble Valley is Lancashire's hidden gem. Even Her Majesty the Queen, in her biography by Sarah Bradford, announced that she would like to retire to this region of rural England.

Situated in The Forest of Bowland, near Chipping, a designated Area of Outstanding Natural Beauty, is The Gibbon Bridge Hotel. More a home than a hotel, this jewel in Lancashire's crown exudes sophistication through a classic mix of the old and new.

The hotel's story is one of passion and pleasure. Once the family farm, the proprietor, Janet Simpson, and her late mother Margaret, transformed it into a luxurious four-star hotel. Sumptuous dining, beautifully decorated interiors and award-winning manicured gardens help create a truly unique atmosphere. And Janet, as the owner of a 1939 Bentley Derby and a Continental GT, certainly knows style.

PASSION: The personal touches that Janet has added over the years are what make the Gibbon Bridge different. Sometimes referred to as a

The hotel's vegetable, fruit and herb garden brings fresh and seasonal fare to its already impeccable dishes

A WARM WELCOME WAITS AT THE GIBBON BRIDGE HOTEL

'magpie', her travels have seen the acquisition of many artifacts that have been woven into the fabric of the hotel. Examples of these include church stonework and stained-glass windows built into its exterior, to iron pillars from the old Preston Public Hall that she saved from demolition and stored for 25 years until finding somewhere suitable for them, which today is the hotel's spectacular orangery.

The orangery is truly something special and lies at the heart of the hotel. Boasting an impressive, modern look accentuated with black and white flocked wallpaper, glassworks from South Africa, mood lighting and a grand piano, this is the place to impress or be impressed, be it for a special occasion or simply dinner. Janet's love for eating outdoors has also led to the installation of many pergolas where guests can dine al fresco; one being particularly large, seating up to 22. On top of the exquisite dining, the hotel's vegetable, fruit and herb garden brings fresh and seasonal fare to its already impeccable dishes.

The Gibbon Bridge was also the first hotel in Lancashire to hold civil marriages, and its ornate bandstand has become a popular place for civil ceremonies, backed by its beautiful gardens.

LUXURY: After a hard day of relaxation, guests can sink into opulent four-poster or Gothic beds and relax in whirlpool baths in one of the 30 spacious bedrooms and split-level suites offering superb, luxury accommodation, each individually designed by Janet and furnished with charm and character.

'The Gibbon Bridge is my passion,' says Janet, 'and it has been since I started; working here is my pleasure. A lot of people who own hotels just do it for the money, but this is my home and I enjoy welcoming people to appreciate it as much as I do.

'Someone once said that staying in a country hotel should be like "being utterly spoilt in your own home". This is, quite simply, what myself and my team aspire to when you stay with us.' ▣

CONTACT: www.gibbon-bridge.co.uk

THE
CASE
IN HAND

PART OF THE GLOBE-TROTTER
EXPERIENCE IS TRAVELLING
THE WORLD IN STYLE

> Sir Winston Churchill used the Globe–Trotter attaché case when he was Chancellor of the Exchequer

Her Majesty The Queen and top model Kate Moss may not appear to have a great deal in common, but they both choose the same brand of quality handmade suitcases when travelling around the world. Globe-Trotter has always been the brand of choice for discerning travellers.

Globe-Trotter is in the business of travelling in style. Globe-Trotter has supplied the Royal Navy, the Army and the Royal Air Force and has been the official luggage supplier to British Airways. The company has an impressive history; it was founded in 1897, and by 1901 Globe-Trotter suitcases and trunks were widely used on the great steam liners of the time.

'Our brand is not only associated with great cruise liners and airlines,' says Creative Director, Gary Bott. 'We also have an affinity to the luxury automotive industry, going back many years. We would design specific cases to fit the interior boot compartment in specific models of cars.'

UNIQUE: Globe-Trotter's manufacturing process, which includes the use of a material called Vulcan Fibre, is so unique that little has changed over the years. The Vulcan Fibre, which was invented in Britain during the 1850s and the manufacture of which is a closely guarded secret making the suitcase impossible to imitate, is so durable that at least one 100-year-old Globe-Trotter suitcase is still in use.

New lines have been added and Globe-Trotter now has an Original line and a Centenary line, launched on the company's 100th anniversary in 1997. 'On Original cases, we use Vulcan Fibre body with Vulcan Fibre corners,' explains Gary. 'On the Centenary line, the corners are leather with additional leather straps, plus a wider range of colour and special print linings.'

Through each innovation, the integrity of the craftsmanship is never compromised. The suitcases are made by craftsmen, some of whom have done so for the last 40 years, which explains why customers remain loyal. 'Some of our customers have grown up with the Globe-Trotter case they've had since their school days,' says Gary. 'Some are over 80 and still own the same suitcase, which they can bring back for repair. The stories some customers tell about the product are not only nostalgic, but are a clear indication of the quality of our products.'

UNIVERSAL: In 2004, Globe-Trotter launched its global flagship store in Burlington Arcade, London, aimed at a new generation of customer. Globe-Trotter suitcases are now available in the USA, Japan, Hong Kong, Taiwan, Korea, Singapore, Australia, Russia, the Middle East and throughout Europe.

No matter what technical and design innovations are made, the Globe-Trotter suitcase remains instantly recognisable. ▣

CONTACT: www.globe-trotterltd.com

FAVOURED BY ROYALTY AND BLESSED
WITH THE PERFECT CLIMATE, IT'S EASY
TO SEE WHY SO MANY PEOPLE RETURN
TO THE GRAN HOTEL ATLANTIS BAHIA
REAL AFTER THEIR FIRST VISIT

Many resorts try to make their guests feel like royalty, but few can actually say that royalty are happy to be treated like normal guests. Such is the calibre of Gran Hotel Atlantis Bahia Real that a European monarch recently opted to stay in a standard double room rather than the 190-square-metre Royal Suite. That simple gesture illustrates the exemplary accommodation and hospitality on offer at this Fuerteventura resort.

Gran Hotel Atlantis Bahia Real's timelessly courteous customer service creates a natural environment where handpicked professionals cater to each guest around the clock with discretion and diplomacy. Even seasoned travellers find themselves surprised at how a visit to this award-winning five-star resort transforms a mere holiday into a perfect lifetime experience.

AMBIENT: Part of the hotel's appeal can be attributed to the local microclimate. The intoxicating island of Fuerteventura enjoys an astonishingly consistent ambient temperature, and this particular setting rarely goes above 28 degrees centigrade or below 20 degrees at any time of year. With more than 300 days of sunshine annually to benefit from, guests can enjoy the outdoors at any time, even as stars shine in the night sky and cool breezes roll in from the Atlantic Ocean. Indeed, Fuerteventura arguably represents the perfect location, with spectacular geology and an extremely high concentration of beaches, all within a four-hour flight from the UK.

Gran Hotel Atlantis Bahia Real stands beside a sandy beach, facing out towards the islands of Lobos and Lanzarote. Behind the extraordinary 19th-century Neo-Mudéjar architecture, there are 242 rooms and suites incorporating a wealth of modern technology and home comforts. These range from a mini-bar and air conditioning through to bathrobes and slippers in the en-suite bathrooms. It's even possible to choose which pillows you would like to adorn your bed.

OUTSTANDING: No discussion of this hotel would be complete without mentioning the Spa Bahia Vital, voted the best spa in Europe and the perfect place for meditation and relaxation. Its amenities include a gorgeous indoor swimming pool, complemented by sauna, steam room, solarium and Jacuzzi, as well as a brace of outdoor pools. A total of 17 treatment rooms join fitness and beauty centres as 'must-see' attractions in this wing of the hotel, and every guest can enjoy a completely bespoke experience within the spa, including hiring it for exclusive private use. That maintains a precedent established elsewhere in Gran Hotel Atlantis Bahia Real, by which any event can be organised, such as a private dinner under the stars with guests' own maître d'. Indeed, with five acclaimed restaurants available, cuisine is one of this resort's outstanding features. With its open courtyard and live cooking, La Alacena Real provides a pleasing counterpoint to the gourmet cuisine of La Cúpula, while the Yamatori Japanese restaurant even features a sushi bar.

Words and pictures can do much to illustrate Gran Hotel Atlantis Bahia Real, but there are so many unique elements of this resort that can only be appreciated in person. Every window offers a different view of the hotel's stunning Spanish architecture or tropical gardens, with the majority of rooms and suites facing directly out across the clear blue waters of the Atlantic Ocean. And with the interior matching the exquisite beauty of the exterior, this resort needs to be seen to be appreciated. ▣

CONTACT: www.atlantishotels.com

SUITE
HARMONY

GRAND RESORT BAD RAGAZ COMBINES EXEMPLARY ACCOMMODATION
WITH A WORLD-CLASS SPA EXPERIENCE

Think of Switzerland, and the first images that generally spring to mind are notions of purity and beauty, crisp air and tranquil mountainsides. It's not often that reality lives up to these heady expectations, but at Grand Resort Bad Ragaz, the beautiful foothills of the Alps form a perfect backdrop to this celebrated spa destination.

It's hard to believe that Zurich is only an hour away by train or car as you stroll along the footpaths that lead to this centrepiece of Swiss excellence – the recent beneficiary of a €100 million refurbishment programme. Much more than a hotel, Grand Resort Bad Ragaz is a well-being and medical health resort, effortlessly fusing together tradition and modernity. It comprises two distinct five-star hotels, Grand Hotel Hof Ragaz and Grand Hotel Quellenhof & Spa Suites. Both are members of the illustrious 'Leading Hotels of the World' group – the ultimate benchmark for luxurious accommodation.

PALATIAL: Both hotels have been exquisitely prepared for the enjoyment of discerning guests. Grand Hotel Quellenhof offers a total of 105 suites, with the calibre of accommodation neatly illustrated by the Spa Lofts. These delightful suites are equipped with everything from Bang & Olufsen TVs to butler service, alongside pamper-friendly 'oasis' bathrooms incorporating such joys as whirlpool baths, steam showers and saunas. Meanwhile, Grand Hotel Hof Ragaz has 106 rooms available, with some of its 21 suites housed in the 'Palais' – a protected historic monument dating back to 1774.

However, the true star of Grand Resort Bad Ragaz is the comprehensively refurbished To B. Wellbeing & Spa, a distinguished member of the 'Leading Spas of the World' list. Extending across more than 5,500 square metres, this is quite simply the finest setting imaginable for restoring your body's balance and beauty, with highlights including an ice cave and the world's first herbal steam bath embellished with Swarovski crystals. There are nine luxurious massage rooms, a Kneipp circuit (a cave-like room designed to stimulate blood circulation), a truly beautiful swimming pool filled with mineral water, and a private spa equipped with everything from a home cinema suite to a Champagne cooler in the sauna. There is even a fully modernised Olympic-standard medical health centre on-site, with a comprehensive menu of services including rheumatology and cosmetic surgery delivered by a team of 70 specialist doctors, consultants and other professionals. All this is complemented by the futuristic Tamina Therme, a public spa covering more than 7,300 square metres with bold architecture and a waterfall surrounding various indoor and outdoor pools.

LEISURE: Grand Resort Bad Ragaz is the only Swiss resort to offer two golf courses, including an internationally acclaimed 18-hole PGA Championship course. The on-site casino has been awarded the title of being the 'Friendliest Casino in Switzerland', and an array of leisure outlets include boutique stores and a cinema, with limousines available for anyone wishing to explore the magnificent Swiss countryside. In winter, this venue is a haven for outdoor sports, with Nordic and Alpine skiing and snowboarding among the most popular options; in summer, it's possible to enjoy everything from angling to horse-drawn carriage rides.

As you might expect from such a lavishly appointed destination, there is a wealth of culinary choice throughout Grand Resort Bad Ragaz. A total of seven restaurants range from the Swiss and international cuisine of Gourmet Restaurant Äbtestube through to the Thai and Chinese dishes of the Namun Asian restaurant. Augmenting this enviable choice of dining environments are half a dozen bars and lounges, some enhanced by live piano music. ▣

CONTACT: www.resortragaz.ch

> Much more than a mere hotel,
> Grand Resort Bad Ragaz is a
> well-being and medical health
> resort, effortlessly fusing together
> tradition and modernity

MAGIC IN THE MOUNTAINS

BY UTILISING THE FINEST RESOURCES AND EMPLOYING ONLY THE
MOST TALENTED STAFF, THIS RESORT IN THE SWISS ALPS HAS
BECOME SYNONYMOUS WITH CELEBRITIES AND CONNOISSEURS ALIKE

Since its doors first opened to guests in 1913, Gstaad Palace has cultivated an unrivalled reputation for discreet, refined hospitality. It has become cherished by many of the world's most discerning clients, who flock to this unspoiled setting high in the Alps. Set within 30,000 square metres of landscaped grounds, with crenellated towers and balconied suites punctuating its frontage, the hotel's dramatic architecture reflects its captivating surroundings, overlooking the beautiful Swiss village of Gstaad.

Over the years, this celebrated resort has hosted countless public figures, from royalty and prime ministers through to some of the world's best-known stars of stage and screen. They have all enjoyed privacy and luxury in equal measure, although many famous performers have waived their anonymity by starring in live performances at Gstaad Palace among them John Cleese, Louis Armstrong and Elton John.

Key to Gstaad Palace's extraordinary roster of famous guests has always been the calibre of accommodation on offer. A total of 104 impeccably decorated and appointed rooms include 19 junior suites, a brace of tower suites and arguably the most luxurious and sophisticated three-bedroom penthouse ever created within an Alpine resort. Every room is specified to the very finest standards, with lavish bathrooms and captivating views. Exemplary customer service is a given for guests in any suite, and a talented team of over 250 staff work around the clock to anticipate and surpass the expectations of even the most particular visitors.

CUISINE: Unsurprisingly, cuisine is taken extremely seriously at Gstaad Palace, with five beautifully appointed restaurants offering everything from traditional Swiss or Italian dishes to exquisite gourmet cuisine and the very finest international menus. A brace of intimate bars offer live music in the evenings, while the famous GreenGo nightclub can accommodate 200 guests.

RECREATION: Gstaad Palace is no ordinary resort, and the activities available to guests reflect this, with heli-skiing and hot-air ballooning available alongside horse-drawn carriage rides and tours of the nearby cheese cathedral. An indoor swimming pool competes for attention against a 50-metre heated outdoor summer pool, itself surpassed only by the 250 kilometres of Alpine slopes awaiting winter sports enthusiasts just beyond Gstaad Palace's gardens.

Exceeding the expectations of even the most discerning spa connoisseurs, Gstaad Palace has created the ultimate retreat. Using 50 tonnes of granite, a 60-metre-long wall was constructed to maintain the mountainous ambience alongside 1,800 square metres of seductive spa facilities. Its features include indoor and outdoor pools, a state-of-the-art gym, a private spa suite and eight treatment rooms. Not to be missed is the relaxation lounge, with comfortable sofas surrounding an open central fire underneath an octagonal timbered ceiling.

Many guests opt for a two-hour visit to the hammam, involving a harmonious progression through seven rooms, commencing with a soothing footbath and culminating in a moisturising oil massage. Throughout its spa, Gstaad Palace utilises only the most select facilities and equipment. Complimentary brands such as Sisley, Cinq Mondes, Niance and L.Raphael are offered within the treatment suites further reflecting the quality of the experience at Gstaad Palace. ▣

CONTACT: www.palace.ch

MAKING
DREAMS
COME TRUE

A wedding is one of life's great occasions, and every bride dreams of a perfect day in a perfect setting. Few locations could be more suitable for a grand marriage ceremony than Hedingham Castle, which has overlooked the Essex village of Castle Hedingham for almost 1,000 years. Unquestionably one of England's most romantic settings, the Norman keep and nearby Georgian country house collectively offer a unique and unparalleled venue for couples on their wedding day, in tandem with an enviable roster of facilities including a vintage Rolls-Royce.

Hedingham Castle was constructed in 1140ad, both by and for the famous de Vere family. These Earls of Oxford lived here for more than five centuries, and to this day the castle remains under the ownership of their descendants, the Lindsay family. As one of Britain's oldest buildings, the stunning keep still overlooks almost the entire county of Essex, with its 12-foot thick walls and original Norman architectural flourishes having

The Norman keep and nearby Georgian country house collectively offer a unique and unparalleled venue for couples on their wedding day

STEEPED IN ANCIENT HISTORY AND ROYAL GRANDEUR, HEDINGHAM CASTLE OFFERS A PERFECT WEDDING VENUE, WITHIN EXQUISITE GARDENS IN THE ESSEX COUNTRYSIDE

been admired by numerous royal visitors including Henry VIII and Elizabeth I. Close by is Queen Anne House, constructed in 1720 and overlooking a lake and glorious wooded grounds which are populated by a profusion of birds, flora and fauna.

ENCHANTING: Both the house and the keep can be hired for corporate functions, private parties and trade shows, yet their grand architecture and timelessness are perhaps best suited to hosting weddings. It is also possible to hire a lodge house and garden cottage, collectively capable of accommodating 20 people within tastefully decorated rooms that seamlessly combine period features and modern accoutrements. Both buildings are situated within mature, private gardens offering a variety of terraces and garden furniture, and both are just a couple of moments' walk from the castle, through the enchanting park grounds. These beautifully landscaped gardens offer a thousand possible backdrops for those all-important wedding photographs, while the romantic garden cottage is an ideal retreat for a newly united husband and wife on their first evening together.

Ceremonies take place within the castle, steeped in the memories of innumerable royal banquets, and with the largest Norman arch in England illuminated by candlelight overhead. Capable of accommodating 130 guests, this room was designed to impress monarchs and heads of state, which makes it a fitting space for any bride to spend her final moments before being joined in matrimony. History permeates every moment of each ceremony, and the nearby Georgian manor house is a superlative setting for the reception afterwards, thanks to its oak panelling, grand piano and portraits of its former occupants.

UNFORGETTABLE: A comprehensive portfolio of bespoke options can be specified to personalise each wedding event, creating an unforgettable day for even the most discerning couple. A team of experts is on hand to augment Hedingham Castle's rich surroundings with everything from jesters to a string quartet or jazz trio. Talented chefs are highly skilled at concocting gourmet cuisine from organic local ingredients, and the extensive wine cellar includes own-label champagne. Such an evocative and unforgettable venue also requires a suitably grand mode of transport – resplendent in its original Cellon blue paintwork, a 1956 Rolls-Royce Silver Cloud I is the Lindsay family's private vehicle, available to hire along with a uniformed chauffeur. From its walnut occasional tables to the gleaming Spirit of Ecstasy adorning its radiator grille, this impeccably presented motor car is the ideal mode of transport for such an extraordinary venue, where every bride's dreams really can come true. ▣

CONTACT: www.hedinghamcastle.co.uk

RYOKAN
HIDEAWAY

A TRANQUIL, TIMELESS OASIS WHICH BLENDS JAPAN'S TRADITIONS AND TODAY'S CONVENIENCES

The waters of the Yukawa River tumble down the forested slopes of Mount Asama to enter a gentle valley. Along its banks rest a small cluster of houses hinting that an old village may have survived into modern times. This is HOSHINOYA, founded as a traditional Japanese hot-spring resort, a 'Ryokan Onsen', almost a century ago.

Five years ago, the resort was reborn as a village that married traditional Onsen hospitality with modern convenience, flexibility and comfort. Guests can bathe in the hot spring waters of the Meditation Bath at any hour, night or day. Complementing this, the HOSHINOYA Spa offers a wide range of massage, oil, bathing and exercise opportunities. Restaurants offer both classical Kaiseki as well as casual dining. Fruits and vegetables are organic, and all ingredients come fresh from neighbourhood farms. The resort is located in Karuizawa Town, only one hour from Tokyo by bullet train or a two-hour drive.

With the village in the midst of a national park and bird sanctuary, many guests spend time walking or cycling the trails. Naturalists from Picchio, a wildlife research centre created by HOSHINOYA, can arrange guided walks and birdwatching to help visitors explore and understand the natural world around them. The rustle of leaves blends with sounds of flowing water to invigorate and refresh the senses. Ecological sensitivity is integral to HOSHINOYA's philosophy; the resort generates 75 per cent of its own power using modern hydroelectric and geothermal technologies.

Despite the modern technology that underpins every aspect of HOSHINOYA, the past still lingers. HOSHINOYA's concept is to explore what Japan might have become if it had modernised while retaining the traditions and ethics of its past. The woods and stone used to construct HOSHINOYA all have ancient traditions. The patterns of light and shade are uniquely Japanese; so too is the simple elegance of the rooms. Many features of the resort are the handiwork of some of Japan's most eminent designers and craftsmen.

The delights of the HOSHINOYA experience are all the more accessible because most of the young staff speak good English, with some fluent in other European or Asian languages.

In December 2009, HOSHINOYA opened a companion resort, based on the same ideas, on the western outskirts of Kyoto. ▣

CONTACT: www.hoshinoya.com

DARING
TO BE DIFFERENT

ACROSS TWO VERY DIFFERENT LOCATIONS, PER AQUUM HAS CREATED THE ULTIMATE LUXURY
LIVING EXPERIENCE, WINNING THE HEARTS AND MINDS OF VISITORS

Nestled on a private island in the North Malé Atoll, and named after the local word for 'dream', Huvafen Fushi is the first of two spectacular retreats created by Per AQUUM. This Maldives retreat comprises 44 bungalows with private pools, surrounded by landscaped pavilions and overlooking the Indian Ocean. As the most exquisite island-chic retreat anywhere in the Maldives, this retreat even boasts its own official soundtrack, courtesy of regular visitor DJ Ravin and his collection of Huvafen Fushi-titled CDs. These typify the spectacular events that take place throughout each year, as part of Per AQUUM's 'Dream Calendar'.

One way to appreciate Huvafen Fushi's glorious surroundings is through guided night snorkelling, although a more relaxing view of the ocean can be obtained from two of the world's only underwater treatment rooms – part of the award-winning LIME spa. Situated 70 metres off-island, LIME features steam and ice rooms alongside those underwater treatment suites, which can even be converted into a wedding venue.

CONTEMPORARY: Creating the same magic in Dubai as Huvafen Fushi has already achieved in the Maldives, the recently opened Desert Palm brings something very different to this glittering Emirate state. Within the Middle East's finest polo estate, lush greenery and palm trees surround a collection of 28 suites and villas, the latter ranging from one to three bedrooms in size. Each is equipped with a profusion of modern technology including espresso machines and an entertainment centre, the latter offering complimentary Wi-Fi and flat-screen satellite TV.

Many elements of Desert Palm can also be found at its Maldivian sister retreat, including the personalised treatments of the sophisticated LIME spa (in this case overlooking four championship polo fields), regular celebrity-led events, and a pair of award-winning restaurants offering the finest cuisine in elegant surroundings alongside a chic lounge bar. ◻

CONTACT: www.peraquum.com

WITH ITS INFORMAL APPROACH TO LUXURY, HOSTELLERIE LA BRIQUETERIE IS THE PERFECT BASE FROM WHICH TO EXPLORE THE DELIGHTS OF FRANCE'S CHAMPAGNE COUNTRY

ON THE CHAMPAGNE
TRAIL

Hostellerie La Briqueterie is set in rolling vineyards just an hour and a half from Paris, outside the small town of Epernay – better known as the capital of Champagne. Epernay's quiet streets are lined with world-famous *maisons de champagne*, such as Moët & Chandon, Mercier, De Castellane and Pol Roger. Wine tours and tastings are organised at these prestigious houses and also at smaller, lesser-known producers. Nearby Reims, with its beautiful Notre Dame cathedral, fine art museum and Jesuit college (of which Condorcet is an alumnus), now links to Paris by rail in just 35 minutes. The region plays host to several luxury and vintage car rallies a year.

CHARM: Affiliated with the prestigious Relais & Châteaux association of *hôtels de charme* and gastronomic restaurants, four-star La Briqueterie maintains the highest standards in hospitality but is 'neither a chain nor a château', in the words of Manager Julien Agnellet. 'Our guests feel at home,' he says.

66

*Affiliated with the prestigious Relais & Châteaux association
of hôtels de charme and gastronomic restaurants, four-star
La Briqueterie maintains the highest standards in hospitality*

'We combine luxury and comfort with a simple, respectful approach.' This is evident in the bar, the hotel's hub, where diners gather for a pre-dinner refreshment. Modelled on an English style, with exposed beams, an open fire, warm red tones and heavy fabric furnishings, it is opulent yet comfortable. Like an ornate winter-garden conservatory, it looks out onto the landscaped gardens and surrounding countryside.

The 40 rooms include four spacious junior suites with vast rectangular baths, balneotherapy showers and dressing rooms. Themes range from Indian, with lavish fabrics and silk wallpaper in vibrant raspberry, orange and yellow, to Japanese, with zen blues and neutrals set off with brilliant blue ceramic and butterfly-print wall fabric.

Owner Alix Philipon carried out major refurbishment between 2004 and 2006. Much of the hotel's exquisite fabric is the work of designer Manuel Canovas. All of the rooms have co-ordinated bathrooms with volcanic stone sinks. The deluxe rooms look onto private terraces where an English-style breakfast can be served in summer.

CUISINE: Head Chef, Gilles Goess, honed his craft at The Ritz and the French Foreign Office in Paris before joining La Briqueterie in 1994. Awarded a Michelin star in 2007, Gilles is influenced by Escoffier. His menu is described as 'classic revisited', inspired by local suppliers. 'I favour local produce: aromatic herbs from the garden, white Champagne asparagus and lentillons (pink Champagne lentils),' he states. Gilles's specialities include *pigeonneau de Fromentières* (pigeon stuffed with cherries, marinated in Reims vinegar and ratafia juice) and variations on traditional French cuisine such as *foie gras au café*.

Non-champagne-induced relaxation can be found in the spa, Bulles de Détente, a haven of calm in wood and neutral tones, encircled by a Japanese garden. The only spa in the region, it employs two beauty therapists and comprises a hammam with a spotlit 'starry' ceiling, sauna, sun terrace and relaxation area. A range of activities is available locally, from golf and hunting to hot-air balloon rides, river cruises on the Marne, and walking and cycling among the vineyards.

WINE: La Briqueterie's heritage is, of course, closely intertwined with that of the region's most prestigious export, the wine of kings (and king of wines). The Champagne list stretches to 200 choices; the seminar rooms are named after various *flacons*; and even the tables in the bar are adorned with bottle-tops in homage to local producers. Expert sommelier, Frédéric Chesneau, is on hand to advise in the relaxed manner that is typical of La Briqueterie. 'There is no set time to enjoy Champagne,' he insists, 'and there are enough varieties to accompany an entire menu.' ▣

CONTACT: www.labriqueterie.fr

DOUBLE **BLISS**

The Hotel Copernicus retains numerous elements of its illustrious medieval architecture while incorporating all the trappings one would expect from a 21st-century hotel destination

Poland is renowned as a fine destination to visit, and in recent times tourists have flocked there in ever-increasing numbers to appreciate the marvels of this historic and architecturally beautiful country. Visitors to Krakow can experience this eternally enchanting city from the comfort and luxury of two of Poland's finest hotels, located in Krakow's Old Town – Hotel Copernicus and Hotel Stary.

HISTORY: The only Relais & Chateaux hotel in Poland, Hotel Copernicus, stands on Kanonicza Street – the oldest road in the city, and famous as the home of the Royal Castle. Among the eye-catching Renaissance buildings lining this famous street, the hotel distinguishes itself with a rich history. The Hotel Copernicus retains numerous elements of its illustrious medieval architecture while incorporating all the trappings one would expect from a 21st-century hotel, recognised by the 'Art of Living Trophy' recently presented to the hotel for the excellence and creativity of the facilities it provides.

LUXURIOUS: Across 29 rooms, Hotel Copernicus offers accommodation presented to the highest standards. Each room welcomes guests with sumptuous period furniture and fine draperies that reflect the character of the hotel's interior, and a personalised service, incorporating concierge and round-the-clock room service, caters for guests' individual needs. The most discerning

STANDING WITHIN WALKING DISTANCE OF ONE ANOTHER, TWO OF KRAKOW'S FINEST HOTELS PROVIDE A WELCOMING BASE FROM WHICH TO EXPLORE THIS MAGNIFICENT CITY

guests can choose from one of four luxury suites, featuring magnificent historical frescoes and each with sitting room, bedroom and spacious bathroom so that guests can truly unwind and feel at home.

Providing a rich and varied interior decoration for the most prestigious suites, the theme of augmenting modern surroundings with historical artefacts extends into other areas of Hotel Copernicus, such as the Chimney Room, where guests can relax among numerous books and ancient prints, or the medieval wine cellar where more than 200 varieties are available to taste in the dedicated Vinoteka bar. The hotel's restaurant serves mouth-watering dishes, created according to the traditional recipes used at the court, while more modern accoutrements at Hotel Copernicus include the glass-roofed terrace cafe and a state-of-the art fitness suite. In more clement conditions, guests can enjoy an extraordinary panorama of Krakow from an open-air rooftop bar with majestic views.

CULTURE: Just a short stroll away through the Old Town, Hotel Stary enjoys a similarly illustrious position on Szczepanska Street. Believed to date back to the 15th century, this building was rebuilt several times during the 16th and 18th centuries, and its present incarnation as a leading hotel was realised in the summer of 2006. The interior reflects this rich history, with gothic undertones contrasted against modern materials such as exotic wood, oriental carpets and silk finishings.

Hotel Stary offers the finest blend of Polish and international cultures, typified by the Trzy Rybki restaurant, where secrets of traditional Polish cuisine are incorporated into a seasonally varied menu, which always uses the freshest and most delicious ingredients including asparagus, artichoke, venison and forest fruits. The hotel's café bars meet more informal dining requirements, where guests can enjoy home-made desserts, great coffee and cocktails, while a summer bar on the top-floor terrace offers an unparalleled view of the main market square. The service at the hotel is tailored to each individual guest's wish, with staff able to recommend and arrange an assortment of cultural activities, from the opera, theatre and concerts to galleries and museums.

UNWIND: Before retiring to their suites, guests at Hotel Stary can relax at its intimate and exclusive Wellness & Spa, which offers swimming and sauna facilities alongside a massage studio, salt iodine cave and fitness club. Fifty-three rooms and apartments range from single bedrooms with bespoke wooden furniture and marble bathrooms with Jacuzzis through to spacious and airy luxury suites with cosy living areas, fresh flowers and (in one case) genuine frescos dating right back to the 15th century. In this magical setting, history is never far away. ▣

CONTACT: www.hotel.com.pl; www.lhr.com.pl

A PALACE IN PARIS

TOURS OF THE CONTINENT TRADITIONALLY BEGIN IN PARIS,
AND THERE IS NO BETTER STARTING POINT THAN THE EXCEPTIONAL
HÔTEL LE BRISTOL

Ideally located on the rue du Faubourg Saint Honoré, just across from the Elysée Palace, Le Bristol was recently described as 'the world's best hotel' by *Institutional Investor* magazine.

Owned by the Oetker family since 1978, the hotel's history can be traced back to the reign of Louis XV, and its most famous guests include Ava Gardner, Marilyn Monroe, Charlie Chaplin and Orson Welles.

NAMESAKE: The name Hôtel Le Bristol was adopted in 1925 in tribute to the Count of Bristol, a British traveller known for his love of the finest things in life. That tradition continues to this day.

The 187 rooms are all filled with sumptuous fabrics and refined woodwork, with the Presidential Suite featuring a private Turkish bath, and the Panoramic Suite including a private gym.

SUPERIOR: In terms of accolades, Le Bristol won the prize for 'Europe's best hotel' at the 2008

Rooms are all filled with sumptuous fabrics and refined woodwork, with the Presidential Suite, featuring a private Turkish bath

World Travel Awards, and was also named 'world's best luxury romantic hotel' at the World Luxury Hotel Awards.

If that were not enough, Head Chef Eric Frechon boasts three Michelin stars, and Le Bristol has been honoured with the prestigious Prix Villegiature Award for 'Europe's best hotel restaurant'. The Gastronomic Restaurant changes its surroundings to match the rhythms of the season. The Winter Restaurant (originally the private theatre of a 19th-century patron of the dramatic arts, Jules de Castellane) and the Summer Restaurant both generate enchanting atmospheres that attract Parisians and international visitors alike.

For something less formal, the elegant bar is perfect for afternoon tea, and the new Le 114 Faubourg restaurant is run by rising culinary star Eric Desbordes.

During the 1960s, chic fashion houses including Yves Saint-Laurent, Givenchy and Lacroix presented new collections at Le Bristol, and its famous 'Fashion High Teas' on Saturday afternoons pay homage to this unique modern history.

SERVICE: The hotel has an international staff of more than 400 employees, and for Head Concierge Carlos Teles the word 'impossible' does not exist. His dedicated team can arrange anything for discerning guests, including reservations on fully booked flights, in-demand theatre tickets and the use of vintage Rolls-Royces.

But there is more to Le Bristol than spectacular service. The magnificent swimming pool on the sixth floor is truly a sight to behold. Designed by world-renowned architect Mr Caesar Pinnau, it is built entirely of teak and glass, giving the illusion of being on a beautiful sailboat. Affording breathtaking views of the Eiffel Tower and the Sacré Coeur, the pool opens onto a vast solarium where guests can relax and take in all of Paris.

FACILITIES: The jewel in Le Bristol's crown, however, is undoubtedly its stunning 13,000-square-foot *à la française* garden, where La Fontaine aux Amours (The Fountain of Love) keeps a watchful eye over the glorious geraniums, impatiens, tulips, heathers and cyclamens. The 18th-century sandstone fountain was restored by masonry expert Franco Ripomonti and has become emblematic of the hotel.

In September 2009, Le Bristol entered a new era by opening a timeless adjoining wing. From the spacious pink Portuguese marble bathrooms to the latest air conditioning and Wi-Fi Internet access, every detail has been carefully considered to guarantee unrivalled luxury.

The state-of-the-art fitness centre and sumptuous Anne Sémonin Spa illustrate Le Bristol's complete dedication to its guests' well-being.

Didier Le Calvez, General Manager of Hôtel Le Bristol Paris, welcomes Rolls-Royce Enthusiasts' Club members who are sure to appreciate this icon of art and refined taste in the French capital. ▣

CONTACT: www.lebristolparis.com

WHERE THE CUSTOMER IS
KING

Enjoying a rarefied ambience 6,000 feet above sea level, the renowned ski resort of Montgenèvre can be found just a couple of miles west of the Italian border. As France's oldest ski resort, and the only French part of the famous Milky Way circuit, this hidden gem offers a huge array of off-piste skiing to suit every level of experience.

REFINED: At the heart of this delightful setting, Hotel le Chalet Blanc more than matches the beauty of its surroundings. This internationally renowned hotel enjoys a rarefied position on a mountain pass. Up to 90 people can be accommodated within the resort's 32 rooms, half of which are suitable for family members and friends to join the main occupants. From classic rooms through to luxury suites, every guest will be able to enjoy refined touches, such as handmade beds clad in the finest linens. As for the numerous communal facilities, an admirably situated mountainside restaurant is

SET WITHIN AN IDYLLIC LOCATION FOR WINTER SPORTS ENTHUSIASTS IS THE LUXURIOUS HOTEL LE CHALET BLANC

staffed by gourmet chefs, who concoct seasonal dishes from local ingredients, augmented by a comprehensive choice of the finest French and Italian wines.

COSSETED: During a stay at Hotel le Chalet Blanc, guests are cosseted and pampered in numerous ways, from the bar and lounge's overstuffed sofas and roaring fireplaces through to the fluffy white robes provided in each suite. The hotel spa is an ideal place to soothe tired limbs, with a combination of Jacuzzi, sauna, hammam steam and a comprehensive programme of massages and even a hair salon. If the hotel doesn't already provide everything guests desire, a concierge service can assist with anything from casino visits through to golf tuition, and this unobtrusive personal service (available at any hour of the day or night) is a hallmark of Hotel le Chalet Blanc – encouraging guests to relax and enjoy this comfortable environment to its fullest.

Inevitably, one of the biggest attractions for any visitor to Hotel le Chalet Blanc is the profusion of winter sports on the doorstep, with the hotel overlooking around 250 miles of pistes. A charming venue at any time of year, Montgenèvre bursts into colour in the summer months, with a golf course, lakes and forest all close at hand. A dedicated bike park offers bespoke challenges for mountain bikers, while there are numerous walking trails past forts and forests, and anglers can take to one of Montgenèvre's three trout-stocked lakes. In winter, pure-white snow creates a strong contrast against clear blue skies, with a variety of ski schools and nursery slopes within a few paces of Hotel le Chalet Blanc. This is an ideal setting for cross-country skiers, with scented forests and alpine meadows among the alternative routes on offer. Everyone from snowboarders to ski-doo riders will appreciate the breathtaking scenery and uncanny silence, with heli-skiing also available for the more adventurous tourists. There is even a dedicated ski route for children – the Jardin des Neiges – complete with a mini-travelator and ski lift.

Anyone would adore the surroundings at Hotel le Chalet Blanc, with the new Hameau de l'Obelisque development proving to be a particularly worthy addition to the resort; but for winter sports enthusiasts, this is surely the perfect setting for the holiday of a lifetime. ▣

CONTACT: www.hotellechaletblanc.com

THE FRENCH
CONNECTION

WITH A WORLD-CLASS ARRAY OF SKIING FACILITIES ON ITS DOORSTEP, THE ATTRACTIONS AT HÔTEL LE LANA ***** ALSO INCLUDE SUMPTUOUS SUITES AND A PEACEFUL AMBIENCE

As you arrive outside Hôtel Le Lana for the first time, there is something quite magical about its setting. Framed by the French Alps with the famous Bellecôte ski slope at its fingertips, this extraordinary location is centred on a collection of buildings that collectively form one of the finest hotel resorts imaginable. It stands at the heart of the sheltered Courchevel ski resort, roughly equidistant between Lyon and Geneva, offering 600 km of runs, 185 lifts and Europe's largest ski school.

Despite all this, it would be wrong to assume that Hôtel Le Lana is simply a venue beloved of ski enthusiasts. This celebrated five-star resort has so much more to offer, from opulent suites to a restaurant run by a chef with two Michelin stars in Paris and Tokyo under his belt. Over the decades, Le Lana has become a revered name among discerning travellers, and today its reputation soars higher than ever, following a complete renovation to celebrate its 50th anniversary.

> 66
>
> *Le Lana has become a revered name among discerning travellers, and today its reputation soars higher than ever*

CUISINE: France is renowned for its exceptional cuisine, and illustrious Head Chef Guy Martin is responsible for the accolades earned by La Table du Lana. Courchevel may have 60 restaurants of its own, but many visitors and locals choose to visit La Table du Lana, taking advantage of a menu packed with gastronomic delights and based around local cuisine made with regional ingredients. Serving lunch and dinner alongside summer buffets and barbecues, meals can be enjoyed on a south-facing terrace at the foot of the slopes.

For many people, the highlight of a stay at Le Lana is the calibre of the accommodation. Even standard rooms offer fine fabrics, flat screen TVs and free Wi-Fi, while superior rooms boast nickel-plated bath taps and queen-size beds. It's even possible to stay in one of the resort's apartments, equipped with a Jacuzzi, sauna and hammam, as well as concierge services.

Every guest at Le Lana receives complimentary toiletries from Clarins, who also manage the sumptuous on-site spa, which was recently enlarged to offer a total of six treatment rooms. The focus is on combining luxury and relaxation to re-establish physical and mental balance, while preserving the skin's natural beauty and vitality. A 15-metre indoor pool completes the spa, and more active individuals can utilise a cutting-edge fitness room.

Relaxation is a recurring theme at Le Lana. Deep sofas make the bar the perfect place to enjoy an evening cocktail, to the soothing sounds of jazz music. Even the breakfast room is peaceful, with a broad spread of continental, English or special 'mountain' breakfasts available from a huge selection of carefully chosen ingredients. And for those guests wishing to unwind by utilising the wealth of ski facilities on the hotel's doorstep, a dedicated ski-room handles everything from equipment hire to cleaning and drying. Premium branded skiwear, accessories and boots are available, and Le Lana will even organise an entire day's itinerary, from morning ski passes to evening restaurant reservations. With babysitting services available on request and a games room for children, Le Lana delivers complete relaxation for the whole family, as a matter of course. ▣

CONTACT: www.lelana.com

NOBODY DOES IT
BETTER

FROM ROLLS-ROYCE TRANSFERS TO GUESTS WHO WON'T STAY ANYWHERE ELSE, ONE ASIAN HOTEL HAS CULTIVATED A DESERVED REPUTATION AS THE ONLY PLACE TO STAY

As the capital of Indonesia and the world's twelfth-largest city, Jakarta is an endlessly fascinating place. With a history stretching back almost 2,000 years, this cultural hotspot attracts huge volumes of visitors each year, particularly to the Senayan district where Indonesia's largest sports complex is situated, alongside a major business district and exclusive shopping centres. With its bustling street vendors, tourist attractions and popular nightlife, Senayan is also the setting for one of Southeast Asia's most celebrated hotels – the locally owned and operated five-star Hotel Mulia Senayan, Jakarta.

Hotel Mulia Senayan, Jakarta opened less than 15 years ago in the city's green belt area, and in that short period of time, this grand hotel has already established a reputation for offering the very finest levels of accommodation and service, becoming the proud recipient of numerous awards and accolades from industry experts and critics alike. Visitors from around the world come to Hotel Mulia Senayan, Jakarta, in the knowledge that a true VIP experience awaits them – right down to the fresh flowers prepared by the hotel's in-house florist.

BESPOKE: In part, the hotel's undisputed success can be traced to its ownership by Mulia Group, one of the largest conglomerates in Indonesia. However, the chief reason this hotel has become so cherished among travellers and locals alike is because of its unashamed focus on luxury and regular refurbishments. In many ways, the Premier Suites are the perfect encapsulation of the philosophy at Hotel Mulia Senayan, Jakarta, and none more so than The Duke Suite. Extending to well over 6,000 square feet, it enjoys a privileged position atop the hotel, boasting panoramic views out across the Jakarta skyline. With a private foyer delineating two distinct living and entertainment areas (including a dedicated massage room), this is commonly regarded as the most luxurious suite anywhere in the region. It's hard to argue with that perception as you discover the 24-carat gold bath and shower fixtures, and the 12-foot wide bed – a bespoke creation draped in elegant silks and furs. The delightfully presented lounge can seat over a dozen people in sublime comfort, and there's even a separate dining room for enjoying the hotel's gourmet cuisine.

GRANDEUR: Considering the luxury of its accommodation and facilities, you would expect Hotel Mulia Senayan, Jakarta to offer impressive cuisine, but the sheer choice and calibre of its gastronomy will still take many guests completely by surprise. Seven food and beverage outlets

have been incorporated into the hotel, ranging from afternoon tea at the Cake Shop through to authentic Italian fare at il Mare. The recently refurbished Orient8, Pan-Asian and French Restaurant, creates a spectacular impression with its pillared corridors and gleaming chessboard tiles, while international cuisine is available at any hour of day or night at The Café – also recently revamped and deservedly revered as one of Jakarta's most sought-after culinary hotspots.

There is, however, one dining establishment that fully encapsulates the ethos of Hotel Mulia Senayan, Jakarta, and that is the recently opened Table8 restaurant, combining Cantonese and Szechuan cuisines. Serving dishes like 'Buddha Jumps Over The Wall Soup' and 'Braised Superior Shark's Fin with Black Truffle and Dried Scallops served in Stone Pot', it's immediately evident that this unique Chinese restaurant has pursued perfection in a way rarely seen in modern life. It's worth taking a moment to admire the award winning architecture as well, which was conceived and completed within five weeks by the Mulia Group's in-house design team. They have created something truly beautiful, with 24 exclusively designed pagodas delicately contrasting against equally bespoke chandelier work in the restaurant's central area.

GLOBAL: Regardless of your chosen dining location, Hotel Mulia Senayan, Jakarta offers a variety of post-prandial retreats, including The Cascade Lounge with its cosy chairs and English afternoon tea, the cocktails and live music of CJ's Bar, or (for those with a truly sweet tooth) the unique Chocolate Boutique, with its dazzling array of edible sculptures and fashion items. As the Director of Sales and Marketing, Rully Rachman, proudly points out: 'Our culinary team has a truly global background, and both hotel guests and Jakarta residents alike are constantly wowed by our ever-changing, and ever-improving, variety of cuisines.'

Stunning though The Duke Suite's accommodation unquestionably is, it's the level of service that lingers longest in the minds of those lucky enough to reside here. Many of the hotel's facilities are at your beck and call, such as exclusive airport transfers in a Rolls-Royce Phantom, and The Duke Suite merely underlines the outstanding levels of service available to each and every guest at Hotel Mulia Senayan, Jakarta. This unswerving dedication to customer service makes the resort a real sanctuary for discerning travellers, as well as cementing its justified status as a five-star resort.

Many guests will be quite happy to remain within Hotel Mulia Senayan, Jakarta for the entire duration of their stay, revelling in distinguished surroundings like the

> *The hotel's facilities are at your beck and call, such as exclusive airport transfers in a Rolls-Royce Phantom*

serene Mulia Fitness Centre. Four tennis courts and a comprehensively stocked gymnasium form the opening attractions of a sanctuary exclusively available to hotel guests and private members. Taking advantage of Jakarta's hot climate and proximity to the equator, a 30-metre outdoor swimming pool and Jacuzzi form the centrepiece of a collection of whirlpools, steam and sauna facilities. These are augmented by state-of-the-art exercise equipment and ten private treatment rooms, where professional massage services including reflexology and Javanese body treatments are available for 16 hours each day. This emphasis on round-the-clock service recognises the unique demands of modern life, and as a consequence, Hotel Mulia Senayan, Jakarta offers corporate guests the use of a well-appointed business centre at any hour of the day or night, complete with high-speed Internet access, a unique information library, meeting rooms and secretarial services.

While the 996 rooms and suites at Hotel Mulia Senayan, Jakarta are undeniably impressive in their own right, the communal areas of this award-winning hotel are bound to leave a lasting impression on even the most experienced traveller, furnished in extravagant materials and populated with international artworks. Consider for a moment the gold and marble-finished ballroom – one of the largest in Southeast Asia, with around 25,000 square feet of floor space. Capable of accommodating up to 4,000 people at a time, the ballroom maintains the spectacular impression created by the hotel's other public areas, such as the towering ceiling and Hollywood-style staircase in the main lobby.

Hotel Mulia Senayan, Jakarta employs more than 2,600 staff, working around the clock to maintain the hotel's reputation as one of Asia's most upmarket destinations. One of these people is Rully Rachman, who began his executive-level career ten years ago. His words form a fitting conclusion to any analysis of this unique business hotel: 'We are proud of our heritage here at Hotel Mulia Senayan, Jakarta, and we hope that our guests receive the best of Indonesian hospitality, along with the finest luxuries and amenities the world has to offer. It is tremendously important to us that each and every one of our guests leaves the hotel having had all of their expectations exceeded beyond their dreams. It is always great to receive feedback from first-time guests who now refuse to stay anywhere else.'

CONTACT: www.hotelmulia.com

WAKING IN
PARADISE

EVEN THE MOST SEASONED TRAVELLER
WILL MARVEL AT THE WONDERFUL INTIMACY
OF THIS RETREAT IN THE MALDIVES

Huvafen Fushi offers something unique and very special to its visitors. Positioned on the edge of its own lagoon on the North Malé Atoll of the Maldives, and managed by luxury brand Per AQUUM Retreats, Resorts and Residences, the atmosphere is informal yet luxurious, with a sense of intimacy and privacy enhanced by award-winning service. The real beauty of what is on offer is the freedom for guests to be themselves, to relax and chill out in the finest surroundings, with a sense of being cut off from the hustle and bustle of everyday life yet with the comforting reality of technology at their fingertips should they need it.

PRIVATE: 'Huvafen Fushi was created around a particular mindset,' explains CEO, Neil Palmer.

'The aim is for guests to be themselves here, to relax and rejuvenate themselves. Celebrities and royalty are the same as everyone else when it comes to holidays and we respect that and also cater for it, ensuring all our guests get the same level of service. There are only 44 rooms here and everything is designed in a way to ensure maximum privacy – it really is like having your own island.' Providing a selection of land-based and over-water bungalows, accommodation is decorated in a cool and minimalist contemporary style, with either a pool or freshwater plunge pool, plasma screen TV and superb surround-sound system, all further complemented by dazzling views of the Indian Ocean.

MAGICAL: No visit here could be complete without experiencing the unique underwater spa, where treatment rooms and a separate relaxation area have breathtaking views under the Indian Ocean. A yoga pavilion, butler service, access to practically any water sport imaginable and a range of wonderful restaurants all add to the magic. Celsius is the main restaurant and overlooks the lagoon, while fine seafood can be enjoyed around the open kitchen at Salt, spa cuisine at RAW, wine-matched meals at Vinum and pizza under the palm trees at Fogliani's. Yet that is not all that is on offer as private dining experiences can also be organised, such as eating beneath the stars on a rock island with a private table for two, or underground in the wine cellar or simply revelling in 24-hour dining in the intimacy of a bungalow.

OASIS: Creating an oasis of peace that people return to time and time again, Neil says: 'We do believe that we make a difference. Our passion is rooted in our confidence that we always strive to attain the ultimate experience for each of our guests and fulfil all their expectations. We create sensual living spaces born from inspirational concepts that are brought to life with naturally modern designs.'

The result is a taste of paradise, with the sun, sea and sand presenting the perfect background to this ideal tropical holiday retreat. ▣

CONTACT: www.huvafenfushi.com; www.peraquum.com

STAR
ATTRACTION

AS THE FLAGSHIP RESORTS OF THE IBEROSTAR BRAND, SEVEN GRAND HOTELS REDEFINE
THE CONCEPT OF LUXURY, IMBUED WITH STUNNING ARCHITECTURE AND SET WITHIN UNFORGETTABLE
COASTAL LOCATIONS

> *The circular reception area in Montego Bay's Grand Hotel Rose Hall in Jamaica is truly breathtaking; and at the Grand Hotel Paraiso in Mexico, the furnishings are all marvellously tactile*

With a family lineage stretching back across four generations and 50 years, the Iberostar Hotels & Resorts name has been displayed proudly outside luxury hotels for many years. Over that time, Iberostar has become synonymous with celebrated resorts in cherished venues around the world, from Brazil to Mexico and from Jamaica to Cape Verde.

PREMIUM: Initially based in Majorca (Spain), Iberostar first expanded overseas in 1993 into the Dominican Republic; and from that point, the company has grown to encompass more than 100 four- and five-star resorts in 16 different countries. In 2007, with a rising emphasis on the quality and refinement of its hotels, Iberostar decided to launch a flagship portfolio of premium resorts – hotels of the finest calibre, chosen for their luxurious surroundings and attentive hospitality. The result is The Grand Collection – seven resorts of true excellence, delivering exclusive holidays to discerning clients in some of the world's finest beach locations.

IBEROSTAR: Grand Hotels can be found in Tenerife, Trinidad, Brazil, Mexico, Cuba and the Dominican Republic. The latter resort is christened Grand Hotel Bavaro, situated in Punta Cana, the country's easternmost province. Served by one of the best-connected airports anywhere in the Caribbean, the Grand Hotel Bavaro neatly encapsulates the appeal and charm of the Iberostar Grand Collection, and an inspection of its amenities illustrates how it and its six siblings elevate themselves above lesser resorts.

MEMORABLE: With Greco-Roman architecture and a music bar designed to resemble a Spanish galleon, Grand Hotel Bavaro's European pedigree is evident even from a distance. Surrounded by mature woodland and constructed in a horseshoe shape around a sweeping collection of interconnected pools, only a cluster of thatched huts along a white sandy beach delineates these pools from the nearby ocean. Memorable sights lie around every corner, nowhere more so than in the hotel's gourmet restaurant (one of four in this resort), with huge timepiece murals suspended from the ceiling above clock-face motifs in the mosaic-tiled floor.

At every Grand Hotel, cuisine is of the finest possible quality, with famous chefs blending local and international flavours to create exquisite food, served by staff whose attentive service makes every meal an occasion. Many of these resorts are in close proximity to outstanding golf courses. Grand Hotel Bavaro features an 18-hole golf course, designed by golf legend P.B. Dye. Coastline surrounds extraordinary landscaping, such as a starfish-shaped green encircled by golden sands and palm trees. Such meticulous attention to detail permeates the suites and communal areas of each hotel as well – the circular reception area in Montego Bay's Grand Hotel Rose Hall in Jamaica is truly breathtaking; and at the Grand Hotel Paraiso in Mexico, the furnishings are all crafted in wood, brass, bronze or limestone. All seven resorts have been individually styled by leading architects, dressed in the most seductive materials and populated with features that linger in the mind long after departure.

More than one-third of departing guests will return to Iberostar resorts in future, a fact that underlines the allure of the company's Grand Collection and its unforgettable nature. People travel from all over the world to stay in these settings, and an international media campaign featuring Spanish actor Antonio Banderas is helping to elevate their profile even further with a simple message – 'On vacation, we're all stars'. With numerous awards received over the last couple of years from the press and industry experts alike, you don't have to spend long in an Iberostar Grand Hotel to understand why every guest really will feel like a star. ▣

CONTACT: www.iberostar.com
IMAGES: (L-R) Iberostar Grand Hotel Paraiso; Iberostar Grand Hotel Rose Hall

GRAND
DESIGNS

IL PELLICANO HOTEL PROVIDES A VERY SPECIAL
EXPERIENCE ON THE TUSCAN COASTLINE

A couple of miles outside the Tuscan village of Porto Ercole stand the cliffs of the Argentario peninsula. With panoramic aspects across the Tyrrhenian Sea, this secluded spot was chosen as the ideal location for a holiday resort in the 1960s by a British army pilot and his American sweetheart, inspired by the Californian promontory where they first met.

WORLD-RENOWNED: Opening its doors for the first time on 2 June 1965, Il Pellicano immediately became an exclusive club that, in its formative years, welcomed the likes of Charlie Chaplin, Henry Fonda, Gianni Agnelli and European royalty. Today, critics and experts regard Il Pellicano as one of the world's greatest resorts, effortlessly combining the ambience of a private home with the luxury of a five-star resort. Described by the hugely respected *Condé Nast Traveler* as the sixth-best hotel in the world, a plethora of other commendations and awards from the world's media and industry experts collectively serve as a glowing testament to the opulence and luxury of this irresistible coastal resort.

Within impeccably landscaped gardens populated by olive and cypress trees, six cottages surround a central building whose architecture draws inspiration from its Tuscan heritage. The hotel's communal areas are all housed in this building, including a conference room and a recently renovated health and beauty centre. In many ways, the latter neatly encapsulates Il Pellicano's continuing emphasis on offering the finest facilities imaginable. Guests can enjoy a Roman-style steam bath known as the Calidarium before heading into one of four dedicated suites where the most advanced beauty therapies are on offer, such as Ayurvedic massages or silk power peels for the skin. An on-site hairdresser and a boutique (stocking everything from swimsuits to designer accessories) provide those all-important finishing flourishes.

GOURMET: Perhaps the finest feature of this exquisite resort is the Il Pellicano Restaurant & Bar. Under the supervision of chef Antonio Guida, who recently received his second Michelin star, the restaurant's elegant surroundings provide a backdrop for celebrated Mediterranean dishes packed with fresh local produce from the hotel's herb and vegetable garden. Alternatively, it's possible to take a seat beside a heated seawater swimming pool in the all'Aperto outdoor restaurant and bar, with a seascape of rare beauty perfectly complementing locally sourced meat and fish, dished out fresh from the grill. Wine connoisseurs will be captivated by the La Cantina wine cellar, with an impressive selection of Italian and international wines and liqueurs served by sommeliers, and the Il Pellicano piano bar offers a blissful environment for the final hours of any evening.

ACTIVITY: Other attractions on offer to guests include wine and oil tasting, cookery classes, a tennis court, horse riding and polo. However, it's the unexpected delights that truly elevate Il Pellicano into one of the world's great resorts – the speedboat excursions, the private rocky beach with its dedicated lift access or the terraced sun loungers with steps leading straight down into the sea. These are the touches that make the hotel so memorable, and draw so many people back time and again.

Each guest suite has been carefully tailored to maintain the levels of opulence delivered by Il Pellicano's communal areas. In total, 35 rooms are augmented by five junior and ten deluxe suites, and the latter are characterised by their sheer size and stunning views over the Italian coastline. The quality imbued into each apartment is visible in stylistic interiors like box radiator covers and intricate cornice work, while the ability to step through arched French doors onto a sea-view terrace provides the final flourish. ▣

CONTACT: www.pellicanohotel.com

SERVICE AND
SETTING

SITUATED RESPECTIVELY ON LAMU ISLAND AND IN THE LAIKIPIA HIGHLANDS, THE EXCLUSIVE
KIZINGONI BEACH HOMES AND LUSH SURROUNDINGS OF MUKIMA HOUSE OFFER VISITORS
AN UNFORGETTABLE AFRICAN HOLIDAY EXPERIENCE

L azing on the unspoilt Indian Ocean coast of northern Kenya, Lamu Island is one of the most beguiling places on earth where its residents are renowned for their warm welcome and hospitality. Little has changed in centuries – its remoteness, tranquillity, rich and colourful maritime trading history and distinctive Swahili culture all provide visitors with a unique amalgam of African, Arabian, Indian and European influences.

Nestling against this serene backdrop and sitting in an old abandoned coconut plantation on Lamu, Kizingoni Beach is a collection of beautifully designed, and perfectly positioned, secluded holiday houses. Surrounded by crystal clear waters, indigenous plants and fruit trees blanket the area and the beach is virtually empty apart from a myriad of crabs, migrant and local sea birds and the occasional donkey. Currently, there are seven privately owned houses to rent, all with four or five en-suite bedrooms, sumptuous interiors, private swimming pools and direct beach access. Watersports are free, with visitors being provided with doughnuts, wakeboards, waterskis and snorkelling equipment. Extras come in the form of massages and beauty treatments, dhow trips and mini safaris.

Meanwhile, far upcountry and in the middle of savannah parkland, Mukima House provides guests with incredible views of Mount Kenya and

*Whether for a couple or a family,
a group of friends or a large
wedding party, Kizingoni Beach
and Mukima House provide
an unforgettable experience*

is only a 15-minute drive from Nanyuki, the gateway to many of east Africa's most beautiful and wild areas. Originally built in the 1940s, the double-storey house, surrounded by vivid tropical flower-beds and expansive lawns, was completely refurbished in 2005 using a traditional colonial style and local materials, while its 360-acre conservancy has been replanted with hardwood and exotic trees.

Sleeping 16 in eight en-suite bedrooms, Mukima guests can enjoy its swimming pool, tennis court, sauna and massage room, dinghies on the dam, badminton, croquet, table tennis, walks and bird watching. Game drives, safaris and horse riding can also be arranged on nearby ranches and reserves, while golf, bird shooting and trout fishing are also available. The nearby Nanyuki airstrip offers effortless access both in and out of the area.

INSPIRED: Interiors of the Kizingoni Beach properties and Mukima House all reflect space, simplicity, comfort and serenity, and boast shady verandas and terraces, welcoming daybeds with lounging areas and freshwater swimming; the tropical hardwood furniture and attractive fabrics, fittings and fixtures are sourced from Lamu, Kenya, Morocco and the Far East.

From their own private, perfectly run home-from-home, visitors are able to enjoy and explore all that the Lamu archipelago and Laikipia have to offer; at Kizingoni a private boat with a captain is supplied to explore the coast or inland waterways and mangrove forests, while at Mukima a land cruiser with a driver is at guests' disposal for safaris.

'We attract independently minded guests who know what they would like to do and appreciate privacy and comfort,' says Director, Leslie Duckworth. 'Our guests do not wish to be herded or hosted. Often, they know Kenya and therefore appreciate what is available in the area.'

'We take great pride in providing luxurious, spacious and private accommodation in inspiring settings and, as all the properties are fully staffed, domestic responsibilities can be left at home. Guests can be as private or as social as they wish, opting to enjoy fine dining on the balcony or join friends in the bar.'

Whether for a couple or a family, a group of friends or a large wedding party, Kizingoni Beach and Mukima House provide an unforgettable experience. As Leslie confirms: 'Once guests have visited, they always return.' ▣

CONTACT: www.kizingonibeach.com; www.mukimakenya.com

GREECE'S BEST-KEPT
SECRET

Domes of Elounda is more than a luxury resort; it immerses guests in the pageantry of one of the world's most vibrant cultures

AS A SUPERIOR LUXURY RESORT IN CRETE, DOMES OF ELOUNDA CAPTURES ALL THAT IS GREEK

Famous not only on the island of Crete but in the entire Aegean Sea, the luxury suite and villas spa resort known as Domes of Elounda is a retreat that encapsulates the essence of the Mediterranean.

Part of the Ledra Hotels and Villas group, Domes of Elounda is a place of extraordinary character. Surrounded by mountains in a secluded bay of crystal waters and soft white sand, its guests enjoy world-class accommodation and privacy. Unique domed structures rise organically from the ground, respecting the contours of the land and creating a picturesque settlement on a hillside of flower gardens, stone pathways and olive groves. Overlooking the sea and nearby historic island of Spinalonga, this was the setting for Victoria Hislop's bestselling novel, *The Island*.

Consisting of 80 suites, eight private residences, three villas and a royal villa, the resort represents the beauty of the area and depicts Cretan culture at its finest. With the motto: 'There's nothing we can't do for our guests', Domes of Elounda offers an extraordinary level of service.

LUXURY: Each resort residence finds its roots in Greek, Carpathian and Syrian architecture. Features such as the domed and pyramidal ceilings help cool rooms, capture sea breezes and create living spaces with traditional, yet opulent and modern, Mediterranean characteristics. Mild, earthy colour tones are found throughout the establishments, which are decorated with fine works of art from international and local artisans. Breathtaking views through large windows form part of the design, and spacious verandas invite guests to feast on the sights and scents.

Lavish villas are freestanding and individually designed with fully equipped kitchens, fireplaces, bedrooms and en-suite bathrooms, terraces, personal swimming pools and panoramic views that add endless luxury, space and complete privacy.

RELAX: A jewel in the resort's crown is the Domes Spa; after all, the Greeks set the standard for modern spas more than 3,000 years ago. A black mosaic seawater pool cocooned by large tinted glass panels provides an inviting welcome; soft lighting sets the scene and areas of treatment achieve isolation, relaxation and tranquillity.

Domes of Elounda is more than a luxury resort; it immerses guests in the pageantry of one of the world's most vibrant cultures. Idyllic surroundings and a distinguished elegance make it the perfect place to rejuvenate in style. ▢

CONTACT: www.domesofelounda.com

FROM BESPOKE ARTWORKS TO BREATHTAKING ARCHITECTURE, LES SUITES DU NÉVADA OFFERS A TASTE OF THE VERY FINEST FRENCH HOSPITALITY, CUISINE AND STYLE

ENJOY
YOURSELF
LIKE NOWHERE ELSE

It is easy to become truly immersed in luxurious surroundings. When every surface radiates quality and every aspect pleases the eye, the trappings of refinement become a cohesive whole, enveloping all the senses. By seamlessly melding quality and exclusivity together, an acclaimed hotel in the French resort of Tignes has created an environment where total luxury is delivered almost subliminally. It's all around you, yet it only becomes fully noticeable when you look for it.

The location of Les Suites Du Névada provides an early indication of the resort's calibre. Close to the famous Val d'Isère ski resort, soaring mountains act as a backdrop to an architecturally spectacular collection of unique suites. The standard suites are compelling in their own right, with heavy fabrics complementing designer sanitaryware in the adjoining bathrooms, while a typical superior suite will encompass exposed wooden finishings, wall-mounted TVs and tub chairs. Opt for one of the suitably titled deluxe suites, and you can expect twin marble sinks and plush corner sofas, while the

Close to the famous Val d'Isère ski resort, soaring mountains act as a backdrop to an architecturally spectacular collection of unique suites

flagship Suite du Névada is a true home from home. This 180-square-metre duplex has a dedicated kitchen wrapping around a huge central island unit, with an illuminated headboard and sweeping windows typifying the focus on providing the best of everything.

PAMPERING: Throughout Les Suites Du Névada, hospitality is of the highest order, yet it always manages to confound both convention and expectations. It is possible, for instance, to bring a pet to stay, with everything from board games to cars available for personal reservation. Some resorts might be happy to simply offer a heated indoor pool, yet this particular example is nothing less than a work of art. Framed with giant stone tablets, a discreetly lit body of water awaits discovery, flanked by designer loungers and augmented by a blend of Jacuzzis, saunas and Turkish baths. Meanwhile, Spas & Beauté Montagne offers a remarkable variety of customised products and treatments in the resort's dedicated beauty centre, from angels' oil massages through to a ninety-minute alchemy facial.

SCULPTED: Just as the pool exceeds expectations, so does the rest of the interior at Les Suites Du Névada. Rather than merely employ an interior designer, a sculptor has been recruited to craft delicately wrought metal features, with the extraordinary reception desk creating a fitting introduction to a resort characterised by exposed woodwork, billiard-smooth tiles underfoot and uniquely styled suites, where signature splashes of red or white in each room create different moods. Wood is also a central theme in Les Suites Du Névada's centrepiece restaurant, La Table en Montagne. Described by the resort's owners as 'a beacon for lovers of creative cuisine', there is a sense of being in the countryside within this expansive area, with trees extending towards exposed timber ceiling beams. Under the Michelin-starred tutelage of Jean-Michel Bouvier, La Table en Montagne and the neighbouring Withney Bar collectively offer the perfect environment to enjoy fine food and drink.

Crafted by artists and artisans, inspired by the neighbouring mountains and styled in a totally unique way, Les Suites Du Névada represents something quite matchless and magical. From even the briefest of visits, it is easy to understand how this legendary resort manages to captivate so many people and hasten their return. ▣

CONTACT: www.les-suites-du-nevada.com

CREATIVE
LUXURY

THE ORIGINAL GREEK BEACH HOLIDAY
HOTEL STILL SETS THE STANDARD FOR
THE ULTIMATE LUXURIOUS GETAWAY

> *In this wonderfully creative setting full of character and originality, Minos Beach Art Hotel offers an intimate holiday with impeccable but unobtrusive service ensuring an experience very close to paradise*

Since 1963, Minos Beach Art Hotel has been the epitome of luxury and style in eastern Crete, offering a holiday experience simply timeless in its app eal. Over the decades the hotel has retained much of its original feel, which was influenced by the traditional architectural style of fishermen's villages in eastern Crete and resulted in the gleaming white bungalows and villas dotted around a quiet peninsula just outside the town of Agios Nikolaos. There is a discreet system of constant renewal and upgrading which ensures that the hotel always feels beautifully maintained and decorated. The minimalist style and muted colours present the perfect retreat from the Cretan sun, while the airy terraces further complement the welcome comfort of the air conditioning.

INTIMATE: While there have been many famous and prominent guests enjoying the hotel over the years, the relationship established with every guest is pivotal, with a policy of ensuring that returning customers use the same rooms and are greeted by the same staff who have been caring for them for years. The intimate atmosphere, luxurious surroundings and warm welcome have always been part of the tradition, as is a strong awareness of all the contemporary requirements of the guests. And the close relationships built up with clients have resulted in generations of the same family returning time after time. 'Our longest-standing guest has been coming here since 1969,' says Manager, Stelios Tamboukos. 'We even have a couple who actually met at the hotel and married, returning to holiday here for the last twenty years.'

CREATIVE: The grounds are spacious and the setting around the lengthy cove idyllic, with banks of beautiful flowers delighting the eye and filling the air with their heady scent. Narrow stone pathways wend their way through the gardens, leading guests to the many stunning sculptures which contribute to the hotel's unique appeal. These world-class works of art are all by renowned Greek and international artists, and add the final perfect touches to the breathtaking views. There is also a private swimming pool, a 100-square-metre covered sun deck and discreet private access to the beach, with some bungalows lying so close to the water's edge that guests can simply step off their terraces into the sea.

Four superb restaurants offer everything from gourmet cuisine to more casual Cretan recipes featuring fresh local ingredients and spices, along with an extensive wine list to complement the meal. The emphasis is always on ensuring that guests enjoy every chance to relax and savour their holiday.

IDYLLIC: The idyllic setting is further enhanced by the Ananea Wellness Spa, which uses Ayurvedic treatments and also offers a sauna and gym for those who want to add a little pampering or some exercise to this perfect experience. 'It all comes back to listening to what our guests want and adhering to the standards we set when the hotel was first opened,' says Stelios. 'When we see guests returning year after year, then we know we're getting it right. I have just had a phone call from a lady who has holidayed here with her husband for nearly twenty years and, sadly, it was to tell me that her husband had died. His wish was to have his ashes scattered over the beach here and it is an honour to know that the hotel meant so much to him.'

In this wonderfully creative setting full of character and originality, Minos Beach Art Hotel offers an intimate holiday with impeccable but unobtrusive service. ▣

CONTACT: www.minosbeach.eu

THE ART OF LIVING

MONTE-CARLO SBM WAS FOUNDED IN MONACO IN 1863
BY SOVEREIGN ORDER OF PRINCE CHARLES III

Rolls-Royce aficionados are inspired by many disparate elements of product design, and the unrelenting pursuit of pure luxury, sublime comfort and state-of-the-art technology remains crucial to the peerless reputation of the world's finest motor car manufacturer. However, such traits are equally vital in establishing excellence within other markets, and it is this constant pursuit of excellence that has inspired Monte-Carlo SBM to such stratospheric heights over the last 150 years.

With its suffix an abbreviation of Société des Bains de Mer, Monte-Carlo SBM was founded in Monaco in 1863 by sovereign order of Prince Charles III. In a principality already synonymous with luxury and refinement, Monte-Carlo SBM stands out for the sheer calibre of its resorts and attractions, by effortlessly delivering world-leading casinos, five-star hotels, gourmet cuisine and much more. The company has cultivated the ultimate indulgence destination, with more than 3,000 staff working tirelessly to ensure the complete approval of each and every visitor.

> **At the heart of the Monte-Carlo SBM empire is a collection of four exquisite hotels, acclaimed as some of the finest anywhere in the world**

EXQUISITE: At the heart of the Monte-Carlo SBM empire is a collection of four exquisite hotels, acclaimed as some of the finest anywhere in the world and each standing within an exceptional location. The oldest resort is the Hôtel de Paris, constructed in 1864 and retaining its sumptuous original architecture, including the Winston Churchill Diamond Suite, so called to honour this prestigious guest. It is a member of The Leading Hotels of the World group, as is the Hôtel Hermitage, with its Belle Époque ballroom, 230 bedrooms and 50 suites. The Monte-Carlo Beach Hotel, built in 1929, was completely redesigned last year by India Mahdavi, retaining only its inter-war façade. It is now a member of the Relais & Chateaux group. Finally, the newest addition to Monte-Carlo SBM's canon of resorts is the Monte-Carlo Bay Hotel & Resort, on the Larvotto Peninsula. Opened in 2005, this 11-storey complex draws inspiration from Mediterranean palaces throughout its 334 rooms, two restaurants, spa, pool, lagoon and casino.

EXCELLENCE: Mention of casinos highlights another area in which Monte-Carlo SBM has developed an unparalleled reputation, even within a city renowned for its love of gambling. Covering the whole spectrum of gaming, two of the four casinos here date back to the 1860s, and nowhere is more spectacular than the magical Casino de Monte-Carlo, where roulette first came to global prominence. Fine cuisine provides a different benchmark of Monte-Carlo SBM's unremitting focus on excellence, with 28 restaurants including the Alain Ducasse-led Louis XV with its three Michelin stars, and Le Grill,

located under a retractable roof and itself the proud recipient of a Michelin star. Just a few steps from these, another treasure is lying in the spectacular wine cellar of the Hôtel de Paris, boasting more than 600,000 bottles, some of which date back to 1860.

SOCIETY: Monte-Carlo SBM is the driving force behind the majority of Monaco's star attractions and high-level cultural events. Monte Carlo's ballet, opera and philharmonic orchestra are all strongly supported by Société des Bains de Mer, while the acclaimed Sporting Monte-Carlo venue combines dining, discos and much more within a lively and elegant environment. Particular mention must also be made of Les Thermes Marins Monte-Carlo – one of Europe's grandest spas with 6,600 square metres of space bedecked with pink marble, pale wood and clear glass – and the Monte-Carlo Country Club, arguably the most beautiful club in Europe.

HOSTS: Since the early years of the 20th century, Monte-Carlo SBM has been a host venue for annual car club meetings and concourse competitions, regularly featuring classic and priceless Rolls-Royce cars. To this day, the resort retains contacts with the RREC around the world, with yearly gatherings of Rolls-Royce aficionados and their prized possessions within a private casino square, allowing owners to display some of the world's finest motor cars within one of the world's most beautiful settings. ▣

CONTACT: www.montecarloresort.com

HOME
FROM HOME

As the fourth largest island in the Bahamas archipelago, West End, Grand Bahama encapsulates the appeal of this exotic region in a single, location. Nestled in the warm waters of the Atlantic Ocean just 60 miles east of Florida, West End is a vibrant place with hidden jewels, none more so than Nandana Private Resort. Discreetly situated within a secluded gated shoreline complex, this magical setting offers a secure retreat for up to a dozen guests, within a series of pavilions whose every surface and component oozes refinement.

Designed by an internationally renowned architect in the style of an Asian beach house, an azure Caribbean backdrop with lapping ocean waves and a private beach awaits through every window and doorway at Nandana, with hundreds of palm trees and tropical plants adding bounteous shade. Asian artworks permeate every corner of the resort, including temple reliefs, hand-carved wooden sculptures and silk treasures from Thailand, Cambodia and Vietnam.

NAMED AFTER THE ANCIENT SANSKRIT WORD FOR 'PARADISE', THIS NEWLY COMPLETED
AND TRULY ASTONISHING COMPLEX IS AVAILABLE FOR EXCLUSIVE HIRE

UNPARALLELED: Many words could be expounded to capture the ethos of this palatial 18,000-square foot resort, but a glimpse of the Great Hall, which forms the centrepiece, speaks volumes. Inside 250-year-old, 20-foot high teak doors (salvaged from a Javanese temple), the Great Hall's vast swathes of hand-carved Burmese teak floors and ceiling extend into the distance, where the Atlantic Ocean appears to glitter atop the central dining table. With massive teak columns supporting the ceiling some 40 feet overhead, a reverential temple-like aura permeates this unparalleled space, which also contains guest areas, a library, a bar and a wine cellar containing 400 bottles of wine. A magnificently appointed kitchen is situated within the Main Hall, opening onto an oceanfront dining area.

The Great Hall is surrounded by five spacious bedroom villas and a unique safari-style luxury tent suite. When the day is done and it's time to retire, each of these pavilions offers a haven of relaxation. From flat-screen satellite TVs, iPod docks and wireless Internet throughout, to computer-controlled lighting and air conditioning, these villas and suites have been furnished with the finest materials. Taking this philosophy one step further is the Canopy Suite, a romantic 2,000-square foot safari-style tent featuring air conditioning, Internet access and the same calibre of furnishings as the neighbouring villas.

One might expect such an opulent environment to offer fitness equipment, but the fully equipped gym with its cardio and weight equipment exceeds all expectations and contains the luxury spa facility where massages are delivered by an in-house masseuse, trained at the famous Aman Resorts.

Nandana's outside areas again surpass what might be expected: a heated 120-foot infinity pool, with a waterfall seemingly melding into the ocean below; and an adjacent Jacuzzi offer a tantalising choice of aquatic environments for enjoying an evening cocktail. From world-class cuisine to a fully equipped business centre, this resort astonishes time and again with its winning blend of residential living and the bespoke amenities of a five-star resort.

EXPLORE: In many ways, it's hard to imagine wanting to leave this opulent haven, but the area surrounding Nandana has its own temptations. Foremost among these are world-class fishing (aboard Nandana's own 50-foot deep-sea yacht), the adjacent Jack Nicklaus-designed 18-hole golf course, and motorised craft including jet skis, a water ski boat, ATVs and a safari-style luxury Land Rover. It's possible to appreciate the pristine clear blue waters and abundant sea life through scuba diving and snorkelling, while more adventurous guests can experience escorted shark or dolphin dives, the richly rewarding Bahamas culture and casino nights.

Security patrols operate around the clock, and this 24-hour service also extends to the resort's staff, including an estate manager, concierge, chef, chauffeur, housekeeper and night butler. □

CONTACT: www.nandanaresort.com

THE BEST OF THE
BEST

THERE ARE FEW PLACES IN THE WORLD THAT LEND THEMSELVES TO MAKING A HOLIDAY TRULY UNFORGETTABLE. OBEROI HOTELS & RESORTS, HOWEVER, OFFER SEVERAL TO CHOOSE FROM

Combining breathtaking locations, luxurious environs, every modern-day amenity with attentive and warm service delivered with genuine care, Oberoi hotels and resorts have become established fixtures in lists of the world's best hotels from authoritative sources such as *Travel + Leisure*, *Condé Nast Traveler*, *Daily Telegraph*'s *Ultratravel*, *The Guardian* and *Observer*.

The Oberoi Vanyavilas, the luxury jungle resort adjacent to the Ranthambhore Tiger Reserve in Rajasthan, has been ranked the best hotel in the world in *Travel + Leisure*'s World's Best Awards 2010 readers' survey. In the same survey, The Oberoi Vanyavilas, The Oberoi Amarvilas, Agra, The Oberoi Rajvilas, Jaipur and The Oberoi Udaivilas, Udaipur have been ranked first, second, third and fourth respectively in Asia and first, fifth, thirteenth and fifteenth respectively in the world.

ENCOMPASSING: It is not only the leisure travellers but also those on business that acknowledge Oberoi hotels as amongst the finest. Oberoi Hotels & Resorts was rated the best hotel chain in the world (outside the United States) in *Condé Nast Traveler*'s Business Travel Awards 2007. This was reaffirmed recently with the overwhelming response to The Oberoi, Mumbai when it reopened after an extensive refurbishment. A signature landmark on Marine Drive, the famed boulevard along the coast in South Mumbai, the luxury hotel offers sweeping views of the ocean and city skyline. With a stunning 14-level atrium lobby, guestrooms that are luxurious havens of contemporary elegance, a 24-hour butler service for each room, dining that includes an Indian restaurant under the direction of the Michelin-starred Chef Vineet Bhatia, an outdoor heated pool, the city's only 24-hour spa and a fitness centre, The Oberoi, Mumbai is the leading choice of business and leisure travellers.

In an endeavour to make travel more convenient and comfortable for the business traveller, the Oberoi city hotels offer the best of facilities with which to conduct business and to unwind at the end of the day. Leisure travel is made more enriching. Each hotel pays tribute to the diverse past and rich heritage of its location, offering guests the opportunity to absorb the history, experience the culture, interact with the local population and delight in their traditions.

Dedicated to offering experiences that are unique and enriching, each Oberoi hotel is distinct, the common element being staff that are committed and inspired to deliver the finest service. Conceived as a traditional Indian palace, The Oberoi Udaivilas showcases the rich heritage of the Mewar region of Rajasthan with its rambling courtyards, gentle rippling fountains, reflecting pools and verdant gardens. The hotel offers the opportunity to indulge in rejuvenating spa therapies, private yoga, meditations and Pranayam sessions, or to explore the city steeped in the romance of the oldest living dynasty in the world.

INSPIRING: Guests at The Oberoi Amarvilas, Agra marvel at awe-inspiring views of the Taj Mahal, located a few hundred yards from the hotel. The Oberoi Rajvilas in Jaipur evokes princely Rajasthan with luxury villas and royal tents in a fort-like setting. Meanwhile, The Oberoi Vanyavilas combines the exhilaration of jungle adventure with the luxury of elegantly appointed and spacious tents. The cruiser Oberoi Motor Vessel Vrinda offers the opportunity to experience the magical backwaters of Kerala in comfort and at leisure, while the Oberoi resort, Wildflower Hall, Shimla in the Himalayas offers a tranquil sanctuary in the mountains.

The Oberoi, Mauritius, located amidst 20 acres of lush tropical gardens and surrounded by a turquoise lagoon, offers a range of water sports such as wind surfing, water skiing, snorkelling and sailing. Guests at The Oberoi, Sahl Hasheesh, the all-suite resort located on the picturesque coastline of the Red Sea, can indulge in a range of water sports and desert safaris. The Oberoi Zahra, featuring the most spacious accommodation amongst boats on the Nile, a full-service spa and a leisurely seven-night itinerary with private docking in most ports, redefined the paradigm of luxury on the Nile when it took to the waters. ▣

CONTACT: www.oberoihotels.com

PARADISE
FOUND

THE ISLAND OF CRETE HAS A HIDDEN JEWEL ON ITS NORTHERN COASTLINE,
COURTESY OF THE PARADISE ISLAND VILLAS RESORT AND ITS UNIQUE APPROACH
TO HOLIDAY ACCOMMODATION

Holidaying overseas is one of life's great pleasures, but sometimes a conventional hotel break isn't necessarily the best option. For those wanting to take the concept of personal luxury one step further, the majestic island of Crete may hold the answer, in the form of Paradise Island Villas – an innovative boutique villa hotel that redefines the boundaries of what is possible…

CONCEPT: Discreetly tucked away in the coastal town of Anissaras, Paradise Island Villas lies just 20 kilometres from Heraklion's airport, yet it could be a world away. Within the lush landscaped grounds of this development, the purity and silence of the air creates a fitting ambience for a collection of twelve individually designed and furnished villas.

Supporting these self-contained properties are carefully orchestrated communal amenities, encapsulated by the stunning swimming pool with an open-sided lounge immediately beside it. It's possible to have meals delivered to your villa, but many guests prefer to enjoy the ambience of the resort's 'Ambrosia' restaurant, named after the ancient Greek term for the food of the Gods. This celebrated centre of gastronomic excellence uses the finest local produce to combine Mediterranean and Greek cuisine within a suitably opulent environment.

Much more than a five-star resort, Paradise Island Villas offers a complete lifestyle service to its guests. From babysitting to beauty treatments, and from dry-cleaning to a doctor on call, guests can experience the rare concept of total relaxation and peace of mind, all courtesy of the grandly named Supreme Paradise Guest Services. Indeed, customer service is perfectly balanced – attentive and comprehensive, yet discreet and personalised.

COLLECTION: As its name suggests, the centrepiece of Paradise Island Villas is a collection of villas, encompassing five different styles of two-storey properties. Named after the Greek Gods, these villas share many common features, from private pools to six-ring hobs and air-conditioning. With Jacuzzi bathtubs and separate shower cubicles, the bathrooms are tiled in polished Greek marble and even come equipped with bathrobes and slippers. However, rather than being generically designed, each has been furnished and decorated by the development's owners – every accessory has a story and every room enjoys its own unique personality. Comfort and privacy are never compromised, and the end result is a dozen completely bespoke properties, reflecting Cretan architecture yet integrating every

modern convenience that guests could hope for, from Italian crystal chandeliers to computers with high-speed Wi-Fi.

The villas range in size from the one-bedroom Artemis and Hephaestus through to the Superior Villas, capable of accommodating up to six people. When guests retire to their bedrooms, they will discover the 'Paradise Bed Concept'. Combining custom-made mattresses, white cotton, silk linens and a variety of pillows, each bed is a haven of softness and sensuality, ensuring a perfect night's sleep in readiness for the next instalment of life in a Paradise Island Villa.

APPRECIATION: As might be expected, Paradise Island Villas has attracted a huge amount of glowing testimonies and positive feedback. Guests are predominantly drawn from Europe and North America, and their appreciation of the finer things in life underlines how compelling this boutique resort's charms really are.

The mesmeric sea and mountain views have entranced many visitors over the years, and the celebrated customer service is a principal reason why Paradise Island Villas receives so much repeat custom. ▣

CONTACT: www.paradiseislandvillas.gr

A MATCH MADE IN

HEAVEN

THE REGENT MALDIVES COMBINES
THE PERFECT INGREDIENTS FOR AN
INDULGENT ESCAPE

From Bordeaux and Berlin to Turks and Caicos, Bali and Beijing, the award-winning legacy of the Regent name encompasses luxury hotels and resorts all over the world. Combine this with the richness, tranquillity and unsurpassed beauty of Maalefushi Island, at the southernmost tip of The Maldives, and you get a match made in heaven.

STRIKING: A cluster of untouched coral islands lined with white beaches and sparkling waters, the beauty of The Maldives defies description. Along the flawless and isolated shores that these gems have to offer, 50 beach and over-water pavilions are skilfully integrated into the natural beauty of Thaa Atoll to preserve its luxuriance and seclusion – alone in their splendour, fronting nothing but the azure seas.

'We have worked around the lush tropics in constructing the property so that when you are in the middle of the island it is like walking in a jungle surrounded by turquoise water and pristine beaches,' explains General Manager, Brice Borin.

LUXURY: Designers, Hirsch Bedner Associates – the name behind The Beverly Hills Hotel, USA – have mingled natural decor with sophisticated contemporary comforts to provide luxury for all the senses – be it sumptuous local cuisine, rich textures or the ultimate serenity of spirit.

Thatched pavilions combine traditional Maldivian architecture with soft, elegant interiors carefully arranged over spacious 310-square-metre villas, each with direct beach access, king-sized bedrooms, private pools with vast wooden decks, and large deep-soaking stone tubs in bathrooms leading on to private gardens or serene ocean panoramas.

'Every piece of furniture has been hand designed; the fabrics are very warm and natural materials are integral to the design, making the villas exceptionally special and intimate,' adds Brice.

Intuitively attending to guests' requirements, the service is custom made to suit the needs of even the most discerning connoisseur, with complimentary use of the 24-hour butler service. As Brice explains, when you step onto the island, tension melts away: 'Before you can breathe a request, the service is there. It is not so much a standard as a philosophy, a kind of attention that is unmatched anywhere else.'

Those seeking indulgent havens need look no further than the 850-square-metre spa overlooking the lagoon, primed with unique, exclusive treatments and tailor-made therapies to pamper and renew.

A 46-metre freshwater infinity-edge swimming pool, watersports equipment, floodlit tennis courts and a glass-walled lagoon-side gym are but a few ways to invigorate body and mind. Thirst for adventure can be quenched by jungle safari, diving and snorkelling, big-game fishing, island hopping and dolphin sighting at sunset.

INSPIRED: World-class cuisine is offered to guests, who can choose from an array of tastes: the over-water grill combines fresh seafood with breathtaking views, while Mediterranean delicacies are cooked to perfection at Izzi's. As the sun goes down, guests can watch the glowing horizon from the Lagoon Bar while sipping exotic cocktails.

Blending the perfect philosophy with an idyllic setting, The Regent Maldives has mastered the absolute luxury experience. As Brice describes: 'An unparalleled sense of freedom and serenity is formed by the luxuriance of space and complete privacy. You are able to feel completely at peace.' ▣

CONTACT: www.RegentHotels.com/Maldives

A NEWLY ESTABLISHED RESORT ON THE PELOPONNESE COASTLINE
COMBINES ANCIENT GREEK TRADITIONS AND CULTURE WITH OPULENT
MODERN FACILITIES

THE PLEASURE
OF LEISURE

To capture the imagination of potential visitors, a successful resort needs a fitting location, and few venues could be more appropriate for relaxation than The Romanos, a Luxury Collection Resort. Surrounded by lush olive groves, this newly opened resort forms the inaugural stage of a 130-hectare mixed-use beachfront development, collectively known as Costa Navarino.

The Romanos Resort's landscaped grounds and indigenous flora extend downhill towards a sweeping sandy beach, framed by the deep blue hues of the Ionian Sea. Bathed in sunshine throughout the year, this glorious Mediterranean setting comprises 321 rooms and suites, with more than 128 individual private infinity pools across the development seemingly merging into the ocean. Drawing architectural inspiration from its historic surroundings in Greece's Messinia region, each low-rise building uses tactile materials such as marble and wood throughout its interior, with thoughtful touches found in every room, wooden-deck terraces and designer garden furniture.

EXTRAORDINARY:
Accommodation at The Romanos Resort ranges from the fittingly named Deluxe Rooms through to the flagship Royal Villa Koroni. Alongside the apartments are a select number of villas, with round-the-clock butler service augmenting interiors of the finest calibre. The two-bedroom Ithomi and Sapientza villas have marble en-suites equipped with tropical showers and separate bathtubs, while the extraordinary Royal Villa represents the pinnacle of these properties. Measuring around 660 square metres internally, it delivers complete privacy and sweeping coastal views from its three bedrooms, each including a balcony and a lavishly appointed en-suite. Private facilities include a gym, spa area and sauna, with a proliferation of water features within the landscaped gardens culminating at an infinity pool.

For many guests at The Romanos Resort, the nearby Anazoe Spa will become an undisputed highlight of their stay. Named after the Greek word for rejuvenation, this lavishly appointed spa aims to reinvigorate both mind and body through time-honoured techniques, some of which extend back two and a half thousand years to the time of Hippocrates. Ice grottos, mist showers and herbal saunas feature alongside hydrotherapy and floating pools, with a variety of indoor and outdoor treatment areas reverberating to the soft melodies of ancient Greek music.

DIVERSITY:
Just as Anazoe Spa offers a diverse array of treatments to suit individual tastes, so The Romanos Resort as a whole provides amenities for guests of all ages. Business visitors can utilise the House of Events, a state-of-the-art centre for conferences, conventions and events that can accommodate up to 2,000 people simultaneously. Nor is The Romanos Resort an adults-only affair, with the Cocoon centre caring for children below five years of age, and the SandCastle offering comprehensive entertainment for 5–12 year olds. Guests of all ages will cherish the fine dining available throughout The Romanos Resort, with gourmet cuisine inspired by traditional recipes and prepared using organic local produce. The beach and swim-up bars also deserve mention, with live piano music in the Anax Lounge creating a fitting ambience for afternoon tea and late-night cocktails alike.

The wider attractions of Costa Navarino also deserve consideration, since this environmentally sensitive development is rapidly establishing itself as one of the Mediterranean's finest settings. A sense of history is indelibly imbued into the surrounding environment, with the Palace of Nestor and Olympia among the famous local landmarks. The Bernhard Langer-designed Navarino Dunes is Greece's first 18-hole signature golf course, with a golf academy, bar and restaurant incorporated into its clubhouse. Other dining facilities can be found at the Agora: named after the ancient Greek assembly area, it combines bars and restaurants of its own with a wealth of boutique and designer retail outlets. ▢

CONTACT: www.romanoscostanavarino.com

MORE
HOME
THAN HOTEL

THE MOMENT SOMEONE ENTERS SERENE PAVILIONS, THEY ARE TRANSPORTED TO A
WORLD OF BLISSFUL TRANQUILLITY

Sumptuous yet unassuming, Serene Pavilions is the only five-star boutique hotel in Sri Lanka that follows an adults-only policy

Serene Pavilions, a luxurious boutique hotel on the coast of western Sri Lanka, is a fine example of serendipity – it came about by accident, and at the whim of its owner, Clive W Leach CBE.

Having been a regular visitor to the country for many years, Clive decided he'd like to spend more time there with his wife and therefore would build a property to match their needs. A sensational seven-acre coconut grove by the sea was identified by his bosom pal and Sri Lankan colleague, Anura Lokuhetty, and after some consideration Clive decided that instead of creating just one luxury abode, why not build 12 and add a magnificent beachside restaurant, a stunning central pool, a spa, a gym and a tennis court, all amidst a lush, private and expansive garden?

And so Serene Pavilions was born. Clive invited Anura to spearhead the project and take on the role of Chief Executive. Anura is recognised as one of the most experienced hoteliers in Sri Lanka, and is also the President of the Tourist Hotels Association of Sri Lanka.

Sumptuous yet unassuming, Serene Pavilions is the only five-star boutique hotel in Sri Lanka that follows an adults-only (15+) policy, in order to ensure that its fundamental aim – to indulge its unashamedly upmarket guests, total privacy, comfort and service without any disturbances or distractions – is guaranteed. 'The reasons why guests who have stayed at Serene have enjoyed their experience is because of the total seclusion, serenity and peace around the place,' says Clive, 'as well as the unobtrusive service from their round-the-clock butler who ensures that nothing is too much trouble.'

OPULENCE: Serene Pavilions is all about indulgence. It becomes easy to get used to meandering past the lotus-filled ponds dotted around the landscaped gardens and through the coconut grove to the beach before returning to the exclusive pavilion to enjoy a refreshing 'as-you-please' dip in the private pool. And at sunset, enjoying a drink and dinner in the beachside restaurant overlooking the illuminated rolling waves is priceless.

Each pavilion consists of either one or two elegant bedrooms with attached dressing room, a spacious sitting room and dining area, a furnished kitchenette, a butler's pantry, a private bar and a large bathroom featuring two vanity units, separate shower room and Jacuzzi. The pavilions also come equipped with their own private plunge pools surrounded by a decking area with Bali-designed sun protection covers. 'Every pavilion has been designed to meet exacting criteria and lovingly christened with a Sanskrit name,' adds Clive. 'Thus, we have blended Sri Lankan culture with the highest levels of service and hospitality to showcase this area of the country.'

RECOGNITION: Even though it opened in late 2009, it is evident, even at this early stage of its life, that Serene Pavilions is one of the most luxurious, exclusive and elite boutique hotels in south Asia. This was confirmed when, shortly after opening, it was added to the prestigious list of Small Luxury Hotels of the World owing to its high quality, style, facilities and service.

The success achieved so quickly by Serene Pavilions might tempt its owners to consider expansion elsewhere using the same model but, as Clive says: 'We aim first to consolidate our position as the leader of boutique hotels in Sri Lanka before we dissipate our energies elsewhere. I am confident that our discerning guests will ensure our continuing success.'

CONTACT: www.serenepavilions.com

HALLMARK OF
SUCCESS

THE UNIQUE SHANGRI-LA EXPERIENCE WILL SHORTLY BE AVAILABLE IN MANY MORE DESTINATIONS WORLDWIDE, ILLUSTRATING ITS WINNING COMBINATION OF UNDERSTATED ELEGANCE AND QUIET CONFIDENCE

As Shangri-La Hotels moves into Europe and North America it is set to delight existing and new customers alike with the unique characteristics that have become synonymous with its name across Asia and the Middle East, best summed up as the ultimate in Asian hospitality.

The warm and welcoming hospitality from caring and interested staff, which sees every need and requirement not just met, but often anticipated and pre-empted, keeps guests returning time and again and the company considers this to be the cornerstone of its reputation as a world-class hotel group, setting it aside from its peers. 'Exciting times lie ahead for Shangri-La as we start to open new hotels in great European cities such as Paris, Vienna and London,' says Brendan Inns, Vice President of Shangri-la Hotels' Brand Communications. 'We will be bringing our renowned Asian hospitality which, from our genuine care and respect for guests and colleagues, mirrors the ideals of our new advertising campaign that launched globally in May 2010.'

PERSONAL: Every hotel revels in its own unique setting, such as the Shangri-La's Barr Al Jissah Resort and Spa in the Sultanate's capital of Muscat, nestling alongside the sparkling bay of Al Jissah in a dramatic desert setting of rugged mountains and inviting beaches. Visiting the resort's Turtle Beach is an absolute must, with a dedicated turtle ranger on hand to teach guests about protecting the turtles and how their life begins at the beach. In an excellent example of Shangri-La's personal service, the ranger will phone guests at just the right moment to save them waiting for hours to see hatchlings.

TRENDSETTING: Shangri-La's Villingili Resort and Spa Maldives is a unique all-villa resort property located in a spacious, boutique-style environment, set amidst sensational sandy beaches and lush tropical foliage. A refreshing change from the usual watersports that every resort offers is the opportunity to be taken to neighbouring atolls on a delightful day out with bicycles and packed lunches provided by the hotel. Shangri-La was also the first resort in the Maldives to open tree-house villas, which are perched high on stilts, along with a private pool at the same level, offering the ultimate in privacy.

INDIVIDUAL: The Island Shangri-La Hong Kong is a welcoming Hong Kong luxury hotel retreat in the heart of the city, soaring 56 floors above Hong Kong's most prestigious shopping, cultural and business addresses, with memorable views of the Peak and Victoria Harbour and unforgettable airport transfers in a Rolls-Royce Phantom.

Each Shangri-La Hotel and Resort makes a great effort to represent the destination that they are in, rather than the standard replications which are normal practice with so many large chains.

Key to the group's success is CHI The Spa, which is featured in many of the key properties. A sense of place is reflected in each location's spa treatments, which either use a local, traditional technique or locally sourced products and indigenous ingredients.

The hotels and resorts also find other ways to distinctively represent the destination that they are in, be it through interior design or local cuisine, such as the Rasa Sayang Resort which offers traditional Malay desserts, where guests can choose from an array of local syrups, rose water and fruit to sprinkle over ice.

'We are proud to have led the way in many concepts,' says Brendan 'Furthermore we were the first luxury hotel group to develop a spa concept intrinsically linked to a specific, evocative theme created in literature, namely the mythical land of Shangri-La. With over 40 projects under development, we are looking forward to introducing Shangri-La Hotels to many more destinations across the world.' ▣

CONTACT: www.shangri-la.com

A GOLFER'S
PARADISE

Nestled among the rolling hills of Kunming, Yunnan, southwest China, lies a breathtaking residential and golfing paradise known as Spring City, a natural sanctuary that is home to luxury residences, a hotel and world-class, award-winning golf courses.

Singapore developer Keppel Land has selected the perfect location for this upmarket, resort-style haven. Here, the mild climate of Kunming allows comfortable golfing all year round, set against the backdrop of a truly spectacular, natural landscape. Spring City boasts two world-class 18-hole golf courses designed by internationally renowned golf masters Jack Nicklaus and Robert Trent Jones Jr.

Both courses have won more than 70 prestigious awards and commendations over the last ten consecutive years, making Spring City Asia's number one. To preserve that status, the courses are kept in a constant state of perfection by the professional management and maintenance team who apply meticulous standards.

The quality of these championship golf courses is enhanced by their awe-inspiring natural setting: the enticing fairways and manicured greens are gently woven into the curvaceous shoreline of the beautiful Yangzong Lake, a glistening, tranquil water feature that is the shimmering centerpiece in the landscape. Overlooking the clear water are private residences, ideal as a luxury retreat for the privileged few.

WITH A YEAR-ROUND TEMPERATE CLIMATE, STUNNING VIEWS AND A MOUNTAINOUS BACKDROP, SPRING CITY GOLF AND LAKE RESORT IS THE PLACE TO RELAX AND PLAY

ESCAPE: Seamlessly integrated into the lush mountain greenery are the villas, terraces and apartments that command views of the unfolding expanse of undulating landscapes. For nature lovers, the elevated mountain perch of these exclusive homes also offers a chance to get close to nature.

The high-quality exterior architecture of the residences at Spring City perfectly complements the surroundings, while the interiors capture true contemporary style. The simple and unpretentious lines create a smooth, visual rhythm consistent with the environment in which they sit. Each blends the charming character of natural stone and wood with the tasteful use of glass. Spacious and thoughtfully designed, they reflect western aesthetics and provide comfort, privacy and first-class amenities.

Spring City offers a supreme quality of life. Residents can spend leisure time in the club houses, with a swimming pool, gymnasium, tennis courts, karaoke rooms, mah-jong room and golf simulator. Other facilities include two restaurants, a trendy cafe, a convenience store and a function hall. In keeping with the high standard of living and service, Spring City also provides concierge services to satisfy the needs of residents.

NATURAL: Spring City is renowned for rigorously adhering to strict ecological principles. Every aspect of its planning involves responsible use of environmentally friendly building materials and many other eco-protective initiatives. It consistently employs energy-saving practices and stringent water resource management, and firmly complies with environmental-protection policies during construction and daily upkeep.

In recognition of such responsible eco-management, Spring City has been awarded numerous certificates. In April 2008, it received the ISO14001 environmental-protection certificate. Then, in 2009, it attained Classical Habitation certification and is now a member of Audubon International co-operative sanctuaries. In November 2009, Spring City added to its list of impressive achievements by being bestowed the prestigious Green Mark Award by Singapore's Building & Construction Authority.

Spring City has elevated the standard of golfing and luxury living in China to a new level. It is, in short, a golfing masterpiece painted on nature's beautiful canvas. It offers the perfect environment for Asia's business elite and socially affluent to reside, play and escape from the rest of the world. ▣

CONTACT: www.springcityresort.com

A PLACE
TO DREAM

DESIGNED TO OFFER THE COMFORTS OF HOME WITHIN AN UNFORGETTABLE COASTAL ENVIRONMENT ON THE ISLAND OF PHUKET, SRI PANWA IS AN OASIS OF LUXURY AND CALM

The huge success of Sri panwa, a resort in southeastern Phuket, can be attributed in part to its philosophy of creating a home-from-home. With the first part of its name meaning 'auspicious', Sri panwa enjoys an idyllic setting within 30 acres of lush tropical rainforest, on the tip of Cape Panwa. With each villa carefully designed to showcase the true beauty of its coastal environment, this secluded resort has been hailed as one of Thailand's greatest venues.

Alongside seven suites, a total of 51 villas range from one to six bedrooms, catering for parties of all sizes, and each offering a different take on Oriental luxury. Larger residential villas have exclusive infinity-edge swimming pools extending around glass-walled bedrooms, with outdoor bathing areas overlooking the Andaman Sea and its picturesque sprinkling of islands.

REFINED: Luxury is a core component of the Sri panwa experience, and numerous refined touches emphasise the calibre of this spectacular resort. Each villa has been designed and specified to the standards of an executive family home, with handcrafted furniture complemented by the finest bed linens and toiletries. Broadband wi-fi and satellite TV allow guests to keep in touch with events back home, and pre-loaded iPods channel a rich variety of music through Bose speaker systems in each living area.

Like the villas, Sri panwa's communal areas offer a comprehensive array of entertainment, and one undisputed highlight is a swimming pool on the estate's breathtaking private beach, complete with moorings for yachts. Land-based facilities include tennis courts, a fully equipped fitness suite and the tranquil Cool Spa retreat. This pampering paradise provides a full portfolio of treatments, ranging from Thai and Swedish massages through to aromatherapy and reflexology, all administered by master therapists using locally sourced ingredients. Anyone wishing to maintain their privacy can request treatments to take place in the comfort of their own villa.

ADVENTUROUS: For those guests eager to explore their surroundings, Phuket is blessed with excellent shops and a vibrant nightlife. There are seven golf courses on the island, and Sri panwa's knowledgeable staff can customise numerous other excursions to suit the specific tastes of adventurous guests, from elephant trekking and safari adventures through to two-day journeys around the Andaman Sea on the resort's own yacht. Keen anglers can lay out fishing lines during the daytime and see their catches being incorporated into a bespoke five-course dinner.

DELECTABLE: Fine dining is a celebrated cornerstone of the Sri panwa experience, with two very different restaurants catering for discerning palettes with a finely honed blend of Oriental and European cuisine prepared daily by gifted chefs. Specialising in comfort food with a twist of luxury, Baba Dining Lounge occupies opulent surroundings complemented by spectacular sunsets. Its on-site rival is the Baba Poolclub – now acclaimed as one of Phuket's finest locations, combining a 25-metre infinity lap pool, business facilities and the acclaimed BabaQ restaurant. Using ingredients sourced from around the world such as Japanese king crab and Australian Wagyu beef, a light and simple menu is crafted within an open kitchen. Anyone wishing to be more directly involved in the culinary process can attend evening cooking-school classes, where guests prepare their own meals under the expert supervision of BabaQ's talented chefs.

With a dramatic location, opulent surroundings, welcoming staff and a very personal service, Sri panwa can bring even the most exotic dreams to life. ▣

CONTACT: www.sripanwa.com

THE COAST IS CLEAR

A HUGE NEW DEVELOPMENT ON A STUNNING PENINSULA
OFFERS THE CHANCE TO ENJOY THE VERY BEST ELEMENTS
OF PORTUGUESE CULTURE, CLIMATE AND CUISINE

> *Ocean waves caress the golden beaches of a compact peninsula whose backdrop is the brooding mountains of Arrábida National Park*

An hour's drive from the vibrant city of Lisbon, a very special Iberian treasure awaits discovery. The Portuguese capital may be geographically close to the tróia peninsula, but there the similarity ends. Sculpted over countless centuries on one of the most southerly latitudes in Europe, ocean waves caress 15 kilometres of golden beaches on a compact peninsula whose backdrop is the brooding mountains of Arrábida National Park. Undisturbed and tranquil, this exquisite setting is the venue for troiaresort – a newly created 486-hectare amalgam of luxury apartments, townhouses, villas, hotels, golf course, marina, casino and congress centre.

Despite the presence of the Atlantic Ocean just yards away, troiaresort enjoys a climate so mild that palm trees and pine trees intermingle. Indigenous plants and bounteous wildlife are the only neighbours of this entirely new resort, conceived with total respect for the environmental sensitivity of its surroundings. Carefully designed to maximise the coastal aspects of the Tróia peninsula, cycle paths and pedestrian walkways intertwine across a series of distinctly demarcated zones. Foremost among these is the Central Area, combining retail and restaurant facilities with four- and five-star hotels and modern apartments. Immediately to the east, 186 villas and townhouses are flanked by beach and country clubs, with a five-star hotel and golf course enjoying close proximity to an eco-resort.

ENCAPSULATE:
Set amid Roman ruins and ageless sand dunes, an eco-resort, currently in development, perfectly encapsulates Tróia's environmental ethos. Every component of these delightful homes has been chosen to complement and support the surrounding environment, with properties scattered amongst pine groves and lagoons. It's little wonder that troiaresort has received ISO 14001 certification, in recognition of its environmental sensitivity.

Housing all the resort's principal amenities, the Central Area will be the heart in every sense. Many people will arrive by boat, mooring in the 184-berth marina and enjoying the unparalleled sense of occasion such an arrival always generates.

From here, the carefully chosen amenities of Tróia's main public areas are a short stroll away, with a casino complex rivalling the bars and restaurants for visitor appeal. Thanks to the mild year-round climate, outdoor amenities are plentiful, while the conference centre and shops add a more commercial flavour to this district. Restaurants draw on the rich diversity of local seafood, and a variety of bars offer the opportunity to see and be seen in this exclusive environment. A free shuttle bus is also available to transport people to tourist attractions.

AMENITIES:
Perhaps the finest embodiment of troiaresort's charms can be found inside the beach apartments and coastal villas. Full-height windows bring spectacular views of sandy beaches and the majestic Atlantic Ocean into the living quarters. Every property has been designed to feel like a true home, rather than a mere holiday venue, with generous room sizes augmented by terraces for al fresco dining and socialising. As might be expected, a comprehensive portfolio of communal services is on offer – from concierges and factoring through to pool, garden maintenance, 24-hour security and a medical centre, clients can be freed from responsibility to simply appreciate their surroundings, or enjoy aerobics classes on the beach, outdoor cinema sessions or workshops for their children.

While the coastal setting will encourage many people towards the comprehensive portfolio of watersports available at troiaresort, others will be drawn irresistibly to one of Portugal's finest golf courses. Nestled between the ocean and the Sado River, this par-72 championship links course, designed by Robert Trent Jones Snr and considered by *Golf World Magazine* as one of the 20 best golf courses in Europe, represents a true challenge, and four other 18-hole courses are situated within a 20-mile radius of Tróia. Sports enthusiasts may consider this the perfect environment, but in truth, troiaresort is a dream destination by anyone's standards. ▣

CONTACT: www.troiaresort.pt

ESCAPE
SOMEWHERE
TRULY
RELAXING

> *We grow a lot of our own salad and vegetable crops, as well as the herbs we need, right here within the grounds'*

TY'N RHOS COUNTRY HOUSE & RESTAURANT IS THE REASON TO TAKE A BREAK AWAY

How can one best escape the daily grind, re-energise and rediscover a zest for life? Taking a break somewhere that offers exquisite comfort and impeccable service surrounded by rugged, awe-inspiring natural beauty is a great place to start. Ty'n Rhos Country House does just that.

LANDSCAPE: Ty'n Rhos Country House is surrounded by some of the most breathtaking landscapes in Wales. Nestled comfortably on the wide-open lush plain between Snowdonia and the Isle of Anglesey, Ty'n Rhos is perfectly poised to allow visitors to explore their surroundings.

Few places have such variety on their doorstep: from castles at Harlech and Anglesey to glorious beaches; from narrow-gauge steam railways to the rugged invigorating beauty of Snowdonia itself.

But what lures people back time and again to Ty'n Rhos is the sense of returning home.

Martin, Jan and their son Phil (along with Susie the terrier), and their friendly staff, extend a warm welcome to visitors.

Bedrooms are individual, distinctive and stylish with names such as Welsh Poppy, Corn Cockle, Cornflower and Dog Violet, and homely touches that are instantly comfortable.

To stay here is to recharge and re-energise with a warm and friendly atmosphere, breathtaking views and delicious cuisine.

DINE: Hotel guests dine alongside non-residents on freshly sourced local produce cooked in subtle, imaginative and simply mouth-watering ways. Here at Ty'n Rhos, the quality of the food speaks for itself.

'We grow a lot of our own salad and vegetable crops, as well as the herbs we need, right here within the grounds,' says Martin. To complement this, Martin and his team select only top-quality meat from local farms and butchers and freshly caught local fish.

Turning the best local ingredients into a gourmet's paradise is something Martin is very skilled at; he trained at the Dorchester under the tutelage of Anton Mosimann before refining his skills at a variety of five-star and Michelin-star country houses and hotels in Britain and abroad. It is this experience that he brings to bear in his own kitchen at Ty'n Rhos. The results are exquisite.

SURROUNDINGS: Of course there is more to Ty'n Rhos than fine dining and lovely rooms. The breathtaking surroundings offer a host of leisure activities including fishing, bird watching and golf.

For guests who wish to enjoy a little more privacy, there are spacious cottages within the grounds that can provide ample accommodation for family and friends. Ty'n Rhos has a fabulous, relaxed ambience, while also catering for the jet set – there's even a helipad in the grounds.

Most of all, Ty'n Rhos is all about one word: *Croeso*, which is 'Welcome' in Welsh. For all guests, no matter how long their stay, can expect a very warm Welsh welcome and a chance to escape from the hustle and bustle of everyday living. ▣

CONTACT: www.tynrhos.co.uk

EMPIRE
IN THE SUN

THE FORMER HOME OF THE JODHPUR ROYAL FAMILY
HAS BECOME A RESORT QUITE UNLIKE ANY OTHER,
FROM ITS WHISPERING GALLERY TO ITS WORLD-
FAMOUS BUTLER SERVICE

As one of the world's largest private residences, Umaid Bhawan Palace has been the principal home of the Jodhpur Royal Family since 1943. Standing within 26 acres of lush grounds and conceived on the grandest of scales, it was designed for Umaid Singh, a maharaja granted full monarchical powers at the tender age of 21. One of Umaid Singh's lasting legacies to his home country was the creation of an enduring symbol for the Jodhpur region of India and the last of the country's great palaces – a breathtaking sandstone edifice sprinkled with turret rooms and terraces, and centred on a 105-foot high cupola in the reception lobby.

MAJESTIC: Behind that colossal Art Deco frontage, Umaid Bhawan Palace today offers visitors 64 rooms and suites that were once the sole preserve of princes and kings. The aptly named historical and royal suites and palace rooms have been recently revitalised, while retaining generously scaled furniture and opulent fabrics in keeping with the majesty of their surroundings. However, nothing can compare with the Maharaja Suite – formerly Umaid Singh's personal chambers, and decorated with frescoes of leopards, tigers and horses. As might be expected, this suite is equipped with huge Art

Deco furnishings, a dining area and private bar, spa therapy room, a luxurious bathroom with adjoining steam room and a large veranda overlooking one of the palace courtyards.

As befits a former maharaja's residence, the cuisine on offer at Umaid Bhawan is second to none, with three restaurants and a bar. Inspired by the famous Jodhpur lancers, Risala's à la carte menu provides an array of contemporary European and Indian fare, while Pillars offers an all-day dining facility with an eclectic menu and spectacular views of Baradari Lawns and the city skyline. The rooftop Sunset Pavilion restaurant is the highest dining point in Jodhpur, with an array of delectable grills served in a spectacular ambience, and the Trophy Bar celebrates Jodhpur gallantry through the ages, with trophies adorning its walls. However, it is also possible to dine and drink anywhere within the palace's grounds, with private dinners served by a personal butler. Indeed, the hotel's butlers have become legendary for arranging anything their guests desire with minimal fuss.

UNIQUE: Such exemplary service is part and parcel of the Umaid Bhawan Palace experience. The entire complex is overflowing with unexpected delights, such as a vintage car collection that includes a 1947

Buick convertible and a Rolls-Royce Silver Ghost. The Jiva Grande Spa offers the opportunity to experience the royal art of India's ancient healing wisdom, with indoor and outdoor pools. The amphitheatre has been named after the renowned court musician and maestro Ali Akbar, and it can be reserved for lectures and movie shows alike. Many guests also relish the opportunity to explore the Palace Museum, which is filled with Victorian and Edwardian timepieces, miniatures, porcelain and objets d'art from the maharaja's personal collection. Even the sporting facilities boast luxurious interiors, from marbled squash courts to a panelled billiard room.

Guests wishing to venture beyond the palace boundaries can easily become more intimately acquainted with this corner of India. Local treasures range from the intricacy of the 15th-century Meherangarh Fort through to the colourful bazaars of Girdikot and Sardar, while many people choose to explore the lovingly embellished 12th-century Sachya Mata temple. The artificial lake and lush fruit groves at Balsamand Palace are a perennial attraction, as are safari tours of local villages. ▣

CONTACT: www.tajhotels.com/Palace/UMAID%20 BHAWAN%20PALACE,JODHPUR/default.htm

CONTEMPORARY
ELEGANCE

A place of serenity in the midst of Bond Street's bustle, The Westbury Mayfair is one of London's best luxury hotels. Like the surrounding area, this five-star establishment embodies style, discretion and impeccable service. Each floor has a distinctive collection of chic black-and-white vintage portraits adorning the walls – for example, the third floor has images of the fashionable elite of the 1930s and the sixth floor showcases hipsters from the 1960s – and a stay at this prestigious hotel entitles guests to a unique discount or gift from the exclusive boutiques nearby, which include Burberry, Chanel, Hermès, Prada, Stella McCartney, Vivienne Westwood and Louis Vuitton.

PERSONAL: Young, dynamic and less traditional than some other hotels you would find in the district, The Westbury is a place where service and discretion walk hand-in-hand. And, in the past two years, this prestigious hotel has become the address of choice for Mikhail Gorbachev, Martina Navratilova, Carla Bruni and the iconic Grace Jones, who loves the discretion The Westbury offers.

Modern in design, mixing classic chic and contemporary elegance, The Westbury's rooms and suites are all individually created with natural, calming colours and sumptuous textiles. The suites provide the ideal living space for those who intend to stay at the hotel that little bit longer. With their own private dining and relaxing areas, they are a home from home. The Berkeley Suite's terrace offers breathtaking views across its namesake, Berkeley Square, and the penthouse St George Suite has panoramic views of London, butler service, interconnecting rooms, two bedrooms and a walk-in wardrobe – a must for any dedicated fashionista.

THE WESTBURY MAYFAIR COMBINES MODERN LUXURY AND THE FINEST COMFORT
WITH TIMELESS STYLE

The hotel has recently doubled in size following the acquisition of the adjacent Washington House, launching the Westbury Gallery and unveiling new function rooms to host extravagant events that can accommodate an extra 400 guests, and opening an impressive brand-new destination restaurant. By the end of 2011, it also plans to have a new spa, 30 extra suites and another bar.

SOCIAL: The place to meet for a drink, snack or cocktail is The Westbury's Polo Bar, which is not only famous for its extensive cocktails, malts and Cognacs, but also boasts the most expensive bottle of Champagne in the UK. This is where the movers and shakers of the world – celebrities, hedge-fund managers and oligarchs – escape the rigmarole of daily life.

Then there's The Artisan, a dining experience for people that enjoy the finer things in life, with innovative mouth watering, expertly prepared dishes by executive chef and Roux scholar Andrew Jones, accompanied by an astounding wine list of nearly 400 varieties. Additionally, The Westbury recently launched Tsukiji Sushi, providing the freshest hot or cold Japanese style fish and seafood delicacies.

Meanwhile, The Lounge is the ideal place to just be for a while, to gather one's bearings for a day out in the city. Set within sumptuous surroundings, its soft furnishings and soothing atmosphere make it the perfect place to enjoy a delicious breakfast, mid-morning, lunch or pre-theatre meals, with a stunning art nouveau mirror being its central focus.

SPORTING: The Westbury is actively involved with many charities. The Westbury Shield (above left), a polo tournament, has raised more than a quarter of a million pounds in the last two years for charities that were founded by the late Diana, Princess of Wales, and are now supported by the two princes. It also supports the Staying Alive Foundation, which globally is helping to conquer HIV and AIDS. The Westbury also has presence in the global hospitality arena, entertaining guests at events that include the Cannes Film Festival and the Cartier International Polo Day.

As The Westbury's owner, Azad Cola, explains: 'Clients coming to The Westbury feel like members of a private club. It is the combination of like-minded individuals sharing the same tastes and preferences, coupled with highly personalised service, that makes it our clients' favourite place to indulge themselves. The Westbury is not just a hotel, it's a way of life.' ▣

CONTACT: www.westburymayfair.com

PROPERTY

6 » Real Estate, Timeshare & Construction

6» PROPERTY

WELCOMING NEW
HOME

RE/MAX LIVING IS A LEADER IN LUXURY PROPERTIES IN ONE OF THE WORLD'S MOST DESIRABLE DESTINATIONS

Gerlinde Moser first arrived in Cape Town from Vienna some 40 years ago and promptly fell in love with the city. 'It has a wonderful fusion of European and African elements,' she says. 'The city presents a wonderful opportunity for anyone looking for a secure and appreciating investment in a first-world environment with a relaxed lifestyle, pleasing climate and on the same timeline as Europe.'

Gerlinde, co-founder of the Cape Town franchise of the global real estate company RE/MAX, operates with a team of dedicated property professionals and was the first agent outside of North America to be inducted into the RE/MAX Circle of Legends in 2008. This is the highest and most prestigious award given to a small number of the leading members of the company's global network of more than 100,000 agents – RE/MAX offers exceptional property investment opportunities in more than 70 countries in locations including Europe, North and South America, Australasia, Asia and Africa.

When RE/MAX announced its intention to open the South African operation in 1995, RE/MAX Living became one of its first offices to open in the region. 'Today we are the largest property group in South Africa and RE/MAX is the world's largest real estate organisation,' says Gerlinde. 'The international network is managed so well that we are able to assist people to sell, buy or rent properties wherever they are in the world. There is vibrant communication between the various franchises across the globe.'

*Cape Town remains a first-class
location attracting the elite traveller
and wealthy retirement investor*

LOCATION: Lying in the shadow of the National Heritage site, Table Mountain (nominated as one of the Seven Natural Wonders of the world), Cape Town is fast becoming South Africa's premier tourist destination. Unlike many destinations that attract mass tourism, Cape Town remains a first-class location attracting the elite traveller and wealthy retirement investor. The Mediterranean climate and wealth of attractions, such as stunning landscapes, national parks, traditional architecture, magnificent wine farms and distinctive white sandy beaches, are a draw that ensures a steady annual growth of discerning visitors to the region.

The Cape Peninsula is South Africa's second largest economic centre and has recently experienced an unprecedented boom in the construction of real estate developments due to the 2010 World Cup football tournament. South Africa is a land full of opportunities and the success of this, the biggest sporting event on the globe, is proof that Cape Town can compete on the world stage.

LIFESTYLE: Many visitors, including pensioners, are buying summer homes in the city or relocating permanently. When investing in Cape Town, investors are buying into a lifestyle that offers cultural interests such as the Cape Town Symphony Orchestra, ballet, theatre, first-class education, world-class medical facilities, exclusive shopping outlets and exhilarating leisure pursuits including yachting, hiking and surfing. Cape Town, in fact, boasts one of the few Royal Yacht Clubs, the renowned RCYC, and investors will find some of the world's finest golf courses.

Focusing on properties in the Waterfront, Atlantic Seaboard coastline and scenic Table Mountain areas, as well as Cape Town city centre, Gerlinde and her team are well respected within the industry because of their intimate understanding of property and their commitment to providing customers with the best possible advice.

Cape Town offers an amazing choice of properties, ranging from multimillion-rand villas and sophisticated ocean apartments to compact cottages and exclusive studio apartments. ▣

CONTACT: www.remaxliving.co.za

THE PERSONAL
TOUCH

INVESTORS CAN CHOOSE FROM THE BEST SOUTH AFRICAN
PROPERTIES WITH AYLESFORD INTERNATIONAL

Settled in the shadow of Table Mountain, Cape Town in South Africa is selected by many as the destination of choice for holidaymakers and second home owners. Its Mediterranean climate, stunning landscapes, cosmopolitan atmosphere and distinctive beaches drawing visitors to the region that Sir Francis Drake once described as, 'the fairest Cape in all the world'.

Cape Town is experiencing a boom in the real estate market, with South Africans and overseas investors looking to purchase property in the area. Well placed to provide this service is global real estate company Aylesford International, which can provide potential buyers with an excellent service and wealth of experience. As South Africa's credit markets were more sheltered by the global banking crisis when compared with other countries, the most recent real estate performance index by IPD/Sapoa demonstrated that potential investors were able to benefit from an average total return of 8.7 per cent from South African property; properties in the Cape Town Atlantic seaboard area have seen benefits of up to 15.9 per cent return, which can be compared to 3.5 per cent from the UK and a loss of 17.5 per cent in the USA.

Aylesford International has offices in London, Spain, France, Switzerland and South Africa, as well as interests across the globe. Representing some of the best residences in Cape Town and the surrounding areas, property prices start from 2.5 million rand (£220,000) and encompass vineyards, golf estates and game farms. 'We really focus on the high end of the market,' explains Director, Sally Wilson. 'All the properties are very high quality and clients get five times more for their money than they would in a place such as London.'

RAPPORT: Cape Town is famed for its hospitality, and the Aylesford team reflects this in the service it offers. While finding properties for discerning clients such as international sports stars, high-profile businesspeople and celebrities, the emphasis is on providing a discreet and personalised service. Sally says that the team aims to build up a long-lasting relationship with clients: 'We work very closely with clients and spend a lot of time entertaining them – they can drop into the office for a coffee and informal chat. The better we get to know our clients, the more successfully we can meet their needs. Many of our buyers/sellers and most new clients approach us due to recommendations. We are trying to create something very special and unique, while changing the whole culture of real estate.'

STRIKING: Benguela Cove Lagoon Wine Estate is a 210-hectare development that allows people to live on a wine estate, with stunning ocean and mountain views, surrounded by lavender fields and olive groves. The resort is ideally situated just 45 minutes from Cape Town, so residents can enjoy the perfect balance of quiet countryside life and bustling city living.

Sally is keen to emphasise what makes Benguela so exceptional: 'It's a great place for cycling, walking and watersports, and if you feel like a round of golf the famous Arabella Country Estate is on the opposite side of the lagoon.' Properties are scattered across the estate; located in the vineyards and olive groves, on the beach and settled on hillsides. Buyers have the choice of purchasing a ready-built house or choosing a plot and working with the developers and designer throughout the whole construction process. The popular historic seaside resort of Hermanus is also within easy driving distance of Benguela Cove.

A unique aspect of Benguela Cove is undoubtedly the award-winning wine it produces. Visitors are invited to indulge in wine tasting as well as to try some of the farm's delicious olives and wonderful red-wine jellies. 'People can buy the produce, but also visit the estate in peace and view properties without any kind of hassle or pressure,' says Sally. ▣

CONTACT: www.aylesfordsa.com

THE
ITALIAN
CONNECTION

FOR THE NON-ITALIAN BUYER, CASE IN ITALIA OFFERS A FULL AND BILINGUAL SERVICE, MAKING THE ACQUISITION AND MANAGEMENT OF A PROPERTY IN ITALY A SIMPLE AND PLEASANT EXPERIENCE

Recent media coverage of the Italian property market has done a great deal to boost the interest and confidence of non-Italian buyers. Yet most buyers still place a very high premium on the support of someone they can trust throughout the process of acquiring and managing a property, and a growing number of international buyers are discovering exactly such a partner in Case in Italia.

Case in Italia is a leading property agency in the Italian market, mainly covering Lazio, southern Tuscany, southern Umbria and the Amalfi coast. 'I established Case in Italia in 2003 with the aim of creating a full-service company, side-by-side to its clients at every step,' explains Pietro Giella, a Partner in Case in Italia. 'We search for properties, arrange viewings, undertake full technical, legal and financial checks, ensure there are no unpleasant surprises and guide buyers through the whole purchasing process. We also handle property restoration and management, as well as set up bank accounts, act as an interface with local authorities, pay bills, and organise for the collection of olives and the making of olive oil.'

VALUED: Offering what Pietro describes as a 'five-star service' through attentive consultation, ethical practices and outstanding service delivery, Case in Italia has secured a favourable position in a highly competitive market. 'We succeed by adopting a listening attitude that allows us to satisfy our clients' requirements,' explains Pietro. 'Sometimes this isn't easy as requests can be unusual and demanding. But we try our best and most of the time we succeed.'

Defining the central values of his business, Pietro is insistent on the importance of transparency and efficiency in all activities, and eager to provide examples. 'Before purchase, we take the documents of the property to a notary where they're checked,' he explains. 'Most agencies do this after a preliminary agreement is signed and money is paid, but that's too late. And when we agree the text of the preliminary agreement, in original and translation, we make it as similar as possible to the deed of purchase, which is only in Italian, so our buyers know exactly what's going on. As for the properties we manage, these are situated across Italy so we rely on local cleaners, gardeners, electricians, and plumbers. Importantly, though, we only develop relationships with reliable people who can offer our clients priority: when a problem arises, it has to be solved immediately.'

FRIENDSHIP: With this level of service, it is no surprise that Case in Italia frequently develops particularly close relationships with its clients. 'We've had many of our clients for years, some since 2003,' says Pietro, 'and this often means developing a friendship that goes beyond business. We've invited some clients to our happenings, even family occasions, and certain clients have hosted my family in their countries. One client has on a couple of occasions lent my family his house in the middle of the Indian Ocean. Another client has hosted part of my family in the UK for long periods, offering them work to help them learn English.'

Despite recent challenges to the global economy, Case in Italia has continued to develop and is today a trusted name in the Italian property market, powered by the enthusiasm of Pietro and his staff. 'I've sold some great properties to some very nice people, and it's been a real pleasure to watch them enjoy their house, their pools and their olive oil,' he says. 'It's also been exciting to sell properties to some very well-known people. But really, for me, it's making friends and developing our network that is the best part of our business.' ▣

CONTACT: www.caseinitalia.net

CIRCLE OF LIFE

CREATING A BESPOKE LIVING ENVIRONMENT,
A FLAGSHIP DESTINATION IN THE HEART OF DUBAI
WILL COMBINE THE BEST OF EVERYTHING, FROM
LEISURE AND RETAIL TO WORK AND HOMES

In a city already blessed with an abundance of landmarks, Dubai Pearl is set to become one of the undisputed highlights of this glittering Emirates state. Nestling between Palm Jumeirah and Dubai's eponymous Media City, Dubai Pearl will be a destination without precedent, where culture and liveability are every bit as important as the buildings and amenities.

INCLUSIVE: The heart of Dubai Pearl, in every sense, is a single structure standing 73 storeys high, dominating the urban skyline and supported by four imposing towers, whose boldness and elegance reflects the ambition of this integrated lifestyle project. It was conceived as the ultimate mixed-use development – a walkable city within a city, where people can live, relax, socialise and work in a single location, minimising commuting and thereby maximising leisure time. A third of Dubai Pearl's total ground space will be dedicated to high-tech offices, with almost 1,400 different units offering an outstanding workplace that complements the neighbouring residential and leisure space – like the dedicated Gourmet Boulevard containing 60 cafés and bistros, ranging from casual dining to Michelin-starred restaurants.

Groundwork began in the summer of 2008, with construction of the superstructure starting in January 2010. The guiding philosophy behind the development is to deliver a sustainable urban community, without compromising on quality or luxury. Through sensitive, intelligent design and a mature approach to placemaking, Dubai Pearl sets a precedent for environmentally-friendly urban design in the region.

Water is recycled and heated by solar power, cars are discreetly tucked away in one of the world's largest undercover car parks, and built-in smart technologies allow for the highest standards of connectivity. Every component has been meticulously planned for maximum efficiency and effectiveness, and nowhere is that truer than in the residential accommodation.

VARIETY: Homes at Dubai Pearl come in an impressive selection of sizes and themes, including some of the world's best lifestyle and luxury brands, in which the very essence of the brand's DNA has been uncovered to offer residents the best that life has to offer. Buyers can choose from apartments and penthouses through to palaces in the sky. With optional bespoke finishings adding a truly personal ambience, each made-to-measure home will feature advanced 21st-century technology and a portfolio of amenities including security, concierge, valet and housekeeping services.

Dubai Pearl will cater for the hectic and fast-paced lifestyles that are synonymous with modern-day living. Leisure time for hard-working business people, students and pupils is a precious commodity, so easy and efficient access to a wide range of high-quality amenities and facilities is essential.

Residents at Dubai Pearl will be able to enjoy a unique wellness centre offering everything from nutritional advice through to ayurvedic medicine, and a high-tech sports complex offers a full portfolio of athletics, fitness and sporting amenities for adults and children alike. With an art boulevard and an indoor games centre, a 1,800-seater theatre, a 10-screen cinema and several internationally renowned spas, Dubai Pearl will appeal to every age group.

EXCLUSIVE: Drawing inspiration from the great centres of the world – London's Covent Garden, the Champs Elysées in Paris and the bay area of San Francisco – the downtown district of Dubai Pearl will comprise a winning combination of leisure, shopping and entertainment across a panoply of boutiques, galleries and theatres. Visitors can enjoy these surroundings while staying at one of seven five-star hotels – an integral part of the Dubai Pearl experience.

The Bellagio Hotel will symbolise the emergence of Dubai Pearl as a truly global destination. Iconic and exhilarating, the hotel embodies the Italian philosophy of 'la Bella Figura' – the Beautiful Form. The Dubai Pearl setting is the perfect complement to the world famous Bellagio brand.

Energy, excitement, indulgence and escape are the watchwords for the MGM Grand Pearl Dubai, where magnificent architecture infuses an unparalleled guest experience.

Skylofts Dubai Pearl will provide guests with a unique private sanctuary with high-altitude penthouse suites that offer panoramic views across Dubai. More than any other hotel in the region, the Skyloft experience is centred on the guest room, defining flexible, open spaces which offer both a sense of physical space and well-being.

To complement Dubai Pearl's unrivalled collection of luxury brands, residents will be offered membership of an exclusive, private, members' concierge club, offering services in keeping with the elegant and sophisticated lifestyles that will be enjoyed by all who embrace the Dubai Pearl. ▣

CONTACT: www.dubaipearl.com

OCEANFRONT
LIVING

EXPERIENCE LIFESTYLE EXCLUSIVITY AND SOPHISTICATION IN SOUTH AMERICA

Punta del Este, Uruguay, is a fashionable beach resort and international hot-spot where jet-setters, celebrities and famous business, art and fashion personalities meet each summer season to enjoy a glamorous lifestyle. The resort is renowned for a unique charm that offers a variety of activities combining luxury, sophistication, social events, gastronomy and nightlife while surrounded by a magnificent and rustic countryside, extensive white sand beaches and clandestine residences. There are many options to enjoy life outdoors, such as golf, polo, tennis, water sports, and sailing. The resort's strikingly beautiful port is a destination for numerous international regattas. Many of the visitors and residents who come to 'Punta' take advantage of the opposite seasons, where summer is in its full splendour during the months of January and February.

EXCLUSIVE: Designed by world-renowned architect Rafael Viñoly, the award-winning residential building, Acqua, meets the standards of the most discerning international homebuyers and investors. Overlooking the South Atlantic Ocean, Punta del Este's

finest architectural marvel offers exclusive beachfront living at its most majestic; a combination of endless blue sky, exceptional sunlight, rippling water and distant vistas. Each of the building's private residences features superb finishes and advanced engineering touches, such as a terraced elevation with an impressive staircase effect leading the residents straight to the water's edge.

The spacious oceanfront apartments include penthouses, duplexes and manors, from 300 to 1,500 square metres, with sundecks and private infinity swimming pools seemingly suspended in mid-air and extending to the ocean. The residences are built with the highest-quality materials imported from Europe and feature wine cellars, home theatres, walk-in closets and service quarters. The natural light-filled interior spaces boast incomparable design details while the floor-to-ceiling windows blur the line between interior and exterior.

LUXURIOUS: The refined property exudes residential charm and comfort, while integrating all the amenities that would be expected from a world-class resort. Residents enjoy services such as year-round concierge, 24-hour security, daily housekeeping, the Acqua Spa complete with a Jacuzzi and sauna, private gym, and a large outdoor infinity pool immersed in a private garden surrounded by a century-old pine forest.

With access to the trendy Acqua Beach Club, located just in front of the building, residents can relax in the sun in the comfort of their lounge chairs and umbrellas, or indulge in a seaside massage listening to the sounds of the crashing waves. A restaurant and bar provide guests with delicious gastronomical selections and refreshing drinks served at the beach club or delivered straight to their lounger.

Offering an ideal second-residence option, the exclusive Acqua development provides owners with the opportunity to just relax and be pampered or explore the picturesque surroundings and sophisticated lifestyle of Punta del Este.

CONTACT: www.acqua.com.uy
IMAGES: Jack Nozewnik and Roman Viñoly

" The refined property exudes residential charm and comfort, while integrating all the amenities that would be expected from a world-class resort

MODERN

COMMUNITIES

HALIFAX, NOVA SCOTIA, OFFERS A LEISURELY LIFESTYLE WITH AN ABUNDANCE OF POTENTIAL

Located on Canada's south-east coast and named after Scotland, Nova Scotia is almost entirely surrounded by water – resulting in a number of harbours and bays which provide the ideal location for water lovers to live, socialise and enjoy their surroundings. Nova Scotia is a province with a rocky coastline encompassing isolated sandy beaches and sheltered bays. As the region's largest populated county and economic centre, Halifax is an area that, according to real estate entrepreneur Francis Fares, has 'hardly felt the global economic crisis; there are plenty of government jobs, it has a stable banking sector and a lot of technology firms.'

Francis is also quick to point out the leisurely positives to Halifax: 'It is situated on the spectacular

> *With a complementary mix of boutiques, European-style grocers and pedestrian-friendly streets, the development is designed to create a welcoming, people-centred community*

Atlantic Ocean, the weather is warmer than many people perceive Canada's climate to be, and it's just a couple of hours from New York and only five hours from Europe. A lot of people are looking at this region as a place to move to; it offers a lot of potential.'

LIFESTYLE: Fares Inc, Francis' real estate company, is based in Halifax and its developments are situated in and around the region. 'With real estate it's all about location, location, location,' he says. 'Our challenge is to stay ahead of the game and ensure we are up-to-date with the latest trends.'

With 20 years' experience in the industry, Francis prides the company on the high-quality service it offers to customers, with agents in touch with clients on a daily basis, listening and responding to their needs. Foreign buyers are also given help with obtaining visas, and all clients are offered a consultation as part of their contract, which allows them input on the interior of their residence with a variety of choices of colours, tiles, cupboards, carpets and other fittings.

KINGS WHARF: With many developments situated in Halifax, Fares Inc's latest project has moved across the harbour to Dartmouth. The mixed-use development of Kings Wharf contains residential, commercial and retail spaces as well as an on-site hotel. The attractive and vibrant waterside location is well connected to walking and biking trails, and downtown Halifax is easily accessible via water taxi. With a complementary mix of boutiques, European-style grocers, parks and pedestrian-friendly streets, the development is designed to create a welcoming, people-centred community.

The design and construction of Kings Wharf has also been devised to be as environmentally friendly as possible. For example, cooling energy from the harbour-side location has been used to create geothermal heating. 'By focusing on green issues and sustainability, the buildings will run more efficiently and be more economical for those who live there,' adds Francis.

'The demographic that are most likely to be interested in investing in developments such as Kings Wharf, either for personal use or rentals,' he continues, 'are young professionals and what I call the "empty nesters".

'People who care about the environment or don't need/want a car and are happy to jump on the ferry, and those who are moving from big homes and don't want to worry about home maintenance or a garden – those two segments of the population are really our core clients.' ▣

CONTACT: www.faresinc.com; www.kingswharf.ca

Each mansion has its own European-trained butler, who ensures that proper etiquette and mansion protocol is maintained

FIRST-CLASS
LIVING

MANSION LIVING OFFERS A LIFESTYLE FIT FOR A KING

Luxury and prestige are the pillars of a new aristocratic-style living concept in sun-drenched Central Florida. Offering the opportunity to either lease or buy a grand mansion suite, Mansion Living© provides its residents with comfort, tranquillity and elegance.

'Traditionally, generations have moved into institutional-style dwellings to rid themselves of burdensome responsibilities and large house expenses; this is no longer necessary,' says the company's Director, Allan Meyer. 'Mansion Living gives them the chance to experience a care-free lifestyle, similar to that of nobility, without giving up living space or compromising their social status.'

PERSONAL: Mansion Living places a distinct emphasis on its white-glove service provided to residents. Each mansion has its own European-trained butler, who ensures that proper etiquette is displayed and mansion protocol is maintained. Residents can rest assured that the mansion's staff will anticipate and respond to every request in the highest standards possible. Alongside personal valets – who are professionals in holistic lifestyles – there is an elegant culinary service offering the finest in European cuisine and a distinct selection of private-label international wines. Spa appointments, using Mansions Living's own range of exclusive spa products, may be enjoyed at the Mansion Hotel or in residents' private suites. Car valet service is always available to arrange personal travel in one of the mansion's exclusive sedans, and the concierge can prepare

a personalised private yacht charter along the Atlantic, Caribbean or Gulf coasts. By getting to know residents, the mansion staff are able to provide an individualised service comparable with that for aristocracy. 'Personal valets cater exclusively to the resident, knowing exactly what they desire,' adds Allan. 'If someone has a specific dietary requirement, the chef will devise a menu accordingly.' A lifestyle of health, prosperity and longevity is Mansion Living's health criterion.

Although there are multiple suites, residents can be confident of privacy through pre-scheduling of mansion amenities. There is a high level of security to ensure the safety and privacy of each resident, and they are able to choose a private suite with multiple entrances and access to upper floors via an elevator. Mansion Living offers studio suites, spacious mansion wing suites and opulent penthouses for sale or for lease.

LOCATION: The Florida mansions are all situated on one development site, set in a forest reserve and surrounded by lush gardens, water features, courtyard enclaves and an expansive pond. Based on European models, each mansion has its own international architectural theme, and these are carried over to the interior and reflected in furnishings, artwork and even cuisine.

The mansions also offer more than just suites; each has a full complement of libraries, formal dining halls, games rooms, spas, theatres and galleries – and one even has its own ballroom. 'It's everything you would expect from a mansion,' says Allan, 'the

grand lobby, the striking winding staircases. Residents can purchase a variety of square footage of living space; however, there is a further 30,000 square feet of amenities available for private use.' The central location also makes it convenient for residents to enjoy the area's many restaurants, theatres and shopping.

INTERNATIONAL: In addition to the development in Florida, Allan is already working with planning departments across the USA and Canada to take the Mansion Living concept to other locations. Mansion residents can experience international living while enjoying the same prestigious surroundings and professional staff. With an expected influx of clients from across the globe, the immigration EB5 USCIS government-approved programme will allow Mansion Living's foreign investors and residents to receive a Green Card so that they and their families can permanently live in the USA. 'A World Bank statistic states that $400 billion is going to be spent annually by individuals who wish to experience life internationally; Mansion Living will give these world citizens a peaceful, luxurious and relaxing lifestyle,' says Allan. 'We have set precedents for luxury living, efficiency and for energy sustainability in our mansion designs.' Foreign clients and Mansion Living residents will have the opportunity to invest in other mansion locations for a return on investment, with the income property used to enhance residents' portfolios when they become part of Mansion Living's family of friends. ▣

CONTACT: www.mansionliving.com

NEW MARKET,
NEW VISION

With our intimate knowledge of the market... we can even structure a higher share for experienced developers and investors

MINH VIET INVESTMENT CORPORATION PROVIDES A REAL ESTATE OPPORTUNITY

Vision is the watchword at Minh Viet Investment Corporation (MVIC), an innovative company led by a group of dynamic Vietnamese Americans who are spearheading the next generation of real estate development in one of the world's most exciting, emerging markets.

Vietnam's young, well-educated citizens (the median age is 27.4 and the literacy rate is more than 90 per cent) are driving a burgeoning cash economy that has bounced back from global recession far quicker than many old-world economies. Property prices in Hanoi and Ho Chi Minh City are among the highest in the world.

Now looking ahead for far-sighted partners to share vibrant investment experiences, Danny Nguyen, MVIC's Chief Operating Officer, says: 'Our strength comes from partnerships. We're continuously looking for new ideas to develop with partners. And out of this creative fusion, we forge products that Vietnam has never seen before. That's what keeps us innovative.'

True to its word, innovation is at the heart of MVIC's $US195 million Tricon Towers development in Hanoi's prestigious, newly developing urban area, 'Splendora'. Scheduled for completion in the second quarter of 2012, Tricon Towers comprises three 44-storey lakeside towers offering 732 luxury apartments and associated high-end recreational facilities.

ICONIC: MVIC's most exciting project to date is the iconic Bay View Towers development in Ha Long Bay. Designated a UNESCO World Heritage site, Ha Long Bay's 120-kilometre coastline overlooks a unique scattering of 1,982 limestone islets formed 500 million years ago. Bay View's twin, 30-storey towers contain 518 luxury apartments offering unrivalled views of the bay's peerless seascape. Bay View Towers is also an environmentally friendly development, complying with the Singapore Government's internationally recognised BCA Green Mark.

In addition to its role as an international partner investor, MVIC also offers comprehensive real estate services to individuals or companies wishing to purchase single or multiple apartments.

The company's trailblazing approach to the Vietnamese property market is underpinned by its strategic partnership with Coldwell Banker, a 104-year-old international real estate brand with its roots in the United States. MVIC is the exclusive operator of the Coldwell Banker brand throughout Vietnam.

PROFESSIONALISM: Adhering to a strict code of conduct is central to the way MVIC does business, as Chairman and CEO, Edward Chi, who has 12 years' experience of Vietnam's property market, explains: 'Our goal is to act as the trusted bridge to Vietnam's real estate market, to be an entry partner with the professionalism and integrity that international investors can rely upon.

'Offering potential investors a transparent route to Vietnam's exciting investment opportunities, is key,' continues Danny. 'We take the risk upfront, and with our intimate knowledge of the market, we can transparently negotiate land purchases and obtain development permits. It is after this that an investor can jump in as a partner. We can even structure a higher share for experienced developers and investors, in order to retain control of the project.'

With around 1,300 kilometres of prime coastline, Vietnam is full of promise. Other MVIC projects in the pipeline include development concepts for Cam Ranh Bay and Da Nang Beach, two of Vietnam's most highly prized coastal locations.

'I have a sense of real belonging here,' says Danny, who was born in Vietnam before being brought up in the United States. 'I look at the opportunities in Vietnam and I think: wow, what can we bring here?'

CONTACT: www.mvi.com.vn; www.thebayviewtowers.com; www.tricontowers.com

BEYOND
EXPECTATIONS

REDEFINING THE STANDARDS OF LUXURY LIVING AROUND THE WORLD, MORAVIA GROUP HAS BECOME SYNONYMOUS WITH PUSHING THE BOUNDARIES OF WHAT CAN BE ACHIEVED

You can tell a great deal about a company from its head office. In the case of the Moravia Group, their international headquarters are sited in Monte Carlo, one of the most prestigious and admired locations imaginable. From this glamorous base, Moravia Group has become a world leader in luxurious living, on land, sea and air.

ORIGINAL: From its inception almost 150 years ago, Moravia Group has been a pioneer, tirelessly pushing back the boundaries of what can be achieved. In the 1860s, this nascent organisation was at the forefront of the production and sale of anti-fouling paint for boats and ships. In the 1960s, the newly created Moravia Yachting company became a world-leader in developing the first superyachts, and today the renamed Moravia Group provides unparalleled solutions for yacht owners, from purchase and registration through to crew management and refitting. Alongside this, Moravia Group has also become synonymous with property and

*'Good is not good when better is expected'
recurs throughout Moravia Group literature,
reiterating the constant pursuit of perfection*

real estate in recent times, applying the same design and construction standards to homes on land as the Monte Carlo division invests in its bespoke superyachts.

Only the very best will do for discerning purchasers, which is why the phrase 'good is not good when better is expected' recurs throughout Moravia Group literature, reiterating a constant pursuit of perfection. The finest minds and materials are employed to continually surpass the expectations of discerning and demanding clients. In the real estate sector, this involves constructing exceptional homes in unique locations. Similar priorities apply on the water, with Moravia Monte Carlo now offering a global service, from Miami to Moscow.

PERSONALISED: Moravia Lab is a division of the eponymous parent organisation, with responsibility for creating living environments that satisfy the requirements of even the most discerning and selective customers. With extensive experience of working within space or design constraints, Moravia Lab can provide everything from a particular piece of artwork to a complete interior design service for residential properties, yachts or even private aircraft.

Moravia Lab can also do the same in the field of architecture – constantly pushing the envelope of design and construction and setting new industry standards in the process. Even when clients have moved into their bespoke home, for example, a fully integrated development management service is on hand, providing complete turnkey solutions to the demands of modern living, from housekeeping to pool maintenance. For yacht customers, the company organises everything from worldwide service and management through to a full interior personalisation programme, completed to exquisite standards and providing a lifetime's comfort and pleasure. A dedicated yacht management division prides itself on offering clients 'only the pleasure' of yacht ownership, while new craft can be designed and specified to suit the specific demands of their future owners. Older yachts, meanwhile, are purchased and sold through a world-leading brokerage division.

Moravia Group works alongside its clients at every step, even offering help with areas such as financing, tax, family office and other financial matters. The aim of this meticulous planning is to create completely bespoke possessions, tailored to the precise requirements and preferences of each individual owner. An illustrious roster of delighted former clients bears testament to how successfully Moravia Group and its specialised sub-divisions achieve this over arching aim – creating true luxury to meet the needs of the individual. ▣

CONTACT: www.moraviagroup.com

MYTHOLOGY COMES TO
LIFE

LIVING 'GREEK STYLE' IS RELAXED AND STRESS FREE – NAUTILUS
PROPERTY REAL ESTATE HELPS YOU MAKE THAT TRANSITION
TO AN EASIER LIFE

G reece is gifted with great natural beauty. It is a country that satisfies the senses through all seasons. A vast number of islands, thousands of kilometres of sandy coastline, emerald waters, mountains and rivers help collectively to paint a magnificent picture of this Mediterranean paradise.

Now, more than ever, due to the drastic price reductions of quality property, Greece has become attractive to overseas buyers who seek an idyllic seaside home or a profitable investment project. Nautilus Property helps people to live their dreams and offers only the highest-quality houses on selected coastal and island areas of the country, especially in Halkidiki.

'We have a portfolio of the best and most unique properties,' says Calliope Gougoussi, a director at Nautilus, 'which are not your average town or country houses, but ones with special qualities, traditional

or modern architecture. If the properties don't measure up to a high standard, they are not for us.'

TRUST: While Greek laws regarding real estate agents are rather loosely defined, Nautilus follows very strict rules that it sets itself. 'We are completely transparent and don't treat clients like sheep, driving them around showing them property after property just to try and get a sale,' says Calliope. 'We treat them as friends and come to understand them, their requirements, their situation and their personality – maybe they're a musician; maybe its someone who likes the arts – all these things make a difference in finding the right place.

'Because of our experience and understanding of the market, 95 per cent of the time we show clients properties that they truly wish for, and many new clients come through referrals. 'Additionally, when clients' express interest in a house we try to offer them the chance to stay in it for a couple of days to get a feel for it – the chance to wake up in the villa and experience it first hand. When the correct match between property and client is made, it's like the perfect marriage.'

LOCATION: The high standard that Nautilus offers is demonstrated by a spectacular Cycladic-style estate situated in Kasandra, Halkidiki.

This grand, white villa on a flat, sun-drenched cape was inspired from the simplicity of the traditional Greek island Cycladic style. Open-plan galleries and archways create the perfect conditions for the hot Mediterranean summers and add to the creation of an atmosphere of tranquillity and relaxation. The famous architect Santiago Calatrava once stayed here to study its form.

Another property on Mykonos, an island that needs no introduction, is undoubtedly one of the finest jewels of the Mediterranean. Located on one of the most highly sought after and desirable parts of the island, its view of the sunset over Delos, the most sacred of the ancient Greek isles, is uniquely spectacular.

As well as sourcing the right property, Nautilus also provides an extensive after-sales service. 'We can assist you with renovation, finding someone to look after the garden, clean or maintain the house – anything you can imagine, we can take care of,' enthuses Calliope. 'Only when the clients have everything they want and need are we truly satisfied.' ▣

CONTACT: www.nautilusproperty.com

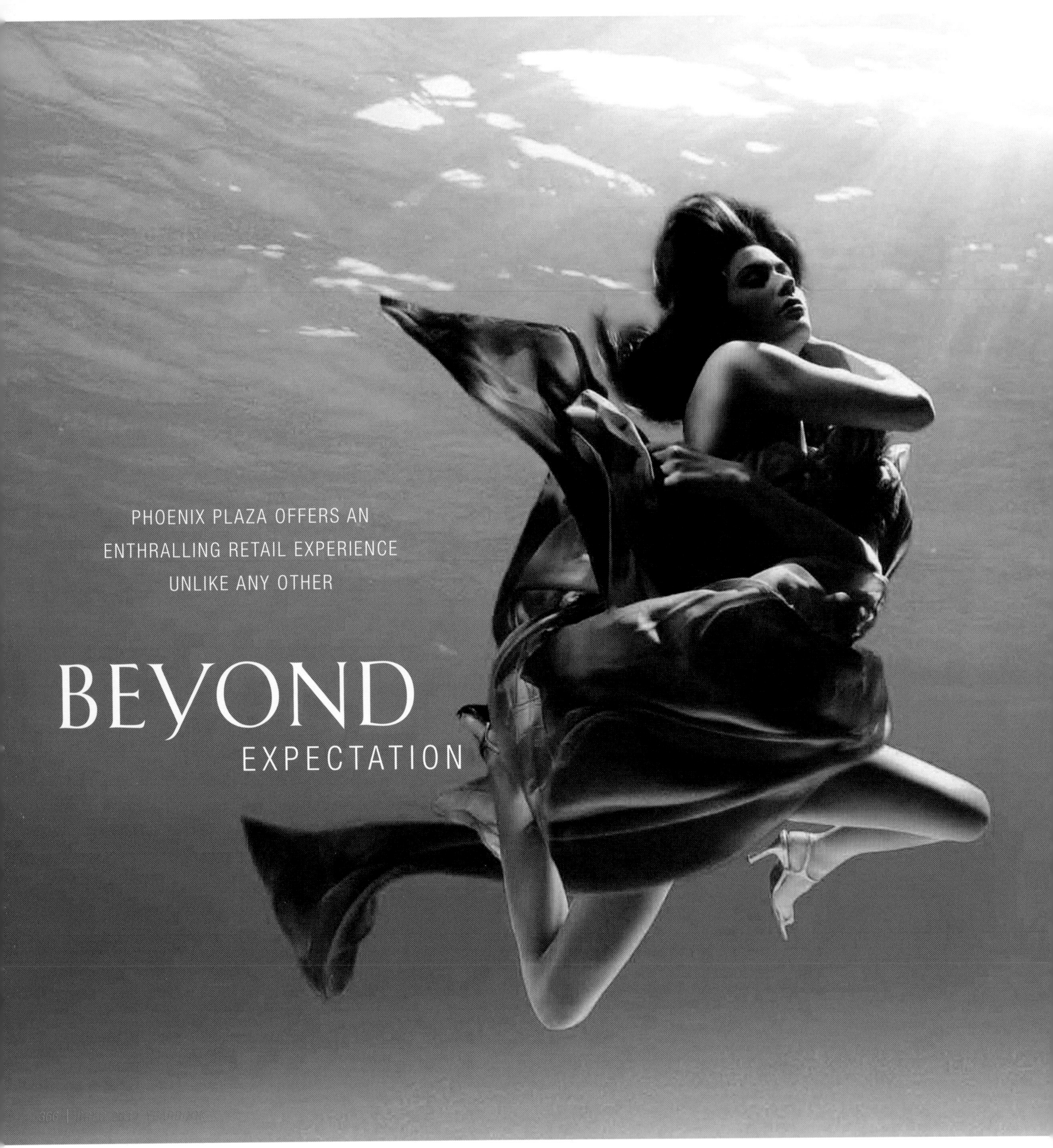

PHOENIX PLAZA OFFERS AN
ENTHRALLING RETAIL EXPERIENCE
UNLIKE ANY OTHER

BEYOND
EXPECTATION

> *While the mix of retailers inside Phoenix Plaza initially draws customers in, the additional leisure facilities and attractions on offer will make it an unforgettable experience*

Modern retail centres have evolved to offer more than just shopping; they are inviting and exciting entertainment venues where visitors can dine in a number of restaurants, pamper themselves at spas and salons, or watch the latest blockbusters.

DESTINATION: In Zagreb, the capital of Croatia, there is a complex that will fulfil all of these desires and more – Phoenix Plaza. Due to open in Autumn 2011, Phoenix Plaza enjoys a great location in the eastern part of Zagreb, within walking distance of the city centre and close to major road, rail and air connections.

The 100,000-square-metre, supra-regional shopping, tourist and leisure destination will offer visitors a vast range of exciting opportunities and activities, including 130 shops and boutiques encompassing fashion, beauty, sports and electronics, as well as cafés, bars, restaurants, nine state-of-the-art multiplex cinemas, bowling, and a tropical aquarium and oceanarium.

STIMULATING: While the mix of retailers inside Phoenix Plaza initially draws customers in, the additional leisure facilities and attractions on offer will make it an unforgettable experience. The centrepiece of the development is Europe's largest tropical aquarium, containing 1,900 cubic metres of sea water and more than 80 species of tropical fish, including sharks. Taking inspiration from the breathtaking aquariums in the Dubai Mall and the luxurious Atlantis Hotel, also in Dubai, Phoenix Plaza's aquarium will be a magnet to tourists in Zagreb. It is complemented by an oceanarium featuring a lecture room, educational centre and interactive museum, which will prove fascinating to those who wish to learn more about life under the sea.

When visitors to Phoenix Plaza wish to take a break from shopping, its Open Green terrace, designed as a relaxation zone, allows them to rest and enjoy a coffee, while the cinema, entertainment and pop lounge – boasting computer games, 3D and virtual technologies, and many modern gadgets – can provide hours of fun.

PURPOSE: Designed by renowned Croatian architectural studio, Ćurković&Zidarić, and London-based retail specialist, Chapman Taylor, the focus for Phoenix Plaza is on sustainability. Natural materials such as stone, brick and wood are complemented by sophisticated technology, and the exterior combines brick and glass to form shapes that are inspired by a unique aspect of Croatian cultural heritage – lace made on the island of Hvar.

The development will also be environmentally friendly, and therefore ensure low business costs for tenants, using an advanced air-conditioning system that lowers typical energy consumption levels by 71 per cent. This has seen it awarded a GreenBuilding Certificate and the highest certificate for energy efficiency.

It has also received further accolades, such as the Best Retail Development at the European Commercial Property Awards; and in March 2009 Phoenix Plaza, and the surrounding Phoenix Park area, was recognised by property professionals MIPIM as one of six mixed-use projects in Europe with the highest potential.

With plans for Phoenix Plaza's neighbouring area to include a gallery, hotel, kindergarten and even a church, the development will be at the heart of the local community and an appealing must-see for all visitors to Zagreb. ▣

CONTACT: www.phoenixplaza.com.hr

MORE THAN
SHOPPING

Property developer Prime Development has a very special focus on city development – in particular a huge passion for shopping centres. The retail sector plays a particular role in the way cities provide specific and specialised development opportunities for modern living spaces where working, living, leisure, culture and trade come together in a modern marketplace. On the one hand it is historically at the heart of the economy, and on the other it offers a meeting and communication point, while it can also provide a one-stop attraction for an entire region. 'Prime Development works as an intermediary between the city, citizens and investors,' says Philipp Von Wilmowsky, CEO of Prime Development. 'We can empathise with the people and acquire the solutions that bring the best benefits for all. We are the bridge between the old and the modern.'

EFFECTIVE: The planning and preparation behind Prime Mall Antakya in Turkey, which is scheduled to open in 2011, is an excellent illustration of Prime Development's expertise in developing shopping centres down to the last minute detail. The company's reputation is built on that attention to detail in every area of its property development, which covers all aspects of the services involved in getting such projects completed on time and within budget.

THIS STUNNING DEVELOPMENT PRESENTS ALL
THE BENEFITS OF MODERN LIVING WHILE KEEPING
THE BEST TRADITIONS OF THE PAST ALIVE

Architecture, centre management, leasing, construction management and development are all elements which need to work effectively together, and specialised project management facilitates that interaction. Prime Development's team also has the skills and experience required for the most cost-effective handling of operating expenses, and the contacts needed to ensure easy access to the network of service providers required throughout all stages of the project.

INTEGRATED: Prime Development addresses the particular challenges and complexities of modern urban living, planning the required urban spaces and design. An integrated management approach is applied to every need, including constant supervision of all phases as well as effective management. The company has a skilled and experienced team of architects, developers and marketing experts for shopping centres and retail, with more than 15 years of experience delivering solutions across Europe developing commercial buildings that blend in gently with existing civic content.

SIGNIFICANT: Antakya is one of the oldest cities in the world, with significant cultural treasures from early Christianity. Approximately 1.7 million people live within one and a half hours' travelling distance from the city. With the facilitation of visa procedures between Syria and Turkey, the city has seen a dramatic increase in the number of visitors and it serves as a significant intersection between the international commerce routes that reach beyond the borders of Turkey into the Middle East and the Mediterranean. The development of Prime Mall Antakya is designed in a way that will integrate modern architecture with the authentic elements of the local culture and create value in a newly developing area of the city. Retail will be more a pleasure than a need, enhanced by activities that make it more like a lifestyle centre with excellent parking, a multiplex cinema, children's play area, food court, restaurants, cafés and bistros.

The shopping itself will have a European flavour, with international brands and local retailers alike showcasing a new, modern lifestyle. 'It will be an exceptional place to visit,' says Philipp. 'As well as the shopping experience there will be wonderful architecture, beautiful surroundings and an exciting range of leisure activities. But the traditions of the past will still resonate with people coming together in something which is not just a shopping centre, but the heart of the community.' ▣

CONTACT: www.pd-global.com

BUILDING
EXCELLENCE

R. W. ARMSTRONG & SONS BOASTS UNRIVALLED EXPERIENCE IN THE LUXURY BUILDING INDUSTRY

The well-known phrase, 'an Englishman's home is his castle', accurately describes the approach R. W. Armstrong & Sons takes towards its work. This traditional building company specialises in the renovation, extension or new build of prestigious period and country homes. With the majority of these homes worth many millions of pounds, undoubtedly owners only want the best for their 'castle' and they will find this with R. W. Armstrong.

Established more than 50 years ago in 1957, this family-run business has built an enviable reputation. Based in Hampshire, R. W. Armstrong also caters for the surrounding areas of Surrey, Berkshire, Wiltshire, Sussex and south-west London, working on properties that can include family homes, gothic mansions, medieval buildings, country manors and contemporary townhouses. 'The company is now run by the third generation of the family – with the fourth generation waiting in the wings – and this, alongside our experience in the industry, shows stability,' says Chairman, Nigel Armstrong. 'During this time, I think we have also experienced every conceivable

"

R.W. Armstrong encourages its talented craftspeople to take up further training

building and design specification, as well as any problems that could possibly arise.'

EXPERTISE: The family ethos is very strong throughout the business, with a large number of employees committing to the company for the whole of their careers – some from when they first join as apprentices until they retire and several following their fathers and grandfathers into the business. Since 1957, R. W. Armstrong has taken on a number of trainees each year, who gain expertise in carpentry, decorating, bricklaying, plastering and joinery.

R. W. Armstrong encourages its talented craftspeople to take up further training, which can see them develop from skilled tradesmen to qualified site and contract managers, leading to the company being awarded Investors in People status.

CONNECTION: When handling a project, R. W. Armstrong works closely with the client as well as architects, interior designers and landscape gardeners to ensure all work is carried out to the highest standard. 'The service is personalised and a dedicated manager is on site, overseeing the project the whole time,' explains Nigel. 'We have also built up long-term relationships within the industry, such as specialist sub-contractors and suppliers.' This comprehensive service also includes extensive joinery workshop facilities, owned by R. W. Armstrong, which manufactures purpose-made joinery for all of its projects.

TRADITIONAL: As well as private houses, the company works on historic structures and listed buildings, such as churches and monuments. 'Development on listed buildings has to be done sympathetically and in keeping with the style, but they can be extended,' says Nigel. 'Our tradesmen are highly skilled in traditional building methods and materials, such as lime-hair plaster, flint work and lead work. However, we are increasingly coming across more sustainable techniques in modern builds.'

R. W. Armstrong recently acquired E A Chiverton of Chichester which, similarly, has a long family history and ethos. 'We expand organically – if opportunities come along, we embrace them,' adds Nigel. 'We have a reputation for producing a high-quality product, being reliable and providing a professional service; to ensure this we need to have the experience, staff and resources – which we do.

'Clients come to us knowing that they will receive the best service and a superior product. Every job we take on is carried out in order to enhance our reputation.' □

CONTACT: www.rwarmstrong.co.uk; www.eachiverton.co.uk

COMFORT AND
Luxury

CREATED BY TEAK S.A., THESEUS BEACH VILLAGE IN CRETE OFFERS THE MOST LUXURIOUS SEASIDE PROPERTIES IN GREECE

With its stunning 1000 kilometre-long Mediterranean coastline, Crete is the largest of the Greek islands, and Theseus Beach Village is located near Heraklion, the island's capital, on the sun-drenched north coast. When finished, this self-contained international-standard development will boast an incredible array of top-class facilities, including two Olympic-size swimming pools, three floodlit tennis courts and round-the-clock security.

350 properties of varying sizes and designs will be grouped together into a series of neighbourhoods, each with its own distinct architectural style. Blending seamlessly into the natural environment, these neighbourhoods have been cleverly designed to protect the privacy of residents while also delivering panoramic sea views.

A stone's throw from a multitude of soft, sandy beaches, secluded coves and spectacular peninsulas, the project also includes a small commercial centre and all of the dwellings are equipped with the fastest Internet connection available.

To date, 97 of the housing units have been completed, one of the swimming pools and two of the tennis courts are operational, and the beach beckons enthusiastic sun-worshippers. Teak S.A.'s aim is to allow prospective buyers to view a completed section of the development before making any commitments. Site visits can be arranged to verify the nature and quality of the work that is under way in accordance with the plans.

INSPIRED: Named after the legendary hero of Greek mythology, Theseus Beach Village is a comprehensive real estate development. It offers high-spec properties for sale, either for permanent residences or for use as holiday homes. The project is not mortgaged and is free of any loans and other impediments.

While the site's total area is 165,000 square metres, actual construction will cover only 40,000 square metres, with the remaining 75 per cent reserved for private and common green areas, roads and walkways.

The area immediately to the west of Heraklion is blessed with eye-catching slopes stretching down to a beautiful beach. Teak S.A. has engaged landscape architects who have produced plans to further enhance this amazing environment.

DETAILS: The plans include: Creating 80,000 square metres of common green areas; transplanting 2,000 trees both within the development and along its boundaries; creating water features, paths, bridges and gazebos – complete with custom-designed lighting; two treatment plants for recycling wastewater for the purpose of irrigating the common green areas; special development of the 200m beachfront pertaining to the site; underground utility lines; a children's playground, resting areas and sports grounds in specially designated areas. This self-contained high-end development is fully fenced, with access through a controlled, permanently guarded gate. A maintenance crew ensures the best possible after sales service.

The Theseus Beach Village resort offers well-designed high-quality properties ranging from apartments to luxury villas, all offering breathtaking views. Inviting interest from Rolls-Royce Enthusiasts' Club members, Teak S.A. promises a land of comfort and luxury, guided by quality of life. ▣

CONTACT: www.theseusbv.com

THE NEW FACE OF
BUDAPEST

AN ENTIRELY NEW CITY CENTRE IS BEING CREATED ON THE
WESTERN FRINGE OF BUDAPEST, FORMING ONE OF EUROPE'S MOST
SIGNIFICANT CONSTRUCTION PROJECTS FOR GENERATIONS

In recent times, Budapest has experienced a renaissance unmatched by almost any other European city. Divided into two by the Danube, the Hungarian capital's unique blend of historic architecture and modern investment has transformed it into a leading international city admired by businesses, investors and residents alike. Into the heart of this vibrant setting comes one of the most ambitious new developments ever seen in the construction and property markets. Covering an area roughly the same size as the principality of Monaco, this brand new 'city within a city' has an estimated construction cost of €2.4 billion, with a projected end value of double that figure.

POTENTIAL: TóPARK will stand at the western gateway to Budapest, at the intersection of three motorways and beside the suburban railway network. It is situated in the heart of the Budapest Business Region – a burgeoning region that is developing at an accelerated pace, with exceptional economic potential for investors. Centred on a 37-hectare lake

The whole district is supplied purely by renewable energy within the next 20 years

surrounded by landscaped parks, the scale of the TóPARK project is quite staggering. For example, a 1.5-kilometre tiled pathway has been constructed for the €400 million office park that will occupy 92,000 square metres and form a cornerstone of the first phase of development. Around 18,000 square metres of retail area will be created at the same time, alongside 150 leased apartments for those foresighted enough to become pioneers in this unprecedented project.

With an estimated completion date of 2020, these plans comprise just the first phase of TóPARK. Future additions will include Hungary's largest shopping and entertainment centre, additional office buildings and further swathes of upmarket apartments aimed at professionals and families alike. An indoor and outdoor sports complex will complement the longest covered pedestrian street anywhere in Europe, alongside an exhibition space and an education/events centre. With such an illustrious master plan, it's perhaps unsurprising that TóPARK was voted the 'best real estate project in the world' at the 2009 CNBC Arabiya International Property Awards – the Oscars of the real estate industry.

STYLISH: TóPARK has been designed to meet all the future needs of Hungary's business, retail and residential markets, but architecturally it draws inspiration from the past. Office buildings evoke the heydays of leading cities like London, Rome and Paris, blending disparate elements such as Art Deco and neo-classical design together. Meanwhile, an array of leading interior designers has handled everything behind those elegant façades, inspired

by the world's top fashion brands. The covered retail street will also feature designer labels and stores, making it one of Central Europe's finest shopping destinations, and this recurring theme of exclusivity suggests that comparisons to Monaco extend far beyond mere geographical similarities.

Every conceivable element has been carefully scrutinised, right down to the environmental impact of this new hub – extensive landscaping features alongside CO_2-reduction technologies, the use of renewable energy sources and selective waste collection. With thousands of car parking spaces, an integrated transport hub for buses and trains will encourage the new district's 40,000 workers and residents not to drive into TóPARK, while international travellers will have minimal transfers from three major airports. One notable long-term aim is to ensure the whole district is supplied purely by renewable energy within the next 20 years.

The driving force behind TóPARK is Walker and Williams Investment Group S.A. Luxembourg. This privately owned real estate investment specialist has made its name in urban projects exceeding €1 billion in value. As such, it is perfectly placed to offer investors at every level the opportunity to be part of one of Central Europe's most exciting and significant investment opportunities at TóPARK. ◙

CONTACT: www.topark.eu

INVESTING IN
LUXURY

Occupying a prime position on the Spanish coast, the Costa del Sol is a draw for millions of people across the world. The Andalucian hotspot boasts in the region of 325 days of sunshine a year, hosts an impressive 50 golf courses, and is home to six world heritage sites, as well as a large variety of shops, restaurants and leisure activities.

SETTING: In the heart of the Costa del Sol is the exclusive development known as Tropical Hill. This peaceful and relaxing complex consists of just 34 houses, each individually designed by award-winning architect, Melvin Villarroel. 'Tropical Hill is like a little oasis in the middle of the Costa del Sol,' explains Director, Arantxa Pérez. 'It's somewhere people can relax but they have the vibrancy of the resort on their doorstep, where they have the choice of many different activities.'

Tropical Hill is located atop a hill in Mijas Costa, moments away from the marinas, shopping and nightlife of Fuengirola and Marbella, and close to Malaga's international airport and train connections. Its position ensures breathtaking views of the surrounding area, taking in the Spanish countryside, the Sierra Blanca mountain range and the Mediterranean Sea.

EXTRAVAGANCE: The development has been designed so that every property can make the most of these views, as well as the space and light. 'The townhouses are in little blocks of four or five, but each one is positioned at an angle that will maximise its surroundings,' adds Arantxa. The two- or four-bedroom houses are built to the highest specifications, using natural materials. A solarium on the top floor features a pergola, Jacuzzi and barbecue, where residents can relax or entertain guests, while the rest of the four-storey homes are spacious, have whirlpool baths, terraces with automatic watering systems, state-of-the-art appliances and private parking. 'Each house also has what we refer to as a "multifunctional" area in the basement,' explains Arantxa, 'and the owner can decide what it will be used for – whether that's a home cinema, gym, playroom or simply an extra bedroom.'

The houses are surrounded by lush tropical gardens, abundant with tall palm trees and fragrant, colourful plants and flowers. Residents only need to step just outside their front door to take advantage of Tropical Hill's large swimming pool, which has the added bonus of a waterfall, and summer bar, as well as a communal fitness room and sauna.

VISION: Tropical Hill's emphasis on combining luxury with natural features is due to its architect, whose input, explains Arantxa, 'is one of the most important aspects of our development. He has a particular vision in the way that he integrates architecture with nature – the way he uses light, space and plants is very interesting. He is also able to take a traditional Spanish design and modernise it.'

With phase one of the development completed and a second phase of 33 homes due to begin construction shortly, Tropical Hill is ready to be a home or holiday getaway for many families. 'It's a good option for investors because it's very unique,' says Arantxa. 'Residents have everything within their reach, and the location and climate are outstanding – it's a very beautiful and easy place to live.' ▣

CONTACT: www.tropicalhill.es

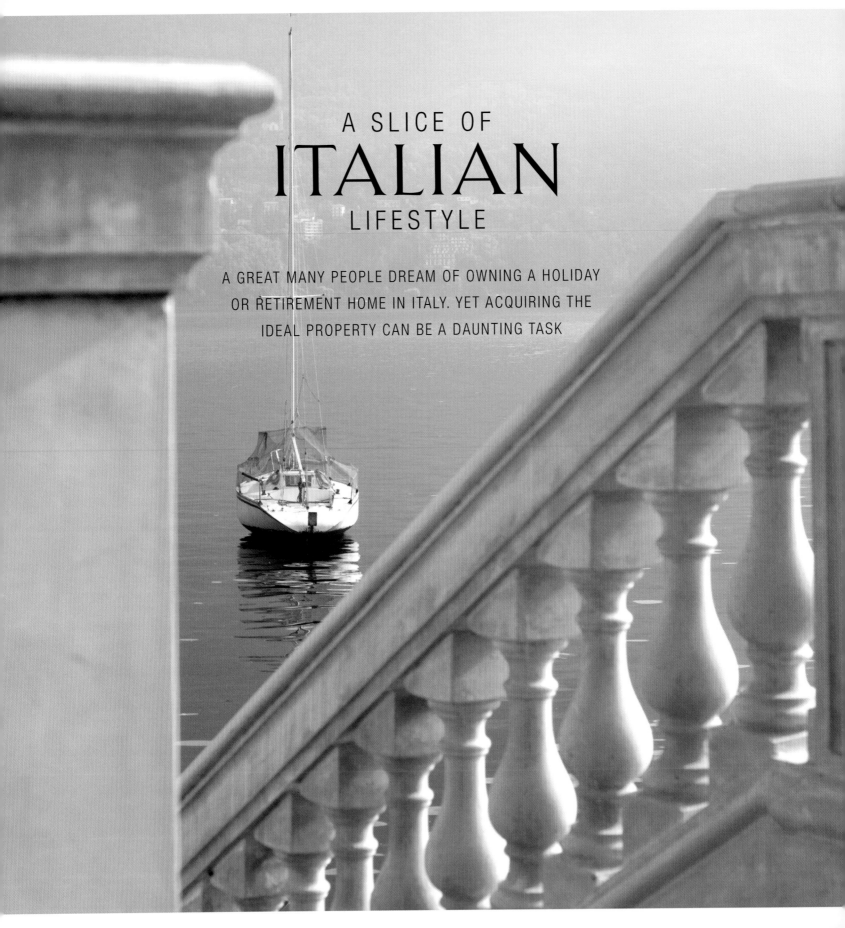

A SLICE OF
ITALIAN
LIFESTYLE

A GREAT MANY PEOPLE DREAM OF OWNING A HOLIDAY
OR RETIREMENT HOME IN ITALY. YET ACQUIRING THE
IDEAL PROPERTY CAN BE A DAUNTING TASK

At Ultissimo we begin by finding out how people want to live and translate that into a specification for their home

Defined by its breathtaking landscapes, plentiful sunshine, welcoming people and outdoor lifestyle, Italy has a fantastic amount to offer its homeowners. But for many property seekers based abroad, finding and buying a home in Italy is a notoriously slow and confusing process. 'There are many potential obstacles to owning a home in Italy, and would-be buyers are often deterred by geographic, linguistic, cultural or bureaucratic factors,' explains Paul Belcher, founder and Managing Director of Ultissimo. "I'm told there are something like 180,000 laws in Italy compared with only 15,000 in Britain, for instance. But anyone wanting a dream home in Italy can rely on Ultissimo to provide the solution.'

Ultissimo is an award-winning developer of Italian properties for the international market, focusing primarily on Lake Como and central Italy, Umbria, Tuscany and Le Marche. Founded in 2006 when Paul, a former management consultant, acquired a collection of derelict Italian farm houses for restoration, Ultissimo set out to fill a gap in the market for restorations and new-builds. 'We were not interested in large apartment developments,' Paul clarifies. 'We were interested in individual character properties and small communities consisting of no more than eight properties.' And the gap was not just in the quality of property: 'There was also a need for a truly client-centric service for finding and buying a property in Italy, and offering support to the owner afterwards, whether that be in terms of maintenance, rental management, repairs or stocking the fridge before the owner's arrival. The concept is simple: your home in Italy should be a pleasure; it should never be a burden or worry.'

KNOWLEDGE: With an architect for a father and a property investor for a mother, Paul acquired an appreciation for property during his formative years; and this, together with his experience as an internationally active management consultant, has been integral to the ongoing success of Ultissimo. 'I've always been driven by an ethos of client satisfaction, and I've enjoyed working across cultures and territories,' says Paul. 'So Ultissimo really provided the ideal opportunity to use existing passions and skills to take on a great challenge – the challenge of delivering someone's dream home.'

And that challenge begins right at the first consultation. 'Consulting with clients on a dream home can be complicated as there's often a difference between what they think they want and what actually suits them,' Paul explains. 'It's not uncommon for an English client to initially request a south-facing property for maximum sunlight, not realising what this means at the height of the Italian summer. It's also not uncommon for a client to request a property in a particular village without realising how busy, or how quiet, that village is at different times in the year. So at Ultissimo we begin by finding out how people want to live and translate that into a specification for their home.'

EXCLUSIVE: Since 2008, Ultissimo has found itself increasingly focused on Lake Como, a major international destination renowned for its many celebrity homeowners, including George Clooney. 'Lake Como is a spectacular location, with simply unbelievable properties,' says Paul. 'We're currently renovating the last unrestored Liberty Villa on Lake Como with a view from 600 metres above the water. In fact we were receiving so many enquiries for homes on the lake that we developed a tailored search service. With our extensive local knowledge and contacts, we find the perfect homes for our clients; many of the finest properties never reach the public market. Our clients tell us time and again how easy we have made the acquisition of a slice of perfect Italian lifestyle.' ▣

CONTACT: www.ultissimo.com

THE PERFECT INVESTMENT

A SPECTACULAR PROMONTORY ON A SOPHISTICATED ISLAND PARADISE PROVIDES SMART
INVESTORS WITH THE CHANCE TO OWN SOMETHING TRULY SPECIAL

Though inhabited since the fifth millennium BC, the endorsement of Aristotle and Jackie Onassis and friends in the 1960s first propelled Mykonos to the status it holds today as one of Greece's (and the world's) most desirable locations. It offers elegant partying, gourmet dining, high-end shopping, plus relaxation, sun, beautiful beaches and more.

Despite its reputation as a hedonistic paradise, with some of the best clubs and bars in Europe, and the ability to attract world-famous entertainers, Mykonos is about more than just nightlife. It is considered one of Greece's most cosmopolitan islands and can boast more than 300 days of sunshine each year. The island has an alluring combination of a city centre with its charming old Chora atmosphere (Mykonos Town), and the natural beauty of crystal-clear water and sandy beaches. »

> A 25-acre promontory has become home for Villas Amrit, a new development of beautiful villas whose unique location is protected by Greek law as a place of exceptional natural beauty

BEAUTY: Positioned between the pristine beaches of Fokos and Myrsini, a 25-acre promontory has become home for Villas Amrit, a new development of beautiful villas whose unique location is protected by Greek law as a place of exceptional natural beauty, lying as it does in peaceful seclusion on the less-inhabited end of the island.

The privacy and serenity of the area is safeguarded against future building, a welcome and unusual aspect that translates into an ongoing increase in value at the highest level. The headland cradling Villas Amrit is elevated directly above the cerulean Aegean Sea with two golden beaches on either side – one with a small, quaint Greek taverna serving high-quality, traditional food, in season.

The villas follow the traditional architectural style that is seen throughout the rest of the island: white, softly rounded houses built over two floors with arches and curves, plus spacious basement levels for entertainment, spas and workout facilities. Every villa is individually developed by an international designer with exquisite attention to detail, and superbly done. Verdant foliage complements each building, with landscaping on the promontory merging into the natural flora.

Built using the best-quality materials and the finest appliances, the villas have between five and seven bedrooms with en-suite facilities, wet bars and many amenities – all master bedrooms contain fireplaces. These villas are completed at a rare level of excellence, not seen before, and are truly exceptional. Features include heated, non-chlorine, ionised private pools (many of which are infinity pools), saunas, steam baths, hot tubs, gyms and recreational areas. Personal roof terraces, verandas and balconies provide breathtaking views of the sea, while built-in outdoor kitchen facilities and barbecues – consisting of two complete kitchens and barbeques, one facing the sea, the other tucked away facing the mountains – equip the properties perfectly for full entertaining.

Villas Amrit places an emphasis on meeting its clients' needs: each villa has an automatic booster to ensure constant and strong water pressure, generators are in place in case of power cuts and provisions have been made to have green, alternative energy sources fitted. For when it may become slightly chillier, the villas have under-floor heating for extra comfort and all windows are double-glazed.

RELAXATION: On-site property management options include security, maintenance, concierge services and rental arrangements, if desired. Villas of this calibre on Mykonos, with such superb amenities, can attract €10,000, or more, per day in rental income (Mykonos enjoys high occupancy rates).

The island of Mykonos is sophisticated yet utterly unpretentious – attracting celebrities, *bon vivants*, the avant garde and many others. Away from this excitement, on the other side of the island, via a short drive and permanently protected, lies Villas Amrit, the jewel of the Aegean. ▣

CONTACT: +30 6989 80 2120

Mykonos is considered one of Greece's most cosmopolitan islands and can boast more than 300 days of sunshine each year

IDYLLIC
ALPINE
ESCAPES

The legendary Four Valleys region of Switzerland has long been acclaimed as one of the world's most beautiful settings, adored by winter sports enthusiasts and offering people the chance to truly escape from their busy lifestyles. Resorts located within the region include Verbier, Nendaz and Thyon-Les Collons, which is at the region's heart, just 20 minutes from Sion international airport, and a true Alpine venue with exceptional views of the Matterhorn and the Swiss Alps.

Just below Thyon-Les Collons lies Village des 4 Vallées, a remarkable and innovative development by V4V. Drawing inspiration from the silence of its surroundings, this collection of 12 opulent mountain residences is being constructed in three distinct stages at an altitude of 1,575 metres. The first properties to be built here measured around 200 square metres internally, incorporating four bedrooms, three bathrooms, a large kitchen and a vast open-space living room with a fireplace. With patios and lawns outside, the elaborate frontages of these sophisticated family homes create a striking contrast against the raw beauty of their surroundings. It's well worth taking a moment to admire the randomised stonework and diminutive matching chimneys, with pagoda-style eaves suspended above intricately sculpted timber balconies that wrap right around each property.

The elaborate frontages of these sophisticated family homes create a striking contrast against the raw beauty of their surroundings

BESPOKE CHALET VILLAS ARE BEING CONSTRUCTED IN AN IDYLLIC LOCATION WITHIN THE SWISS ALPS, CREATING LUXURIOUS HOMES IN AWE-INSPIRING SURROUNDINGS

PERSONALISED: The degree of personalisation available with a V4V chalet is such that the client can modify everything from its interior design to the layout, to suit their personal tastes or requirements. Some features are universal, however, such as stunning views over the Matterhorn and Dent Blanche. Jacuzzi baths and fully integral parking spaces have been engineered into each traditionally constructed property, with landscaped gardens offering barbecues and fountains among their various decorations. Environmental matters have also been at the heart of the V4V design philosophy – every property is energy-saving thanks to features such as thick stone walls and geothermal heating, while a further touch of luxury comes courtesy of a full security and maintenance service, handled by on-site staff.

VARIETY: Other amenities on the doorstep of Village des 4 Vallées include thriving restaurants, bars, shops and a new spa, underlining this region's popularity at any time of year. In summer, tranquil days and cool nights provide ideal conditions for outdoor activities, from walking and mountain biking through to paragliding, mountaineering and golf. The medieval town of Sion and its castles collectively boast a wealth of heritage, while the artificial lake at Grande Dixence and the Pyramids of Euseigne draw in tourists from around the world. In colder seasons, this area truly comes alive as one of Europe's largest winter sports areas, offering 400 kilometres of pistes and more than 90 ski lifts linking the resorts of Thyon-Les Collons, Verbier, Nendaz and Veysonnaz. With two cross-country skiing tracks in the local vicinity, the winter sports season extends between late November and mid-April, with artificial snow readily available to counteract any mild weather.

The brooding Alpine backdrop will provide a sufficient incentive for many people to consider purchasing a property at Village des 4 Vallées, especially when fresh snow glistens under flawlessly blue skies. Alongside the chalets, constructible land is also for sale, ranging from 1,000 to 14,000 square metres in plot size and offering the opportunity to construct something completely bespoke. However, there are also pragmatic reasons for investing in this region, with the absence of inheritance taxes one of several fiscal advantages that result from choosing to domicile here. Village des 4 Vallées is that most unusual of phenomena – an investment opportunity that appeals equally to the head and the heart. ▣

CONTACT: www.v4v.ch

GROOMING

7 » *Tailoring & Men's Grooming*

7» GROOMING

66

*The name 'Aramis' derives from an
exotic Turkish root used in folklore
as a stimulant and aphrodisiac*

aramis

EAU DE TOILETTE
NATURAL SPRAY

VAPORISATEUR

A
GENTLEMAN'S
BLEND

THE DEFINITIVE LUXURY MALE FRAGRANCE, ARAMIS IS THE PERFECT
BLEND OF SOPHISTICATION AND SEDUCTION

As the American physician, poet and Harvard professor, Oliver Wendell Holmes, mused: 'Imagination, sentiments and associations are more readily reached through the sense of smell than through any other channel.' It was this philosophy that brought Aramis into being as the first men's fragrance and grooming collection to be sold in department stores, and the brand that took men's grooming to the next level of luxury, beyond the traditional barbershop.

Aramis was created for Joseph Lauder, husband of Estée Lauder, in 1964, after he refused to use his wife's face cream to soothe his winter-raw skin and asked her to make him his own products. Before long, Aramis had developed the first men's 'master plan for grooming' line on the market, with more than 22 products from shaving creams to shampoo, antiperspirant and deodorant – everything a man could possibly want for his daily grooming routine.

LUXURY: Classic, sophisticated and distinctly masculine, Aramis has made its mark as the definitive gentleman's scent. As Ms Trudi Loren, Vice President of Corporate Fragrance Development Worldwide, explains: 'The brand has kept its character and strength throughout its evolution by keeping the classic gentleman interested time after time – the man who wants to make a statement with his scent. Classic Aramis fragrances have timeless connotations of rich leathers and oak-panelled reading rooms, which are reminiscent of a gentlemen's club.'

DISTINCTION: A first-class fragrance, Aramis works with the finest-quality raw materials that the industry has to offer; and after 46 years of developing powerful yet understated scents that have withstood the test of time, it remains one of the best-selling men's luxury fragrances around the world.

Fragrances are blended to evoke specific impressions and emotions. Creative developers work with leading fragrance houses in formulating scents with characters and moods catered to different cultures. 'The art is in blending the oils together and composing a formula which is almost like a musical composition, where the notes interplay with each other to form the overall impression,' says Trudi Loren. 'Englishmen tend to prefer woodier notes with cedar, sandalwood and patchouli, as well as the slightly sweeter woody blend and strong lavender quality of the *fougère* category. These fragrances are inspired by a long tradition of discerning preferences in the English aristocracy. King Henry VIII and Queen Elizabeth I were heavy users of fragrance, for example; so the English sentiment for select scents is rooted in their history and culture.'

The name 'Aramis' derives from an exotic Turkish root used in folklore as a stimulant and aphrodisiac. 'I think there is a strong connection between scent, emotion and perception; and a well-dressed man who smells as wonderful as he does wearing Aramis is definitely an aphrodisiac,' adds Trudi. Creating every gentleman's ideal blend, Aramis pays tribute to Holmes' statement, finding the ultimate inspiration in men's fragrance. ▣

GREAT
BRITISH
EXPORT

DRAKES LONDON'S HANDMADE TIES COMBINE TRADITION WITH STYLE

Tucked away on a quiet street in east London is a building that, from the outside, seems pretty unremarkable. But inside, among rolls of exquisite material and reams of coloured thread, hundreds of high-quality handmade ties of various patterns and shades are created every day for discerning customers across the globe.

The company that produces this multitude of ties, Drakes, first entered the market in 1977 as a scarf manufacturer, offering an alternative to the basic tartans and solids that were the only quality scarves available at the time. 'It struck me that nobody was doing anything different or special with scarves,' explains the firm's founder, Michael Drake. 'Ours became popular because they were unusual; we were reputed to be the first to produce larger-sized scarves and the first to introduce brighter and more interesting colours.'

FLOURISHING: Finding success in the scarf market, Michael and his partners decided to branch out into the unfamiliar territory of ties, which grew into, he says, the company's major focus: 'Ties now represent 70 per cent of the turnover although scarf sales remain very strong.'

Today, as the largest independent producer of handmade ties in England, Drakes' collections are sold in more than 500 outlets worldwide, with over 200 of those based in Italy alone. Having formerly worked for Aquascutum, a company focused on the export of goods, Michael and his joint founders not only gained expertise, but acquired a global vision for the company.

> **"**
> *With hand-crafted ties – from*
> *the first cut to the last stitch –*
> *the emphasis is on quality*

QUALITY: Michael describes the brand's style as 'English, but the way Italians imagine it to be', and it is thoroughly British; handmade in London using materials produced in the UK. 'The majority of the ties are made from silk, 85 per cent of which is woven in the UK,' says Michael. 'Anything we can't get done here is carried out by specialist mills in Italy.' Different fabrics are used across the seasons as well, with pure cashmere and fine woollen ties made in winter, and linen in the summer. Each season the collections also start afresh with more than 100 designs in at least 8–12 colours, some of which are screen printed by hand exclusively for Drakes. Ties that are longer or shorter than the brand's standard 148 centimetres can also be specially made for customers, ensuring they have a tie that fits them well.

With hand-crafted ties – from the first cut to the last stitch – the emphasis is on quality and Michael considers the whole outfit when he designs: 'I think very carefully about who is going to wear the tie and what it will go with; I have in mind the suit, the shirt and all the other accessories. I don't think anyone who has bespoke hand-tailored suits would be interested in wearing a machine-made tie.'

Drakes' ties and scarves, together with other products, are stocked at tailors on Saville Row as well as The Shop at Bluebird, Selfridges, Monocle and Emma Willis. However, although the brand's products appeal to conservative dressers, they are also fêted by the fashion industry – being available at stylish, high-end stores, Dover Street Market and Comme des Garçons, for whom Drakes also produces a range of scarves.

PROSPERITY: Launched in 2007, Drakes' website has seen online sales increase by 100 per cent each year, with those in the UK expanding significantly. Michael is focused on building on the success of the website: 'It has given us the chance to experiment with products we may not have considered in the general collection, such as socks, belts, shirts and knitwear, which have proved particularly popular. 'The website has also brought us closer to our customers, allowing us to build up personal relationships; we have many loyal, returning customers who are passionate about what we are doing and enthusiastically anticipate the new collections. We even know many of them on a first-name basis!' ▣

CONTACT: www.drakes-london.com

THE
HEIGHT OF
FASHION

TIMELESS DESIGN IS COMBINED WITH IMPECCABLE
QUALITY IN EACH PRODUCT ASSEMBLED BY THIS
LEADING LONDON TAILOR

Like many fine crafts, bespoke tailoring is an art form that requires great skill and precision from its practitioners. Throughout the ages, people have laboured over individual garments to achieve the best possible results, and even in this increasingly disposable modern age there are still experts in the field of tailoring who will take all the time necessary to produce a perfect piece of clothing.

DISCERNING: With four decades of expertise obtained from a variety of backgrounds, Graham Browne epitomises the constant pursuit of perfection that is associated with the finest bespoke tailoring. From its headquarters in central London, the reputation of this company, which is synonymous with garments of true quality, has spread far and wide. The spacious showroom and production centre at 12 Well Court can surpass even the most discerning expectations, seamlessly blending elements of tradition and modernity together in the best Savile Row traditions.

Suits are the bedrock of Graham Browne's business, and the customer is rightly at the heart of every key decision when a new suit is commissioned. This timeless process begins with the client making a selection from a broad range of fabrics. Wool is the most common choice, and many people are unaware that materials as diverse as tweed and fresco are crafted from it. The next decisions to be made concern the cut of both the suit and trousers – how many buttons and pockets are desired, which type of trouser pleat to incorporate, how the jacket's inner lining should be styled, and so on.

Once precise customer measurements have been acquired (to ensure a perfect fit at every joint and limb), a paper outline is created. This is also stored as a template, in case the client subsequently requests further items of clothing. Greater formality can be injected through the addition of a waistcoat, an item of clothing that is presently experiencing a renaissance. Waistcoats represent an opportunity to create a striking contrast against the matching materials of the jacket and trousers. When the design process is complete, master tailors set to work, and the finished garments are meticulously assembled with an unswerving focus on detail augmented by stitching that will last for generations. Indeed, the company's shirts are handcrafted in a similar vein, to individual specifications and with a huge array of personalisation options available. Almost all of the pure cotton used is sourced within the UK, and despite their handmade exclusivity, each shirt is affordably priced.

CLASSIC: Customers return to Graham Browne time and again, not only for the calibre of clothing on offer but also because of the personal service they receive. Client expectations are always exceeded, irrespective of how intricate a particular design may be and regardless of the quality demanded from a certain fabric. Each piece of clothing is fashioned using classic tailoring skills that should ensure it lasts a lifetime and, in this respect, it additionally represents real value for money.

As might be expected, Graham Browne offers a comprehensive collection of accessories, and other apparel, to complement its bespoke tailoring division. From bow ties to braces and from cufflinks of cummerbunds, it's possible to completely co-ordinate one's wardrobe, with shoes provided by Loake – another great British brand, with origins extending back to the 19th century. As for Graham Browne, its history grows more enviable with every passing year, and a steady focus on contemporary design ensures that its products will continue to be timeless in the most modern sense of the word. ▣

CONTACT: www.grahambrowne.co.uk

QUINTESSENTIALLY
ENGLISH

Eighty-five years ago in a small room above a pub in Wilmslow, English tailor Harold Humphreys founded Umbro with a big vision: sports tailoring. Ten years later, Umbro established the success of that vision when Manchester City won the 1934 FA Cup. The team that day were fitted out in football kits crafted using the same techniques and materials as the immaculate Umbro-tailored suits of the dignitaries they were shaking hands with as they went to lift the trophy.

This iconic juxtaposition aptly articulated how Humphreys heralded a new epoch in which traditional tailoring could go hand-in-hand with sportswear. His ideas revolutionised the sportswear industry and spread quickly. By 1966, 85 per cent of all British clubs and 15 of the 16 teams at that year's World Cup were sporting Umbro.

Today, Umbro reasserts itself as the definitive English football-tailoring brand, binding the tailoring creed of its heritage with cutting-edge design and an unparalleled insight into the great game. The epitome of understated style, Umbro is characteristically English, crafting superior quality into every product.

CRAFTSMANSHIP: As Chief Marketing Officer Trevor Cairns explains: 'Extensive insight and artistry is devoted to each and every product that Umbro creates.' This craft makes Umbro completely unique next to other football

UMBRO EMBODIES THE CHARM AND REFINEMENT OF THE ENGLISH GENTLEMAN
IN LUXURY TAILORED FOOTBALL-WEAR TO BE SPORTED ON AND OFF THE PITCH

brands that focus instead on replication or needless garnishing of their products. 'Our exhaustive research and development combines creative and scientific expertise from the very start of the process right through to when it arrives in the hands of the customer, covering everything from wear testing to fabrics, fit and construction,' affirms Trevor. 'Umbro's dedication to craft ensures a reassuring level of quality as well as the classic aesthetic. The new shirts are made with a polycotton fabric that looks and feels very different to other kits, and are sold in chest sizes for a much better fit, like any formal shirt.'

ENGLAND: For the 2009 England national-team shirt, Umbro combined the forward-thinking design skills of conceptual designer Aitor Throup with traditional Savile Row tailor Charlie Allen. 'We created a clean, bold aesthetic which Fabio Capello felt had a real psychological benefit for the players; we then tailored the shirts to the exact specifications of each player's body,' Trevor adds. 'Umbro is carving out a unique niche, redefining the marketplace with bespoke garments as tailored to the individual as possible.'

Aitor, who also crafted the iconic England away kit, uses a unique three-stage process in his designs, beginning as an exploration of human anatomy through drawings. 'I then introduce narratives and concepts into those drawings,' he explains, 'after which I create a bridge from the two-dimensional drawings to a three-dimensional concept through sculpture – the initial drawings become the negative space around which the garments are placed; I'm giving them a skin, and that skin becomes the garment itself.'

STYLE: Timeless and effortlessly stylish, Umbro's new tailored England shirts have caught the attention of both devoted football fans and those with only a passing interest in the beautiful game. Now, with the future in mind, Umbro is revisiting iconic moments from its archives that underline the tailoring concept that has flowed throughout the company's history. 'We are reissuing faithful reproductions of our most iconic products, that are equally as iconic today,' says Trevor. 'We've also enlisted some of the most inventive designers around to collaborate with us, finding inspiration from these moments in our history to create new items that will inform our future.'

Developing this idea with the new England home kit, Umbro has enlisted iconic designer Peter Saville to create a graphic panel on the shirt that reinterprets the St George's Cross as a symbol of modern England. Matching a cultural awareness with the latest in fabric technology, the shirt epitomises Umbro's distinctly English approach to sportswear tailoring. ▣

CONTACT: www.umbro.com

CENTURIES OF
EXCELLENCE

INSPIRED BY ITS RICH BRITISH HERITAGE, WOLSEY HAS
BECOME A NATIONAL INSTITUTION WITH A MODERN
RANGE OF CLOTHING INSPIRED BY TRADITIONAL VALUES

I t's certainly not luck that has seen Wolsey reach 255 years in the clothing business, and it's fair to say that much has changed since those very early years. Today, there's a new spirit about the brand that is bound to ensure an equally strong future, while the heritage of this great British institution reads like an historical document of our time, and an intriguing one at that.

Wolsey has been woven into the fabric of our lives, including supplying garments to our brave soldiers of the First and Second World Wars – some with bespoke pieces to cater for our war heroes' missing limbs as they returned home from duty on the front line. Wolsey also supplied essential kit to Captain Scott and his team for the British Antarctic Expedition to the South Pole a hundred years ago. A commemorative collection of 15 pieces celebrating such British endeavour has been produced in 2010, drawing inspiration from original designs, but modernised for the discerning consumer of today.

HERITAGE: Royal Warrants have been aplenty for Wolsey over the years, ever since its first appointment as hosiery manufacturers to His Majesty King George V in 1935. The brand also revolutionised the industry by producing the first unshrinkable pure-wool underwear in the early 1850s. Setting the benchmark for a company that has always embraced new technology, Wolsey is renowned as a manufacturer of products such as 'aviator' jumpers and football jerseys that date back as far as 1920.

The Wolsey name was adopted as the brand name for a manufacturing company in 1897, inspired by the highly powerful statesman Cardinal Wolsey, who died and was buried in the brand's home town of Leicester. His grave sits next to the old Wolsey factory. Leicester has been the home of the company from day one, but strong links with Scotland, initially forged in the company's early years, have remained. Wolsey produces knitwear, scarves and socks in England and Scotland to this day, and is very proud of that fact. The phrase 'Made in Britain' is something to be rightly proud of in the modern age.

The emphasis now is on style inspired by Wolsey's illustrious and colourful history, and while some try to create a feeling of history, Wolsey is the real deal in every sense. Originally from the 1930s, its 'Sportsman' logo has been revisited for this year, but it's the brand's 'fox' logo – first introduced in the early 1970s – which is back at the forefront. Leicester is synonymous with the fox, and English golfer, Tony Jacklin, wore Wolsey knitwear bearing the fox logo during his many victories, becoming the most successful British player of his generation and also the most successful European Ryder Cup captain ever. Golf clothing remains a huge part of Wolsey's global appeal, with modern classics such as Argyle v-neck knits and classic polo shirts produced in a fantastic array of colours.

Wolsey is a modern brand as well as a vintage one, and there's a full collection that really does cater for the man about town. There are sharp, heritage-inspired polo shirts and 'ruggers', laundered 'weekend' casual shirts, stylish outerwear pieces and socks featuring classic contrast toe and heel designs and bold stripes. There's also a beautifully crafted line of modern leather goods and accessories, from bags and belts to hats and gloves. You can be sure that the Union flag will be flying high from Wolsey's Leicester HQ for many years to come. ◻

CONTACT: www.wolsey.com

Wolsey is a modern brand as well as a vintage one, and there's a full collection to cater for the man about town

INDULGE

8 » *Food, Drink & Hospitality*

8» INDULGE

A COGNAC
BEYOND
COMPARE

RICHARD HENNESSY IS AMONG THE WORLD'S RARE AND
PRECIOUS LIQUEURS – HELD TO RIGOROUS STANDARDS,
IT IS THE CORNERSTONE OF THE COGNAC WORLD

The Irishman, Richard Hennessy, was an 18th-century pioneer who enjoyed pushing the boundaries. As a soldier, entrepreneur and visionary, the French King, Louis XV, promoted him to the rank of captain but he traded his arms for adventure, settling in the town of Cognac in 1765, where he established Hennessy Cognac.

This highly ambitious man, obsessed by the notion of heritage, had a vision that extended far into the future. A born trailblazer, he travelled the world in search of new markets and selected the very finest *eaux-de-vie* and preserved them for forthcoming generations, signing the first recorded sale of cognac in the United States in 1794. Enthusiasm, high standards and courage are Hennessy's values that still honour his name today.

200 YEARS: The latest and top of the Hennessy range is a homage to the company's founder. Richard Hennessy is a unique blend of more than 100 exceptional *eaux-de-vie* matured to their fullest expression. The oldest of these are extremely rare and date back to the early 19th century; some hail from grape varieties that disappeared in 1870, when the phylloxera disaster devastated many of Cognac's precious vines. These *eaux-de-vie* were carefully selected and nurtured by the ancestors of Yann Hillioux, the House of Hennessy's seventh-generation master blenders. Refining Richard Hennessy Cognac is thus based on a process that draws on nearly 200 years of knowledge, ingenuity and expertise, handed down through the family. This dynastic tradition is without equal in the world of cognac.

An unparalleled range of aromas gives Richard Hennessy its unique complexity, which is structured to achieve perfect harmony. Balanced, complex and intense, its rich bouquet slowly releases a succession of essences that have built up over the years: vanilla, spices, pepper and delicately fragrant flowers.

INSPIRED: With Hennessy in search of a talented designer that befitted the brand, French designer Inga Sempe created the Richard Hennessy carafe and exquisite strongbox. A fellow at the Villa Medicis in Rome and recipient of the Grand Prix de la Creation design from the city of Paris, she has worked with the most reputed designers and her talent is recognised worldwide. Inga's creative expression fuses power and mystery, innovation and tradition. Her work is bold, but also draws on a deep respect for skilled artisans, combining vision with a respect for the Cognac values that are rooted in the 18th century.

PEERLESS: Each Richard Hennessy carafe is unique, numbered and faceted. The bottle's striking form is made of pure, hand-blown crystal by the town of Baccarat's most skilled glassblowers. Made of the finest ash, each carafe strongbox is hand-worked by a master engraver, and requires 30 hours of labour before being covered with 14 layers of lacquer.

Richard Hennessy is a work of art: cloaked in majesty and nestled in its dark hollow, it reflects contemporary design and is crowned with a silver stopper; only those who hold the engraved metal key to the strongbox have access. Continuing a dialogue between the past and the present, Richard Hennessy is a blend of the *grands siècles* that cannot be explained, only understood. ▣

CONTACT: www.hennessy.com

AN EVENT IN
TIME

A 29-foot-long bench table is believed to be a gift from Elizabeth I after she dined in the hall

MIDDLE TEMPLE HALL PROVIDES THE OPPORTUNITY TO HOST FUNCTIONS IN SURROUNDINGS THAT ARE VIRTUALLY UNCHANGED SINCE THE TIMES OF THE TUDORS

Having survived the Great Fire of London and both world wars, Middle Temple Hall is one of the country's finest examples of Elizabethan architecture and one of the grandest places in the city to host any occasion.

Built between 1562 and 1573, Middle Temple remains virtually unchanged since its last stone was laid. Located in the heart of London's legal quarter, it's one of the four ancient Inns of Court that have the exclusive right to call men and women to the Bar. Continuing to service the legal profession today as members of the Bench, Bar and law students meet there daily for lunch, it houses some of the most impressive event spaces in London available for formal dinners, weddings, meetings, receptions, garden parties and outdoor functions. Just a few minutes from Fleet Street and overlooking the River Thames, the secluded environment lends itself to corporate and private events in a rare and peaceful haven tucked away from the hustle and bustle of the fast-paced city.

Flaunting a double hammer-beam roof chiselled from the oak of Windsor Forest and an elaborately carved screen made in 1574, its traditionally panelled walls are festooned with coats of arms and the impressive windows are made from heraldic glass-memorials to notable Middle Templars. At its centre is a 29-foot-long bench table that is believed to be a gift from Elizabeth I, made from a single oak tree that was floated down the Thames from Windsor. The first performance of Shakespeare's *Twelfth Night* is also recorded as having taken place here in 1602.

LAVISH: Offering a dramatic backdrop for events that can accommodate up to 500 people, the hall can be configured in a wide variety of layouts to suit individual requirements, while personal, attentive and friendly staff afford helpful guidance for a client, from the initial enquiry through to the end of an event.

The award-winning Middle Temple gardens can also be used for a relaxing pre-dinner reception followed by a meal in the hall or, alternatively, a marquee can be erected for larger parties.

Surrounded by intricately manicured borders and expertly maintained lawns, an outdoor event at Middle Temple is a spectacular sight. It also provides an idyllic backdrop for corporate events, filming and wedding photography.

Meanwhile, Middle Temple's first-class in-house caterers create stylish, imaginative and sumptuous cuisine, carefully constructing the menus to provide organisers with the flexibility to choose courses to suit the palate of their guests.

'The venue is luxurious and unique within London,' says Director of Catering and Marketing, Colin Davidson. 'With each event being bespoke, we at Middle Temple offer a personal service to each individual client and will always deliver to the highest standards.'

For any occasion, Middle Temple, a hidden gem at the centre of the city, will surpass all expectations and help create memories to be treasured.

CONTACT: www.middletemplehall.org.uk

A PIECE OF
HISTORY

JJ FOX HAS EXPERIENCE IN THE TOBACCO INDUSTRY THAT DATES BACK CENTURIES

Sir Winston Churchill is arguably one of the most prominent figures in British history, famous for his inspirational speeches as Prime Minister and leading the Allies to victory in the Second World War. Also known for his love of cigars, there are few photos of him without one in his hand or slanting from the corner of his mouth. It has been recorded that at his family home, Chartwell Manor in Kent, he kept boxes containing between 3,000 and 4,000 cigars in a room adjacent to his study so that he would never run low of his favourite indulgence. Many of these cigars would have been purchased from JJ Fox – the cigar emporium where Churchill was a treasured customer.

ESTABLISHED: JJ Fox is the oldest cigar merchant in the world, operating from its flagship store on London's prestigious St James's Street since 1834, an area famed for its luxury shopping and wealth of gentlemen's clubs. The company was established through the union of Robert Lewis

As a specialist in its field, over the years JJ Fox has amassed an impressive eight Royal Warrants

and James J Fox – two of the most respected names in the tobacco and cigar world – and can also count Oscar Wilde, Napoleon III, royalty, tsars, actors and foreign dignitaries among its past and present customers. As the specialist in its field, over the years JJ Fox has amassed an impressive eight Royal Warrants.

With a long and illustrious trading past, encompassing links with countries including Jamaica, Cuba, Brazil and Honduras, tradition is very important to JJ Fox and the store is bursting with history. Customers entering the premises will find a wide range of cigars and tobacco, and a plethora of accoutrements, such as pipes, cigar cutters, books and cases. They are also encouraged to descend stairs in the corner and explore the treasures in the Freddie Fox Museum, which details the history of the company and the tobacco industry over the past 200 years. Items on display include the oldest box of Havana cigars in the world, which first arrived in the UK in 1851; Oscar Wilde's outstanding bill for purchases made between 1892 and 1893;

past correspondence from various members of the Royal Family; and Winston Churchill's account ledger and the chair he would sit in as he sampled and chose his cigars. 'The history and tradition behind the company delights our customers and gives them a sense of security,' says Head of Retail, Bogusha Kopec. 'We are specialists whose expertise and products they know they can trust.'

Many customers return time and again to JJ Fox because they appreciate the high-quality service and the relaxed atmosphere of the St James's Street store – many regulars are happy to wait until the particular member of staff they usually speak to is free, knowing that they will be offered reliable and informed advice.

CHANGING: While its location among the gentlemen's clubs traditionally meant many local businessmen stopped by, the store is increasingly attracting both a younger and a female clientele. As JJ Fox is also responsible for the cigar departments in Harrods and Selfridges, it is able to cater for a wider range of cigar aficionados.

Although the emphasis at JJ Fox is firmly placed on heritage, the company is embracing the modern world through its website, which sells products worldwide. 'The website is very much our future,' explains Bogusha, 'but we will not forget about JJ Fox's history because it has defined who we are and what our customers have come to expect.' ▣

CONTACT: www.jjfox.co.uk

" On the palate, Cristal is characterised by its great finesse and elegance, with a delicate bouquet and a perfect balance

WITH ITS ORIGINS EXTENDING BACK TO THE 18TH CENTURY, LOUIS ROEDERER HAS CREATED A TRUE MASTERPIECE IN CRISTAL, ITS PREMIUM CHAMPAGNE BRAND

CRISTAL
CLEAR

Many great brands carry with them an illustrious history, where their finest achievements have a lineage and a cachet that imbues their name with connotations of timelessness and peerless quality.

This is certainly the case of the celebrated French champagne house Louis Roederer. Situated in the country's Champagne-Ardenne region, this father-and-son enterprise was founded in the French city of Reims and produced sparkling wine. In 1827, it was taken over by a gentleman named Louis Roederer and since then has not looked back.

IDENTITY: At the opposite end of Europe, Russia was governed by the ruling tsars, who had developed a penchant for Champagne; Tsar Alexander II had become such an admirer that, in 1876, he asked Louis Roederer's son (also called Louis and, by now, in charge of the business) to create a completely new and unique blend of Champagne for his own personal consumption. The aim was to elevate himself and his friends above the Russian nobles who drank established Roederer products.

The tsar's wish was granted and, to visually identify this new blend and set it apart from its siblings, it was supplied in flat-bottomed, white crystal bottles. The name 'Cristal' was an obvious name choice, befitting the world's first *cuvée de prestige*.

In 1917, the Russian Revolution brought about the fall of the tsarist autocracy, but by then the world was ready for a new brand of premium Champagne and Louis Roederer swiftly set about introducing the delights of Cristal to a far wider audience. The reaction was hugely favourable and Cristal became acknowledged around the world as one of the finest wines ever made. To this day, it retains its reputation of exclusivity and purity, served in the best venues and appreciated by true connoisseurs.

METICULOUS: A great deal of Cristal's appeal flows from the meticulous production techniques involved in its creation. By using premium grapes from the best vineyards, an improbably high standard is maintained in each unique bottle. Every grape is sourced from one of three Roederer-owned vineyards – Montagne de Reims, the Vallée de la Marne and the Côte des Blancs – and if the weather conditions are insufficiently favourable in a particular year, Cristal is not produced at all.

When conditions are just right, oak casks are filled and left to mature for an average of five years, with an additional eight months of rest after disgorgement allowing the taste to develop perfectly. On the palate, Cristal is characterised by its great finesse and elegance, with a delicate bouquet and a perfect balance. Its flavours range from toasted hazelnuts and candied citrus fruits through to white chocolate and caramel, and it forms the perfect accompaniment to fish and seafood such as scallops, caviar and oysters.

With Cristal as its flagship product, the Louis Roederer brand has become synonymous with the finest Champagne known to man. Almost three million bottles are produced each year and sold in 80 countries worldwide. Retaining its family lineage to this day, and still blessed with an unparalleled vineyard collection, Louis Roederer has become a truly iconic name. ▣

CONTACT: www.louis-roederer.com

CHAMPIONS
9 » Best of British & Royal Warranty Holders

9 » CHAMPIONS

INTERNATIONAL
ACCLAIM

WHENEVER YOU WRAP A PRESENT, BUY A CARD OR PULL A
CHRISTMAS CRACKER, THERE'S A HIGH CHANCE THAT YOU'LL BE
USING THE PRODUCTS OF INTERNATIONAL GREETINGS

Even the largest companies can generally trace their lineage back to humble beginnings. Global brands always start as local enterprises, and a classic example of this can be seen in the meteoric rise of International Greetings, a world leader in the fields of gift wrap, cards, crackers and related accessories.

The origins of this Royal Warrant holder go back to 1979, when a small Swedish ribbon and bow manufacturer relocated to the UK, under the direction of a young and ambitious man by the name of Anders Hedlund. Anders was continuing a family tradition extending back to the 1920s of producing packaging materials for gifts and special occasions. From a tumbledown base in the Welsh village of Crosskeys, this modest enterprise would go on to become a trailblazer in a variety of market sectors, with manufacturing facilities on four continents representing some of the world's largest brands.

> *During 2008-09, International Greetings produced enough gift wrap to extend around the world 20 times more than 800 million metres of wrapping paper*

GREETINGS: The International Greetings name was chosen in 1989 to reflect the burgeoning success of this specialist in greetings cards and present-wrapping materials. The company had already pioneered unique innovations like selling gift wrap by the roll rather than by the sheet (a first in the UK market), and British high-street retailers underpinned the first ten years of growth. By the 1990s, a relentless programme of brand acquisition had begun, with companies joining the International Greetings family in countries as disparate as the USA, Australia and Holland.

Today, International Greetings is one of the world's leading designers, manufacturers, importers and distributors of everything from gift wrap and bags through to greetings cards and stationery. Considerable focus has been invested in obtaining licences to work with brands such as Marvel, *The Simpsons* and Disney, with the wildly successful *Toy Story 3* offering the opportunity to develop new product lines and extend character concepts across a diverse range of items. Examples of the company's current scale can be glimpsed in its output figures: during 2008–09, International Greetings produced and sold more than 30 million gift bags, as well as creating enough gift wrap to extend around the world 20 times – more than 800 million metres of wrapping paper.

CRACKERS: A combination of productivity and perceptive design has seen International Greetings firmly establish itself as a market leader in various industry sectors, such as branded, licensed and bespoke Christmas crackers. In 2005, the company received a Royal Warrant as the official supplier of crackers to Her Majesty the Queen, drawing on almost two decades of unimpeachable expertise in this field. From a wholly owned manufacturing facility in China, a huge portfolio of designs are sold by leading national and international retailers, eventually taking pride of place on festive tables around the world. Another area of proficiency is the gift card sector, ranging from high-volume budget designs through to glittery embossed die-cut cards, for the premium end of the market.

International Greetings trades under a variety of brand names, with Tom Smith perhaps the most famous example that traces its origins back to London 1847. Both the parent organisation and its various subsidiaries have received acclaim from numerous quarters, for their successful product design and corporate ethos. Flagship honours have included the 'Company of the Year' and 'Decade of Excellence' awards from London's Alternative Investment Market, following a 1995 flotation there. With more than 30 years of expansion and excellence already achieved, the future of this innovative organisation looks bright. ▣

CONTACT: www.internationalgreetings.co.uk

PEDIGREE
REPUTATION

NATIONAL MILK RECORDS HAS A LONG AND
VALUED HISTORY IN THE DAIRY INDUSTRY

> *The health benefits of milk are endless; it contains numerous amounts of vitamins and minerals including calcium, Vitamin D and magnesium*

From birth, milk is an integral part of our daily diet. As a natural source of nutrition, we continue to enjoy milk beyond childhood and through other dairy products including cream, yoghurt, butter and cheese.

Such are the health benefits of milk – it contains numerous vitamins and minerals including calcium, Vitamin D and magnesium – that the government encouraged milk consumption following the Second World War; the post-war population needed to be fed and milk was one of the easiest and most nutritious ways of achieving this.

HERITAGE: Around this time, proposals were introduced for milk recording in England and Wales to fall under the remit of the Milk Marketing Board (MMB) to enable dairy farms to operate more efficiently. The goal was to 'assist and encourage milk producers to record milk yields of cows in their herds in order that the management and performance of the dairy herds shall be improved for increased milk production in wartime and thereafter'. The previous milk recording societies, which each looked after a specific county, were combined in 1947 to create National Milk Records (NMR). 'In those days, everything to do with being a dairy farmer was taken care of by the MMB,' explains NMR's Finance Director, Chris Hughes. 'All a farmer would have to do is milk the cows, then the milk would be collected and he would be paid by cheque each month. Farmers subscribed to National Milk Records through a small deduction from their milk cheque.'

REPUTATION: NMR's business is still underpinned by recording information on the individual cow. It records the yields of around 50 per cent of the UK's estimated 12,000 dairy herds, and will shortly be offering its services in Ireland as well.

Chris points out that, as research and technologies advance, the business has also become more sophisticated: 'We also take samples from the cows, send those to a laboratory to be analysed, and compare them with the farmer's other records such as births, deaths and inseminations. Our database can trace the ancestry of every cow on our records back to 1947.'

These records are an integral part of the dairy farmers' operations because they help them to make decisions that drive efficiency into their milk production and improve the standard and quality of the milk.

Recently developed tests for disease and saturated/unsaturated fats are helping farmers maintain a healthy herd, and address concerns about the volume of saturated fats in the UK diet. 'We are constantly running trials and monitoring information to ensure it is correct,' affirms Chris. 'It is vital to our business that we are providing accurate data because these farmers are making critical decisions based on it. We wouldn't go into the market and sell these tests unless we could absolutely prove they work – which we can.'

MODERNISATION: NMR always strives to be at the forefront of cutting-edge research and technologies to offer valuable solutions to farmers. One of its latest innovations is an electronic collar that alerts farmers when cows are receptive to insemination. 'It's very useful for farmers because otherwise they can waste a lot of money trying to inseminate cows that aren't ready or may already be pregnant,' adds Chris. 'We are also part of a project in Carmarthenshire, which has EU funding via the Welsh Assembly, to trace lambs from birth to supermarket shelves by means of an electronic ear tag that holds information.'

As Royal Warrant Holders, NMR records the herds of both HM The Queen and The Prince of Wales, emphasising its reputation for providing a high-quality and reliable service. 'NMR is an important part of the food industry,' says Chris. 'Our main source of pride is making sure that the milk we drink comes from clean, cared-for animals and is of the highest standard possible.' ▣

CONTACT: www.nmr.co.uk

WEALTH

10 » *Investment Management & Philanthropy*

10» WEALTH

A HOME
FOR ALL

SINCE 1860, BATTERSEA DOGS & CATS HOME HAS BEEN INTRODUCING
ABANDONED ANIMALS TO A LIFE FILLED WITH LOVE AND CARE

C oncerned about the number of stray animals roaming the streets of London 150 years ago, Mrs Mary Tealby decided to open 'The Temporary Home for Lost and Starving Dogs' in a stable yard in Holloway. Sadly, Mary Tealby died in 1865, aged 64, but the home she founded continued caring for dogs and, in 1871, moved to its present site in Battersea. It was renamed The Dogs' Home Battersea, and also began taking in cats in 1883. Two years later, Her Majesty Queen Victoria became patron of the home and it has remained under royal patronage ever since.

Battersea has always been thought of as a rehoming centre for dogs, and many people are still unaware that it rehomes hundreds of cats every year, so in July 2002 the home changed its name to Battersea Dogs & Cats Home to reflect this.

CARING: Battersea Dogs & Cats Home accepts stray dogs and cats at any time, day or night, 365 days a year. Dogs and cats are also brought in by owners

> 66
>
> *Every year the home takes in around 11,000 dogs and cats and, since its establishment, has cared for more than three million animals*

who are unable, or unwilling, to care for them any longer. On arrival, all animals are given a thorough health check by a veterinary nurse and scanned for a microchip. Battersea's Animal Welfare, Veterinary and Behaviour staff constantly monitor the animals to throughout their stay at the home, ensuring that all their needs are met, caring for them until new homes can be found, and providing shelter and the highest standards of kennelling and veterinary care. Prior to rehoming, all dogs and cats receive a full behavioural and temperament assessment to find out as much as possible about each animal's character and to build up a picture of the type of home that would suit them best.

Currently made up of three centres – the London site, Old Windsor in Berkshire and Brands Hatch in Kent – Battersea rehomes dogs and cats across the whole of the UK, using a process made easier by the recent introduction of an online application form. Those interested in rehoming a dog or cat can fill out the form on Battersea's website and it will be assessed remotely by dedicated rehoming staff. All prospective owners are interviewed and this information is used to match them with the dog or cat which best suits their home and lifestyle. Although the majority of Battersea's dogs are rehomed to family homes, it is sometimes felt that a particular dog would benefit from the added stimulation of a working home, and a number of Battersea dogs have thrived in a wide range of working roles such as assistance dogs, sniffer dogs and working sheepdogs.

DEDICATED: As well as rehoming animals, Battersea Dogs & Cats Home reunites lost dogs and cats with their owners through its Lost Dogs & Cats Line. It also offers extra training and socialisation to those that need it, and detailed help and advice to new pet owners with behaviour programmes and through its Behaviour Advice Line.

Every year the home takes in around 11,000 dogs and cats and, since its establishment, has cared for more than three million animals. It relies heavily on public donations and gifts in wills to carry on providing this dedicated care, as well as purchasing vital veterinary equipment, maintaining kennels and catteries, raising awareness and funds, and educating the public in responsible pet ownership.

COMMEMORATION: Battersea Dogs & Cats Home celebrates its 150th anniversary in 2010. The animal rescue organisation is one of the most famous and longest-serving charities in the country, and the home is proud to be London's leading animal rehoming centre and looking forward to many successful years to come. ▣

CONTACT: www.battersea.org.uk
CHARITY NUMBER: 206394

SERVICE
TO RAISE A GLASS TO

ATTRIBUTES SUCH AS EXCLUSIVITY, DEPENDABILITY AND INNOVATION ARE NOT USUALLY ASSOCIATED WITH INSURANCE, BUT THEY FIT COMFORTABLY WITH CHARTIS

Chartis has its origins in Shanghai where founder, Cornelius Vander Starr, became the first westerner to sell insurance to Chinese people in 1919. To put his achievement into historical context, it was the same year British aviators, Alcock and Brown, made their first transatlantic air crossing – in a Vickers Vimy aircraft powered by two Rolls-Royce Eagle engines – and the year in which electric lighting and starting motors became standard on Rolls-Royce cars.

From its earliest days Chartis has been committed to expansion and is now one of the world's leading general insurers, serving more than 45 million clients in over 160 countries and jurisdictions. It offers an extensive range of products and services, high-quality claims expertise and excellent financial strength.

66

Elegant solutions for the risks posed by clients'
ownership of fine art, jewellery, wine, antiques,
homes, cars, superyachts and planes

EXCLUSIVE: Chartis created its Private Client Group in 2000 to meet the insurance needs of affluent clients. It is founded on a simple premise: the understanding of international lifestyles and the unique backgrounds and perspectives of its clients. Each member of the team has specialist expertise so that an appropriate solution can be delivered to each individual client. Private Client Group has offices in 11 countries and provides elegant solutions for the risks posed by clients' ownership of fine art, jewellery, wine, antiques, homes, cars, superyachts and planes.

'Our client base is cash-rich but time-poor, and we have designed our products to recognise that,' explains Vice President David Smith. 'They have bought the best and want to know they are receiving best-quality service and protection.'

DEPENDABLE: Private Client Group is proud of its 'concierge-level claims service' – a claims team dedicated to its affluent clients. Claims are assessed individually in the same way that each insurance programme is individually underwritten. 'Our clients don't necessarily want a cheque for their claim,' adds David. 'They frequently want the lost or damaged item replaced, restored or repaired and our concierge-level claims service assists that in a fuss-free way.'

INNOVATIVE: When a serious leak in a clients' cellar resulted in the loss of a considerable number of bottles of wine, including vintage champagne and port, one of the world's top wine specialists was hired-in and replaced the collection, bottle for bottle. According to the estate manager: 'The understanding of a challenging situation such as this... together with the recognition of the needs and requirements of the exclusive clients... was complete.' And when there was severe flooding, clients who might be affected were identified from their postcodes. One was away on business so, with their permission, their property was sandbagged and pumps installed to help hold back the potential floodwater.

'Our clients want to know that if something happens, it is going to be handled efficiently and with complete professionalism,' says David. It's this anticipation of clients' needs, and attention to detail, that demonstrates the Private Client Group's commitment to providing the most responsive and incisive claims service in the industry. A service to raise a glass to. ▣

CONTACT: www.chartisinsurance.com/PCG-Home-Page_911_217283.html

BIRDS
OF A FEATHER

BEING A RARE BIRD CLUB MEMBER AND SUPPORTING BIRDLIFE INTERNATIONAL MAKES A HUGE DIFFERENCE FOR THE WORLD'S BIGGEST PARTNERSHIP OF CONSERVATION ORGANISATIONS

The Rare Bird Club is an exclusive international community of concerned individuals who are determined to make a difference

Birds are vital indicators of the well-being of environments and the human populations that they support. Sadly, just like the canary in the coalmine, they are warning humans of huge changes occurring in ecosystems across the globe. The Rare Bird Club provides support to BirdLife International – the world's biggest partnership of conservation organisations. This vital support delivers a lasting difference for birds, nature and humanity.

At present, one-in-eight bird species – over 1,200 in total – is at risk of extinction, under relentless pressure from habitat destruction and degradation, alien species, hunting, climate change and much more. Saving them not only preserves these wonderful animals and their habitats, but also contributes to the preservation of natural ecosystems which are vital to all life on earth.

Helping to protect biodiversity, BirdLife International is a global partnership of 114 organisations with a supporter base of ten million people from across 120 countries. It delivers long-term conservation programmes on the ground and works with civil societies towards sustainability in the use of their natural resources.

SUPPORT: The Rare Bird Club is for people from all over the globe, who gather to share their love of wildlife and the natural environment, and aspire to make a lasting difference for nature.

Members are invited to exclusive events and there have been dinners and receptions in New York and London hosted by Queen Noor of Jordan, in Japan hosted by HIH Princess Takamado, in the UK with The Duke of Edinburgh, and in Austria with Princess Von Hohenberg. HIH Princess Takamado, the Honorary

President of BirdLife International says: 'The Rare Bird Club is an exclusive international community of concerned individuals who are determined to make a difference. Through BirdLife International, it provides the resources which help to deliver successful projects to reverse the global decline in species and improve the quality of people's lives.'

SUCCESS: The global BirdLife Partnership is proving highly effective and it is making a huge difference. A number of species have been saved and are now off the danger list. The size of protected areas is growing. However, there is still much to do. This is why The Rare Bird Club plays a crucial role in providing the resources to support BirdLife International's priority programmes.

Luigi Prins, a car enthusiast and Rare Bird Club member, says: 'In a rapidly changing world, I believe in the value of history and technological advancements made by previous generations, which together fuel my interest and excitement in classic cars, restoration of wooden sailing ships and renovation of buildings with architectural importance.

'I also believe in the conservation of natural habitats as the best way of saving species from extinction, especially the tropical rainforests of the world, which are home to many interesting and threatened forms of biodiversity. By being a Rare Bird Club member, car enthusiasts can also be proud to make a lasting difference to the natural world.' ▣

CONTACT: www.rarebirdclub.org

IMAGES: (L–R) Pete Morris / Birdquest; Robert E Fuller

FORGING
NEW PATHS

SCM PRIVATE IS EVOLVING THE MANNER IN WHICH INVESTMENT MANAGEMENT IS CONDUCTED

Progressive wealth management firm SCM Private is changing the DNA of the world of investment in terms of what clients need and expect. Traditionally, there have been two approaches to investment management: active or passive. SCM offers a third choice, something it calls Fusion Management, which is a combination of passive investment instruments that are continuously and actively managed.

Even though SCM is relatively new, the experience its team musters is vast and its rise has been meteoric. Taking a modern approach to fund management, SCM is designed around investors and grounded on common sense, academic research and the experience of its Fund Manager and CEO, Alan Miller, who has an unprecedented 20-year track record of outperformance using his vast, active stock-picking knowledge to conduct 'under the bonnet' research. His contrarian style means he does not simply follow the herd, preferring to investigate thoroughly any latest trend or fad and go against the flow if necessary.

DIFFERENT: SCM uses Exchange Traded Funds (ETFs) – a fund that tracks an index, but can be traded like stock – to offer investors a choice of two portfolios in a diversified range of assets including equities, bonds, property, commodities and cash via exceptionally liquid indexes. ETFs reduce the extra costs of dealing commissions, price spreads and taxes which such activity normally produce.

As well as making sensible and shrewd investment decisions, SCM knows that investors' security and peace of mind are paramount. Therefore, all monies and investments are held in clients' names with portfolios accessible online 24 hours a day. 'Because it's our own money invested in exactly the same way, it's much easier for us to take the client's point of view and consider how money should be run,' says Partner at SCM, Gina Miller. 'The most important things are security, liquidity and fair fees. Everything is clear and easy to understand.'

UNCONVENTIONAL: Many large wealth management brands in the City offer very little transparency, hiding behind a wall of complexity. SCM goes against this grain and, additionally, has among the lowest fees and costs in the industry. There is also the added reassurance that SCM is 100 per cent staff owned, with the founding partners investing a significant amount of their own wealth in exactly the same portfolios and on the same terms as clients. Its corporate structure is extremely lean and highly efficient with key non-investment functions outsourced to large specialist companies.

'Our investment model gives investors high liquidity, transparency and a real alternative to pure active or passive fund management,' says Alan. 'I am very pleased that not only have we delivered performance that exceeds our benchmark, but that it has been achieved at a fraction of the costs of most traditional wealth managers.'

EXCEPTIONAL: because of its unique market approach, SCM has been recognised as 'Firm of the Year' by *Spear's Wealth Management*.

'We believe our offering can significantly benefit individuals, pension funds, family offices and charities,' says Gina. 'Particularly if they are suffering the double hit of poor performance and excessive fees. This is a family business and we want it to be so for generations to come; we are here for the long term and we are confident that SCM offers a unique investment approach.'

Gina also launched SCM Philanthropy, a foundation that funds small charities and individuals who undertake benevolent work in their community. The foundation is underwritten by SCM Private so 100 per cent of all funds donated or raised go to benefactor charities. ▣

CONTACT: www.scmprivate.com

A LIFETIME
OF SUPPORT

Our work is more important than ever before and it is vital that our troops know they can rely on SSAFA to provide direct practical support when they, and their families, need it

THE SOLDIERS, SAILORS, AIRMEN AND FAMILIES ASSOCIATION SUPPORTS THOSE WHO SERVE, OR HAVE SERVED, IN THE ARMED FORCES – EVEN IF ONLY FOR A SINGLE DAY

For 125 years our servicemen, women and their families have known they can rely on The Soldiers, Sailors, Airmen and Families Association (SSAFA) Forces Help in times of need. From the elderly Second World War veteran with mobility problems, to the young marine seriously injured in Afghanistan, SSAFA provides much-needed practical, financial and emotional assistance to more than 50,000 people every year through its network of professional staff and 7,000 trained volunteers. SSAFA believes that bravery, dedication and loyalty deserves a lifetime of support.

COMFORT: The charity's two new SSAFA Norton Homes offer 'home-from-home' accommodation to the families of seriously wounded servicemen and women being treated in Headley Court and Selly Oak. The houses mean partners, parents, children, siblings or grandparents can be close at hand no matter where they live. They also allow service personnel to spend quality time with their families away from the hospital environment as they come to terms with life-changing injuries and begin to look towards the future together.

Linda Sheridan's son, Ranger Andrew Allen, lost both legs serving in Afghanistan in 2008. The family travelled from Belfast to a SSAFA Norton House each weekend to spend time with him. 'It's nice to be able to do normal family things,' Linda says. 'I can get up in the morning and cook us all breakfast like I would at home.'

CARING: SSAFA's many support groups allow those coping with loss or serious injury to a loved one to meet and talk with others who have had similar experiences, sharing information, advice and mutual support.

Karen Thornton's eldest son, Gunner Lee Thornton, 22, was killed in Iraq in 2006. 'I can't thank SSAFA enough for setting up the groups,' she says. 'It has been such a benefit to me to meet people who totally understand how I feel.'

SSAFA Chief Executive, Major General Andrew Cumming, says: 'We are very proud of our lifelong commitment to our servicemen and women. Our work is more important than ever before and it is vital that our troops know they can rely on SSAFA to provide direct practical support when they, and their families, need it.' ▣

CONTACT: www.ssafa.org.uk
IMAGE: (L–R) Sgt Simon Harmer, photographed by Ed Miller; Wally Harris, photographed by Eli Dean

FIVE-STAR
SERVICE

THE SERVICE THAT ANTHONY JONES INSURANCE BROKERS
OFFERS IS TAILORED TO EACH INDIVIDUAL CLIENT'S NEEDS

For the past 30 years, Anthony Jones Insurance Brokers has been steadily building a reputation as a trusted and professional insurance company, creating valued relationships with both clients and insurers. The company deals mainly in general insurance, while specialising in a number of niche areas.

PERSONALISED: One of these specialist divisions concentrates on providing cover for the company's most affluent customers, incorporating their homes, motor vehicles, yachts and aviation among other items into the policy. 'A whole lifestyle package is created for our high-net-worth clients,' explains Managing Director Terry Marshell. 'Whatever the starting point may be, we can put in place bespoke arrangements to meet all of their requirements.'

Terry says the company prides itself on offering clients a 'concierge service', which caters for them globally and round the clock. 'For example,' he adds, ' one of our customers needed us to arrange his cover on a worldwide basis and that included everything – homes in the UK and overseas, contents, travel and movement of art around the world – and we were able to take care of it all for him.'

EXPERTISE: With a wealth of experience behind Anthony Jones, clients are also provided with a small but dedicated team of personal account handlers whom they can contact 24/7. This builds up personal relationships with clients, ensuring that the team can anticipate and meet their needs better – a stance that has paid off as many clients have been with the company for 20 years or more, and the majority of new business is via word-of-mouth recommendations.

'We aim to provide a discreet and personalised service because many people do not want to shout about what they have got and certainly do not want to share that information with third parties,' says Terry. 'Do we ever receive a phone call out of hours? Very rarely, but our clients are safe in the knowledge that should they need us we will be here for them.' ▣

CONTACT: www.anthonyjones.com/concierge

ROLLS-ROYCE ENTHUSIASTS' CLUB
CREDITS

PRESIDENT
Lt Col Eric Barrass OBE

CHAIRMAN
Tony James

CHAIRMAN ELECT
Duncan Feetham

YEARBOOK EDITOR
Wg Cdr Julian Spencer

SUB-EDITOR
Julia Meadowcroft

FINANCE/DISTRIBUTION
Jaclyn Smith

**CLUB HEADQUARTERS
MANAGEMENT COMMITTEE**
Tony James
Duncan Feetham
Gerwald Anderle
Trevor Baldwin
Roger Cockfield
Jim Fleming
Philip Hall
Steve Hubbard
Rolf Kuhnke
Steve Lovatt
Benno Th Müller
David Towers

GENERAL SECRETARY
Wg Cdr Julian Spencer

COMPANY SECRETARY
Keith Lanchbury

BUSINESS ADMINISTRATION MANAGER
Jaclyn Smith

BULLETIN EDITOR
Wg Cdr Julian Spencer

BULLETIN PRODUCTION EDITOR
Julia Meadowcroft

LIBRARIAN
Philip Hall

CLUB SHOP MANAGER
Linda Housden

WEBMASTER
Ailsa Plain

ARCHIVIST AND CHASSIS HISTORIES
Barbara Westlake

ADMINISTRATION & SEMINARS
Penny Thorburn

MEMBERSHIP SUBSCRIPTIONS
Martika Andrzejow

OFFICE SERVICES
Sandra Harris

ROLLS-ROYCE ENTHUSIASTS' CLUB
The Hunt House, High Street,
Paulerspury, Northamptonshire, NN12 7NA

Telephone: +44 (0)1327 811 788
Fax: +44 (0)1327 811 797
Club Shop: +44 (0)1327 811 489
Email: admin@rrec.org.uk
Website: www.rrec.org.uk

The name Rolls-Royce, the Rolls-Royce badge and
the linked RR device are trademarks of Rolls-Royce
plc and are used by the RREC under licence.
Where photographs have not been accredited, the
source and copyright remain with RREC Ltd.

PUBLISHER
St James's House
(Regal Press Limited)
298 Regents Park Road
London, N3 2SZ
Tel: +44 (0)20 8371 4000
Email: production@stjamess.org
Web: www.stjamess.org

MANAGING DIRECTORS
Richard Freed
Gary Worden

EDITORIAL & CREATIVE DIRECTOR
Chris Maillard

EDITORIAL & CREATIVE CONSULTANT
Annie Prior

St James's House would like to thank all the
sponsors in this publication for their support.
©2010 Regal Press Limited

ISBN: 978-1-906670-13-9

INDEX

392 Drakes of London
www.drakes-london.com

352 Dubai Pearl
www.dubaipearl.com

124 E-Watch Suisse Sàrl
www.myriad.ch
www.cyma.ch

264 Eastern & Oriental – Penang, Malaysia
www.e-o-hotel.com
www.seritanjungpinang.com

354 Edificio Acqua
www.acqua.com.uy

166 Eva Solo
www.evasolo.com

266 Fairmont Royal Pavilion, The
www.fairmont.com/royalpavilion

356 Fares Real Estate Inc
www.faresinc.com
www.kingswharf.ca

268 Fisher Island Hotel and Resort
www.fisherislandclub.com

210 Fleming Yachts
www.flemingyachts.com

126 Francesca Sibylla Augusta FSA
www.FSAugusta.co.uk

272 Gibbon Bridge Hotel, The
www.gibbon-bridge.co.uk

274 Globe-Trotter
www.globe-trotterltd.com

212 Gore Design Completions Ltd
www.goredesign.com

394 Graham Browne
www.grahambrowne.co.uk

276 Gran Hotel Atlantis Bahia Real
www.atlantishotels.com

278 Grand Resort Bad Ragaz
www.resortragaz.ch

280 Gstaad Palace
www.palace.ch

168 Hästens
www.hastenswestend.com

282 Hedingham Castle
www.hedinghamcastle.co.uk

404 Hennessy
www.hennessey.com

406 Honourable Society of the Middle Temple, The
www.middletemplehall.org.uk

284 HOSHINOYA
www.hoshinoya.com

286 Hostellerie La Briqueterie
www.labriqueterie.fr

288 Hotel Copernicus / Hotel Stary
www.hotel.com.pl
www.lhr.com.pl

290 Hotel le Bristol Paris
www.lebristolparis.com

292 Hotel le Chalet Blanc
www.hotellechaletblanc.com

294 Hôtel Le Lana *****
www.lelana.com

296 Hotel Mulia
www.hotelmulia.com

300 Huvafen Fushi
www.peraquum.com
www.huvafenfushi.com

302 Iberostar Hotels & Resorts
www.iberostar.com

304 Il Pellicano Hotel
www.pellicanohotel.com

416 International Greetings
www.internationalgreetings.co.uk

172 Jenny Edge
www.jennyedge.co.uk

114 Jesper Velling
www.jespervelling.com

408 JJ Fox (St James's) Ltd
www.jjfox.co.uk

128 Kaja Gjedebo Design
www.kgd.no

174 Kinari Design
www.kinaridesign.com

KINARI

306 Kizingoni Beach & Mukima House
www.kizingonibeach.com
www.mukimakenya.com

308 Ledra Hotels & Villas
www.domesofelounda.com

310 Les Suites Du Névada
www.les-suites-du-nevada.com

130 Liana Pattihis
www.pattihis.com

214 Lombard Aviation
www.lombard.co.uk/assets/aviation

410 Louis Roederer
www.louis-roederer.com

358 Mansion Living
www.mansionliving.com

132 Matthew Foster Fine Jewels
www.matthew-foster.co.uk

216 metrica® aviation INTERIOR
www.metrica-aviation.de

360 Minh Viet Investment Corporation
www.mvi.com.vn

312 Minos Beach Art Hotel
www.minosbeach.eu

218 Mobius Design Group Inc
www.mobiusdesigngroup.com

314 Monte-Carlo Resort – SBM
www.montecarloresort.com

362 Moravia Group
www.moraviagroup.com

Moraviagroup

220 Morristown Municipal Airport
www.mmuair.com

316 Nandana Private Resort
www.nandanaresort.com

418 National Milk Records Plc
www.nmr.co.uk

364 Nautilus Property Real Estate
www.nautilusproperty.com

134 Nina Koutibashvili
www.ninakoutibashvili.com

318 Oberoi Hotels & Resorts
www.oberoihotels.com

222 Ocean Alexander Yachts
www.oceanalexander.com

224 Oryx Jet / Rizon Jet
www.oryxjet.com
www.rizonjet.com

320 Paradise Island Villas – Prodromos SA
www.paradiseislandvillas.gr

226 Pensum Ltd
www.PensumOffshore.com

285 Per AQUUM
www.peraquum.com

366 Phoenix Park d.o.o.
www.phoenixplaza.com.hr

228 Pilatus Aircraft Ltd
www.pilatus-aircraft.com

176 Pippa Toledo Design Ltd
www.pippatoledo.com

178 Plan Associated Architects
www.planassociados.pt

368 Prime Development
www.pd-global.com

426 Private Client Group, Chartis Insurance UK Limited
www.chartisinsurance.com/PCG-Home-
Page_911_217283.html

428 Rare Bird Club of BirdLife International, The
www.rarebirdclub.org

346 RE/MAX Living Cape Town
www.remaxliving.co.za

322 Regent Maldives, The
www.RegentHotels.com/Maldives

230 Rockwell Collins
www.rockwellcollins.com

232 Rolling Stock Group
www.rollingstock.es

324 Romanos Resort, a Luxury Collection Resort, The
www.romanoscostanavarino.com

234 Royal Jordanian Airlines
www.rj.com

180 Royal Mansour
www.royalmansour.com

370 R.W. Armstrong & Sons Ltd
www.rwarmstrong.co.uk
www.eachiverton.co.uk

182 Sarah Davenport Ltd
www.davenportinteriors.co.uk

Davenport

430 SCM Private
www.scmprivate.com

184 Selvaggio
www.selvaggio.ch
www.crandsv.com

326 Serene Pavilions
www.serenepavilions.com

136 Sevan Bicakci
www.sevanbicakci.com

380 Shamballa Jewels
www.shamballajewels.com

328 Shangri-La Hotels and Resorts
www.shangri-la.com

186 Showerlux UK Ltd
www.showerlux.co.uk

140 Singhal Gems
www.singhalgems.com
www.mirabellejewels.com

432 Soldiers, Sailors, Airmen and Families
Association (SSAFA) Forces Help, The
www.ssafa.org.uk

236 Special Projects and Services Limited
www.specialprojectsandservices.com

330 Spring City Golf & Lake Resort
www.springcityresort.com

332 Sri panwa, Phuket
www.sripanwa.com

372 Teak S.A.
www.theseusbv.com

146 Tillberg Design
www.tillbergdesign.com

TILLBERG DESIGN

374 TóPARK
www.topark.eu

238 Tottenham Hotspur
www.tottenhamhotspur.com

334 troiaresort
www.troiaresort.pt

376 Tropical Hill
www.tropicalhill.es

336 Ty'n Rhos Country Hotel
www.tynrhos.co.uk

378 Ultissimo
www.ultissimo.com

ULTISSIMO
defining italian living

338 Umaid Bhawan Palace
www.tajhotels.com/Palace/UMAID%20BHAWAN%20
PALACE,JODHPUR/default.htm

396 Umbro
www.umbro.com

380 Villas Amrit
+30 6989 80 2120

*Villas Amrit, Mykonos
Jewel of the Aegean*

188 VitrA UK
www.vitra.co.uk

384 V4V S.A.
www.v4v.ch

340 Westbury Mayfair, The
www.westburymayfair.com

398 Wolsey Ltd
www.wolsey.com

190 Zil Pasyon Seychelles
www.zilpasyon.com

St James's House
QUALITY IN PUBLISHING

As communications specialists, one of the core activities of St James's House is publishing, with creativity and our clients' goals at the heart of our business.

St James's House has produced numerous official publications for and with the Home Office, Royal Air Force and Royal Navy, securing our position as a market leader in the publication of high-quality media. Recent publications include: The Oxford & Cambridge Careers Guide, 60 years of the National Health Service and Britain's Aviation Heritage in association with The Royal Air Force – an award-winning 90th anniversary commemorative album.

Our public-sector customers include HM Treasury, MoD, The UK Intellectual Property Office and HMRC. Corporate customers encompass the BBC, Clifford Chance, Goldman Sachs, M&S and MasterCard. At the time of writing, we are working with around 30 per cent of the FTSE 100 and 40 per cent of FTSE 350 companies.

For more information, and to enquire about partnership possibilities, contact Richard Freed on + 44 (0) 20 8371 4000; richard.freed@stjamess.org. ▣

The Oxford & Cambridge
Careers Handbook

CONTACTS: www.stjamess.org